Children's Literature

Volume 25

6/19/97

Armand Hammer
Museum of Art
and Cultural Center

for Joe
Mitzi Myers

Volume 25

Annual of
The Modern Language Association
Division on Children's Literature
and The Children's Literature
Association

Yale University Press

New Haven and London

1997

Children's Literature

The editors gratefully acknowledge support from Hollins College.

Editorial correspondence should be addressed to The Editors, *Children's Literature,* Department of English, Hollins College, Roanoke, Virginia 24020

Manuscripts submitted should conform to the style in this issue. An original on non-erasable bond with two copies, a self-addressed envelope, and return postage are requested. Yale University Press does not accept dot-matrix printouts, and it requires double-spacing throughout text and notes. Unjustified margins are required. Writers of accepted manuscripts should be prepared to submit final versions of their essays on computer disk in XyWrite, Nota Bene, or WordPerfect.

Volumes 1–7 of *Children's Literature* can be obtained directly from John C. Wandell, The Children's Literature Foundation, P.O. Box 370, Windham Center, Conn. 06280. Volumes 8–25 can be obtained from Yale University Press, P.O. Box 209040, New Haven, Conn. 06520-9040, or from Yale University Press, 23 Pond Street, Hampstead, London NW3 2PN, England.

Set in Baskerville type by Tseng Information Systems, Inc., Durham, N.C.
Printed in the United States of America by Vail-Ballou Press, Binghamton, N.Y.

Library of Congress catalog card number: 79-66588
ISBN: 0-300-07000-4 (cloth), 0-300-07001-2 (paper); ISSN: 0092-8208

A catalogue record for this book is available from the British Library.

The paper in this book meets the guidelines for permanence and durability of the Committee on Production Guidelines for Book Longevity of the Council on Library Resources.

10   9   8   7   6   5   4   3   2   1

Contents

Varia

Reviews

From the Editors: "Cross-Writing" and the Reconceptualizing of Children's Literary Studies

The Victorian satirist and evolutionist Samuel Butler once tried to depict ancestral genes at cross-purposes with each other. These "former selves," wrangling for "possession" of a single psyche, create a din of jarring voices: "Faint are the far ones, . . . loud and clear are the near ones. . . . 'Withhold,' cry some. 'Go on boldly,' cry others. 'Me, me, me, revert hitherward. . . . Nay, but me, me, me'" (Butler 43).

The notion of "cross-writing" we advance in this special issue of *Children's Literature* resembles Butler's dramatized crossover in one important respect: we believe that a dialogic mix of older and younger voices occurs in texts too often read as univocal. Authors who write for children inevitably create a colloquy between past and present selves. Yet such conversations are neither unconscious nor necessarily riven by strife. Instead of the competing ancestral voices that Butler posits, we stress creative cooperation. Most of the writers, artists, and editors we consider in this volume manage to integrate the conflicting voices they heed. Their constructs involve interplay and cross-fertilization rather than a hostile internal cross fire.

Cross-writing is not limited to texts written for children. In an "adult" novel such as *The Mill on the Floss*, George Eliot's Mr. Tulliver is puzzled by the genetic "crossing o' breeds" that makes the dark daughter to whom he gave his own mother's name so unlike his blonde wife. Yet the man who sees everything in terms of contraries cannot help his precocious child cross into a new order of reality. The adult is at odds with the child in an inimical world that has no room for Maggie Tulliver. In contrast, George Eliot's next child-man, Silas Marner, who also gives his mother's name to the orphan who has crossed his threshold, benefits from the reactivation of hitherto dormant childhood memories. Like that other solitary, Robinson Crusoe, whose family name was *Kreuzner* (crosser), Silas mends a wounded psyche by reverting to a more elementary and childlike world. Given its pastoralism, George Eliot's fable was at one time deemed as suitable for child readers as Defoe's romance. Yet, as two generations of American schoolchildren discovered to their chagrin, the book remains preeminently "adult." Despite its primitive setting and fairy-tale elements, the novel relies on the authoritative voice of an ultra-sophisticated expositor. This linguistically adroit narrator brings out existential complexities that the tongue-tied Silas can bypass, but which her readers cannot read as merely a "simple twist of fate."[1]

Indeed, it might be argued that any text that activates a traffic between phases of life we persist in regarding as opposites demands, yet seldom receives, readings that should reflect a similar critical elasticity. Whether addressing adult or child audiences, or both, such fluid texts often rely on settings that dissolve the binaries and contraries that our culture has rigidified and fixed. Crusoe's island hut and Marner's valley cottage offer blendings not possible in the civilizations each man has fled; and although the raft that acts as a temporary haven for Huck and Jim cannot remain immune to the divisive communities that dot the river, the boy who plans to cross into still open territories at the end of Twain's novel refuses to succumb to the new form of enslavement that Jim accepts.

In transcending the binaries imposed by culture, Huckleberry Finn thus anticipates that other strange pilgrim-navigator, E. B. White's Stuart Little. Himself a cross between different species, the mouse-boy resists the allurements of a human mate his own size, the pretty dwarf child of Ames's Crossing. Instead, he prefers to pursue an elusive bride of still another order, Margalo the Shelleyan (or Mater-linked?) bird who never was on land or sea. Were he to find her, his new family would be as cross-grained as that formed by the hunter, the mermaid, and the furry and non-furry foundlings in Randall Jarrell's *The Animal Family*, an enigmatic fairy tale enhanced by Sendak's equally enigmatic crosshatched drawings.

As a writer-artist whose ability to maintain contact with "the psychic reality of my own childhood" shapes an original classic such as *Where the Wild Things Are* (Lanes 247), Maurice Sendak's wonderful understanding of the interplay between adult and child has also made him a key interpreter of such diverse figures as the Grimms, George MacDonald, Lewis Carroll, Melville, and many others. His shrewd grasp of the "cross-writing" at work in Wilhelm Hauff's sly and delightful *Dwarf Long Nose* even exceeds, as Maureen Thum points out in the first essay in our collection, that of the story's translator. Like Sendak's own Max, whose mother sends him away for being too wild, Hauff's boy-protagonist Jacob is repudiated by his biological mother when he returns to her in an alien shape. And yet, like the boy in a wolf suit, the deformed Jacob can adopt a maternal identity. As one who has learned to feed others, he follows the career of the misshapen herb-fairy he now physically resembles. For his part, Max also tries out the adult identity of one more powerful than he. As undaunted by the monsters he unleashes as his mother had been by her own wild thing of a boy, he fashions a self by blending child and adult—the rebel rumpus dancer and the authoritarian grown-up who can keep wildness in check. When this Mowgli-like wolfboy and king of the jungle returns to maternal domestication and restraint, his recrossing ratifies the blending he has achieved.

One of the delights of teaching children's literature is to ask college students, those recent "adults" still in contact with earlier selves, how their present, more analytical reencounters with texts such as *Where the Wild Things Are* or *Charlotte's Web* ratify, alter, or complement their childhood responses. Their accounts vividly confirm the duality of such texts. One reader notes that the terrible claws and gnashing teeth of the Wild Things had never disturbed her as a child, when she trustfully regarded the creatures as "incredibly kind and unthreatening." Pondering about this discrepancy, she adds a long postscript:

> Perhaps this was because I focused more on Sendak's illustrations than on his verbal description of the Wild Things. I always thought they were heading towards Max to welcome him when his boat arrived. The most remarkable thing in comparing my responses, then and now, is the realization of the willing suspension of disbelief that I extended to the book when I was young. There is a different gratification in reading children's books as an adult. One marvels at the wit of an author who can delight the child's parents as much as the child. While the development of analytic faculties has afforded me the opportunity to enjoy children's books from fresh perspectives, I also like to believe that I could sit in my room and have a wild rumpus with some terrible looking beasts.[2]

Using *Charlotte's Web* for their comparison of childhood and adult readings, two other students recall near-opposite responses. Whereas Andrea M., a psychology major, remembers that she and all the other students in Mrs. Murray's first-grade class had joyfully identified with Wilbur, Douglas M., an English major who was first exposed to the book in "Mrs. Hutching's third grade classroom," privileges Wilbur's two caretakers, Charlotte and Fern. In rereading the book at age twenty, Andrea realizes that her investment in Wilbur's survival had totally obscured the importance of Charlotte's role; she even recalled "being slightly angry at Charlotte for leaving Wilbur all alone." Now, however, Wilbur seems less important to her than the spider's "so enviable and admirable ability to accept the natural course of life."

Douglas M.'s impressions also underwent a radical revision. Although as a third-grader he had regarded Fern "as a heroine, not only in the beginning, but throughout the story," as a grown-up he faults her for failing to "fling herself at her father" a second time, when Mr. Arable assures Homer Zuckerman that this "wonderful" pig would yield "some extra good ham and bacon" (126). Yet the self-pitying Wilbur himself now seems diminished: "he is not 'Some Pig,' 'Terrific,' or 'Radiant,' and thus did not really qualify to be saved while all other pigs are slaughtered. As an adult reader, you start to wonder why Charlotte went through all the work to save a pig who never considered the fragility of her own life until death became readily apparent." If the six-year-old Andrea and the eight-year-old Douglas once regarded Wilbur as a threatened fellow-child, both now preeminently identify themselves with the nurturance and wisdom of the adult Charlotte.

Charlotte's ability to metamorphose a "humble" pig into a radiant, special child through the criss-crossings of her intricate web is, of course, inseparable from White's own craft as a cross-writer. Although adult and child readers of his text express discrepant priorities, it is the web that allows both constituencies to believe in talking animals and in a spiderly interest in pigs. Whether read as an assault on the credulity of adults for whom advertising has replaced religion or as a Thoreauvian document that celebrates continuity and renewal, *Charlotte's Web* will continue to appeal to the child in us all.

White is a humorist, as are Hauff, Kipling, and Nesbit, the writers taken up in the first third of this collection. Like the *New Yorker* ironist who so strongly identifies with children and animals, Hauff uses indirection to question the norms imposed on the young by their elders. Yet if the deceptively conventional and benign surface of his children's stories allows Hauff, as Maureen Thum shows, to evade adult censorship, Kipling's invention of a genre of his own in the *Just So Stories* opens up a meeting place for father and daughter, an adult survivor and a dead—but ever living and infinitely renewable—child. Moreover, as U. C. Knoepflmacher demonstrates in his analysis of Kipling's composite drawings, the writer's graphic wit, like Sendak's, amplifies his verbal text and frees a space for endless interplay. Kipling and his children revered the work of E. Nesbit, his fellow cross-writer. Although her own attitude toward the "Mowgli-man" was more ambiguous, the Bastable children are uncritical of *The Jungle Books* they act out. Nesbit transports the Bastables into an adult novel, *The Red House,* and the significance of that transportation is assessed here not by one, but by three different interpreters—Mavis Reimer, Erika Rothwell, and Nesbit's most recent biographer, Julia Briggs. We felt that a volume devoted to polyphonic texts should include at least one colloquy by different voices. And, as an author whose wonderfully individualized children are typically treated as dynamic members of a larger group, E. Nesbit seems the ideal candidate.

"Salutations" is the first word uttered by the spider who immediately apologizes for her Latinism: "it's just my fancy way of saying hello or good morning" (White 35). Yet Charlotte's contravention of Strunk and White is deliberately implanted. The spider who knows that "humble" is related to "humus" and hence to one who lives close to the ground surely also knows that "salvus" is embedded in her choice of greeting. After salving a boy pig's wounded self-esteem and soothing his night fears, she will use her steadying voice to bring about his salvation. White's mentoria thus follows the path of those wise and impeccable dames who supervised the growth of English and American children in the eighteenth and nineteenth centuries. Four of these influential figures are taken up in the second third of our collection of essays. That the first, Charlotte Smith, should share the name of the hairy-legged Charlotte A. Cavatica may merely be a felicitous coincidence. But the fact that the other three, Maria Edgeworth, Margaret Gatty, and Mary Mapes Dodge, were also involved in revisionary cultural work does make them the foremothers of White's weaver of words. Charlotte the wordsmith is, after all, based on the brilliant Katharine White, "a true friend and a good writer," whose discriminating yet nurturing stewardship at the *New Yorker* helped bring distinction to those she supervised.

As Donelle Ruwe's analysis of the Lambs and Smith demonstrates, the cross-writing of genders and generations can reinforce or challenge existing cultural ideologies. If our historical positioning makes us notice textual fissures papered over by the Lambs, recent feminist theory enables us to appreciate Smith's artistry and cultural ambitions. But Ruwe notices what contemporary resuscitations of Smith's

literary achievement have undervalued: how much of her poetic vir-
tuosity is grounded in her work for young persons. Smith (who gave
birth to twelve children) could use juvenile relatives for both inspiration and critical reception. Similarly, as Mitzi Myers reminds us,
the twenty-two children produced by her father's four marriages provided Maria Edgeworth with an ongoing supply of juvenile readers,
critics, and potential story subjects and allowed her to reexperience
childhood and continually reactivate her own child self. Moreover, as
Myers maintains, Edgeworth's Anglo-Irish identity, her hybrid literary careers, her cross-disciplinary curiosity, her conflicting political
allegiances, and her allusive intertextuality also coalesced to designate her as a paradigmatic border-crosser.

Like Smith, Edgeworth, and many other women writers, Margaret
Gatty melds scientific and literary interests. Her multidisciplinary
parables not only conspire against later "adultist" notions of aesthetic
purity, but also address dual audiences and fulfill surprisingly ambitious dual aims. As Alan Rauch notes, this wife of a provincial clergy-
man has designs on a British national consciousness and can debate
"big" issues like evolution: not all Victorian sages are named Car-
lyle or Ruskin, nor do they all inveigh in strident polemics. Engag-
ingly oblique and scientifically informative, Gatty remains indubitably
political. Her work confirms the profound impact exerted by works
all too often ignored in current cultural reconstructions. As Graham
Greene and so many others have testified, "It is only in childhood
that books have any deep influence on our lives. What do we ever get
nowadays from reading to equal the excitement and the revelation of
those first fourteen years?" (13).

Rauch, Ruwe, and Myers, as well as Susan R. Gannon in her subsequent study of the dual readership of *St. Nicholas Magazine*, remind us
that child readers produce adult thinkers and writers. Given the critical attention paid to texts read by adult writers in their later years, it
seems odd that what they imbibed as children has gone unremarked.
The memoirs, autobiographies, and letters of a host of eighteenth-
and nineteenth-century figures defy our modernist clichés about the
deadening effect of all those boring, adult-chosen works shoved down
the throats of unwilling tots. Despite invectives against one's youthful reading, like Nesbit's own *Wet Magic* (1913), what impresses about
these reminiscences is how beloved many writers we now dismiss
were and how influentially they shaped future audiences—and future
writers.

Perhaps no periodical production succeeded so well in amalgamating the aims and needs of a dual audience as did *St. Nicholas.* Gannon's rich analysis of the magazine as a bi-text urges us to explore what happens to the *adult* audience for all ambiguous writings directed at multiple readers. As she shows, Dodge converted *St. Nicholas* into a meeting ground: generations of future adults could interact in its pages with their young peers as well as with their elders. This harmonious coalition, befitting a nation beginning to insist on its identity as a "melting pot," thus offers one more example of the transformative spaces created by the cross-writing contributors to Dodge's journal. Frances Hodgson Burnett and Kipling, for example, not only transport boy heroes into England and India, the remembered lands of their respective childhoods, but also open up new terrains for girls: the fantasyland in Burnett's "Behind the White Brick" anticipates the secret garden Mary Lennox will revitalize (see Auerbach 133), and the Whale, Camel, and Rhinoceros tales are preludes to the story in which Taffy can create a sign-system of her own. Here, adult and child, as well as girls and boys, can become reconciled, mutually strengthened.

Young and mature audiences, however, could also meet in other kinds of ventures—undertakings that perfected the "art of teaching in sport" long before our own multimedia artifacts and even before the educational innovations rightly celebrated by Carolyn Steedman and Juliet Dusinberre.[3] The virtually complete teaching tool assembled by Lady Ellenor Fenn, discussed in our "Varia" section by Andrea Immel, is just one example of the extraordinary teaching devices that delighted our ancestors of all ages. Fenn's charming box miniaturizes the extravagant devices and exhibits examined by scholars such as Richard D. Altick and Barbara Maria Stafford. Her visual and verbal cornucopia opens out an entire Lilliputian world that parent and child can reassemble and deconstruct as their whimsy takes them. As innovative in its day as post-modern hypertextuality is today, and certainly requiring a more active and imaginative participation, this specimen of child-adult interplay challenges the constructions of our own media culture by the sophistication of its high literary and intellectual standards.

The last two essays in the collection, however, stress fissures as much as coalitions. Can *Goblin Market* and *The Lord of the Flies* be read as child-texts, or are they irrevocably shaped by an adult understanding? Like so many of her fellow Victorians, Christina Rossetti aligns herself with the traditions of folklore in order to recover a female space. Even more important, she razes the distinction between child and adult when she has a cured Laura wake up from her trance: laughing and tossing "gleaming" locks that show "not one thread of gray," Laura is a sexualized woman who has fully recovered her "innocent old way" (Rossetti, ll. 540, 538). But even though Rossetti conflates girlhood and maturity, she also tries to cleanse Lizzie's and Laura's world of all male contamination, of the unsavory fraternity of goblin men who are both sexually threatening and childish. As Lorraine Janzen Kooistra shows, the transpositions at work in this masterpiece thus affect its readership. As she notes, the poem's blending of near-pornographic descriptions with materials highly attractive to child readers resulted in a dual marketing that persists to this day.

If merchant men are barred from Lizzie's and Laura's agrarian world, women are absent in an island world where British boys degenerate into goblin-like sadists. Maternal memories fade as the blinking Piggy—a Wilbur without a Charlotte—is immolated by his peers. Golding's irony is exacerbated by his cross-references to an antecedent text, a boys' book, Ballantyne's *Coral Island*. As Minnie Singh notes, this earlier robinsonade exulted in the Crusoe-like resourcefulness of civilized Victorian boys. Yet Golding, who has a uniformed officer wonder whether such feral creatures could once actually have been British boys, has shifted genres. *The Lord of the Flies* not only harks back to Defoe via Ballantyne; it also takes its readers into the fourth book of *Gulliver's Travels*, the one omitted from all those children's editions that feature the voyages to Lilliput and Brobdingnag. Mowgli the boy who feasts with wolves and Max the boy who dances with wild things have, in Golding's own alchemy, turned into Yahoos. And yet this so emphatically "adult" text owes its power to its own distinct mode of cross-writing.

Cross-writing, we believe, has a dual value for those eager to gain for children's literature the recognition now given to formerly marginalized fields such as women's literature or ethnic literatures. It helps us conceptualize this emerging scholarly discipline more clearly and more globally. And it will help us to relocate children's literature at the center of the curricula at our schools and universities. The pioneering interdepartmental program in Children's Studies instituted at Brooklyn College by Gertrud Lenzer, professor of sociology at the City University of New York Graduate School and University Center, features courses in children's literature at its core. If a greater attention to cross-writing in such courses can benefit fields that are themselves in need of cross-fertilization, mainstream courses in literature might be equally enriched. We received essays on writers whose "adult" works are much taught and reprinted, but whose work for the young has persistently been segregated: Hawthorne and Kate Chopin, Stein and Ionesco. As Sandra Lee Beckett noted in a special Modern Language Association (MLA) session on cross-writing we sponsored in 1993, a writer like Michel Tournier (who, like Golding, returns to the Robinson-story from a modern perspective) persistently rewrites his children's books for adults and his adult books for children.[4]

Only when current revisionists of all stripes—feminists, Americanists, modernists—count children in will we be able to see the full cultural space that we continue to subdivide into separate little parcels. Even though formerly neglected adult female poets of the period between the late eighteenth-century Revolutions and the reformist 1830s are currently undergoing serious revaluation, the Romantic depictions of childhood—masculinist and anti-masculinist—still go unquestioned. When Charlotte Smith or Letitia Barbauld write grown-up poems, they are hot; yet as authors of work for the young, they are passed over. Despite the success of adult fictions such as *Turtle Diary* (1975) and *Riddley Walker* (1980), Russell Hoban seems to have been denied a place in American literature courses. His many children's books, including the one that, according to him, could just as well have been marketed as an adult fiction, have unquestionably contributed to that neglect: a pair of mechanical mice who resemble Huck and Jim and a living rat as obsessed as Captain Ahab seem to lack the "high seriousness" demanded by Arnoldian academics.

Without too much overstatement, we hope to claim cross-writing as an unlocker of doors that have shut off and devalued our field. More than a simple key, however, cross-writing offers the versatility of a critical Swiss Army knife. That versatility, we feel, is well exemplified by the essays we have collected. As delineated in this special issue, cross-writing is not just one topic among others. Currently proliferating articles on gender and postcolonialism anticipate what might be the eventual place of children's cultural studies. Cultural studies itself, as most centrally the study of *relationships* within and between cultures, has to go back to how cultures produce and construct citizens and consumers. Thus cross-writing, as developed in the following essays, involves more than one topic. To study the relationships within and between cultures, we need to go back and consider how cultures that transform children into citizens and consumers produce and reproduce themselves through literacy and the literary.

Our coinage brings together many disciplines and lines of inquiry. The playful yet sophisticated cross-weavings undertaken by the contributors to this volume cheer our utopian vision that children's literary studies will eventually be recognized not as a peripheral field annexed to an established canon, but as a "radiant" central core much like the concentric web against which Charlotte (and Garth Williams) placed a smiling Wilbur. Cross-writing may even help us revise, once and for all, the notions of a "Romantic" natural childhood which still tend to dominate most readings of children's literature and the child. But such airy projections are premature. We prefer to stay "humble," which, in Charlotte's helpful gloss, means "near the ground" as well as unproud (White 140).

U. C. Knoepflmacher
Mitzi Myers

Notes

1. Steve Martin's recent film by that name is a laudable attempt to "update" *Silas Marner*, and yet his "translation" cannot capture the existential dimensions of George Eliot's text.

2. C. D., an English major at Princeton University, 12 May 1995.

3. Despite their sophisticated critical attention to juvenile writing and representation in nineteenth- and twentieth-century culture, Dusinberre and Steedman start too late: the history of cross-writing begins long before the Victorian period. Although Steedman's 1995 book, *Strange Dislocations*, ostensibly begins in the 1780s, she looks at Goethe's Mignon rather than actual maternal educators.

4. As Marilyn Fain Apseloff notes in *They Wrote for Children Too*, most readers seem astonished by the sheer number of major authors who also wrote for children.

Works Cited

Altick, Richard D. *The Shows of London*. Cambridge, Mass.: Harvard University Press, Belknap, 1978.

Apseloff, Marilyn Fain. *They Wrote for Children Too: An Annotated Bibliography of Children's Literature by Famous Writers for Adults*. Westport, Conn.: Greenwood, 1989.

Auerbach, Nina, and U. C. Knoepflmacher, eds. *Forbidden Journeys: Fairy Tales and Fantasies by Victorian Women Writers*. Chicago: University of Chicago Press, 1992.

Butler, Samuel. *Life and Habit*. Vol. 4. The Shrewsbury Edition of the Works of Samuel Butler, Ed. Henry Festing Jones and A. T. Bartholomew. 20 vols. London: Jonathan Cape, 1923–26.

Dusinberre, Juliet. *Alice to the Lighthouse: Children's Books and Radical Experiments in Art*. New York: St. Martin's, 1987.

[Fenn, Lady Ellenor.] *The Art of Teaching in Sport: Designed as a Prelude to a Set of Toys, for Enabling Ladies to Instill the Rudiments of Spelling, Reading, Grammar, and Arithmetic, under the Idea of Amusement.* London: J. Marshall [not before 1785].

Greene, Graham. *The Lost Childhood and Other Essays.* London: Eyre and Spottiswoode, 1951.

Lanes, Selma G. *The Art of Maurice Sendak.* New York: Harry N. Abrams, 1980.

Rossetti, Christina. *Goblin Market,* in *The Complete Poems of Christina Rossetti: A Variorum Edition,* ed. R. W. Crump, vol. 1. Baton Rouge: Louisiana State University Press, 1987.

Stafford, Barbara Maria. *Artful Science: Enlightenment Entertainment and the Eclipse of Visual Education.* Cambridge, Mass.: MIT Press, 1994.

Steedman, Carolyn. *Strange Dislocations: Childhood and the Idea of Human Interiority, 1780–1930.* Cambridge, Mass.: Harvard University Press, 1995.

White, E. B. *Charlotte's Web.* New York: HarperCollins, 1980.

Articles

PLAYFUL TRAFFIC

Misreading the Cross-Writer: The Case of Wilhelm Hauff's Dwarf Long Nose

Maureen Thum

> *The grotesque . . . discloses the potential of an entirely different world, of another order, of another way of life. It leads men out of the confines of the apparent (false) unity of the indisputable and stable."*
> M. M. Bakhtin (*Rabelais*, 48)

In their appeal to a dual audience, the literary fairy tales of Wilhelm Hauff (1802–27) epitomize the problematic nature of cross-writing. Hauff's three cycles of literary fairy tales, *The Caravan* (1826), *The Sheik of Alexandria and His Slaves* (1827), and *The Inn in Spessart* (1828, posthumously published), are directed at two seemingly disparate but by no means mutually exclusive readerships: an overt audience of bourgeois children, the "sons and daughters of the educated classes" (Hinz 112) to whom Hauff dedicated the three fairy-tale "almanacs,"[1] and an implied audience of aesthetically and politically sophisticated adults, whom he expected to be alert to his strategies of ironic reversal and indirection.

In the history of the *Kunstmärchen*, Hauff has been seen as an unusual and even a puzzling case. Insufficiently known to English-speaking readers, Hauff's tales, from the time of their publication, have nonetheless enjoyed an unabated popularity in German-speak-

Children's Literature 25, ed. Francelia Butler, R. H. W. Dillard, and Elizabeth Lennox Keyser, guest ed. Mitzi Myers and U. C. Knoepflmacher (Yale University Press, © 1997 Hollins College).

ing countries, where they continue to rank just behind the *Children and House Tales* of the Brothers Grimm (Klotz 210).[2] German critics have taken at face value Hauff's dedication of the tales to the off-spring of the educated classes, as well as his claim, made in a letter to his publisher, that the tales are exclusively aimed at an audience of "girls or boys from twelve to fifteen years of age" (Pfäfflein 15). They have therefore dismissed Hauff's tales as inconsequential children's fantasies, ascribing his "juvenile popularity" (Koopmann 491) and "puzzling" success to his production of a presumably superficial and inferior product designed to cater to the tastes of an uncritical and aesthetically naive audience.[3]

In rejecting the tales as puerile fantasies, Hauff's German critics have disregarded the satirical and subversive intent expressed in the poignant allegory "Fairy Tale as Almanac," which Hauff deliberately placed at the beginning of *The Caravan,* the first of his three cycles. They have thus greatly underestimated the author's craft—and his craftiness—as a cross-writer who wishes both to explore and to test the shifting relation between the child and the adult reader.

Hauff assumes the role of children's author precisely because it allows him to question the norms that an audience of children—prospective adults—are expected to adopt in order to fit into the world of their elders. During a period when severe sanctions were imposed on those who transgressed strictly enforced censorship laws, donning the mask of the children's writer allowed Hauff to conceal his critical stance from adult view, and thus to evade the vigilance of censors. Disguised as a writer for "mere" children, he could undercut the contemporary status quo with relative impunity.[4]

Still, precisely because Hauff's tales consciously transgress generational boundaries by engaging the child on one level while undertaking an ironic and satirical dismantling of societal norms on another, critics have been at a loss to categorize his works either as children's or as adult literature. Dismissing Hauff's tales as inferior "juvenile" fare, commentators have failed to look beyond their seemingly conventional and innocuous surface.

Thus, the German editors of two relatively recent scholarly editions of Hauff's collected works, published in 1962 and 1970, have characterized Hauff's writings as the productions of a hack writer whose mental horizon was circumscribed by the petty bourgeois prejudices of a literary and cultural philistinism. In full agreement, Volker Klotz, a respected German literary critic, sums up the prevailing consensus

when he professes to be dismayed by Hauff's failure to vanish from
the literary and popular scene. "Nowhere else in the history of the
literary fairy tale," states Klotz, has such "dubious literary quality"
been accompanied by such "an immense and continuous popularity
among the reading public" (210).[5]

Viewing Hauff's literary fairy tales from the perspective of literary
cross-writing, however, can provide a far clearer understanding of the
author's intentionally ambiguous authorial stance. Neither a second-
rate "children's" author nor a petty bourgeois ideologue, Hauff provides in his tales an astute, highly sophisticated exploration of that
uncertain area between seemingly antithetical poles of experience:
the area of wonder, of free-floating potentialities and magical inter-
cessions associated with the child's "unreal" world of fantasy, and the
area of social realities, psychological restrictions, and responsibilities
so often identified with the "real" world of the adult. Indeed, Hauff
repeatedly blurs the binary oppositions on which his contemporaries
based their constructions of identity; thus he can be said to "hover,"
much like William Blake, between the opposed "states of perception" that the English poet had "labelled innocence and experience"
(Knoepflmacher 497).

Hauff's novella-length tale *Dwarf Long Nose* is a case in point. In
Dwarf Long Nose, Hauff deliberately enlists a juvenile protagonist in
order to chart the ambiguous territory of a consciousness suspended
between the world of the child and that of the adult. In its exploration
of this in-between state, Hauff's tale furnishes a perfect example of
Knoepflmacher's notion that the boundaries between a literature directed toward the child and that intended for the adult are uncertain
at best—if indeed such clear lines of demarcation are at all discern-
ible.

Dwarf Long Nose first appeared in Hauff's second cycle, *The Sheik of
Alexandria and His Slaves,* but it has, at least in part due to its novella-
like length, been frequently issued by itself. Much reprinted, the tale
is as familiar to German speakers as are *Alice in Wonderland* and *The
Wind in the Willows* to a British audience, or *Little Women* and *Huckle
berry Finn* to Americans. English-speaking readers, however, may only
know Doris Orgel's 1960 translation of *Dwarf Long Nose,* a book noteworthy not so much for Orgel's misleading and in some areas mis-
translated rendition of Hauff's text as for Maurice Sendak's rich
and highly suggestive illustrations, which are faithful to Hauff's own
mockery of "pretension and stiffness" (Lanes 61). Indeed, Sendak's

graphic interpretation of Hauff's text not only surpasses Orgel's translation, but also reveals that his understanding of this highly complex, multilayered work goes far beyond that of his academic critics, who have persistently overlooked the story's subtle, playful (and often acerbic) subversions.

In *Dwarf Long Nose,* Wilhelm Hauff conceals his subversive intentions beneath the deceptively benign surface of a conventional text. Camouflage is crucial to his concealments. The narrator first appears to establish a conventional portrait of a seemingly harmonious society and to rely, uncritically, on an entire repertoire of ostensibly familiar folk- and fairy-tale motifs and stereotypes. But Hauff soon upsets the expectations of his readers. He violates the generic codes he had seemed to invoke at the outset of his tale by engaging in a steady process of unmasking and ironic reversal. By the conclusion of the narrative, the conventional fairy-tale images and the petty-bourgeois idyll seemingly endorsed in the initial scenes have been dismantled and radically turned on their heads. The narrator thus destabilizes fixed views of identity, undercuts traditionalist codes, and exposes the underlying injuriousness of what had appeared on the surface to be an idealized portrait of community life.

The tale opens with what seems to be a typical fairy-tale scenario. Jacob, a good little boy who appears to embody all the proper social virtues, confronts a hoarse-voiced Herb Fairy, who ostensibly displays the malignancy of the stereotypical "wicked witch." Overly trustful, Jacob appears to fall victim to this bizarre stranger: he finds himself imprisoned for seven years in her enchanted house, where, transformed into a squirrel, he undergoes an apprenticeship as kitchen helper and chef. Released after his captivity, he is again transformed, this time into an ugly dwarf. As Jacob now discovers, he has acquired all the deformities he had formerly derided in the Wise Herb Fairy when she had first appeared on the marketplace seven years before. When he returns home, he is cruelly repudiated by his parents and by his entire community, none of whom can recognize the abducted boy.

Only by falling back on the culinary skills he acquired in the house of the Wise Herb Fairy can this creature—no longer called Jacob, but now known only as Dwarf Long Nose—find a place in a society that spurns misfits. He enters the service of a demanding duke and rises to the position of master chef, becoming a figure of widespread renown. But his career as court cook turns out to be precarious. On a whim of the finicky and capricious duke, Dwarf Long Nose is sentenced to death for "bad cooking." Aided by the extensive herbal lore of another outsider, an enchanted goose called Mimi, whom he had saved from the butcher's block, Dwarf Long Nose manages to recover his normal shape and to slip secretly out of the palace, leaving pandemonium in his wake. After the couple returns to her father's house, Mimi, too, is restored to her normal state.

Hauff's conclusion appears to present the conventional return to harmony and order, the expected happy ending of fairy-tale lore. Richly rewarded by Mimi's father, the sorcerer Weathergoat, Jacob returns home. Now joyfully recognized and received by the parents who had rejected him in his previous incarnation, Jacob sets up shop with the money from Weathergoat. As an adult, Jacob forsakes the fantasy world of his childhood and settles for the peaceful yet colorless realities of a petty bourgeois existence.

Pointing to its concluding return to "normalcy," critics have argued that *Dwarf Long Nose* is nothing more than a conventional children's tale. It is dominated, they contend, by a didactic author who promulgates a narrowly philistine mindset. If Hauff allows his child readers to indulge briefly in escapist fantasizing, he does so only in order to teach them that fantasy has no ultimate place in the adult bourgeois world he presumably endorses.[6]

Such a reading underestimates Hauff's relation to both his child and his adult readers. Restricted by harsh censorship laws that forbade any form of social or political criticism, Hauff was forced to resort to subterfuge: he concealed his subversive intentions beneath the seemingly innocuous cloak of fairy tales for children. A careful attention to the cues Hauff implants in his text reveals that he has no intention of indoctrinating the "sons and daughters of the educated classes" with bourgeois values. Instead, he values them as potential future allies. Like Jacob in the story, they are to be wrested away from a smug conformity; yet, unlike Jacob, who forgets his magical apprenticeship, they may remember after becoming adults their tutelage as momentary outsiders.

Hauff provides an important cue to his intentions in "Fairy Tale as Almanac," the brief prologue to his first cycle of tales. He adumbrates his strategies of subversion and dissent in this brief, parable-like narrative in which Fairy Tale reports to her mother, Queen Fantasy, that her lot on earth has become increasingly difficult. As Fairy Tale explains, "intelligent guards" at the gates of the city—that is, of society—have barred her entrance. The guards are unequivocally censors whose "sharp eyes" and "sharp pens" (Hauff, *Sämtliche Werke*, 2:8–10), probe into "everything" that comes from the realm of Queen Fantasy. As Fairy Tale plaintively explains, "If someone arrives who does not share their opinions, they raise a great clamour or murder him, or slander him . . . so that nobody believes what he says" (Hauff 2:8). On the advice of Queen Fantasy, Fairy Tale resorts to a ruse to gain entrance into the city. Masked by the fabulous cloak of the fairy-tale almanac (the title that Hauff gave each of his cycles), she lulls the guards to sleep with her magical images. She then steps over their prone bodies and slips through the gate unobserved, aided by a friendly and enlightened adult who comments acerbically, pointing to the sleeping guards, "Your beautiful things mean nothing to them. Come quickly through the gate; then they will have no idea you are in the country, and you can continue your way undisturbed and unnoticed" (2:11). The kindly man takes Fairy Tale to his own children, and shelters her secretly in his house. Accessible to all the other children in the neighborhood, she can now carry out her forbidden activities undetected (2:11).

Hauff's parable not only indicates the subversive potential of his fantasies for the young, but also acknowledges his authorial strategies of concealment. In order to challenge the status quo, Hauff must, like Fairy Tale, slip past the censors, whether these are the real censors in the Duchy of Württemberg, where Hauff resided, or the internalized censors within the minds of his German readers. Internalized censors are, as Hauff implicitly recognizes, far more widespread and pernicious than those of any enforcement agency; they stir up prejudices that stifle any alternative, dissenting view of the world. "Fairy Tale as Almanac," appearing in a prominent position as the preface to the first fairy-tale cycle, indicates that Hauff's dedication to the "sons and daughters of the educated classes," so carefully foregrounded on the frontispiece of the three fairy-tale "almanacs," acts as a screen for his desire to appeal to a far more diverse alliance between children and enlightened adults—here represented as coauditors of Fairy Tale—than critics have allowed.

As "Fairy Tale as Almanac" suggests, Hauff's narratives for children are characterized by a dialogic interplay between two implied audiences. *Dwarf Long Nose* is no exception. As a reader of this tale, the child is invited to empathize with the story's marginalized boy protagonist and to share the metamorphic process Jacob undergoes when he is transformed into a grotesque dwarf. Compelled to view the familiar world from Jacob's estranged perspective, the child adopts a potentially critical view. The adult, too, participates in a process of defamiliarization, yet is more likely than the child to engage the text intellectually and analytically. The adult reader is thus invited not only to partake of Jacob's alienation, but also to observe the dialogic process itself and thus to go beyond the child reader, who might welcome Jacob's final return to normalcy. The adult, by contrast, is encouraged, by concealed authorial cues, to decode Hauff's sharp critique of communal prejudice and stereotyping.

As part of his cross-writing strategy, then, Hauff has created a double-voiced text in the sense understood by Bakhtin: his carnivalized discourse "serves two speakers at the same time and expresses simultaneously two different intentions" ("Discourse," 324). Yet these "intentions" also overlap, for the "two voices" in the text, like Hauff's two kinds of readers, cross each other and are "dialogically inter-related" (324).[7] Cross-writing thus invites cross-reading.

II

As Hauff's parable suggests, a careful reading of *Dwarf Long Nose* as a double-voiced text reveals that the author, like Fairy Tale, has taken pains to lull the censors to sleep before slipping past them with the aid of the child and the enlightened adult reader. The opening scene—the ostensible encounter between a "witch" and her "victim"—is paradigmatic of the author's consistent strategies of carnival unmasking and ironic reversal throughout the tale. The narrator first establishes a deceptively "normal" and conventional textual surface that relies on conventional images; he then proceeds to undermine these images. In the dismantling process, he unmasks himself as a subversive writer who challenges rather than reinforces the contemporary status quo.

In the initial pages of the tale, the narrator takes pains to depict a conventional petty-bourgeois idyll peopled by what appear to be stereotypical fairy-tale figures. The shoemaker, his wife, and their son Jacob form a small, modest family resembling the virtuous poor depicted in such tales as the Grimms' "The Shoemaker and the Elves." These are generally good, kind people who, as the reader expects, are bound to be rewarded for their charitable behavior.[8] Jacob, in particular, seems to be cast as an ideal, universally pleasing child. Kind, polite, hard-working, and obedient, he helps his mother at the

marketplace, calling out her wares with his clear voice, attracting customers by his beauty, and earning large tips from the wealthy market
patrons whose purchases he helps to carry.

The harmony of this scene appears to be disrupted by the arrival of
an intruder, an old woman who has all the characteristics associated
with the stereotypical wicked witch: "She looked rather ragged and
tattered, had a small, sharp face with deep lines from old age, red
eyes and a bent and pointed nose reaching down toward her chin.
She walked, leaning on a long stick; and yet it was impossible to say
how she moved, for she limped and slid and swayed" (Hauff, "Zwerg
Nase," *Sämmtliche Werke,* 2:113). The arrival of this ungainly stranger
not only proves threatening to the burghers of the small town, but
also shows its self-complacent ethos to be a total fraud. Jacob is now
unmasked as being less innocent or childlike than the reader had
expected. Conversely, the old woman, whom Jacob assumes to be a
wicked witch, will reveal her true identity as the Wise Herbalist, or
the Wise Herb Fairy, whose role is—as her name suggests—therapeutic rather than malevolent.

Jacob's response to the repulsive, hoarse-voiced old woman provides the first clear signal that all is not right in this harmonious
world. The good, polite, kind child, habitually praised by his mother's
clients for his pleasing and tractable manners, suddenly shouts at
the old woman and derides her seemingly bizarre appearance: "Look
here, you are a shameless old woman," he cries. "First you shove your
horrible brown fingers into the beautiful herbs, then you squeeze
them and hold them up to your long nose, so that anyone who sees
wouldn't want to buy them any more" (2:113).

Jacob's anger and revulsion at first seem understandable to a reader,
whether child or adult, who has been schooled in the ways of wicked
witches, and who is therefore familiar with the drastic measures to
which fairy-tale characters resort in order to banish or to destroy such
undesirables. Only in retrospect, when the reader is led to question
the stereotypically malignant image the old woman seems to represent, does the boy's indignant response appear out of place, going
far beyond the apparent cause: the rude handling of market wares by
a thoughtless customer. His knee-jerk response reflects the distrust
and communal hatred of the outsider—a hatred that Jacob himself
is forced to experience when he reappears in the marketplace as a
grotesque dwarf whom the townsfolk no longer recognize as one of
their own.

Symptomatic of his mindset, the boy does not recoil from making a thinly veiled threat to decapitate the old woman: "Don't wag your head so horribly back and forth. Your neck is as thin as a cabbage stem," he shouts, "It could easily break off and fall into the basket" (2:114). These expressions of communal hatred are all the more disturbing because Hauff has placed them in the mouth of an ostensibly innocent, spontaneously kind, and enviably comely boy. Equally if not more disturbing than his ghoulish comment is Jacob's final taunt, a rhetorical question indicating that the old woman's death would be at most an economic inconvenience, because it would frighten away the other customers: "And who would want to buy anything from us then?" (2:114).

Jacob's angry and rude outburst demonstrates that he has already been shaped by the narrow outlook of the provincial society whose material values he so unthinkingly espouses. Like a ventriloquist's puppet, Jacob utters words that are not his own. Because the old woman deviates from his society's norms, Jacob feels justified in attacking her as someone unprotected by the codes and courtesies extended to those accepted as fellow human beings. He also knows that everyone in the marketplace, including his mother, shares this view of the outsider. Indeed, Jacob's mother implicitly validates her son's statements by demanding that the woman either buy or leave: "If you want to buy something, make it quick. You are frightening away my other customers" (2:114). Only later when Jacob returns to the marketplace as an ugly dwarf does the pain inflicted by such conditioned responses fully come to light. Only then will Jacob be forced to the excruciating recognition that his community's hatred of Otherness applies even to one who can prove, like Jacob, that he was formerly one of its "normal" members.

In this process of unmasking and reversal, Hauff assigns the role of catalyst to the Herb Fairy. She wears a conventional mask herself and thus allows not only Jacob, but also Hauff's readers, to misread her as a stereotypical witch. Previous critics, taking the mask at face value, have seen the Herb Fairy with Jacob's prejudiced eyes. Doris Orgel goes so far as to reinforce the stereotype by substituting the misogynist label of "old hag" for Hauff's more neutral term "old woman" ("altes Weib") throughout much of her 1960 translation. She even adds the adjective "wicked," which is pointedly absent from the German text (Orgel 28).[9]

Yet the old woman is neither a witch nor a symbol of evil. Instead, this seemingly grotesque figure allows Hauff to expose the hostility toward aberrant behavior shown by the virtuous citizens of a community ready to malign all strangers as diabolical outsiders. Her malevolence is revealed to be an identity imposed on her by a community that projects its superstitious dread of the unknown on the grotesque stranger. Hauff implants sufficient authorial hints to challenge this arbitrary superimposition. Her actual name, "die Fee Kraüterweis"— literally "Wise Herb Fairy" or "Wise Fairy"—does not betoken the evil and destructiveness of a demonic figure, as Doris Orgel's translation suggests (Orgel omits the word "wise" from her name). Rather, the name suggests her mastery of herbal lore. The narrator thus signals that the Wise Herb Fairy is a figure in the tradition of the female healer, a tradition epitomized in German culture by the well known and much revered medieval mystic and intellectual Hildegard von Bingen.[10]

Contrary to the impression created by Orgel's translation, the narrator does not reinforce misogynistic stereotypes; instead, he eschews antifeminist labels, consistently avoiding such charged words as "Hexe" (witch), "Unholdin" (crone), or "Scheusal" (hag). This intentional avoidance signals the narrator's dissociation from those characters in the tale who call her "böse" (evil), a word that appears only twice in the text, and in a context that challenges its applicability.[11] Furthermore, by casting the Wise Herbalist as a fay (from the Latin *fata*, or "fate"), Hauff converts this misunderstood creature into one of those "goddesses of destiny" so prevalent in Continental folklore (Harf-Lancner 13). Far from exerting a malign influence, the Wise Herb Fairy is a severe female mentor or "mentoria" who initiates a therapy designed to "cure" Jacob of his blindness, a disability caused by his adoption of his elders' narrowly restrictive and prejudicial views.[12]

Just as the Herb Fairy defies antifeminist stereotypes of the diabolical old hag, so is her domain anything but conventional. Her enchanted house bears little resemblance to the expected evil witch's house familiar to readers of "Hänsel and Gretel." On the contrary, her dwelling is a transformative site—an extraordinary, magical realm of fluidity and mind-altering dreams. There, after drinking a fragrant broth she prepares for him, Jacob falls asleep and experiences the equivalent of a dream vision. Traditionally, dream visions have been portrayed as spiritual quests that often bring about a radical change in the perspective of the dreamer. As Bahktin has noted, the dream world suspends the rules and values governing ordinary reality and prepares the way for the dreamer's new vision of the world (*Problems,* 147).

Jacob's dream vision not only alters his original fix on the world, but also leads the reader to question a status quo to which the sleeper can no longer return. Awakened, Jacob epitomizes the solitary, insightful, and talented outsider who sees his society with alien eyes; in short, he is analogous to the writer or artist who views his society through defamiliarizing lenses. Hauff has the Wise Herb Fairy initiate Jacob into secrets known only to the greatest of chefs, so that he becomes an expert in his culinary "art." (The narrator repeatedly uses the word "Kunst"—art—to refer to Jacob's newly won skills.) Hauff thus relies on a metaphor for the writer that he also employed in his "adult" prose.[13] That Jacob is being trained as an "artist" is soon corroborated by his need to cater to the tastes of his patron, the local duke. Both the talented master chef and the talented writer must equally draw on their imaginative capacities to appeal—as Hauff emphasizes in his satire "Books and the World of Readers"—to the finicky taste of spoiled and pampered consumers. Furthermore, Jacob as master-chef must operate under prohibitions similar to those that an absolutist regime places on the creative artist.

In this context, the Wise Herb Fairy may be seen as a rather unconventional muse. Sendak's representation of her as she hovers over a fragrant broth—the source of Jacob's dream-vision—catches the anomaly of this figure. Ugly and homely the Herb Fairy may be, but in Sendak's rendering, she appears as big-bosomed, maternal, and smiling (Orgel 12).[14] She is Jacob's new "mother" and teacher, and her enchantments and chastisements facilitate Jacob's radically altered view of his former world.

Although a child reader may not respond analytically or intellectually to Hauff's strategies of unmasking and reversal, he or she cannot avoid participating in the changes *Dwarf Long Nose* dramatizes. Seeing the world anew through the eyes of Jacob—renamed Dwarf Long Nose—the child reader responds with a shared sense of precariousness and an equally strong desire for reempowerment. Parental rejection and fear of abandonment, so real to the child, are offset by the text's reassurance that the ugly dwarf who no longer resembles Jacob has nonetheless acquired skills and insights that make him unique. But in depicting Jacob's plight, Hauff's text also is unsparing. Thus, although a child may not remember or know what the word "preju-

carving knives sticking in their belts. After them a
crowd of squirrels came skipping in; these wore wide
Turkish pantaloons, walked upright, and had little
caps of velvet on their heads. They seemed to be the
kitchen boys, for they scrambled with great speed
up the walls and brought down pans and bowls, eggs
and butter, herbs and flour, and carried them to the
stove. There the old woman herself was walking back
and forth in her slippers of coconut shell, intent on
personally preparing the little boy's soup.

Now the fire was burning high, smoke was coming from the pan, and a pleasant odor pervaded the
room; but the hag was still running about with the

Figure 1. The old woman stirs the pot. Illustration by Maurice Sendak in *Dwarf Long
Nose* by Wilhelm Hauff. By permission of HarperCollins and the artist. Copyright ©
Maurice Sendak 1960.

dice" means, he or she cannot but respond viscerally to the experience of a boy who weeps bitterly when his father treats him as an
imposter and whips him out of the shop and down the street, shouting invectives and showering blows on his humped shoulders.

If the child's perceptions of the normal and normative world are disturbed by such a scene, then Hauff has achieved his purpose: to provide an alternative view of reality informed by greater tolerance, enlightenment, and understanding. I have at least anecdotal evidence from two German-speaking readers who remember their childhood reading and rereading *Dwarf Long Nose* with startling clarity and vividness. Upon hearing the present interpretation, one of them stated, "I like to flatter myself that even as a child I perceived the concealed critique, and that I took it with me from the text." The other reader remembered that Jacob's final recovery of his former shape and identity, though satisfying, failed to offset the empathy he had felt for the ostracized and lonely dwarf.

III

Although the Herb Fairy ostensibly disappears from view in the next phase of Hauff's narrative, her attributes are retained by Jacob, who has now assumed her identity as a deformed, yet knowing, outsider. Child and adult, Self and Other are telescoped in this hunched, neckless figure. Dwarf Long Nose, no longer "little Jacob," is a hybrid figure caught in a liminal zone between a childhood he has already abandoned and an adulthood he has not yet reached. Dwarf Long Nose epitomizes Bakhtin's description of the grotesque as "a phenomenon in transformation" and "an as yet unfinished metamorphosis of death and birth, growth and becoming" (*Rabelais*, 24), which is quite different from the "ready-made completed being" (25) associated with traditional views of how identity is fashioned.

When Jacob emerges from his period of enchantment and reenters the everyday world, his age, like his identity, has become indeterminate. Although trapped in the body of a grotesque adult, he is still mentally a young boy of eight or twelve years old—Hauff gives conflicting ages, thus further blurring the time frame—who believes he left the marketplace just a few hours earlier.[15] Seven years have elapsed in the ordinary world; nevertheless, only a single afternoon appears to have passed during his dream vision. Jacob is chronologically fifteen (or nineteen?) years old, but having experienced no maturation from childhood to adulthood, he is mentally still a "child."

Jacob remains childlike in another sense as well. As an eight- or twelve-year-old boy in the marketplace, Jacob was already formed as a carefully conditioned adult. With all his preconceptions and prejudices fully developed, he was Bakhtin's "ready-made, completed being." Now, however, in the body of a grotesque adult, he finds that his former "grown-up" prejudices no longer fit an estranging universe. He has thus been "reborn" and must start over again by reliving a childhood based on different premises and assumptions. He must return to the position of a naive, unformed infant who has been "birthed" after a gestation period of seven years by an ancient and aged, yet wise, Herb Fairy. Hauff refers, if obliquely, to a relatively well-known European carnival figure: that of the pregnant and laughing "old hag" who "combines a senile, decaying and deformed flesh with the flesh of new life, conceived but as yet unformed" (Bakhtin, *Rabelais*, 25–26). (Unlike the traditional carnival figure, however, the Wise Herb Fairy is no hag, and she is far from senile.) Dwarf Long Nose, the child produced by this bizarre pregnancy, is a similarly anomalous figure. He combines the features of age and youth in a single grotesque being who is nonetheless neither child nor adult; and, by the same token, he crosses genders with the wise old woman whose powerful phallic nose he has inherited.[16] He is thus neither male nor female. Finally, as a figure with whom the reader empathizes and identifies, but who is nonetheless trapped in a deformed body, he is neither Self nor Other.

When the boy reenters the ordinary world, he still believes himself to be unchanged. Ironically, as the narrator's comments stress, he still tries to view the world and his place in it from his accustomed perspective. Very rapidly, however, his former view must give way to an unfamiliar and estranged outlook. Bakhtin refers to such shifts in perspective as "experimental fantasticality" and argues that such a disjunctive point of view permits the writer to depict "a radical change in the scale of the observed phenomena of life" (*Problems*, 116). In *Dwarf Long Nose*, the misshapen dwarf is forced to shed both his former values and his former view of himself, a drastic alteration in which the reader is invited to participate.

In order to elicit a visceral response from the (perhaps unwilling) reader, Hauff charts Jacob's gradual process of discovery and enlightenment in chilling detail. As he runs through the streets, hurrying back to the marketplace and to his mother, the former Jacob is hampered by gathering crowds who are shouting, "Hey look at the ugly dwarf. . . . Hey, look what a long nose he has, and see how his head sticks down in his shoulders, and his ugly brown hands" (Hauff, *Sämtliche Werke*, 2:119). Assuming that these exclamations are directed at some passing freak, Jacob is filled with curiosity. Only his haste prevents him from joining the crush of curious onlookers: "On any other day he would have run along with them, since he had loved to see giants or dwarfs all his life" (2:119). Unaware as yet that *he* is the misshapen outcast who will later be known by the metonymic name of "Nose," he still regards himself as a comfortable member of a majority who regards such freaks as a source of "innocent" entertainment.

When he at last looks into a mirror and sees the grotesque object he has become, Jacob experiences an estrangement from his own body and from his former hold on the world: in this depiction of doubled consciousness, symbolized by Jacob as he observes his altered image, the Self has literally become the Other. In the bizarre body reflected before him, he immediately recognizes an exaggeration of the old woman's features, and he remembers how, while still a comfortable member of the normal world, he had spurned and insulted her:

> His eyes had become small, like the eyes of a pig. His nose was monstrous, and hung down over his mouth and chin; his neck seemed to have been removed altogether, since his head was stuck deep into his shoulders. He could move it to the right and left only with great pain. His body was still the same size as it was seven years before, when he was twelve years old. But, while other children grow taller from the age of twelve to twenty, he had grown wider. His back and chest were buckled outward, and gave the appearance of a small over-stuffed sack. This heavy trunk sat upon two weak and spindly legs, which appeared incapable of carrying their burden. But his arms, which hung down his body, were all the larger for that; as large as the arms of a big, strong man. His hands were coarse and brownish-yellow, his fingers long and spidery. If he stretched them out, he could touch the floor without bending over. (2:123)

His Kafkaesque sense of self-estrangement brings about a radical shift in Jacob's view of himself and his place in the world. He suddenly feels older and "wiser," and, when he thinks of the old woman in the marketplace, he understands how and why this transformation has occurred.

The reader, whether experientially as a child, or experientially *and* analytically as an adult, can now see clearly the formerly idyllic, harmonious, petty bourgeois social order through the dwarf's defamiliarizing eyes. The small community of women in the market square is no longer friendly and welcoming, but hostile, angry, and vituperative. Jacob discovers that his grotesque appearance automatically excludes him from their society. His mother, Hanna, showers him with imprecations, just as Jacob had insulted the old woman seven years before. Calling him a "Missgeburt" (literally a misbirth, or a child born monstrously deformed), Hanna cries out, "What do you want from me, you ugly dwarf?" and orders him, "Get out of here!" (2:119). Soon Jacob's father, as noted, does not limit his response to verbal abuse.

Jacob's transformation allows Hauff to expand his critical scope by including an entire German duchy. Abandoned, rejected, and destitute, Jacob applies at the court of the local duke for the position of cook. His elevation to master chef, however, only underscores the continued precariousness of his position. Like a writer, this kitchen-artist must uneasily navigate between two seemingly separate worlds —a world of fantasy and imagination associated with the child, and a world of economic necessity and political machinations associated with the adult. Upon first entering the palace, Jacob is invited to become the duke's personal "pet" or "court dwarf," a position he proudly refuses because it does not allow him to exercise his genius in the art of cooking. As soon as Jacob is hired, the duke confers a new name upon what is now his creature by calling him "Zwerg Nase," which may be translated either as "Dwarf Nose" or simply, "Nose." The label not only signals the fact that Jacob is known only as an appendage to his own grotesque body; it also indicates Jacob's formal loss of individual identity and dignity. As a servant whose sole purpose is to cater to the sovereign's palate and submit to his lord's mindless whims, he exists only as an extension of the ducal will. Only as long as he can provide new recipes to enhance the duke's already bloated self-image is this kitchen-artist treated well. In (fig. 2) one of Sendak's most memorable illustrations (Orgel 43), Dwarf Long Nose is seated, dog-like, his mouth open, as the duke feeds him morsels from the table—a privilege, the narrator notes sarcastically, that Jacob "knew well how to treasure" (2:130).

The satirical portrait of petty German princes during the early decades of the nineteenth century is unmistakable. In its precariousness and short duration, as well as its threatened outcome, Jacob's career parallels that of many a court favorite in eighteenth-century German duchies. Whether chef, financier, or court writer, the court favorite watch him cook, and a few of the noblest gentry managed to get the Duke to allow their chefs to receive instruction from the dwarf, which brought in not a little money, for each of them paid half a ducat a day. And in order to keep the other cooks in good humor and to prevent their feeling envious, Long-Nose let them have this money which the gentlefolk paid for their chefs' tuition.

Figure 2. The Duke and the dwarf at dinner. Illustration by Maurice Sendak in *Dwarf Long Nose* by Wilhelm Hauff. By permission of HarperCollins and the artist. Copyright © Maurice Sendak 1960.

frequently rose only to suffer an abrupt fall.[17] Thus, after two years of faithful and impeccable service, Dwarf Long Nose is set an impossible task. The duke demands that he prepare a pâté whose secret ingredients are known only to a visiting prince whom the duke wishes to impress. When Jacob presents the dish, the visitor smiles "scornfully and secretively" as he tastes it, then pushes it away. Even though only a single ingredient has been omitted, the visitor claims that the savory dish is an unequivocal failure. Infuriated that his creature has punctured his self-image, the duke immediately withdraws his former praise: "You dog of a dwarf," he shouts, castigating his former favorite: "How dare you do this to your master?" (Hauff, *Sämtliche Werke*, 2:134). In punishment for the dwarf's "bad cooking" the duke threatens to "hack off his great head" (2:134). Threatened with death, Jacob falls on his knees and pleads, movingly, that the visiting prince reveal the secret ingredient: "Don't let me die for a handful of meat and flour" (2:135). His poignant plea indicates the absurdity of a political structure in which human life is worth nothing in the face of a princeling's most trivial and capricious whims.

Satirizing the numerous internecine and territorial squabbles among the dukes and princelings who competed for power and prestige throughout eighteenth-century Germany, Hauff depicts the bad cooking incident as triggering a war. The narrator wraps up the incident with playful yet pointed irony: "The Herb War," as it was named, was finally brought to an end by the "Peace of Pâté," so designated in the "annals of history" because during the feast celebrating their reconciliation the prince's chef prepares the pâté that Jacob had earlier failed to produce for the duke (2:137–38). The narrator's final comment, "Thus the tiniest causes often lead to great effects" (2:138) intentionally echoes, albeit more playfully and far less savagely, Voltaire's satirical lampoons in *Candide* against the misunderstood application of cause and effect. The intertextual echo, one of many references to Voltaire in Hauff's tales, points implicitly to Hauff's own covert satirical stance.

The conclusion of the Jacob and Mimi tale represents a complete anticlimax. When the two former outcasts escape and regain their normal shapes, the reader, schooled in fairy-tale paradigms, may well expect them to marry and live happily ever after. But they do not. The anticipated ending is aborted; Jacob returns home without Mimi. Seemingly forgetting his fantastic adventures as Dwarf Long Nose, Jacob opens up a little shop in his hometown and becomes old, respected, and prosperous—the epitome of a satisfied, upright, industrious, and colorless burgher. His previous years of suffering and rejection have left no trace on the tranquil surface of small-town existence.

But Hauff's ostensibly happy ending by no means signifies the author's resigned acquiescence to petty bourgeois values, as critics have contended (Schwarz 130; Klotz 210). Instead, it marks the last ironic reversal in this carnivalized tale. The intentionally abrupt and ironic ending suggests that the problems raised in the narrative have merely been set aside, not resolved. Again, Maurice Sendak's illustration catches the overlay of irony and whimsy that characterizes the final, folksy picture of Jacob as a happy burgher, smoking his pipe at the window of his shop and smiling contentedly (Orgel 63).

Wilhelm Hauff's *Dwarf Long Nose* exemplifies the difficulties encountered in the reception of cross-writing, as well as the transgressive potential of such writing. Misread as second-rate children's writing, Hauff's fairy-tale cycles have yet to be fully recognized by an academic and critical audience, and they have yet to be translated adequately into a modern English version that would include not only the tales themselves, but also the stories in which they are framed. Reading Hauff's tales without the frame stories is a little like reading Chaucer's *Canterbury Tales* without the General Prologue or the Head Links to each of the tales. Although the novella-length *Dwarf Long Nose* can certainly be read in its own right as a consummately crafted and multilayered work, a great deal of the wider context is necessarily lost in the absence of the frame tales.

Hauff's indirections as a children's author have unfortunately played into the prejudices of those who tend to segregate children's literature from "serious" adult literature. Thus, critics have regarded *Dwarf Long Nose* with the same condescension and distrust met by the aberrant Jacob/Dwarf Nose in the tale itself. Forced to disguise his voice and to conceal his subversive and dissenting stance beneath an innocuous mask, Hauff creates unusual barriers for any reader who approaches his texts with the preconceived notion that children's literature is neither worthy of nor susceptible to the careful analysis automatically granted to "adult" texts. Thus since the initial publication of his *Kunstmärchen* Hauff's artful mask has remained, for many readers, firmly in place; the signposts that mark the author's ironic strategies have yet to be noticed.

In making the case for a rereading of *Dwarf Long Nose*, I also wish to argue for a thorough reassessment of Hauff's other literary fairy tales. Modern readers who enter into Hauff's imaginative realm find his dual appeal to child and adult to be as resonant as is his attack on the mechanisms of stereotyping. They will appreciate him as did those initial readers, who—before the long critical silence and his subsequent rejection by academic scholars—had hailed him as a genius whose tales rival those of Brentano, E. T. A. Hoffmann, and Tieck.[18]

Notes

1. All translations of the German texts are my own. The citations from "Zwerg Nase" follow the text of *Sämtliche Werke*.

2. Hauff was a younger contemporary of the Grimm brothers. Although his literary and editorial activities spanned a mere three years, he was extraordinarily productive. Just ten months after becoming editor of J. F. Cotta's *Morgenblatt*, he died on November 18, 1827, at age twenty-four. His works, which were for the most part written and published between 1826 and 1827, demonstrate a remarkable variety and range. They include extensive journal entries, parodies, poems, sketches, a two-part satirical novel, half a dozen novellas, a historical romance in the manner of Sir Walter Scott, as well as three cycles of novella-length literary fairy tales. See Hinz (1989), Pfäfflein (1981), Beckmann (1976), and Hofmann (1902).

3. For Koopmann, "the history of literature has closed its files" on Hauff and has forbidden "any serious consideration of his works" (491).

4. During the post-Napoleonic restoration of absolutist forms of government in German-speaking countries, the Vienna Congress (1814–15) and the Karlsbad Decrees (1819) radically curtailed freedom of speech, imposed rigid censorship on publication, and ordered the dismissal of all teachers who undermined public order or who questioned the reestablishment of an absolutist status quo (Reinhardt 467). Although Wilhelm I of Württemberg, the duchy where Hauff resided, was among the less despotic of the absolutist petty princes, he often silenced critics by resorting to imprisonment without trial (Elias 312–13). Hauff's father and a cousin, Friedrich Hauff, were both victims of repressive measures. Imprisoned without trial, Hauff's father never recovered from the experience (Pfäfflein 8), whereas Hauff's cousin died shortly after being released, his health impaired by the imprisonment (Hofmann 39). Hauff, who was forced to rewrite his novella *Jew Süss* numerous times to escape censorship, thus had first-hand knowledge of the censors' destructive power.

5. Thus, for example, Fritz Martini dismisses Hauff as a "fabulizing improvisor" (535) whose work is marred by a narrow, petty bourgeois mindset. Egon Schwarz's astute discussion of *Dwarf Long Nose* grants Hauff some sharp flashes of irony but fails to recognize them as part of a sustained critical stance (130).

6. See Klotz, who argues that Hauff stifles fantasy with convention. According to Klotz, Hauff "draws on essential forms of the literary fairy tale and folk tale" but "weakens" and "strangles them, or wastes their former poetic energy" (210).

7. For certain aspects of the present study, I have adopted Bakhtin's concept of the multivoiced (carnivalized) text as opposed to the univocal (authoritarian, monologic) text, particularly as set forth in his *Problems of Dostoevsky's Poetics* and *Rabelais and His World*. For Bakhtin, multivocal literature expresses subversions akin to the questioning spirit of the European pre-Lenten Carnival, during which conventional and authoritarian structures are overturned through "a temporary suspension of all hierarchic distinctions and barriers among men and of certain norms and prohibitions of usual life" (*Rabelais*, 15). Unlike Bakhtin, however, I argue that such reversals are not necessarily free-floating and temporary phenomena. They are not confined to a carnival "time-out," which some anthropologists argue is merely a venting mechanism that permits authorities to stabilize and reaffirm the status quo (Davis 131–50). Instead, such dismantlings may lead—as historian Natalie Zemon Davis and medievalist Susan Crane argue—to a permanent state of questioning and subversion, if not an outright revolt against an authoritarian and unjust status quo (Crane 129–30; Davis 131–50).

8. Also known as "The Elves," the tale concerns a poor but charitable and virtuous cobbler and his wife who are aided by elves. After the couple returns the favor, the elves depart. Nevertheless, business continues to improve: "as long as the shoemaker lived, all went well with him, and all his efforts prospered" (Grimm 198; Pantheon ed.).

9. Although this is the *only* area where Orgel consistently mistranslates the original text, it is a significant error because her mistranslation inserts anti-feminist labels absent in the German text and thus "corrects" Hauff's text by reinstating the binaries—Good Mother versus Wicked Stepmother; Good versus Evil; Self versus Other—that Hauff set out to abolish.

10. The medieval abbess Hildegard von Bingen not only produced poetry and music, but also authored scientific treatises, including a learned lexicon of herbs in which she explained the curative properties of numerous medicinal plants used in the abbey infirmary and provided them with their vernacular German names.

11. The townspeople, scarcely credible witnesses, refer to the Herb Fairy as "evil," as will Jacob—after he first discovers his grotesque transformation, but before his adoption of a radically altered mindset.

12. I have adopted this term from Mitzi Myers's telling discussion of female guides or "mentoria" (31–59).

13. In a short story "Books and the World of Readers," Hauff refers to the writer who must cater to a mass audience of consumers as a "chef" who is required to "prepare something tasty" in a vain attempt to please the "spoiled palates" of a fickle reading public (Hauff, *Romane*, 730).

14. She thus resembles the buxom Jewish mother Sendak later memorialized by reproducing a photograph of Sadie (Sarah) Sendak holding little Maurice within the Blakean panorama he created for Randall Jarrell's *Fly by Night* (1976). His mother, he told Selma Lanes, had a "gruff, abrupt manner," and hence may well have been associated in his mind with Hauff's uncouth nurturer (Lanes 18).

15. Hauff mentions Jacob's age on two different occasions. In the initial scenes, when the boy meets the Herb Fairy, he is eight years old (2:112). Later the narrator depicts Jacob as remembering that he was twelve (2:123) when these events took place. Doris Orgel, interpreting Hauff's intentional blurring of chronological time as an "error" on the part of the writer, "corrects" the age to twelve. Compare Orgel, who states that Jacob was "rather tall for his twelve years" (3) to Hauff's original: "for a boy aged eight, he was already quite big" (2:112).

16. In his discussion of "antique and medieval grotesque," Bakhtin notes the repeated and intentional association of the nose with the phallus throughout the carnival tradition (*Rabelais*, 87). Hauff clearly refers to this familiar linkage in his depiction of Dwarf Long Nose as crossing age and gender barriers.

17. See, for example, Barbara Gerber's discussion of Jewish financiers who rose to power in German duchies and who, after supplying money for the coffers of various dukes and princes, suffered a fall from favor and public approbation, often as the scapegoats for their masters' misdeeds. Hauff's novella *Jew Süss* demonstrates how one of these figures, Joseph Süss Oppenheimer, was scapegoated and judicially murdered. See my article on Hauff's dismantling of stereotypes in *Jew Süss* (Thum, "Re-Visioning"). Although he is not an ethnic outsider, Dwarf Long Nose is a grotesque Other who enjoys a parallel rise and fall when he is unfairly blamed for something he could not possibly have known about or have corrected.

18. Unlike Brentano, whose anti-Semitic stereotypes are so prominent in his story "Gockel, Hinkel and Gackeleia" (in which Jewish engravers are the villains), Hauff identifies with the superior yet maligned outcast both in *Dwarf Long Nose* and in a tale from the same collection entitled "Abner, the Jew who saw Nothing." It is surely no accident that the two tales should have appeared back to back as companion pieces in *The Sheik of Alexandria and His Slaves*. In "Abner, the Jew who saw Nothing" Hauff uses a tale from Voltaire's *Zadig* as the point of departure for his own demonstration of the mechanisms of stereotyping. Hardly the "naive" anti-Semite that Leon Feuchtwanger took him to be (quoted in Gerber 282), Hauff attacked not only Jews but also Christians and Christianity in his *Memoirs of Satan*, a two-part Rabelaisian satire. But if his heavy-handed Jew-

ish caricatures—put in the mouth of Satan—are undeniably alienating to a twentieth-century reader, Hauff's subsequent works demonstrate a radical distancing from such Jewish stereotypes. In *Jew Süss*, he not only dismantles stereotypes and demonstrates the perniciousness of scapegoating, but also expresses his philo-Semitism by portraying Lea Oppenheimer, Joseph Oppenheimer's sister, unequivocally as the most intelligent, charitable, and heroic figure in the entire novella (see Thum, "Re-Visioning").

Works Cited

Bakhtin, Mikhail M. "Discourse in the Novel." *The Dialogic Imagination: Four Essays by M. M. Bakhtin.* Ed. Michael Holquist. Trans. Caryl Emerson and Michael Holquist. Austin: University of Texas Press, 1981. 259–422.

———. *Problems of Dostoevsky's Poetics.* Ed. and trans. Caryl Emerson. Minneapolis: University of Minnesota Press, 1984.

———. *Rabelais and His World.* Trans. Helene Iswolsky. Bloomington: Indiana University Press, 1984.

Beckmann, Sabine. *Wilhelm Hauff: Seine Märchenalmanache als zyklische Kompositionen.* Bonn: Bouvier Verlag, 1976.

Clark, Katerina, and Michael Holquist. *Mikhail Bakhtin.* Cambridge, Mass.: Harvard University Press, 1984.

Crane, Susan. *Gender and Romance in Chaucer's "Canterbury Tales."* Princeton, N.J.: Princeton University Press, 1994.

Davis, Natalie Zemon. *Society and Culture in Early Modern France.* Stanford, Calif.: Stanford University Press, 1965.

Elias, Otto Heinrich. "König Wilhelm I (1816–64)." In *900 Jahre Haus Württemberg,* ed. Robert Uhland. Stuttgart: Verlag W. Kohlhammer, 1985.

Gerber, Barbara. *Jud Süss, Aufstieg und Fall im frühen 18. Jahrhundert: Ein Beitrag zur Historischen Antisemitismus-und Rezeptionsforschung.* Hamburg: Hans Christians Verlag, 1990.

Grimm, Wilhelm, and Jacob Grimm, eds. *The Complete Grimms' Fairy Tales.* Trans. Margaret Hunt and James Stern. New York: Pantheon, 1944 and 1972.

———. *Kinder und Hausmärchen: Ausgabe letzter Hand mit den Originalanmerkungen der Brüder Grimm.* 3 vols. Ed. Heinz Rölleke. Stuttgart: Philipp Reclam, 1980.

Harf-Lancner, Laurence. *Les Fées au moyen âge.* Geneva: Editions Slatkine, 1984.

Hauff, Wilhelm. "Die Bücher und die Lesewelt." *Romane, Märchen, Gedichte.* Vol. 2 of *Wilhelm Hauff: Werke.* 2 vols. Stuttgart: J. B. Cotta, 1962. 727–43.

———. *Dwarf Long Nose.* Trans. Doris Orgel. Illus. Maurice Sendak. New York: Random House, 1960.

———. "Zwerg Nase." *Sämtliche Werke in drei Bänden.* Vol. 2. Munich: Winkler-Verlag, 1970.

———. *Tales by Wilhelm Hauff.* Trans. S. Mendel. 1890. Freeport, N.Y.: Books for Libraries, 1970.

Hinz, Ottmar. *Wilhelm Hauff: Mit Selbstzeugnissen und Bilddokumenten.* Hamburg: Rowohlt Taschenbuchverlag, 1989.

Hofmann, Hans. *Wilhelm Hauff: Eine nach neuen Quellen bearbeitete Darstellung seines Werdeganges.* Frankfurt a. M.: Moritz Dieterweg, 1902.

Klotz, Volker. *Das europäische Kunstmärchen.* Stuttgart: J. B. Metzler, 1985.

Knoepflmacher, U. C. "The Balancing of Child and Adult: An Approach to Victorian Fantasies for Children." *Nineteenth-Century Fiction* 37.4 (Mar. 1983): 497–530.

Koopman, Helmut. "Nachwort" (Afterword). In Hauff, *Sämmtliche Werke in drei Bänden.* Vol. 3. 491–510.

Lanes, Selma G. *The Art of Maurice Sendak.* New York: Harry N. Abrams, 1980.

Martini, Fritz. "Wilhelm Hauff," in *Deutsche Dichter der Romantik*. Ed. Benno von Wiese. Berlin: Erich Schmidt Verlag, 1983. 532–62.

Myers, Mitzi. "Impeccable Governesses, Rational Dames, and Moral Mothers: Mary Wollstonecraft and the Female Tradition in Georgian Children's Literature." *Children's Literature* 14 (1986): 31–59.

Orgel, Doris, trans. *Dwarf Long Nose* by Wilhelm Hauff. Illus. Maurice Sendak. New York: Random House, 1960.

Pfäfflein, Friedrich. *Wilhelm Hauff, der Verfasser des "Lichtenstein": Chronik seines Lebens und Werkes*. Stuttgart: Fleischhauer und Spohn, 1981.

Reinhardt, Kurt F. *Germany: 2,000 Years. The Second Empire and the Weimar Republic*. Vol. 2 of 2 vols. New York: Frederick Ungar, 1962.

Schwarz, Egon. "Wilhelm Hauff, 'Der Zwerg Nase,' 'Das Kalte Herz' und andere Erzählungen (1826–27)." *Romane und Erzählungen zwischen Romantik und Realismus*. Ed. Paul Michael Lützeler. Stuttgart: Philipp Reclam, 1983. 117–35.

Thum, Maureen. "Kunstmärchen or Menippean Satire? Wilhelm Hauff's 'Abner der Jude, der nichts gesehen hat.'" Paper presented at the Kentucky Foreign Language Conference, Lexington, 23 Apr. 1993.

———. "Re-Visioning Historical Romance: Carnivalesque Discourse in Wilhelm Hauff's *Jud Süss*." In *Neues zu Altem: Novellen der Vergangenheit und der Gegenwart*. Houston German Studies. Ed. Sabine Cramer and Gertrud Pickar. Frankfurt a. M.: Peter Lang, 1995.

Kipling's "Just-So" Partner: The Dead Child as Collaborator and Muse

U. C. Knoepflmacher

It seems worth remembering that texts with impeccable "adult" credentials may enlist the intense attachments of a vanished youth in the service of growth and maturity. Tennyson opens *In Memoriam A.H.H.* (1850) by trying, characteristically, to find a gain in loss: "I held it truth, with him who sings / To one clear harp in diverse tones, / That men may rise on stepping-stones / Of their dead selves to higher things" (i.1–4). Although referring to Goethe here, the future laureate may also have thought of the laurels bestowed on an ideal female Other by a much earlier predecessor, Francis Petrarch (1304–74). Petrarch's *Rime*, after all, was divided by later editors into two parts, "In vita" and "In morte di Madonna Laura"; lyrics that celebrated a living lady as an infatuated young lover's better "self" thus could become stepping stones for tributes on a higher plane. A sequence built out of meticulously crafted, compact, yet psychologically and tonally diverse units thus serves both Petrarch and Tennyson in fashioning ascending—and assenting—structures of memorial homage.

I am deliberately invoking these "adult" constructs as analogues for a very different narrative sequence addressed to a very different audience. For the impulses that gave shape to both *In Memoriam* and the *Rime* bear more than a passing resemblance to the rationale behind Rudyard Kipling's own artful arrangement of the twelve tales, separately composed from 1897 to 1902 and collected in that year—together with twelve supplementary poems, twenty-three captioned full-page drawings, and many other smaller illustrations—under the title of *Just So Stories for Little Children*. This much-reprinted collection neither activates a male "dead self" such as Tennyson's best beloved Arthur Hallam nor an idealized female alter ego such as the adult paragon whom Petrarch called Laura; instead, it animates a child-self imbedded in all grownup psyches and yet also recognizable as a juvenile Other.

For Kipling, this child-self, preserved from the happiest era of

Children's Literature 25, ed. Francelia Butler, R. H. W. Dillard, and Elizabeth Lennox Keyser, guest ed. Mitzi Myers and U. C. Knoepflmacher (Yale University Press, © 1997 Hollins College).

the writer's own childhood, is intricately identified with "Effie" or Josephine, his first-born American daughter. That Effie acted as a catalyst for some of Kipling's finest work as a children's author is a point that has not been wasted on previous critics (Green 182, for example), although her role in the *Just So Stories* has yet to be fully assessed. Kipling publicly identified his daughter as a listener and collaborator when he celebrated her fifth (and his thirty-second) birthday in December 1897 by publishing the first of "The 'Just-So' Stories" (as he then called them) as the leading piece in *St. Nicholas Magazine*. Yet he expanded and redefined Effie's role upon her unexpected death in New York on March 6, 1899, after the trans-Atlantic passage that almost claimed his own life.

Kipling's decision to transform his prime auditor into the "Best Beloved" he addresses throughout stories written after her death gave him unusual insights into the process of cross-writing child and adult selves. Indeed, as we shall eventually see, several of these later stories can be read as dramatizing an alliance or collaboration designed to counter not only the separation between adult and child, but also gaps between the sexes and between the living and the dead. Although born of acute personal loss, Kipling's buoyant tales resist sentimentality in ways that seem saner and more self-knowing than the nostalgia for a lost childhood that sometimes seeps into classics such as the *Alice* books or *Peter Pan*. Because 1997 marks the hundredth anniversary of the self-contained trio of "Just-So Stories" Kipling offered to *St. Nicholas,* a fresh look at the "stepping-stones" through which he so brilliantly dramatized concerns taken up throughout this issue of *Children's Literature* seems an especially apt contribution.

I

When Kipling first flirted with the idea of writing children's stories for *St. Nicholas Magazine* he was not yet a father, and the child reader he envisioned was not a girl but a boy. He had himself read the magazine as a boy and had even tried to contribute to it at age thirteen. Catharine Morris Wright stresses the adult writer's excitement on finding himself sought out by Mary Mapes Dodge, the same editor who had rejected a poem he had submitted in 1879 while still an "English schoolboy." At that time, Kipling had hoped to get his American peers, "wisely allowed more liberty than we enjoy"—to "sympathize" with the predicament he had tried to dramatize (autumn 1879, cited by Wright 259). In agreeing to write something for *St. Nicholas* in February 1892, Kipling reminded Dodge that his chief "advantage" over other prospective authors stemmed from his having "read St. Nicholas since I was a child." He can thus do more than compose "slick" stories *about* children for "a Wee Willie Winkie audience" of adults; instead, he can directly address "a People a good deal more important & discriminating—a peculiar People with the strongest views on what they like and dislike" (21 Feb. 1892, cited by Wright 265). This sincere respect for the child's acuity was retained when a few years later he considered the interests of the precocious Effie.

Initially, however, the fictions Kipling offered Dodge released the boyish exuberance of his early years in Bombay. A story such as "The Potted Princess" (Jan. 1893), ecstatically welcomed by Dodge, becomes a playful antidote for the unbearably painful "Baa Baa, Black Sheep," the 1888 story Kipling had intended for adults.[1] And the Mowgli and non-Mowgli stories that Dodge published before they made their way into the two *Jungle Books* similarly rely on the empowering exploits of boyish Indian heroes such as Mowgli, Toomai, or Rikki-Tikki-Tavi. Wright wonders whether "these stories, like 'Wee Willie Winkie' and 'Baa Baa, Black Sheep'" actually might not have been "too powerful for the young" audience of *St. Nicholas* (286). She points out that no American child reader ever referred to them in communications sent to the magazine's "Letter Box," and she also notes that Dodge balked at publishing "Servants of the Queen," the ironic critique of imperialism that Kipling then promptly placed in the "adult" *Harper's Weekly* (Mar. 1894) and used as the closing tale for the first *Jungle Book*.

By 1897, however, there was an entirely new start. When "the first three 'Just-So Stories' came to a grateful Mrs. Dodge from A. P. Watt, Kipling's agent" (Wright 287), the author who had by August of that year become the father of three children was ready to produce a rather different fare. While in Vermont, he had vividly recalled his Indian childhood in order to chart a wolf-boy's adolescent empowerment. Now, back in England, he drew on his more recent memories of New England story sessions in order to dramatize a much smaller child's passage into self-consciousness and linguistic mastery. This new interest, empirically acquired, did not involve fantasies of compensation such as those that underlie the *Jungle Book* stories. Instead, they led to the development of an entirely new narrative persona and to the gradual refinement of a form that allowed him to capture the joyousness of a parental investment in the curiosity and creativity of the child.

In his valuable bibliographical essay on the illustrated versions of the book, Brian Alderson rightly stresses the distinctiveness of the initial unit of three stories that Kipling offered to *St. Nicholas Magazine* in 1897. He notes how Kipling placed an opening paragraph—directed at the adult, rather than the child, reader—before the narrative of "How the Whale Got His Throat" in the 1897 Christmas issue of *St. Nicholas* in order to insist "that these stories originated in the living—and private—exchange between a teller and a listener" (Alderson 148). Kipling's preamble, also meant to introduce the next two installments, "How the Camel Got Its Hump" (Jan. 1898) and "How the Rhinoceros Got Its Skin" (Feb. 1898), asserts the privileges due to that original listener, the vibrant Effie. She holds the rights to stories that must, according to her father, be set down and retold by the adult exactly in the way in which she first heard them—"just so."

Although Alderson excerpts the salient portions of this long introductory paragraph, it deserves to be reproduced in its entirety if one is to savor the authority that Kipling confers on his little prime auditor. The narrator's five references to Effie suggest that, far from being regarded as a passive listener, such a child must be granted a status that approaches that of a collaborator. Just as the bossy boy Punch in the 1888 "Baa Baa, Black Sheep" tries to orchestrate his Indian ayah's storytelling, so does tiny Effie exercise an imperious control over the stories told in her Vermont nursery. But if the narrator of the earlier "adult" tale ironically looks back at Punch's self-aggrandizements in a Bombay he must soon leave, the narrator of "How the Whale Got Its Throat" defers to the girl's controlling stake in narratives that involve an active partnership between teller and listener:

> Some stories are meant to be read quietly and some are meant to be told aloud. Some stories are proper for rainy mornings, and some for long, hot afternoons, when one is lying in the open, and some stories are bedtime stories. All the Blue Skalallatoot stories are morning tales (I do not know why, but that is what Effie says). All the stories about Orvyn Sylvester Woodsey, the left-over New England fairy who did not think it well-seen to fly, and who used patent labour-saving devices instead of charms, are afternoon stories because they were generally told in the shade

of the woods. You could alter and change these tales as much
as you pleased; but in the evening there were stories meant to
put Effie to sleep, and you were not allowed to alter those by
one single little word. They had to be told just so; or Effie would
wake up and put back the missing sentence. So at last they came
to be like charms, all three of them,—the whale tale, the camel
tale, and the rhinoceros tale. Of course little people are not all
alike, but I think if you catch some Effie rather tired and rather
sleepy, and if you begin in a low voice and tell the tales precisely
as I have written them down, you will find that Effie will presently curl up and go to sleep.

Now, this is the first tale, and it tells how the whale got his tiny
throat:—

Once upon a time there was a whale, and he lived in the sea
and he ate fishes. . . ("The 'Just-So' Stories," 89).

Kipling realized that the Mowgli and non-Mowgli stories he wrote
for St. Nicholas might easily find an even wider audience if they were
expanded, collected in book form, and published in England as well
as in America. He appears to have entertained no such marketing considerations, however, after fashioning the Whale, Camel, and
Rhinoceros stories; instead, he regarded them as a complete unit, a
memento of "charms" shared with a four-year-old. Although Kipling
surely told more just-so stories in 1898 to Josephine and to her special "bosom friend," Angela Thirkell, the latter's account is limited to
the telling of the Whale story she remembered in its printed version
(Thirkell 309, 312). In her memoir, Elsie Kipling (Mrs. George Bambridge) claims that the "*Just So Stories* were first told to my brother
and myself during those Cape winters, and when written, were read
aloud to us for such suggestions as could be expected from small
children" (Carrington 396). Yet it remains difficult to determine the
exact number of stories specifically invented for Kipling's surviving
two children. Born in February 1896, Elsie Kipling and certainly John
(born in August 1897) would not have been told "The Elephant's
Child" while vacationing in Capetown in January 1898; because that
story, "The Beginning of Armadilloes," and "The Sing-Song of Old
Man Kangaroo" were not written down until later in 1899 (Green 176)
and published in the first half of 1900, all three may well belong to a
store of tales originally devised for Effie.[2]

There is no reason, however, to distrust Elsie Kipling's contention that all tales, "when written," were read aloud for "suggestions" to be made by herself and John. Kipling had to devise a new format to blend the published *St. Nicholas* tales and unpublished Effie stories with tales told and written after her death. When he eventually chose to use the original trio of Whale, Camel, and Rhinoceros stories as "stepping-stones" for the ambitious twelve-story, pyramidal structure of the 1902 book, he was compelled to make several important re-adjustments. The "you" he had addressed in these first three stories now became a "Best Beloved" invoked at the very outset of the book. As a result, the casual opening of the original Whale story ("Once upon a time there was a whale, and he lived in the sea and he ate fishes") became more formalized and incantatory: "In the sea, once upon a time, O my Best Beloved, there was a Whale, and he ate fishes" (*Just So Stories* 25).[3] Even the parenthetical interjections of the original text—"(you must *not* forget the suspenders)"—became less casual: "(you must *not* forget the suspenders, Best Beloved)" ("The 'Just-So' Stories" 90; *Just So Stories* 25).

The playful captions for the full-page drawings Kipling introduced for the book version more than compensated, however, for the stateliness of such invocations. Adroitly anticipating the many questions that an inquisitive child might pose, Kipling delights in further stimulating his young readers with a bountiful store of never-gratuitous additions. The names of Whale ("Smiler"), Mariner ("Mr. Henry Albert Bivvens, A.B."), and 'Stute Fish ("Pingle") may seem extraneous to an adult, but not to the child who relishes such verbal extensions and also accepts the invitations to let its visual fancies range beyond the limits of an illustrated page. Kipling's drawings rely on cryptic images that the artist-writer points out in his captions and then encourages both child and adult to decode. The recast stories of Whale, Camel, and Rhinoceros can therefore no longer be read in the purely linear fashion called for by their *St. Nicholas* originals. The "plot" of each tale comes to a halt whenever the reader, arrested by an intricate drawing, is seduced into becoming a viewer. And that viewer must subsequently turn into a reader of a different sort when invited to absorb the verbal amplifications and annotations in the full-page caption that faces each such drawing. As in a Talmudic commentary, the progress of the main narrative thus must defer to lateral coruscations. And even when that narrative finally stops, the poem placed at the end, far from providing a definitive closure, only opens up possibilities for further associations.[4]

Kipling's renewed attention to the creative input of young inter-locutors who want all details to cohere "just so" went far beyond the relatively simple instructions he had given to adult transmitters of his *St. Nicholas* tales. By 1899, such instructions had become obso-lete, superseded by his much more dramatic demonstration of ways to handle the imaginative hunger of the astute "little people" he respected more than ever. Yet the introductory paragraph of 1897 had also become undesirable for another, more painful, reason: after Effie's death and Kipling's months of convalescence, the personal ori-gins of the three animal tales obviously needed to be obscured.

Still, even though these private origins no longer could be explic-itly acknowledged, it was Kipling's unabated attachment to his dead child that led him to reinvest his creative energies in stories about growth and adaptation. Deflected to other children, his communion with the girl who had been the primary recipient of his first three stories is often handled indirectly in the later additions. Yet in "How the First Letter Was Written," "How the Alphabet Was Made," and "The Tabu Tale," he allowed himself the luxury of a more direct expression of his feelings by transforming Effie into Taffy, a best be-loved child he deposited in the safe haven of a prehistoric past. The joy and loss of a father, who was not a Briton or an Indian, or even an American, which he well might have been, could thus be ascribed to a Neolithic man who was "not a Jute or an Angle, or even a Dravid-ian, which he might well have been, Best Beloved, but never mind why" (*Just So Stories* 95).

Given that Effie had permanently fallen asleep after returning to her native land, Kipling could hardly be expected to continue posing as a dispenser of sedatives helpful to adult readers equipped with drowsy little girls. In a way, however, the 1897 *St. Nicholas* introduction had already anticipated the process of transference that now became such a major feature of the expanded *Just So Stories*. After acknowl-edging that "little people are not all alike," Kipling had appealed to a wider audience by offering other parents and other Effies oral nar-ratives that he had designed for the ears of a single child. If the tales he had told to that special child could already be transcribed for a dual audience in 1897–98, then they also could, as Kipling came to see, readily be assimilated after 1899 into an expanded sequence that might itself stress the dynamics of assimilation and accommodation.

By celebrating the child's adaptability and its gradual mastery of verbal and visual signs, Kipling could also partake in a transformative process of obvious therapeutic value to himself. He had previously transferred to Effie his memories of a self-centered little rajah by becoming her paternal playmate. It now remained for him to take the more difficult step of rechanneling his deep emotional attachment by transferring it to maturing children as bright as she had been. To do so, he required a new set of listeners—the effigies of Effie, as it were—Elsie and John Kipling, the many girls and boys he continued to befriend, and all those faceless children he could charm and help to grow beyond the age at which Effie's life had stopped. The child— and childhood—he had now twice lost could therefore be recaptured once again, kept alive through the agency of an undying fictional Other who was his personal Best Beloved as well as a universal Everychild.

Kipling's bold decision to return to a cross-writing project that he might well have abandoned after the three *St. Nicholas* stories had appeared must have been difficult to manage. Yet the decision seems to have been made quickly: he was composing "The Elephant's Child" in October 1899, a mere seven months after Josephine's death (Carrington 235n). Was the story, which he sent to another American journal, *Ladies' Home Journal,* among those he had previously told her? Although one need not share Howard R. Cell's belief that "despite the masculine pronoun" the Elephant's Child is "in fact . . . a female" (Cell 143, n. 2), it is true that the "person small" celebrated in the poem Kipling eventually placed at the end of that story is a girl who is every bit as inquisitive as the observant Taffy (or the "little girl-daughter" of "The Crab That Played with the Sea"): "She keeps ten million serving-men / . . . / One million Hows, two million Wheres, / And seven million Whys!" (*Just So Stories* 72).

Whether or not "The Elephant's Child" belonged to a group of tales originally fashioned for Effie, it marks a distinct departure from the emphasis of the *St. Nicholas* trio. Although the comic transformations of the Whale, Camel, and Rhinoceros were as pronounced as was the metamorphosis of a short "bulgy" nose into a versatile trunk, those earlier changes were punitive rather than beneficial to the selfish protagonists. The omnivorous Whale, gluttonous Rhinoceros, and uncooperative Camel are made to pay for their childish and egotistical behavior. But if the Whale must curb its insatiable appetite, the little elephant who is beaten for asking questions is amply rewarded for his " 'satiable curtiosity." Although its higher form of hunger may offend punitive adults, it is clearly endorsed by an author who de-

lights in the barrage of Hows, Wheres, and Whys produced by rest-
less young minds. Kipling grants the Elephant's Child an appendage
that proves to be as handy as the skinning knife that the Mariner—
or Mowgli, another quick learner tutored by a rock python—wielded
to such great effect. Mowgli's older animal acquaintances came to
fear the superiority of this precocious manling. The superiority of
the Elephant's Child, on the other hand, not only allows him to carry
out a Mowgli-like revenge against abusive elders, but also soon inspires other elephants, old and young, to emulate him by becoming
equipped with "new noses" as powerful as his own (71).

Like the initial story of the Whale, "The Elephant's Child" dramatizes a collaboration in which the small and weak can outwit those
who are in power by sheer virtue of their larger size. By directing the
huge Whale to the ingenious Mariner, the little 'Stute Fish creates
an alliance between smaller marine creatures and the "man" whom
Kipling figures as a boy who had "his Mummy's leave to paddle"
in the water (28); the little 'Stute Fish can save himself and other
threatened creatures from being eaten. Yet if this alliance can be
read as merely pitting two children against a stronger third child,[5]
the Elephant's Child rises above his rigid elders after being aided by
the "mournful" Kolokolo bird and by the sententious Bi-Coloured-
Python-Rock-Snake. It is not the Crocodile, a hungry predator much
like the Whale, but rather the python (an ironist who, like Kaa, is
endowed with a mocking intelligence much like Kipling's own) who
becomes primarily responsible for furthering the little elephant's
growth. The transference of the python's superior powers is symbolized by the child's acquisition of that elongated, snakelike trunk.[6]
This phallic, yet bigendered (as well as bicolored) tutor thus takes the
place of elephant parents who ought to have supervised, rather than
inhibited, their precocious child's growth. And, in a pachydermous
twist of the old Wordsworthian paradigm, the evolved Child can now
become Father of the Elephant.

II

"The Elephant's Child," written first yet placed second, is central to
the four-story unit that follows the trio of Whale, Camel, and Rhinoceros tales. All four stories dramatize beneficial mutations: if the trunk
gained by the Elephant Child gives it a greater maneuverability and
new powers of self-defence, the evolutionary advantages obtained by

the new colorings assumed by the Leopard and the Ethiopian, by the longer hindlegs gained by the Kangaroo, and by the conversion of Tortoise and Hedgehog into a new species are just as significant. Less childish than Whale, Camel, or Rhinoceros, this new set of protagonists can nonetheless retain childhood strengths that are crucial to their development. Their resilience is encouraged not only by the narrator, but also by his surrogates. With the notable exception of the Tortoise and Hedgehog, who manage their own transformation, the members of this group require the advice or intervention of adult-like superiors: Baviaan, the dog-headed Baboon "who is Quite the Wisest Animal in All South Africa" (52); the pithy Python; and the Big God Nqong.

Although collaboration is highlighted throughout this sequence, it is especially prominent in the first and last tales, "How the Leopard Got His Spots" and "The Beginning of the Armadilloes," which also act as pendants for "The Elephant's Child." Yet if the plain-spoken Leopard and the verbose Ethiopian simply learn that camouflage can make them better predators, the "mixy" verbal games that save the lives of the word-twisting Hedgehog and the artfully literal Tortoise anticipate an even higher accomplishment in the art of survival. Whereas the Leopard and Ethiopian merely regain their former superiority as fellow hunters, Hedgehog and Tortoise are fellow victims who help each other become less vulnerable. The flexibility that permits each to develop into a shielded armadillo is contrasted with the rigid upbringing of their confused child antagonist, the Jaguar Mother's overdependent son. In their joyously inventive partnership, Hedgehog and Tortoise thus anticipate the collaborative successes of Taffy and her father in "How the First Letter Was Written" and "How the Alphabet Was Made," the two stories Kipling placed right after "The Beginning of the Armadilloes" in the 1902 collection.

Though seventh in the book, the Armadillo story was actually fifth in order of composition, having appeared in *Ladies' Home Journal* in May 1900, a month after the same journal had published "The Elephant's Child" and a month before it printed "The Sing-Song of Old Man Kangaroo." Kipling links the Armadillo story to that of the little Elephant through deliberate verbal as well as visual echoes. He recalls the opening sentence of "The Elephant's Child" by announcing at the outset of the new tale that "This, O Best Beloved, is another story of the High and Far-Off Times" (82). And by placing Stickly-Prickly Hedgehog and Slow-Solid Tortoise "on the banks of the turbid

Figure 1. Initial *T* from "The Beginning of the Armadilloes."

Amazon" (82), he clearly means to match "the banks of the great grey-green, greasy Limpopo River" (61) to which the Kolokolo Bird had directed the curious young elephant. An even more important connection, however, is established by the ornate capital *T* that Kipling drew for the story's initial letter. Picked up in both of the full-page illustrations for the Armadillo story, the letter will figure prominently, as we shall see, in "How the Alphabet Was Made," where it comes to signify the bond between the father-daughter letter-makers whose first names begin with the same consonant *T*.

Kipling places two heads at each end of the upper crossbar of the capital *T* that he uses to open the Armadillo story (see fig. 1). The crossbar is inclined rather than strictly horizontal, as it will be in the *T* that opens "How the Alphabet Was Made." At the higher extreme right is the stylized head of an adult elephant, with tusks that are considerably longer than those in the representations of the Elephant's Child; it is underneath that mature head that Kipling places his initials, "R K." At the extreme lower left is the head of an embryo whose big eyes resemble those of an unhatched chick. Although looking, Janus-like, in opposite directions, the two heads grow out of an intertwined common *I* stem that could be made out of bone or cartilage, (its helix-like right side resembling a ribcage), or be sprouting from a vegetable organism. If made out of bone, this shaft recalls the carved knives that served as opening letters for both the Whale tale and the Leopard/Ethiopian story. If it is meant to be a vegetable growth, however, the sinuous stalk resembles the sheltering uterine "seaweed" into which Kipling had placed the 'Stute Fish he had drawn in the second full-page drawing for his Whale story.

The symbolic implications of this decorated initial suggest a complexity that befits that of Kipling's two full-page illustrations for the Armadillo story: the overly detailed map of the Amazon delta, which, as Alderson notes, takes (at least!) "half an hour to decipher" (Alderson 155), and the wonderful drawing of the ball of intertwining bodies formed by Tortoise, Hedgehog, and Armadillo "all in a heap" (*Just So Stories* 92), observed by a jaguar child with a puzzled face and a wounded paw. The sites and adventures so minutely labelled on the "inciting map" of "Ye Manie Mouthes of Ye Amazons River" may not literally have "anything to do with the story" itself (84). But it seems significant that all the inscriptions that crowd the page are placed at the border of a blank body of water that Kipling shapes as a giant letter *T*. The child "incited" by the map's puzzling proliferation of details thus is induced to feel "more mixy than before" (86), just as the Jaguar felt after his intended victims cleverly jumbled up his mother's explicit instructions on how to identify and catch hedgehogs and tortoises. But if that "incited" child is inspired, unlike the Jaguar, to learn the benefits of "mixiness," it will hardly be as "much surprised" by the blending of separate species within a single globe. If the Jaguar child is drawn, parodically, as an inverted Atlas who cannot sustain that "mixy" globe, its black snout and mouth form a letter that also seems to parody, in its droopy inversion, the outlines of the initial *T* with which the story began. By way of contrast, the Tortoise seems truly Atlaslike, even though he is at the center and not outside of the globe. Simultaneously bearing the weight of the newly formed Armadillo on his shoulders and propping his four legs to hold up the Hedgehog, this creature's legs act as a sort of intermediary stem between two T-shaped mushrooms, as shown in figure 2.

Because both tortoises and elephants figure as propping up the universe in Hindu representations,[7] the portrait of this *T*-bearer also brings us back to the significance of the elephant's head portrayed in the story's opening letter. The wise elephant and the unreflective

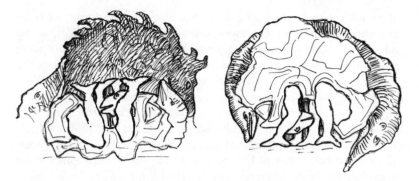

Figure 2. The ball of animal bodies: tortoise, hedgehog, and armadillo.

embryo are no more opposites than are Stickly-Prickly and Slow-and-Solid in the story itself. They evolve from the same vital *I*, and hence can eventually assume a common identity such as that of the Armadillo-self that Kipling confers on two animals who belong to such different species. By way of contrast, the Jaguar mother who relies on a taxonomy that falsely insists on irreconcilable contraries demands a conformity that might well cripple her child. The young Jaguar who finds his mother's mnemonic jingle useless may never grow up. His deference to her authority does not allow him to learn, as Hedgehog and Tortoise do, by adopting fresh defensive tactics. When Stickly-Prickly practices his swimming, he ceases to look like a "chestnut-burr"; when Slow-and-Solid starts his stretching exercises, his back-plates lose their former rigidity. Their "mixy" interchangeability subverts Mother Jaguar's rigidly held conviction that "a Hedgehog is a Hedgehog, and can't be anything but a Hedgehog; and a Tortoise is a Tortoise, and never can be anything else" (90). Kipling's own evolution as an armadillo with protective scales gave him a toughened adult identity he was eager to pass on to children willing to take imaginative risks. At the same time, however, his self-caricature as a wounded Jaguar child suggests that he was too honest to repress his painful memories of adult inflexibility.

III

Kipling appears to have initially regarded the stories of the Elephant's Child, the Armadilloes, and the Kangaroo, all published in *Ladies'*

Home Journal from April to June of 1900, as forming a unit almost as close-knit as that of the *St. Nicholas* stories of Whale, Camel, and Rhinoceros. But the publication history of the three stories that feature Taffy and her father—"How the First Letter Was Written," "How the Alphabet Was Made," and "The Tabu Tale"—suggests no such design. By featuring the same protagonists, these tales are even more closely interrelated than those in the other trios and may well have been composed in a single creative thrust. And yet Kipling seems to have gone out of his way to disperse their publication. He published the first in *Ladies' Home Journal* in December 1901 (on the dead Effie's ninth birthday and hence exactly four years after the Whale story first appeared). It was followed there by "The Cat That Walked Alone" (July 1902) and "The Butterfly That Stamped" (Oct. 1902), but not by the second and third Taffy tales. Instead, Kipling saved "How the Alphabet Was Made," the most important of these tributes to Effie as his collaborator, until he was ready to gather all of his tales for the 1902 edition of the book; in this way, he made it the only story among those collected there never previously published in periodical form. And he kept "The Tabu Tale" out of all standard collections, although he included it, with two full-page illustrations and captions but no final poem, in a 1903 volume of *Just So Stories* published by Charles Scribner's Sons in New York.

When Kipling introduces Tegumai and "his little girl-daughter" Taffy in "How the First Letter Was Written," he minimizes the difference between child and adult. Treated as equal partners—like Hedgehog and Tortoise[8]—the pair also circumvent, as Kipling and his children apparently did in real life, a strong maternal authority that they respect yet half-defy.[9] Covered with mud after one of their romps, father and daughter are pronounced to be totally indistinguishable by Teshumai, the superior guardian of their cave: "Where in the world have you two been to, to get so shocking dirty? Really, my Tegumai, you're no better than my Taffy" (95). Tegumai's childlike carelessness is evident again when he forgets "to bring any extra spears" along (96). Self-absorbed while trying to mend his broken spear throughout the story, Tegumai seems slower than his quick, precocious child. When she volunteers to run back to the Cave to obtain another spear from "Mummy," he refuses to let her go: "It's too far for your little fat legs. . . . Besides you might fall into the beaver-swamp and drown" (96). His refusal stems as much from parental solicitude as from an unwillingness to part from his lively child-

companion. And his response introduces, however lightly, a note of
death that will gradually intensify as the Taffy tales unfold.[10]

Tegumai's passivity is necessary, however, to help set in relief his
daughter's activation of her inventive powers. Although he fusses
with the spear he fails to repair, she composes, with the help of the
Tewara stranger's shark tooth, a narrative entirely made out of pictures. The child-artist's story is misread by both its adult bearer and
its adult recipient—the stranger and her mother. It is therefore as
unsuccessful as the creative effort that Rudyard Kipling himself had
sent to *St. Nicholas* while still a schoolboy. But just as that failed contribution prepared him for his later successes as a writer, so is Taffy's
letter-that-failed rightly honored by the Head Chief of the Tribe as "a
great invention" that augurs well for future accomplishments (103).

Kipling's own adult art thus defers to the nascent achievements
of young artists-to-be. The narrator had previously encouraged his
child readers to take out their paint boxes and loosen their imagination by wildly coloring the drawings his publishers had restricted
to black-and-white. In "How the First Letter Was Written," however,
the artist lovingly reproduces—within the text and without a caption—Taffy's own drawing, "a little berangement of my own, Daddy
dear" (100). And his captioned full-page illustration adopts Taffy's
own pictographs to repeat her story "carved on an old tusk a very
long time ago" (104). Like Tegumai's spear, that tusk—"part of an
old tribal trumpet that belonged to the Tribe of Tegumai"—is frag-
mented and incomplete: "a sort of network of beads and shells and
precious stones" has been "broken and lost" (104). The efforts of a
paternal artist-writer are required to supplement the budding creative powers of a "precious," gemlike child.

Yet Kipling does not want to leave that inventive child at the mere
threshold of her creative achievement. In "How the Alphabet Was
Made" he therefore reenlists Taffy in order to credit her with the
"great invention" that the tribe's Head Chief had predicted. Angus
Wilson contends that all Just So stories "marred by humans" lack the
pleasurable interaction between child and adult found in the animal
tales (Wilson 229). Yet, far from exhibiting a "sentimental whimsicality," the story of the Alphabet actually transcends the "interplay"
that Wilson so aptly describes as a "continuous flirtation between
the two worlds": "Every adult knows the pleasure of suddenly seeing what a child is putting into the game or the reading; equally, I
am sure, children find much of their enjoyment in revelations of the

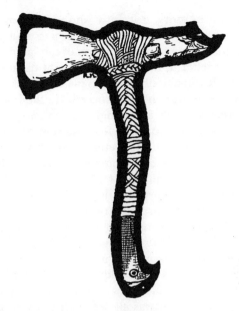

Figure 3. Initial *T* from "How the Alphabet Was Made."

jokes and absurdities that adults add to the stories or games for their own delight" (229). It is the sudden coalescence or overlapping of these complementary pleasures that Kipling manages to produce in "How the Alphabet Was Made." By involving young and old readers in the same playful, yet serious, process that enmeshes Taffy and Tegumai, he allows us to share the joyful immediacy of their discoveries. The "whimsicality" of Taffy's and Tegumai's joint enterprise, far from being "sentimental," thus acts as a universal antidote against the indulgence of an actual father's grief for his lost playmate.

The capital *T* that opens "How the Alphabet Was Made" is no longer drawn as an organic shape as in the Armadillo story; instead, it has become a tool, an artifact constructed for social progress (see fig. 3). The crossbar of the ax is bound to its vertical handle by woven filaments, just as language—a cultural artifact—relies on the ligature of separate letters. Kipling places his initials, "R K," beneath the cutting edge of the axe, and now draws the head of a young chick at the very end of the handle. Adult and child, therefore, now seem farther apart than they were in the capital *T* of the Armadillo story. And yet it is the chick handle that gives the edge of the blade its velocity and power, just as, in the story, it is Taffy who will empower her father as an artificer. Watching Tegumai idly scratching on a piece of bark, Taffy prompts him to refine her depiction of the "ah-noise" they convert into the first letter of the alphabet. Caught up in his daughter's "inciting" game, Tegumai is no longer as inattentive as he had been in the previous tale. He urges her to proceed, "in the voice that grown-ups use when they are truly attending" (*Just So Stories* 108). Soon, the pair have progressed far enough to form short words. Although their task is still incomplete when they return to the cave for supper, they exult in their mastery of "secret" constructions that Taffy's "Mummy" mistakes for meaningless squiggles (115).

Excluded from their enterprise, the mother nonetheless is at first granted a place in the construction of the letter *T* with which father and daughter begin the second day of their collaboration. Yet not only she, but Taffy, too, will drop away, as the *T* gradually assumes the shape of a lonely, cruciform male figure: "When they came to T, Taffy said that as her name, and her Daddy's, and her Mummy's all began with that sound, they should draw a sort of family group of themselves holding hands. That was all very well to draw once or twice; but when it came to drawing it six or seven times, Taffy and Tegumai drew it scratchier and scratchier, till at last the T-sound was only a thin, long Tegumai with his arms out to hold Taffy and Teshumai. You can see from these three pictures partly how it happened" (115). By placing the three drawings that depict the progressive reduction of the *T* next to an inverted *S*, described as a "hissy-snake" placed "the other way round for the Z-sound" (116), Kipling creates a sequence that seems to suggest that this falling off may lead to an ominous end (see fig. 4). No longer attached to either mother or daughter, the lonely figure flanked by a hissing serpent seems as forsaken as Christ on the cross. He is a child without his prime parent and an adult without his prime child. Only a few more "sound-pictures" remain to be completed, among them the "scratchy, hurty, Ka-sound" (116). Reasserting the passage of time, the narrator explains how the "fine old easy, understandable Alphabet" invented by a daughter and her father was later set aside, deformed and forgotten, until it "got back into its proper shape again for all Best Beloveds to learn when they are old enough" (117).

Yet even as he celebrates Taffy's useful legacy to other Best Beloveds, the narrator also insists on the uniqueness of her world: "But *I* remember Tegumai Bopsulai, and Taffimai Metallumai, and Teshu-

Figure 4. How the *T*-sound changed.

mai Tweindrow, her dear Mummy, and all the days gone by. And it was so—just so—a long time ago—on the banks of the big Wagai!" (117). The meaning of "just so," in this last sentence of the narrative, has clearly altered; it no longer carries the resonances of the phrase once used to signify a living child's insistence on verbal accuracy.

But Kipling does not end there. Just as he produced a preface to the 1897 Whale story, he now devises a sort of afterword. Having provided no full-scale, captioned picture in an illustrated story that markedly differs from all the others by its inclusion of no less than thirty-three little "sound-pictures," Kipling surprises the reader by also drawing—and then elaborately describing—a necklace composed of twenty-three letters. He tells us that Tegumai had made that "magic Alphabet-necklace" to be preserved "for ever and ever" by the tribe but that it took father and daughter "five whole years getting the necklace in order" (119). Because five years had also elapsed between the publication of the first "Just-So" story and the collected tales, the analogy to Kipling's own crafting of a necklace of interconnecting stories seems inescapable. Just as Taffy begot the individual letters her father then worked into this fuller construct, so is Effie implicitly credited as the begetter of a mode her father perfected after her death.

"How the Alphabet Was Made," the one story Kipling had saved for the completed book, ought logically to have come last in the sequence. Why, then, does he not use it to close his volume? A hint of an answer, I think, can be found in Kipling's annotations for the letter beads linked in the Alphabet necklace. Tegumai and Taffy may have spent five years ordering the beads, but the order has been disturbed. For the narrator explains that the necklace he professes to have copied so "very carefully" (121) no longer retains its pristine shape. He can joke about the missing "P and Q," lost in a war and replaced by "the dried rattles of a rattlesnake." But the dislocation of several other letters seems more serious: whereas E is still "a twist of silver wire," its successor F (pronounced "ef," as in Effie) "is broken" and "what remains of it is a bit of stag's horn" (119).

Moreover, J and K, Josephine Kipling's initials, are no longer in their proper sequential order:

J is a fish-hook in mother-of-pearl.
L is the broken spear in silver. (K ought to follow J, of course; but the necklace was broken once and they mended it wrong.)
K is a thin slice of bone scratched and rubbed in black.   (120)

Kipling here encodes private meanings he neither wants or expects his readers to fathom.[11] "JLK" are the initials of the jovial father-artist, John Lockwood Kipling, whom his son emulates by drawing his own illustrations. Yet the separation of J and K by the broken silver spear of the letter L also suggests a generational discontinuity: Collaboration Lost. L may well stand for Love, transfixed by a spear, but it also stands for Loss. The K etched on a thin bone splinter thus appears to carry connotations that are as painful as that "hurty Ka-sound" mentioned toward the end of the narrative. Its blackness seems funereal, as does the "black squiggle" designed to set the whole necklace in relief and to "make the beads and things look better" (121). This record of a collaboration comes perilously close to a ritual of mourning.

Mourning is also the note struck in the verses Kipling put after this coda. Lewis Carroll had professed himself to be haunted by his own dream child in the poem he placed at the end of *Through the Looking-Glass*. But whereas Carroll bemoans the loss of an idealized little girl who has turned into an actual woman, Kipling memorializes the loss of an actual child whose exceptional promise might well have been fulfilled as a grown-up. Unlike Carroll's Alice, his Taffy is more than a wishful self-projection; despite her early death, she can still stimulate his hopes that other Best Beloveds might effect a less traumatic passage from childhood to maturity than that which he had been forced to negotiate. If Kipling's final poem is an elegy, it also celebrates the possibility of an imaginative blending. It is therefore closer, as I have already suggested, to Wordsworth's "Lucy Gray" than to Carroll's farewell verse.

Yet Kipling avoids the first person that Wordsworth and Carroll use. He relies, instead, on the figure of Tegumai, who has himself long disappeared, whittled down into thin slices of bone, to dramatize a loss he tries to depersonalize through his art. Indeed, Art—

"the figure" cut by "all the Tribe of Tegumai"—survives artists young and old (p. 123, ll. 1–2). Yet amidst a landscape in which "silence and the sun" remain sole constants, a ghost child can be glimpsed, "dancing through the fern / To lead the Surrey spring again" (123:ll.4, 7–8). This prehistoric child may materialize on British Downs, yet she is suspiciously American, a little Pocahontas moving in her native land:

> In moccasin and deer-skin cloak,
> Unfearing, free and fair she flits,
> And lights her little damp-wood smoke
> To show her Daddy where she flits.   (123:ll.13–16) [12]

The child's perpetual motion directs the adult man she has preceded. She is still the active little girl who speaks in the Taffy stories and who had formerly, in real life, "put back the missing sentence" in her father's narratives. But her voice has been muted:

> For far—oh, very far behind,
>   So far she cannot call to him.
> Comes Tegumai alone to find
>   The daughter that was all to him.   (123:ll.17–20)

IV

Angela Thirkell claimed that much "of the beloved Cousin Ruddy of our childhood died with Josephine" (Thirkell 311). Kipling never returned to the United States after Effie's 1899 death in New York. Back in England, according to John Lockwood Kipling's report, "house and garden" were full of "the lost child and poor Rud told his mother how he saw her when a door opened, when a space was vacant at the table, coming out of every green dark corner of the garden, radiant— and heart breaking" (quoted by Green 175). If the composition of new Just So stories proved therapeutic as a revival of the old father-daughter collaborations, the termination of that project was clearly marked by renewed pain. The text and drawings Kipling provided for the New York edition of "The Tabu Tale," the third Taffy story he had kept out of the 1902 collection, suggest how difficult it became for him to close off, even artistically, his relation to the American "daughter that was all to him."

In "How the Alphabet Was Made," Taffy helped to create a system of signs that could be adopted by adults; in "The Tabu Tale," however, she must master codes that are already known to her parents and have been harnessed by her tribe's powerful shaman, the Head Chief. Whether contained in "magic necklaces" such as the one the Head Chief gives Taffy, in the "Big Tribal Tabu-pole" he places at a spot where fishing is forbidden, or in mere handsigns that she must learn from Tegumai, these tabus involve restrictions and prohibitions. As the Chief tells Taffy, "Tabu doesn't mean anything till you break it" (1903 *Just So Stories* 235). Yet what the self-disciplining Taffy must learn turns out to be as essential for the adult as for the child. Both Taffy and her father need to discipline themselves in the face of death. He places the pair within a world of predation and casts them as hunting partners such as Leopard and Ethiopian—or Mowgli and Bagheera—had been.

But the youthful restlessness that Kipling had previously celebrated can become a liability in an order in which hunters may themselves be hunted. The Alphabet story had ended with a poem in which Taffy's "flitting" still could symbolize the childhood energies Kipling wanted to tap. In "The Tabu Tale," however, her lack of restraint makes her a poor hunting partner. Not until she masters "the Still Tabu sign" will her "wonderhugely pleased" father hail Taffy as "a superior girl-daughter" (1903 *Just So Stories* 248, 247). But her major test does not come when her stillness allows Tegumai to catch a nimble rabbit or even when she puts the Still Tabu on him in order to kill her own rabbit (247). Instead, it occurs when Taffy is herself threatened by death after "her Daddy had taken off all tabus" (248). Seen by Tegumai but not by Taffy, "a big, lean, grey wolf" who seems to have come straight out of Mowgli's Jungle sneaks up on the girl (248). Even before she detects this grisly predator—"something black creeping sideways at her"—Taffy spots her father's "Still Tabu sign" and freezes, thereby allowing both him and the Head Chief to throw their hatchets past her shoulder (249). It is the Chief who now certifies Taffy as a valued member of the tribe: "O Daughter of Tegumai, I saw everything that happened. You are a true tabu-girl. I am very pleased at you" (250). He awards her the wolfskin for a "winter cloak," promises to make her a necklace out of the beast's teeth and claws, and decides to paint this climactic scene "on wood on the Tribal Tabu-Count, so that all the girl-daughters of the Tribe can see and know and remember and understand" (251).

The father-playmate who had fashioned a letter necklace at the end of the Alphabet story thus is replaced by a far more powerful

Figure 5. The killing of the wolf in "The Tabu Tale."

artist figure in "The Tabu Tale." By inserting this thirteenth Just So story between "The Cat That Walked By Himself" and "The Butterfly That Stamped," Kipling may have wanted readers to connect Taffy to the freedom-loving Cat who comes to accept social constraints and to link the Head Chief to Solomon as all-powerful patriarchs who vindicate their ostensible inferiors. Yet the creation of this alternative father figure, who clearly prefers Taffy to Tegumai and whose hatchet would have killed the wolf even if Tegumai had faltered, also suggests that Taffy has approached a phase of existence in which more than a childlike "Daddy" is needed to help her master the art of stillness.

In the illustrations for "How the First Letter Was Written," Kipling purportedly reproduced a child's scribbles; but in the last illustration for "The Tabu Tale," he claims to have rendered the Head Chief's own depiction of the climactic killing of the wolf (see fig. 5). The long caption for this drawing explains that it is "done in the Head-Chiefly style of the Tribe of Tegumai, and it is full of Tabu meanings and signs" (252). The Chief, who stands with lifted hatchet at the top right, "has no face, because the face of a Head Chief does not matter" (252).[13] The faceless Taffy, who is placed closer to him than to Tegumai, is drawn as a mere silhouette who seems to levitate above the ground. The caption laconically suggests that her near invisibility must be accepted as being just so: "Taffy is always drawn in outline—quite white," like the two-headed beaver on top of a T shape that "is meant to be a Tabu tree" (252). The tree, the black wolf at its base, and a horizontal strip that shows the Ark that Kipling had used as a signature in other drawings (Ar/K = R.K.) tend to impinge upon the foregrounded figure of Tegumai in the lower left quadrant. Whereas the floating Taffy looks reposed and free, surrounded by blank space, Tegumai seems crowded and cramped into an awkward position. He is in the act of slaying Death, yet the child who seems to ascend toward the godlike Chief has entered a stillness that somehow belongs to a different order of reality.

Kipling was correct to leave out "The Tabu Tale" from all standard editions of the *Just So Stories*. Closer to an adult ghost story such as "They," this tale hints at an impassable gulf between child and grown-up. The joyous traffic of the other tales no longer seems possible in a narrative that makes the sharing of "meanings and signs" difficult for both kinds of readers.[14] Kipling informs us in the penultimate sentence that the "Still Tabu" was the "chief thing" that Taffy learned. He then offers a concluding paragraph made out of a single sentence: "That was why she was taken everywhere that her Daddy went" (256). The father who had fallen "down flat on the floor and shouted," who had "curled himself up and rolled round" upon infringing on his daughter's space earlier in the story, indulges in one last romp with Taffy and the Head Chief before she ceases to behave like a child (1903 *Just So Stories* 241). He must himself now learn adult self-discipline. In her stillness, Taffy/Effie has taught him the value of a restraint he needs to adopt when carrying her within wherever they go.

Notes

1. For a discussion of "The Potted Princess" and its relation to "Baa, Baa Black Sheep," see Knoepflmacher, 28–32. Dodge wrote to "Dear Mr. Kipling": "How *did* you do it? Children will go wild with delight over the story, and the editor is simply chortling over the bewitching thing. Editors seldom know the joy of thorough satisfaction!"

(19 Oct. 1892, quoted by Wright). For other satisfactions in Dodge's long editorial career, see Gannon's essay in this volume.

2. Still, the African story of "How the Leopard Got Its Spots," printed a year after "The Elephant's Child" and featuring an alliance between two childlike protagonists, may well have been first tried out on Effie's two siblings. In December 1901, they probably were also exposed to "The Crab That Played with the Sea," which was published by itself as late as August 1902, when John was five (Effie's exact age in 1897, when the Whale, Camel, and Rhinoceros stories had appeared in print). December 1901 also saw the publication of "How the First Letter Was Written," the first of three stories featuring Taffy and her father, Tegumai. Back at the Cape in early 1902, Kipling completed the last two stories for the 1902 volume, "The Cat That Walked by Himself" and "The Butterfly That Stamped" (Green 177). The dates of composition of the other two Taffy stories, "How the Alphabet Was Made" and "The Tabu Tale," remain murky. Given their emphasis on his special relationship to Effie, Kipling may not have wanted to share these with Elsie and John.

3. Adding to the formalism, of course, is the decorated opening letter *I* that Kipling drew as a skinning knife, just as in the opening of "How the Leopard Got His Spots," the story he placed right after the *St. Nicholas* trio (although seventh in order of composition). Carved bones also appear in the Taffy stories: the "old tusk" inscribed by Taffy's people "a very long time ago" (*Just So Stories* 98, 104) and the "magic Alphabet-necklace of all the letters" (119) I shall later discuss more fully. It seems significant that these representations of bone, as well as the initial *T* of the Armadillo story and the *H* for "The Cat That Walked By Himself," should all appear in stories that feature collaborations. Depicted as palimpsests that retain engraved memories unerased by time, these relics also preserve the father-daughter relation that more explicitly surfaces in the Taffy tales.

4. The verses at the end of "How the Whale Got His Throat," for example, seem an ebullient, but innocuous, address to a child who refuses to get seasick during a turbulent ocean voyage that even decimates the ship's steward. The hardy "you" ostensibly resembles the resilient Mariner of the story. Yet the last lines, which establish the coordinates for that passage, introduce a more ominous subtext: the steamship careening on the latitude that offered a last glimpse of England and on the meridian that brings the first sight of the American continent is following the same trans-Atlantic course that caused Effie's fatal pneumonia: "When Nursey lies on the floor in a heap, / And Mummy tells you to let her sleep, / And you aren't waked or washed or dressed, / Why, then you will know (if you haven't guessed) / You're 'Fifty North and Forty West!'" Like so many of the other settings in the *Just So Stories,* the space defined here acts as a rather special meeting place.

5. In this sense, the alliance resembles those formed against school bullies in *Stalky & Co.*

6. I defer to Maureen Thum, whose reading of *Dwarf Long Nose* appears in this volume, to expound on the implications that nasal empowerment holds for a young male child. In Kipling's fable of empowerment, the rock python plays the role that Hauff assigns to the long-nosed Herb Fairy, who passed on to Jacob both her culinary powers and her long proboscis.

7. Kipling placed an elephant and a turtle at the top left and top right of the first of the two full-page drawings he devised for "The Crab That Played with the Sea," the tale he placed after the two Taffy stories (127).

8. When we are told that Tegumai's name means "Man-who-does-not-put-his-foot-forward-in-a-hurry" (95), it is difficult not to associate him with Slow-and-Solid Tortoise in the previous story.

9. Given the "difficult temperament" that Elsie Kipling attributes to her mother,

bonding with a playful father may have offered important relief to his children. Elsie claims that her mother's "domination" and "possessive and rather jealous nature, both with regard to my father and to us children, made our lives very difficult." Although she credits Carrie Kipling with "a keen, quick mind and ready wit, a business ability above the average," and a mastery of "pain and sorrow," she prefers to stress the constraints placed on a mate whose "kindly nature, patience, and utter loyalty to her prevented him from ever questioning this bondage" (Carrington 400). Kipling's ambivalent relation to the maternal, discussed in my 1992 essay, clearly affected his own parenting. That ambivalence colors his portraits of mothers in five of the last six *Just So* stories: "The Beginning of the Armadilloes," the two Taffy tales, "The Cat That Walked By Himself," and "The Butterfly That Stamped."

10. As a young man, Kipling had parodied "Lucy Gray"; yet Wordsworth's poem about a drowned girl vainly sought by her grieving parents must have acquired a more serious dimension for him after Effie's death, as the closing verses he placed at the end of "How the Alphabet Was Made" strongly suggest. The Kiplings bitterly reproached themselves for having insisted that Josephine accompany them on their sea journey.

11. The possibilities are multiple: the *L* that takes the place of the *J* might possibly stand for El-sie, who replaced Josephine as a daughter Kipling could address as his "Best Beloved" as late as 1914 (see Gilbert 169).

12. Five months after Effie's death, Kipling wrote to Edmonia Hill: "I don't think it likely that I shall ever come back to America. My little Maid loved it dearly (she was almost entirely American in her ways of thinking and looking at things) and it was in New York that we lost her" (in Wilson 197).

13. Seymour-Smith's remarks about Kipling's quasi-gnostic sense of "personal unworthiness, his granting of all his genius to a daimon outside himself," and Kipling's own remarks to Haggard that "we should become unfitted for our work in the world" if allowed to see God's face (213, 332), seem as pertinent here as in "They," the ghost-story published a year after "The Tabu Tale." In both cases, Kipling seems to follow *In Memoriam, A.H.H.*: striving to "paint / The face I knew" (70:2–3), Tennyson tries to find comfort in thoughts of a deity whose own face cannot be seen ("Prologue" 2–3).

14. The capital *T* that opens "The Tabu Tale" offers a good example of the difficulties posed by what has become a private symbology. With a curved bottom bar as long as its straight top bar, this letter can be read as a *T* even if it is inverted. But why? To capture the dual *T* alliterations of "Tabu/Tale" and "Taffy/Tegumai"? And why are six

Figure 6. Initial *T* from "The Tabu Tale."

black Chinese letters that have no phonetic relation to a *T* placed inside the white letter? Were the outer four thinner signs—the simplest of which resembles the T-shape
of the daggers and axe drawn for the earlier stories—chosen because they belonged
to a more ancient Chinese alphabet that was carved on bones? Were the inner, fatter
ones chosen as more modern representations of continuity and life?

Works Cited

Alderson, Brian. "Just-So Pictures: Illustrated Versions of *Just So Stories for Little Children*." *Children's Literature* 20 (1992): 147–74.

Carrington, C. E. *The Life of Rudyard Kipling*. Garden City, N.Y.: Doubleday, 1955.

Cell, Howard R. "The Socratic Pilgrimage of the Elephant's Child." *Children's Literature*
20 (1992): 132–45.

Gilbert, Elliot L., ed. *"O Beloved Kids": Rudyard Kipling's Letters to His Children*. London:
Weidenfeld and Nicolson, 1983.

Green, Roger Lancelyn. *Kipling and the Children*. London: Elek Books, 1965.

Kipling, Elsie (Mrs. George Bambridge). "Memoir." In Carrington, *Life of Rudyard
Kipling*, 396–403.

Kipling, Rudyard. *Just So Stories for Little Children*, ed. Peter Levi. London: Penguin,
1989.

———. "The 'Just-So' Stories" ["How the Whale Got His Throat"]. *St. Nicholas* 25 (Dec.
1897): 89–93.

———. "The Tabu Tale." *Just So Stories for Little Children*. New York: Charles Scribner's
Sons, 1903.

Knoepflmacher, U. C. "Female Power and Male Self-Assertion: Kipling and the Maternal." *Children's Literature* 20 (1992): 15–35.

Orel, Harold. *Kipling: Interviews and Recollections*, 2 vols. Totowa, N.J.: Barnes and Noble,
1983.

Seymour-Smith, Martin. *Rudyard Kipling*. New York: St. Martin's, 1990.

Thirkell, Angela. "Life at The Elms, Rottingdean." In Orel, *Kipling*, 2:307–16.

Wilson, Angus. *The Strange Ride of Rudyard Kipling: His Life and Works*. New York: Viking,
1978.

Wright, Catharine Morris. "How 'St. Nicholas' Got Rudyard Kipling and What Happened Then." *Princeton University Library Chronicle* 35 (spring 1974): 259–89.

Treasure Seekers and Invaders: E. Nesbit's Cross-Writing of the Bastables

Mavis Reimer

treasure, verb: *1.* transitive *To put away or lay aside (anything of value) for preservation, security, or future use; to hoard or store up* 2. figurative *To keep in store, lay up (e.g., in the mind, in memory).*

Oxford English Dictionary

The power of suggestion which is exerted through things and persons and which, instead of telling the child what he must do, tells him what he is, and thus leads him to become durably what he has to be, is the condition for the effectiveness of all kinds of symbolic power that will subsequently be able to operate on a habitus predisposed to respond to them.

Pierre Bourdieu, *Language and Symbolic Power,* 52

A startling moment in Edwardian children's literature occurs in a book not written for children at all, when a remarkably spelled letter from the Junior Blackheath Society of Antiquaries and Field Club arrives at the breakfast table of Len and Chloe, protagonists of a domestic comedy, *The Red House,* published in 1902 by E. Nesbit. The Antiquaries turn out to be none other than the Bastable children and their friends, who have decided to recast the visit of the Maidstone antiquarian society to the Moat House, a visit that forms the basis of one of the stories in *The Wouldbegoods* (1901). The report of the genesis of the children's plan and Oswald's account of the Red House experience appear in yet another context, one of the stories in the *New Treasure Seekers* collection (1904).

Julia Briggs observes that the Bastables "put in a guest appearance" in Nesbit's adult novel (*WP* 215), a comment implying that the Bastables' presence is somehow incidental to the trajectory of the text. My experience of reading *The Red House,* however, was that the Bastables' eruption into Nesbit's novel radically disrupted the text. Not only does the "free" talk of the children (*RH* 226) generally

Children's Literature 25, ed. Francelia Butler, R. H. W. Dillard, and Elizabeth Lennox Keyser, guest ed. Mitzi Myers and U. C. Knoepflmacher (Yale University Press, © 1997 Hollins College).

undercut the conventionally sentimental and coy tone of Nesbit's narrator, Len, but also the children's discovery of the antique cradle "treasure" in the basement of the house allows the text to introduce, by decorous indirection, the fact of Chloe's pregnancy. Moreover, the Bastables' return by invitation to the Red House at the conclusion of the novel allows readers their first glimpse of the occupant of the cradle—Len's and Chloe's daughter, who is known only as "the pussy kitten" in the text. Nesbit, it seems, uses the Bastables to focus the representation of "the child" for her adult audience. How, I wondered, is that representation the same as and different from the representation of "the child" Nesbit constructs for her audience of children in the three collections of Treasure Seekers stories?[1]

Recent theories of children's literature suggest that such differences and similarities in the cross-writing of the child may point to significant ideological constructions. Jacqueline Rose (1984), James Kincaid (1992), and Perry Nodelman (1992) have demonstrated that Anglo-American culture sets childhood apart as a site of lost innocence and that children are constructed as Other for the benefit of adults. Those benefits include the exercise of power in various guises: the power to know and conceal desire, to preserve values on the verge of collapse, to reproduce children as commodities, and to define adulthood itself. But although the idea of the child as a site of lost innocence may have been produced for the benefit of adults, the relative stability and the persistence of that idea imply that it is not simply a coercive domination, but rather a domination that also manufactures consent.[2] Children's literature would seem to be a primary site for the production and reproduction of this complex subjectivity.

Nesbit's work for children fits into the late nineteenth-century "cult of the child" and what Roger Lancelyn Green (1962) named the Golden Age of children's books. Children's books of the period are distinguished in Green's view precisely by their attitude to childhood, an attitude Green—like Rose, Kincaid, and Nodelman after him—describes by borrowing the metaphor of colonization: childhood suddenly was presented as "a thing in itself . . . a new world to be explored, a new species to be observed and described" (44–45). The difference from earlier texts of children's literature, according to Green, is that there was no longer a sense of the child as an "undeveloped adult" being pushed toward a more fully realized humanity; rather, "you were enjoying the Spring for itself" (44–45). Rose develops her theory that children's literature is "one of the cen-

tral means through which we regulate our relationship to language
and images" (139) in her work with another text of the period, J. M.
Barrie's *Peter Pan*. She remarks a similar change in the texts of children's literature over time: from the eighteenth century through the
works of such nineteenth-century writers as Mary Molesworth, children's fiction delineates the division between the adult's and the
child's "types of language and modes of address" (59), but that division progressively was removed after the late-nineteenth century, "as
the adult intention has more and more been absorbed into the story
and, apparently, rendered invisible" (60). The congruence between
the relative ideas of "the child" and "the adult" that Green finds
in Edwardian literature for children and the ideas that recent theorists describe as persisting in contemporary Anglo-American culture
points to the possibility that texts from the turn of the century, such
as Nesbit's, might demonstrate how this structural relation comes to
be instituted. What cultural function does this formation serve? What
contradictions does it resolve? How do Nesbit's texts represent to the
child his or her position as subject in such a way that the child is
likely to consent to this position?

The primary scene in which the Bastable children establish an important relation with an adult occurs in the first collection of stories.
After spending fourteen chapters trying various ways to "restore the
fallen fortunes of [their] House" (16), the Bastables finally find the
"treasure, and no mistake" (200) they have been seeking in the person of their "Mother's Indian Uncle" (*STS*, 182). Not only does the
Uncle arrive in a fairy-godmother coach laden with boxes and knobby
parcels containing "heaps and heaps of presents" (200), but he also
rescues Father's faltering business with a substantial capital investment and takes the whole family to live with him in the "jolly, big,
ugly red" house "with a lot of windows" on the top of the hill (202).
It is, as Oswald remarks, just like the ending of a fairy tale.

The abundance of treasure and happy surprises unpacked in this
ending almost obscures the sequence of events by which the treasure
seekers transform an irascible old man into a fairy godmother. The
sequence is set in motion because the children make a series of mistakes in interpreting adult language. When their father announces
that their "dear Mother's Indian Uncle" is coming to dinner (*STS*,
182), the children assume that the uncle is "the Red kind" (199), an
imperial subject rather than an imperial functionary. They find evidence for their interpretation in the uncle's description of himself as

"a poor, broken-down man" (186), a description that the Bastables hear as a literal statement about the uncle's material circumstances rather than as a metaphorical description of his health. Corroboration for this train of thought comes from their reading of English literature, specifically the line from Pope's *Essay on Man*—"Lo, the poor Indian!"—which Nesbit uses as the title for the chapter. Again, their misprision is a result of their confusion of Pope's metaphorical judgement of the Native American's "untutor'd mind" with literal pauperism, which exceeds even their own straitened circumstances. By reading literally the adults' figurative language, the children position the uncle with themselves as subjected Other rather than as subject.

In their assumption of equality—indeed, of superiority—to the uncle, the children offer him the pleasures of play. Their "play-dinner" includes teaching him "how to be a dauntless hunter," by slaying the rabbit/deer with "trusty yew bows" and the pudding/wild boar with forks (191); how to be an adventurer in an exotic land, by plucking almonds and raisins "from the boughs of the great trees" at the top of the chest of drawers; and how to be a cosmopolitan consumer, by choosing figs "from the cargo that the rich merchants brought" in their drawer/ship (193). Their play, in other words, reproduces three roles in the colonial project—that of the trophy hunter, that of the European traveler/adventurer, and that of the consumer back home. The uncle's subsequent appearances in the novel make it clear that he literally has enacted each of these "playful" roles before his momentous meeting with the Bastables: his red house is decorated with "swords and guns" and with "horns of stags and other animals" (202); the Christmas dinner he serves them is replete with such exotic comestibles as ginger wine (207); and the cargo disgorged from the coach includes "Japanese china tea-sets" (199) and "yards and yards of soft silk from India" for the girls, "a real Indian sword for Oswald and a book of Japanese pictures for Noël and some ivory chessmen for Dicky," as well as assorted carved fans, silver bangles, strings of amber beads, necklaces of uncut gems, shawls and scarves of silk, cabinets of brown and gold, ivory boxes, silver trays, and "brass things" (200). The children's reading of the metaphorical as the literal has allowed the uncle to release his literal experiences as colonizer into the play of metaphor.

The congruence the theorists find between the construction of the Other in colonial discourse and our discourse about "the child," it seems, not only offers an explanatory analogy, but also is historically apt. Jacqueline Rose, in fact, notes that the oppositional terms in which childhood currently is understood can be traced back from "Thomas Day and Peter Parley to Rousseau" (59) in the colonialist concepts of exploration, discovery, and adventure. A similar structural definition of the "primitive" in relation to the "civilized" was put in place by evolutionary theory in the middle of the nineteenth century. According to Daniel Bivona (1990), the "notions of the 'barbaric,' the 'uncivilized,' the 'primitive,' the 'childlike,' the alien in time and the alien in space overlap constantly in the Victorian imagination of the late nineteenth century" and eventually "the purely analogical relationships . . . begin to be broken down into more literal ones" (76–77).

Seen as "alien in time," the child retains the promise of growing up and crossing into adulthood. Seen as "alien in space," however, the child is fixed as irremediably Other. Peter Coveney insists that this fixity distinguishes the cult of the child as an attitude "wholly different" from the Romantic view of childhood: "their interest in childhood serves not to integrate childhood and adult experience, but to create a barrier of nostalgia and regret between childhood and the potential responses of adult life" (240). What Nesbit does by staging the mechanisms through which her culture produces its version of "the child" is even more consequential than Bivona suggests, for her discourse is not about childhood—about the metaphor of the child— but is directed to actual children. This is a text of children's literature. To some extent, then, Nesbit's writing of the Bastables must be seen as an imperative to children to occupy a place in discourse that allows adults to effect the transaction of the literal and the metaphorical.

The immediate rewards of consent are abundantly obvious in *The Story of the Treasure Seekers:* the Bastables achieve safety, material comfort, the restitution of their class position (Oswald is headed for Rugby and Oxford at the conclusion of the story), and the ability to see themselves as coherent characters. "I can't help it if it is like Dickens," remarks Oswald, "because it happens this way. Real life is often something like books" (*STS,* 205).

The children also gain the illusion of power. They assume that they show the "poor Indian" "how to be a dauntless hunter" (191); it seems to be Oswald's saying so that brings "the coach of the Fairy Godmother" to a stop outside their house (197). That their power is illusory—in the sense both that their power lies in creating illusion and that they are deluded in assuming they have real power—becomes evident in the next book about the Bastables, *The Wouldbegoods*. The collection opens with a story about the children playing *The Jungle Book*, an escalated version of the same game that had captivated their uncle and had brought about the fairy-tale ending to their story of treasure-seeking. In this case, however, the children's playing comes too close to being real. They borrow several of the uncle's hunting trophies as props, even stuffing and animating the tiger skins he has brought from India. When the uncle walks in on this game, far from responding with expansive enjoyment, he madly begins to beat the children with the Malacca cane he is carrying. As a consequence of their misbehavior, the children are sent into the country to "stay till we had grown into better children" (*W*, 25), a resonant phrase for any argument about the constructedness of "the child." It is while they are staying at the Moat House that they meet the Maidstone Society of Antiquaries and Field Club, which inspires their trip to the Red House in the adult novel.

If in the children's novel the children's reading of the metaphorical as literal allows the adult to disperse the literal in play, in the adult novel the reverse transaction takes place: the children's restaging of a "real" event as play allows the adults to reconstitute their own play as reality.

Len and Chloe, writer and illustrator, respectively, are left the grand old Red House by the will of a deceased uncle identified, like the Indian uncle, as a "fairy godmother" (*RH*, 32). Their modest incomes as members of "the noble army of workers" (7) will not stretch to allow them to maintain the rambling house and the country property on which it sits. Yet when they cycle out to see the house, they immediately succumb to its charms and decide to move in. Housed in a manor, but inept at proper household management on such a scale, Len and Chloe repeatedly refer to themselves as "Babes in the Wood" (82) playing at housekeeping. Like "naughty children" (120), they picnic on newspapers in the kitchen, scandalize the vicar's wife by greeting her in bare feet because they are washing their own floors, and succeed in mounting a housewarming party only by borrowing dishes and draping packing cases for a table. At the same time, however, Len as narrator is careful to distinguish their play in the Red House from their play in the "doll's house" they first occupied after their marriage, allowing only the Red House experiences to be thought of as "real" (111). In order to hold together his contradictory definitions of play, he adopts the metaphors of exploration and colonization. The Red House, he muses, is "a new life—a primitive existence where law was not" (66); he and Chloe are "in the position of folk cast upon a desert island" (67). "Like Columbus," he tells Chloe, they must establish their own rules (111).

The visit of the Bastable children legitimizes the proprietary status they have assumed in play and ratifies their rule. The letter the Bastables copy and send to Len and Chloe names the Red House as having "great ihstoric [sic] interest" (*RH*, 212) and has the effect of making the adults feel like "lords of the manor" (215). When the children arrive, they assume the continuity of the house's past owner (a "celebrated amn [sic]" [213]) and its present owner ("a clever writer" (222)) and, despite their "discerning" observations (232) and "free" talk (226), they do not register any incongruities between the house and its occupants—they simply pronounce both to be splendid. That is, they do not register any such incongruities in this text directed to an adult audience. In the retelling of the incident in the children's book, Oswald does remark that "the girls thought [the house] was bare" (*New Treasure Seekers*, 88). In *The Red House*, however, the Bastables are only focalized through the first-person narrator, Len, so that their private judgements are never introduced into the text. Even what Len calls their "very full flow of conversation" (*RH*, 225) is reported in the text in a summary marked by the narrator's insistence that the children's relationship to language is "close and unproblematic" (Rose 44)—a representation of the relation of children and language that Jacqueline Rose suggests underwrites children's literature from its beginnings in the mid-eighteenth century. Len comments: "They now threw away all shyness, and talked to us with simple directness of adventures, of contemporary literature, of the ways of Providence, and their own vital ambitions" (*RH*, 225). "Simple directness" is, I suspect, the last phrase most readers would use to describe Oswald Bastable's language as narrator of the Treasure Seekers stories. What purpose does it serve for Len to describe the children's language in this way in the adult novel?

As in *The Story of the Treasure Seekers*, it is the children's confusion of categories—in this case, their conflation of historical periods—that makes them available as agents of transaction. By suggesting that the children's uncertainty represents a higher truth, a simple and direct account of, among other things, "the ways of Providence," Len and Chloe can insert themselves into a line of historical "lords of the manor." Indeed the children's playful "invasion" of the house uncovers the props Len and Chloe need to give substance to their play: behind the door of an inner cellar, the Bastables locate a store of massive and solid, if somewhat dilapidated, furniture from various eras of the house's ownership. The dynastic cradle is among the treasures. Len's reverential conclusion to his story is an extended metaphor of lineage and inheritance: his daughter is a "usurper," a "princess," the occasion of Chloe's mounting from a "high estate" to "a higher" (*RH*, 274). It is a metaphor made literal by the person of his heir in the cradle.

Why did it become so important for adults to be able to manipulate the linguistic fields of the literal and the metaphorical in turn-of-the-century England? By the late nineteenth century, the Empire was producing unprecedented economic benefits for England, but, at the same time, the imperial project had become fraught with what Bivona calls "epistemological" difficulties, which shook British confidence in the Empire's right to exploit Indian and African territories for British benefit. Jenny Sharpe in *Allegories of Empire* dates this crisis from the Indian "Mutiny" of 1857. She argues that it was in the aftermath of the savage British restoration of order in India that a new discourse about imperialism emerged. Imperialism had long been regarded as a civilizing mission, but that mission unproblematically included "the profit-making enterprise of creating new markets for English manufactures" (7). It was only after the "violent upheavals that encouraged the colonizers to see themselves as the innocent victims of native hostility" that Britain began to figure its mission in terms of the "domestic virtues of self-sacrifice, moral duty, and devotion to others" (8). In Nesbit, the Indian Uncle's restaging of his part in colonial exploitation as play allows him to reproduce himself as a benevolent rescuer of the Bastables, as a fairy godmother.

But play, because it allows for such a reinvention of subjectivity by blurring the boundaries between the literal and the metaphorical, also allows for the opposite transaction, the conversion of game into history. It is this transaction that the Bastables facilitate in *The Red House*. Because adults not only create children in language, but also produce children through procreation, their play can be reified as fact. In *The Red House*, this reification allows Len and Chloe, who not incidentally are makers of texts, to use the pleasures of children's play—and the pleasures of playing with children—to institute a historical entitlement for their child. That the theorists of children's literature should find that we continue to recognize and reproduce this historical entitlement as a structural relation raises many troubling questions about the institution of children's literature and the criticism of it.

Nesbit's representation of "the child" alternatively to audiences of children and adults is literally a cross-writing, a staging and restaging of the chiasmic discursive mechanism by which her culture produced the structural relation of child and adult. Do her texts for children merely manufacture consent? Green himself suggests that Nesbit substitutes "tone for teaching" (46). Although I am not convinced that the two can be separated so neatly, it seems clear that the sceptical, self-deprecating, yet arrogant voice of Oswald Bastable exceeds the category of "this emptiness called a child" (Kincaid 71). The several levels and situations of narration—readers' consciousness of Oswald as Nesbit's creation, Oswald's self-conscious withholding of full information about himself as narrator, and Oswald's alternate reportage of other characters' words and feelings in direct quotation and in the amalgamated narrative voice of free indirect discourse—point to the mediation of language between "the child" and the world and complicate any attempt to read the children's texts as straight instruction or as simple appropriation. Nesbit, after all, gives Oswald the last word on the Red House adventure, a last word he uses to insist on the intractability of actual children to adults' self-serving conceptualizations: "I suppose they thought it was wilful waste to have a cradle and no baby to use it. But it could so easily have been used for something else. It would have made a ripping rabbit-hutch, and babies are far more trouble than rabbits to keep, and not nearly so profitable, I believe" (*NTS*, 104).

Notes

1. [Reimer's point is underlined by Nesbit's chapter title in *The Red House:* the children's visit in ch. 10 is called "The Invaders." Interestingly, Nesbit also separates juvenile and adult texts not only by language and narrative perspective, but also by naming the invasive society in the *Red House* differently. The children style themselves the Maidstone Society of Antiquaries and Field Club in *The Wouldbegoods* and in "The Young Antiquaries" chapter of *New Treasure Seekers*. Eds.]

2. Stephen Slemon and Jo-Ann Wallace (11) suggest that locating the places where imperial power "manufacture[s] a domination by consent" is an important project for theorists of children's literature to investigate.

Works Cited

Bivona, Daniel. *Desire and Contradiction: Imperial Visions and Domestic Debates in Victorian Literature.* Manchester, Eng.: Manchester University Press, 1990.

Bourdieu, Pierre. *Language and Symbolic Power.* Ed. John B. Thompson. Trans. Gino Raymond and Matthew Adamson. Cambridge, Mass.: Harvard University Press, 1991.

Briggs, Julia. *A Woman of Passion: The Life of E. Nesbit, 1859–1924.* London: Hutchinson, 1987.

Coveney, Peter. *The Image of Childhood: The Individual and Society: A Study of the Theme in English Literature.* 1957. Rev. ed. Harmondsworth, Eng.: Penguin, 1967.

Green, Roger Lancelyn. "The Golden Age of Children's Books." 1962. In *Children's Literature: The Development of Criticism.* Ed. Peter Hunt. London: Routledge, 1990. 36–48.

Kincaid, James R. *Child-Loving: The Erotic Child and Victorian Culture.* New York: Routledge, 1992.

Nesbit, E[dith]. *New Treasure Seekers.* 1904. Harmondsworth, Eng.: Puffin-Penguin, 1982.

———. *The Red House: A Novel.* 1902. New York: Harper, 1903.

———. *The Story of the Treasure Seekers, Being the Adventures of the Bastable Children in Search of a Fortune.* 1899. London: Puffin-Penguin, 1958.

———. *The Wouldbegoods, Being the Further Adventures of the Treasure Seekers.* 1901. Harmondsworth, Eng.: Puffin-Penguin, 1958.

Nodelman, Perry. "The Other: Orientalism, Colonialism, and Children's Literature." *Children's Literature Association Quarterly* 17.1 (1992): 29–35.

Rose, Jacqueline. *The Case of Peter Pan or The Impossibility of Children's Fiction.* 1984. Philadelphia: University of Pennsylvania Press, 1993.

Sharpe, Jenny. *Allegories of Empire: The Figure of Woman in the Colonial Text.* Minneapolis: University of Minnesota Press, 1993.

Slemon, Stephen, and Jo-Ann Wallace. "Into the Heart of Darkness? Teaching Children's Literature as a Problem in Theory." *Canadian Children's Literature* 63 (1991): 6–23.

Chronology of Book Publications

1899 *The Story of the Treasure Seekers, Being the Adventures of the Bastable Children in Search of a Fortune.* Narrated by Oswald Bastable. After a series of adventures, the children meet and "win over" the Indian Uncle, their "treasure, and no mistake." Previously published in *Pall Mall Magazine, Father Christmas, Nister's Holiday Annual,* and *Windsor Magazine.*

1901 *The Wouldbegoods, Being the Further Adventures of the Treasure Seekers.* The children are sent to the country for the summer by the Indian Uncle. Among their adventures is the visit of the Maidstone antiquarian society to the house in which they are living. The children decide to ensure that the society's visit is profitable and bury some broken pottery for society members to find. Some of the pottery turns out to be priceless Roman artifacts. Narrated by Oswald. Previously published in *Pall Mall Magazine* and *Illustrated London News.*

1902 *The Red House: A Novel.* The Bastables erupt into this adult novel, restaging the Maidstone Society's visit to their own house in a visit to the Red House, which is occupied by newlyweds Len and Chloe. Narrated by Len.

1904 *New Treasure Seekers.* Oswald tells the story of the children's visit to the Red House. Len, Chloe, and baby also appear at a local "society" picnic in another of the stories in this collection, where Chloe rescues the children from being arrested for peddling without a license by directing the policeman's attention to a neighborhood poacher. Previously published in *The London Magazine, Black and White,* and *Illustrated London News.*

"You Catch It if You Try to Do Otherwise": The Limitations of E. Nesbit's Cross-Written Vision of the Child

Erika Rothwell

Edith Nesbit did not begin writing for children consistently or particularly successfully until she produced *The Treasure Seekers* in 1899. After this success, the majority of her books were children's, but she also continued to write for adults. Nesbit, however, not only alternates between addressing child and adult audiences, but also cross-writes for adult and child *within* and *across* works. The children's books that make up the Bastable trilogy—*The Treasure Seekers* (1899), *The Wouldbegoods* (1901), and *The New Treasure Seekers* (1904)—though told from a child's point of view, address both child and adult readers and focus attention upon the common, but conflicting, experiences of adult and child. Meanwhile, the domestic novel *The Red House* (1902), which is intended for an adult audience, calls attention to the same phenomena of shared, yet conflicting, experience by introducing the child Bastable characters as "guest stars" and telling, from Len's adult point of view, an episode that is later renarrated by Oswald in *The Treasure Seekers.*

Virtually all critical consideration of Nesbit and her view of the child is based solely upon her children's books and does not incorporate the intersection of child and adult books that I have just described. Humphrey Carpenter finds Nesbit's Bastable trilogy "as condescending towards children as are any of the Beautiful Child books of the Molesworth era" (132), but more often Nesbit's children's books are thought of as iconoclastic.[1] Mary Croxson, for example, believes that Nesbit's purpose is to emancipate the child. Nesbit's children "are no longer enslaved by the repressive or over-indulgent adult domination of an earlier age. They converse freely with their elders, are at liberty to develop as they will and have the freedom of personal awareness given by a rich imaginative life" (Croxson 63). In

Children's Literature 25, ed. Francelia Butler, R. H. W. Dillard, and Elizabeth Lennox Keyser, guest ed. Mitzi Myers and U. C. Knoepflmacher (Yale University Press, © 1997 Hollins College).

short, Nesbit is typically defined as a juvenile author who writes for children as equals and as an uncompromising advocate of the child's viewpoint, rights, and freedoms.

I believe, however, that the cross-written vision of the child that emerges from the sum of the Bastable books and the *Red House* reveals that Nesbit's view of the child is more complex and contradictory than is usually acknowledged and that this perspective is neither liberating nor emancipating. It is true that the Bastables are remarkably free of regulations and inhibitions, and that Nesbit clearly does reject some Victorian manifestations of the child when she dismisses evangelical classics like Maria Charlesworth's *Ministering Children* (1854) as the "wrong sort of books" (328).[2] Nevertheless, I do not think that Nesbit's works truly can be said to address the child as an equal or to grant him or her any significant liberation. The Bastable books contain much that is inaccessible to the child reader, and the final picture that emerges from Nesbit's texts reveals the young as separate and powerless beings who are repeatedly subject to failure and confusion. Unable to understand fully or to affect knowingly the adult world, Nesbit's children can hope for no more than amused condescension from the kindest of adults.

Nesbit may well owe her reputation as a child-centered author to the creation of Oswald Bastable, who sees and speaks to the adult world from a child's perspective. Alison Lurie writes that "the decision to tell her story through the persona of Oswald Bastable, a child much after her own pattern: bold, quick-tempered, egotistic, and literary," was a decision which "released Nesbit's genius" (424).[3] Oswald voices the collective opinions, observations, and conclusions of the Bastable children as they attempt to understand adults and the adult world. Thus, Oswald has been considered an "Everychild" who can speak directly to child readers in a way adult narrators cannot.

Oswald's jaunty narration, however, which combines detail, incident, observation, and reflection, balances the Bastable tales between child and adult readers through a style designed to suggest realism to the child reader while simultaneously communicating both realism and humor to the adult reader. Both child and adult readers can relate to the Bastable children's bewildering experiences with adults and respond to Oswald's realistic descriptions of games, meals, and the dynamics of sibling relationships. But many child readers, like the child narrator, will probably fail to appreciate at least some of the humor of circumstance that informs the Bastables' comic disasters or to perceive the motivation for adult characters' actions. In addition, the "mystery" of the narrator's identity, Denny's misquoted poetry, Oswald's misuse of various words and expressions, and the general misunderstanding of the adult world that pervades the trilogy are all jokes seemingly designed to be understood by and appeal to adult readers before child readers—and at the expense of children—because the joke is often between the adult reader and the author at Oswald's expense.

There is an air of quixotism about the Bastables in their first volume of adventures as they attempt to "restore the fallen fortunes of the house of Bastable" through various methods suggested by the children's reading (16). Ultimately, all of these ventures fail, although their amusing misapprehensions often induce kind adults to supply them with pocket money. These adventures also reveal circumstances and create comic situations that Oswald (and child readers like myself) never recognize: the money found in digging for treasure was planted by Albert's uncle; the criminals they capture in expectation of a generous reward are their own neighbors hiding out at home, who are ashamed of not being able to afford their usual sea-side holiday; the "generous benefactor" is a money lender who cannot part with a sovereign; and the "Noble Editor" who admires and buys Noël's poetry is a tabloid journalist using the boys for his own ends. Oswald *is* critical of this journalist's article, which he says "describes [them] all wrong," and "seemed to make game of [Noël's poems]" (71), but he never understands the entire experience, further stressing the disjunction between adult and child worlds: children do not understand adults to adults' satisfaction, and adults do not see children as they see themselves. Thus, adults and children seem to occupy separate spheres that are firmly segregated from each other.

In *The Case of Peter Pan,* Jacqueline Rose suggests that the segregation of child and adult is a defining characteristic of fiction such as Nesbit's, which she identifies as "new realism"—essentially, the portrayal of real children. Rose theorizes that new realism is governed by a subtle rule which "demands that the narrator be adult *or* child" and use that "knowledge to hold the two instances safely apart on the page." This distance enforces the separateness of the child and, by extension, his permeable nature, which Rose believes is attractive to adults (69). Overall, Nesbit's construction of Oswald does provide a child narrator who is unable to interpret the codes of the adult world and who holds the realities of child and adult apart. I cannot completely endorse Rose's rule of total separation in relation to the Bastable chronicles, however, because there are times when Oswald brings the solitudes of child and adult reality together. Oswald has flashes of insight that allow him to perceive the truth of situations like the "Noble Editor's" mockery of him and Noël. Noël, however, is simply "quite pleased" (71). Thus, Nesbit breaks down the categories of "child" and "adult" by distinguishing between the perception of two unique child characters of different ages. This distinction suggests that Nesbit views children as individuals, recognizes graduations in the category of childhood, and under some circumstances, allows the adult and child realities to meet.

Furthermore, the very realism that arises from the inclusion of Oswald's inability to understand what may be easily elucidated by an adult reader brings the worlds of child and adult into collision, and thereby further undermines Rose's theory that the child and adult are purposely separated to provide the adult reader with a safe (that is, completely knowable) incarnation of childhood. When the children visit the moneylender Mr. Rosenbaum, they gain entrance with one of their father's cards and unknowingly touch Rosenbaum's heart. Afterward, Mr. Bastable receives a "kind" letter from Mr. Rosenbaum and declares "that letter took a weight off my mind" (130–31). Oswald "can't think what he meant" (130). He remains the innocent child narrator with no inkling of his father's financial struggles, and thus holds the reality of child and adult worlds apart. Simultaneously, however, Oswald's innocence or ignorance has brought the worlds of child misapprehension and adult reality together on the page. The Bastables cause Mr. Rosenbaum to play some aspect of the role of "Generous Benefactor" and relieve their astonished father of some pressing adult cares. Many child readers are likely to share Oswald's bewilderment over this adventure, but Nesbit's message for the adult reader is that real children like Bastables are separate and unaccountable beings whose decisions, actions, and conclusions are not easily elucidated and who may unexpectedly bring the worlds of child and adult into collision.

Despite such crossovers of influence, however, the Bastables are often forced to remain outside the adult world and are frequently bewildered to find that acting on good intentions results in accusations of naughtiness from adults. The children's naughtiness may be seen as simply an aspect of their realistic nature, and by extension of their lack of understanding, but, as James Kincaid notes in *Child-*

Loving (1992), the naughty child is as much a construction as the angelic one—a "resisting child" that "keeps its distance from the professed standard, remains Other, does not so much rebel as respond more acutely to what is wanted" (246). In other words, although I do not believe that Nesbit presents the child as completely knowable or separate as Rose suggests, I do think that she flatters and appeals to adult readers by constructing child characters who take on the identity of an Other defined by the persistent inability to understand what is easily apparent to adults. Nesbit's Other is not a child who is willfully naughty and allows adults to rebel vicariously against prescriptive social norms, but rather an Other who cannot cope in the adult world and who is helplessly and unintentionally naughty.

This helpless, unintentional naughtiness is best illustrated in *The Wouldbegoods*. In this second volume of the Bastable trilogy, the children form a "New Society for Being Good In" (285), after they are sent to the country following a disastrous game of *Jungle Book* in which Uncle's possessions are the losers. But the gaps in their knowledge and ability make the desired goodness unattainable. Early in the novel, Oswald observes that "grown-up people" like "to keep things far different from what we would, and you catch it if you try to do otherwise" (292–93). Throughout the novel, something always goes wrong in the Bastables' efforts to be good. When Dicky fixes a window in the dairy, the maids fail to notice his handiwork and prop the window with a milk pan as usual. The pan pushes the window all the way open and falls into the moat. The Bastables attempt to drag the moat, and Dora cuts her foot badly on a jagged piece of tin. Oswald observes that they looked for the pan not "to please ourselves, but because it was our duty. But that made no difference to our punishment when father came down. I have known this mistake to occur before" (305).[4]

Children not only "catch it" when they attempt to interact with the adult world; they also must endure the frustration that arises from being caught in a child world that is inherently separate. Alice expresses a child's frustration at this separation from the adult world when she cries, "It's no use! We *have* tried to be good. . . . You don't know how we've tried! And it's all no use. I believe we are the wickedest children in the whole world, and I wish we were all dead!" Albert's uncle assures Alice that although they can be "naughty and tiresome," they are not wicked; observes that they do not tell lies or do mean things; and explains that they "will learn to be good in other ways some day"—or, in other words, when they are adults (378–79).

Children, it seems, are not capable of acts of significant goodness in Nesbit's adult world, but are confined to the separate role of the unintentionally naughty Other.

Anita Moss (226) writes that Nesbit "breathed new and vital life into the Romantic child" with the Bastable stories. Even when the Bastables manage to escape charges of naughtiness, however, their attempts to exercise influence through the traditional Romantic and Victorian child roles of rescuer or redeemer are generally ineffectual or unnecessary—and ultimately undermine, rather than reanimate, the Romantic vision of the child. Often an adult has anticipated their actions. The efforts made to find Albert-next-door's Uncle's sweetheart turn out to be for naught because Albert's uncle has already found her, arranged a Christmas wedding, and deliberately kept these events secret. Nor do Nesbit's children successfully play any of the other roles so often linked to the Romantic portrayal of the child; they do not function as agents of healing, rejuvenation, or salvation. Instead, they require adults to rescue them from the consequences of their actions and provide comfort and guidance. In other words, the Bastables do not exercise any real or lasting influence over the outcome of events in the adult world, nor do they possess any of the innate moral superiority often associated with the Romantic and Victorian visions of the child. The Bastables actually engage in some rather questionable moral activities like arranging to "rescue" Lord Tottenham from the "savagery" of their own dog, orchestrating the "Avenging Take-In" on the porter, or begging for money to enhance the contents of the Christmas pudding. After such incidents, they are inevitably ashamed, often half-realizing that they have done wrong even before an adult makes this clear. According to the definition advanced by Albert's uncle, the Bastables are generally good. They are not mean, selfish, or untruthful. In no way, however, does Nesbit allow them moral superiority, and her limited definition of a "good" child is certainly different from earlier definitions of "goodness," which generally incorporate piety, respectfulness, obedience, neatness, and productive industry.

Furthermore, Romantic and Victorian literature implicitly flatters the child and pays court to his or her superior innocence and sensitivity by granting the child power over adults. Nesbit does not. If she flatters anyone, it is adults, who are shown to be so necessary to children. Like many Victorian and Romantic predecessors, Nesbit's children are basically honorable, truthful, and well intentioned,

in addition to being realistically quarrelsome, mischievous, and ego-
istic; moreover, they are granted new, Edwardian-inspired freedoms
in terms of play and individuality. But ultimately Nesbit undercuts
Romantic elevation and Victorian idealization by showing children as
dependent upon the adult world, which defines and controls them,
however benignly.

This deflation of the Romantic and Victorian visions of the child
is confirmed by *The Red House* (1902). The novel's title page refers
to Nesbit as "the author of *The Treasure Seekers.*" No additional cross-
reference is provided, but Nesbit must expect her adult readers to be
familiar with her children's books or her child readers to graduate to
reading her adult books. Otherwise the joke, the sense of being "in"
on something, would be lost. The joke begins when Len and Chloe
receive a letter they can scarcely read and barely understand.[5] Sent
from the Bastables and inexpertly typed by Noël, it requests permission to view their old country house. As usual, the Bastables are attempting to interact with the adult world as equals, but they lack the
requisite skills and knowledge. Although they are initially stunned
when the children appear, Len and Chloe quickly ascertain and
evaluate their names, class, appearance, and manners and, approving
of the children's imagination and initiative, enter into their visit with
amused and kindly, though condescending, enthusiasm: Len, for instance, notes that the children are "much funnier than they meant to
be" (*RH*, 228). Like an adult reader of the Bastable trilogy, Len sees
that the Bastables are both ignorant and innocent of the adult world:
"They are very trusting. The world must have been kind to them"
(229). The Bastables' visit inspires Len and Chloe to muse briefly on
the nature of children. Chloe, having expressed her emphatic dislike of Albert—whose velvet suits, frilly collar, and priggish manners
seem reminiscent of Little Lord Fauntleroy in particular and the
Victorian conception of the delicate seen-and-not-heard child—asks,
"Why aren't all children nice?" Len replies, "They are—if they have
nice grown-ups belonging to them" (224). In this conversation, Nesbit
expresses a concept that is implicit to the Bastable trilogy's comparison and portrayal of the Bastables, the Ffoulkeses, and Albert—that
the influence of the adult upon the child is an important and determining one. The children occupy similar places and evoke the same
attitudes, themes, and responses in this adult novel as they do in the
Bastable trilogy, but they are further reduced in terms of autonomy
and importance through the sentimental attitudes of Len and Chloe.

Len dwells on the children's picturesqueness—their rosy cheeks, their scarlet Tam-o'-Shanters, and their "young laughter" in the "old garden" (219). Len finds Alice more attractive than Dora because Alice is so pretty, and Chloe gushes over H. O. because he is the smallest, declaring him "simply a duck" (224). Len and Chloe reduce the children to the status of amusing, ornamental playthings that furnish the garden and are pretty to look at. In some ways, Oswald is less childish than these adults. He never mentions his siblings' appearances, and he judges them based upon what they do, not what they look like. To Oswald, each Bastable is an individual, not a trope of childhood that calls forth culturally conditioned, sentimental responses.

By itself in *The Treasure Seekers,* the visit to the Red House is merely another example of the Bastables' insouciant misunderstanding of the adult world, but read in concert with Len's, Oswald's account reveals differences in child and adult perceptions. The children think Len and Chloe are nice, but they see nothing untoward in their own behavior and do not realize that Len and Chloe are really extremely lenient adults stooping to a child's level. Len and Chloe are simply called "Mr. and Mrs. Redhouse." This nomenclature humorously reduces their importance in the child-centered text and suggests that Nesbit may occasionally poke fun at adults' own self-importance, but it is also another example of Oswald's failure to grasp the significance of name and position in the adult world. Furthermore, Oswald's method of naming is a practice that is likely to be deemed amusing and naive by adults who would not indulge in it; thus it enforces once more the child's separation from the adult world. Nor does Oswald reflect on what makes some adults nicer than others or consider what effect the nature of children has on adults. The dual stories of the Red House make it doubly clear that adults have a power of definition and influence over children that is not reciprocated, and that adults can stoop to interact equally with children, but children cannot rise to the level of adults.

The Bastables' third volume of adventures, *The New Treasure Seekers,* is organized around the children's attempts to raise money for their (supposedly) poor landlady. Once again, the Bastables frequently find themselves in trouble in spite of their good intentions, and adults are needed to restore order, give explanations, administer punishments and rewards, and offer comfort and understanding. In *The New Treasure Seekers,* however, Oswald grows into a new consciousness of the adult world. After the "General" lets the children take part in

the "war" and Benenden lets them participate in a "smuggling run,"
Oswald suspects that the adult world is benevolently deceiving him.
Thinking over the military adventures, Oswald uneasily concludes
that "we had made jolly fools of ourselves throughout" and that "the
whole thing was a beastly sell" (586–87). He is perfectly right, but like
a good adult-in-embryo, he does not undeceive his younger siblings.

Contemporary depictions of the child and childhood such as Kenneth Grahame's *The Golden Age* (1895) and *Dream Days* (1898) or James
Barrie's *Peter Pan* (1911) portray growing up as a thoroughly negative
process. Grahame's children refer to the adults as "The Olympians"
and condemn them as "hopeless and incapable creatures" (4) whose
"movements were confined and slow" and whose habits were "stereotyped and senseless" (5). Children are the *"illuminati,"* the only ones
capable of understanding "real life" (7). The opening page of *Peter Pan*
laments the fact that children grow up and declares that "two is the
beginning of the end" (1). Both books feature adult narrators looking
back through time and both have been judged to be *about* rather than
for children. Nesbit's view of childhood is more immediate due to her
use of Oswald as narrator, but her view of childhood is, of course, also
an adult's interpretation. For Nesbit, childhood is a time and a space
set apart, and children are not to be looked up to with reverential
awe as in Wordsworth's romantic vision, but thrown sidelong glances
of condescending sympathy, amusement, and understanding. Growing up is not a tragedy. Oswald loses some of his innocence, but he
gains in perception. Oswald does say that he sometimes feels "grown-
upness creeping inordiously upon him" and rather wishes that "you
didn't grow up so quickly," but these rather trite, literary-sounding
observations seem most likely to have been (imperfectly) culled from
Oswald's reading and are probably intended to mock such sentiments
(610).[6] At other times, Oswald is eager to grow up, to leave school,
to travel, to become a soldier. In addition, I think that the Bastables'
many misadventures teach that in growing up children gain in terms
of power and knowledge, even if they do lose some of their innocence and sense of wonder.

In creating intersections between books for children and adults,
Nesbit crosses the borders and challenges the boundaries separating
children's books from adult books while she explores children's and
adults' continuing and shifting attempts to understand and define
one another. The picture of the child that emerges from Nesbit's
attempts to appeal to both adult and child readers is curious and

contradictory. In the Bastable trilogy, children are granted new freedoms and indulgences but are simultaneously marginalized and disenfranchised from the Romantic child's traditional roles of superiority and influence over the adult. *The Red House,* however, not only reinforces the child's difference, but further undermines the child's autonomy and status through sentimental and condescending attitudes. Therefore, the vision of the child that finally emerges from Nesbit's writing is not liberating, as most commentators suggest, but dominated by limitation and condescension.

Notes

1. All Nesbit references, except to *RH,* are to the 1928 *CHBF.* By late nineteenth-century standards, Edith Nesbit was a cross-dresser as well as a cross-writer. She wore pantaloons, cropped her hair short, and was rarely seen without cigarettes at a time when few respectable women smoked.

2. Daisy and Denny Ffoulkes, who have read such books under the tutelage of a Victorian aunt reminiscent of Miss Murdstone in *David Copperfield* (265), are considered repressed "little pinky, frightened things, like white mice" who must be re-formed through their association with the hardy, independent Bastables (263).

3. Julia Briggs believes that Nesbit splits herself between the characters of the twins: Alice is "morally courageous and determined," and Noël is "vulnerable" and "subject to fits of poetry, fainting, and tears" (*WP* xvii). This is a very perceptive observation; nevertheless, I still concur with Lurie that a great deal of Nesbit's reported personality can be seen in Oswald. It probably isn't necessary to choose between the two interpretations; given that Oswald, Alice, and Noël are the most prominent of the six Bastable children, it is reasonable to suppose that Nesbit identified closely with all three characters.

4. Attempts to fill the empty lock with water after it has been emptied, to bury a fox the hunt was pursuing, to rescue an "abandoned high born babe," to entertain the Antiquarian society by planting relics in their excavation site, and to offer nonalcoholic "free drinks" to thirsty travelers also end in punishments and disasters of varying degrees, outcomes that further illustrate the truth of Oswald's observations.

5. Chloe believes that the writer of the letter must be mad or idiotic, but Len, seeing the children's address, says "I'm almost certain it's a workman's club" (*RH,* 214). These two ideas represent traditional classifications of the child, who has historically been linked with the lower classes and the mentally deficient.

6. Oswald speaks grammatically correct English (a tribute to his middle-class education), which is sprinkled with slang and catchwords culled from his wide reading of children's classics, novels of all descriptions, and newspapers. Oswald is a self-reflexive author who cheerfully admits that his style is influenced by what he reads. In comparing the live farm animals to the mounted ones in his uncle's house, he says: "The stuffed denizens of our late-lamented Jungle pale into insignificance before the number of live things on the farm," and then he comments in an aside: "I hope you do not think that the words I use are getting too long. I know they are the right words. And Albert's uncle says your style is always altered a bit by what you read. And I have been reading the Vicomte de Bragelonne. Nearly all my new words came out of those" (387). Later Oswald tries out a different descriptive style: "In a very short space of time we would be wending our way back to Blackheath, and all the variegated delightfulness of the country would soon be only preserved in memory's faded flowers." He

observes, however, that "I don't care for that way of writing very much. It would be an awful swat to keep it up" (588).

Works Cited

Barrie, James M. *Peter Pan*. 1911. Toronto: Penguin, 1987.

Briggs, Julia. *A Woman of Passion: The Life of E. Nesbit*. London: Century, 1987.

Carpenter, Humphrey. *Secret Gardens: A Study of the Golden Age of Children's Literature*. Boston: Houghton Mifflin, 1985.

Croxson, Mary. "The Emancipated Child in the Novels of E. Nesbit." *Signal* 14 (May 1974): 51–64.

Grahame, Kenneth. *The Golden Age*. 1895. New York: Dodd, Mead, 1905.

Kincaid, James R. *Child-Loving: The Erotic Child and Victorian Culture*. New York: Routledge, 1992.

Lurie, Alison. "E. Nesbit." *Writers for Children*. Ed. Jane M. Bingham. New York: Scribner, 1988. 423–30.

Moss, Anita. "E. Nesbit's Romantic Child in Modern Dress." *Romanticism and Children's Literature in Nineteenth-Century England*. Ed. James Holt McGavran, Jr. Athens: University of Georgia Press, 1991. 225–47.

Nesbit, E. *The Complete History of the Bastable Family: The Story of the Treasure Seekers, The Wouldbegoods, and The New Treasure Seekers*. London: Ernest Benn, 1928.

———. *The Red House: A Novel*. New York: Harper, 1902.

Rose, Jacqueline. *The Case of Peter Pan or the Impossibility of Children's Fiction*. London: Macmillan, 1984.

E. Nesbit, the Bastables, and The Red House: A Response

Julia Briggs

It is at once a pleasure and a responsibility to respond to two papers that address E. Nesbit's cross-writing, as demonstrated in Nesbit's description of the Bastables' visit to the Red House in the novel of that name. It is a pleasure to find Nesbit's work being treated with the seriousness it deserves, and a responsibility because any response risks narrowing, rather than opening up, the field. Mavis Reimer and Erika Rothwell contribute valuably to ongoing theoretical discussions concerning the construction of the child at the end of the last century; they set the figure of the child in the perspectives of empire and of earlier writing for children, and they explore the question of persuasion or even coercion implicit in the adult writer's address to the child reader. These are key issues, and their very centrality permits a response more closely focused upon the initial circumstances of publication of *The Story of the Treasure Seekers* as a text generated by and within a context of cross-writing. I am conscious of pursuing a rather different line of argument, but my approach through intertextuality and publishing history, which is intended to complement rather than to counter the arguments Reimer and Rothwell establish, is made possible by their more fundamental concern to define the relationship between adult and child as figured in Nesbit's *The Story of the Treasure Seekers, The Red House,* and *The New Treasure Seekers.*

> Yes, these stories are good. They are written on a rather original idea, on a line off the common run. Here we have the life of a family of children told by themselves in a candid, ingenuous and very amusing style. Of course, no child would write as E. Nesbit writes, but the result is that we have drawn for us a very charming picture of English family life . . . the stories are individual— they will please every grown up who reads them.
>
> Edward Garnett, Reader's Report to Fisher Unwin
> on Seven Stories from the *Pall Mall Magazine,* 1898

Children's Literature 25, ed. Francelia Butler, R. H. W. Dillard, and Elizabeth Lennox Keyser, guest ed. Mitzi Myers and U. C. Knoepflmacher (Yale University Press, © 1997 Hollins College).

Garnett, a famous talent-spotter, seizes at once on the point made by Erika Rothwell at the outset of her essay: the stories that became *The Story of the Treasure Seekers* were addressed to children and adults simultaneously, with the expectation that they would be read in different ways, like a pantomime that includes different types of jokes for different age groups. Unfortunately Nesbit left no record of the process by which she transformed her writing for children from the flat, simplistic narratives of her early work for Raphael Tuck and Ernest Nister to the complex and self-conscious rhetoric of Oswald Bastable, whose literary sense apparently directs him to relate his own story as a third-person narrative. She was, however, an ardent admirer of Henry James, whose work in the 1890s, particularly *What Maisie Knew* (1897) and *The Turn of the Screw* (1898) exploits the possibilities of literary misreadings created by unreliable narrators and the conflicting interpretations of events by children and adults.

Put to comic purpose, these devices dominate the narrative practice of *The Story of the Treasure Seekers* (1899), creating a cross-writing that simultaneously addresses adult and child readers by conferring on Oswald (and through him on his siblings) the full subjecthood implicit in a first-person narrative, a narrative that invites the child-reader to identify with Oswald or his siblings. (When he is referred to in the third person or as a child among children confronting the adult world, however, Oswald is seen from an adult perspective as comically smaller and less significant than he supposes, as an amusing little boy, as "Other"; as Rothwell puts it, "the joke is often between the adult reader and the author at Oswald's expense.") Nesbit's introduction of the Bastables into her sentimental novel *The Red House* (1902) could thus be considered the logical outcome of a narrative strategy that had originated with their invention. Chloe's exclamation, "Aren't they perfect dears? . . . I don't like the Morrison boy— but the others are lovely" (175) is thus in danger of overstating what adult readers have already observed for themselves, and for a moment the speaker within the fiction and the author outside it betray an uneasy complicity.

If Henry James offers one literary paradigm, Kenneth Grahame affords another. *The Golden Age* (1895) and its successor *Dream Days* (1898) were outstandingly successful books written about children for adults, though they were soon passed on to children as well: Oswald considers *The Golden Age* "A1 except where it gets mixed up with grown-up nonsense" (*Wouldbegoods*, 94). Grahame's celebration of the child's world of imaginative play owes something to Stevenson's essay "Child's Play" (*Virginibus Puerisque,* 1881) and more to Richard Jefferies's evocation of childhood in *Bevis: The Story of a Boy* (1882), both texts written about rather than for children by writers who also wrote for children directly. *The Golden Age* established childhood as a pastoral or nostalgic world for adults and later lent its name to a particular way of writing for children that marks a distinctive development within the history of children's books as well as in the construction of the child—the point at which the adult, searching for a lost childhood, vicariously recovers it through a particular child's experience.

Such a pattern is always potentially present in the relation of child to adult—for example, when Wordsworth interrogated Basil Montagu in "Anecdote for Fathers," or when Dickens sought his own healing through exposing society's victimization of children—but it takes an intensified, even exaggerated form in Carroll's use of Alice, and later in Barrie's use of Peter Pan and "the Lost Boys." Positioning the nostalgic adult reader over the child's shoulder decisively alters the narrative voice and the angle of address. Whereas romantic poets and essayists recalled the *Arabian Nights* or chapbook heroes such as Jack the Giant-Killer with affection, a later generation of adult readers sought books they had enjoyed in childhood, while adult writers for children deliberately rework themes from earlier children's books. C. S. Lewis, who did both these things, even enunciated the principle that "a children's story which is enjoyed only by children is a bad children's story" (59). Adults gladly surrendered the "Olympian" status conferred on them by Grahame and joined in children's games in many "Golden Age" texts including Nesbit's, Kipling's *Just So Stories* (1902), and the opening sequence of *Winnie the Pooh* (1926).

The 1880s and 1890s saw an increasing overlap between writing addressed to children and that meant for adults: "boys' stories," adventures at the outposts of empire, historical tales, and detective stories, as well as ghost stories and sentimental or romantic narratives, were widely read and published in the illustrated magazines aimed at middle-class "family" reading. Here popular romance of all kinds was published alongside the serialized work of Thomas Hardy or even Henry James. E. Nesbit wrote up memories of her schooldays for *The Girl's Own Paper,* but the adventures of the Bastables appeared in the *Illustrated London News* (initially in the "Father Christmas" supplement, but later in the regular pages) as well as in the *Pall Mall Magazine,* the *Windsor Magazine, Crampton's,* and the *London Magazine* (where *The New Treasure Seekers* was immediately followed by the serialization of *The Railway Children*). Her closest association, however, was with George Newnes's best-selling and high-paying magazine *The Strand,* where her children's stories appeared more or less continuously from 1902 to 1912.

Nearly all of the Bastable stories were published in magazines of this kind before they reached book form, as the appended list indicates. Unlike *Aunt Judy's Magazine,* recalled by Edward Garnett in the course of his reader's report, none of these magazines was addressed to children, though nothing they included would have "brought a blush to a young person's cheek." Nesbit herself also published short stories for adults in them, and these were often illustrated by the same artists as her stories for children: for example, Frances Ewan illustrated "The Nobleness of Oswald" when it appeared in the *Windsor Magazine,* as well as Nesbit's story "A Perfect Stranger," later reprinted in a collection of short stories for adults, *Thirteen Ways Home* (1901). Another story from that collection, "G. H. and I," was illustrated by Lewis Baumer for the *Pall Mall Magazine,* for which he also illustrated the episode "Being Detectives," later to become chapter 3 of *The Story of the Treasure Seekers.* Arthur Buckland, the main artist for *The Wouldbegoods* as it appeared serially in the *Illustrated London News,* also illustrated her romantic short story "The Letter in Brown Ink" for the *Windsor Magazine.*

All these magazines situated the children's stories they published within a context of adult reading and thus could be said to constitute a locus of cross-writing. Surprisingly, there seems to have been little anxiety to identify the readership being addressed in any individual piece of writing, presumably because it was evident from the outset and none of the material published was obviously "unsuitable for children." When the individual episodes that later made up *The Story of the Treasure Seekers* first appeared in the *Pall Mall* or the *Windsor Magazine,* they were not explicitly identified as stories for children. "Noël's Princess," the third episode of the Bastables to appear in the *Pall Mall Magazine,* was subtitled (inaccurately, as it happened) "Passages from the life of Oswald Bastable, Esq., of Lewisham, in the County of Kent. No 2." This title was probably intended to indicate the humorous tone of the child aspiring to adult status; possibly it was intended to distinguish it from the comparable episode in *The Golden Age.* In any case, the experiment was not repeated.

One way in which the illustrated magazines conveyed the nature of their articles was through the subject matter of their illustrations. Another was the use of illustrative blocks appearing at the head and foot of a particular story or poem. These blocks were not specifically drawn for that piece, but served rather as indicators of mood or subject. The Bastable stories as they appeared in the *Pall Mall Magazine* were introduced by rather stiff little scenes in period costume of the type appropriate for a history book or for a series of historical episodes. These headers bore no relationship to the stories they introduced; they usually changed from month to month, though episodes published in July and August 1898 were introduced by the same picture. Dated four years earlier and signed "Gilbert James, '95," they had presumably been drawn for an earlier set of articles. *The Windsor Magazine* did not make use of introductory headings.

Many, but by no means all, of the illustrations made for the Bastable stories when they first appeared were reproduced when they were published in book form (*STS* 1899). Lewis Baumer and Gordon Browne, who illustrated episodes for the *Pall Mall Magazine,* were included, whereas the *Windsor Magazine* illustrators, Frances Ewan and Raymond Potter, who worked with wash rather than in line, were not. *The Wouldbegoods* (1901) reprinted the work of Arthur Buckland and John Hassall, first published in the *Illustrated London News*. Later, Wells, Gardner, and Darton, who published *Oswald Bastable and Others* (1905), appear to have commissioned Charles Brock to provide some extra pictures for stories such as "An Object of Value and Virtue," which had originally appeared without illustrations. Nesbit's early illustrators, Lewis Baumer and Gordon Browne, have subsequently been overshadowed by H. R. Millar, who worked mainly for *The Strand* and illustrated the fantasies she published there. Browne, in particular, was an excellent artist in his own right: the son of Dickens's illustrator "Phiz" (Hablot K. Browne), he was particularly good at conveying movement: in his pictures the nursemaid sweeps out of the frame carrying the screaming German princess, or the Indian uncle attacks the pudding in high style. He did not illustrate *The Wouldbegoods* (which was mainly serialized in the *Illustrated London News*) but the drawings for *The New Treasure Seekers* (1904) were his, having originally appeared in the *London Magazine.* It was Gordon Browne who depicted the encounters between Len and Chloe of *The Red House* and the Bastables.

Children's books of this period tended to be illustrated more fully and often in a more decorative or stylized manner than those in-

HER VOICE WHEN SHE TOLD US WE WERE TRESPASSING WAS NOT SO FURIOUS.

THE LUNCH WAS A BLISSFUL DREAM OF A.1.-NESS.

Like the stories themselves, the original illustrations for the Bastable children's inter-
play with the adult world teasingly evince both condescension and community. Gordon
Browne's illustrations were used for the stories collected in *The New Treasure Seekers*.
Original captions are from the adult novel *The Red House*.

tended for adults, but the kind of periodicals referred to above were heavily illustrated, and adult books often included some illustrations, usually at least a frontispiece. *The Treasure Seekers* is cross-written insofar as it addresses adult readers in a magazine published for adults at the same time as it addresses child readers (or perhaps it speaks to the parent reading to the child; Kipling enjoyed reading Nesbit's stories to his children). It also reproduces features of its original publication context as part of its structural form and content. Journals and newspapers figure repeatedly in the text and are used in a variety of ways. Dicky's proposals for moneymaking, adopted in chapters 9 and 11, are inspired by "small ads" of various kinds, especially those that promise instant cash, offer lucrative partnerships in return for an investment of £100, promise loans without security, or give assurances that you can make £2 a week in your spare time (the sums involved should be multiplied by at least one hundred). Invitations of this kind, telltale signs of a degenerate capitalism, were (and still are) addressed to the gullible, and thus naturally appeal to the Bastables. In the following chapter (12), they study the commercial techniques displayed in patent medicine advertisements, inventing and bottling "Bastable's Certain Cure for Colds," a mixture of peppermint and nontoxic paint which they hope will bring in a clear profit, if marketed effectively.

One of their earliest projects for making money is a visit to Fleet Street to sell Noël's poems. It is on this occasion that Oswald and Noël meet Mrs. Leslie, who, like Albert-Next-Door's Uncle, is a professional "author" (what other job would allow him to make himself available whenever he was needed?). The Bastables also write and edit their own journal, *The Lewisham Recorder*: its wide range of forms and genres closely parallels that of magazines such as the *Windsor* and the *Pall Mall* where the stories originally appeared (although this episode, ch. 7, had a significant forebear in Nesbit's "The Play Times," published as a series in *Nister's Holiday Annual* from 1894 to 1896.) Also composed by a family of children, "The Play Times" includes a number of pieces later attributed to the Bastables and written in imitation of the conventions of adult journalism; both newspapers deliberately rework the equivalent scenes in Dickens's *Holiday Romance* (1868). *The Lewisham Recorder* reveals the children's sensitivity to literary languages: in their different contributions, they recreate a variety of styles and genres as a mode of imitative play. All writing is stylized, and although particular languages are appropriate for particular games, they also shape the children's expectations and suggest to them a particular interpretation (or misinterpretation) of the events they encounter. This process is vividly displayed in chapter 3, "Being Detectives," where literary fictions are used to expose social fictions. There the highly distinctive conventions of the detective story lead Oswald and Dicky to uncover their neighbors' guilty secret: that they are too poor for all of them to go on holiday. The girls' cheap meal is comically underlined by an engraving of the Prodigal Son that hangs on the wall above (*STS*, 44).

Nesbit could count on her readers' familiarity with a range of literary styles, a reliance that can be an obstacle for many of today's child readers. The Bastables are portrayed as avid readers who are delighted when they can communicate with adults through the shortcut of shared allusions: Albert's Uncle regularly scores by "talking like a book" and Mrs. Leslie knows her Kipling; the Jewish moneylender, on the other hand, is baffled by being addressed as "G. B.," short for "Generous Benefactor, like in Miss Edgeworth" (137, 142). The world of children's reading provided familiar reference points not only for child readers, but also for middle-class adults, a generation who had grown up with children's books. Nesbit's allusions are often substantial: she sets up either an announced or a concealed playing-out of an episode from an earlier text — *Sintram and His Companions*, Charlotte M. Yonge, Grahame, or Kipling — by drawing on its plot outline or perhaps its opening sequence of events. Such borrowings allow her to economize on original plot invention while she sets up a series of intertexts that create further moments of comedy or recognition.

Cross-writing implies a double perspective, lending complexity and richness while increasing uncertainty. There is an effect in Nesbit's works of being simultaneously inside and outside a story-shaped world, because books are "acted out" even though they are explicitly recognized as fictions. Oswald undercuts the implausible happy ending of *The Story of the Treasure Seekers* by observing "I can't help it if it is like Dickens, because it happens this way. Real life is often something like books" (294). Elsewhere the adult world seems as arbitrary as any game (a point of view that underpins the *Alice* books), so that the clichés of fiction provide at least one stable system of referents in an incomprehensible world, even though the expectations fiction creates also lead to difficulties: in *The New Treasure Seekers*, Noël and H. O. cut the wires Father has just installed for electricity on the assumption that "It is dynamite . . . to blow up Father because he took part in the Lewisham election, and his side won" (156). The Bastables see themselves as empowered and independent, with an obligation to restore the family fortunes or to help those less privileged than themselves; yet, as Erika Rothwell observes, their assumptions are always undercut by adult interventions that reduce them to the status of children once more, leaving them intimidated or outmaneuvered, even ritually punished: "His face wore the look that means bed, and very likely no supper" (*Wouldbegoods,* 167). Their uncertain status defines the Bastables as closer to Carroll's Alice than to those children of the evangelical tradition whose spiritual resources give them unexpected power over the fallen adults around them.

Both Rothwell and Reimer read *The Red House* episode and its reworking in *The New Treasure Seekers* in terms of a redefinition of the power relations between adult and child, although they each approach the topic from rather different angles. "Treasure Seekers and Invaders" asserts the centrality of the Bastables' disruptive intervention to the structure of *The Red House* and defines the relationship between *The Red House* and the Bastables' earliest appearance in *The Story of the Treasure Seekers* in terms of a close reading of the latter's final chapter. Reimer comments on their differences: "If, in the children's novel, the reading of the metaphorical as literal allows the adult to disperse the literal in play, in the adult novel the reverse transaction takes place; the children's restaging of a 'real' event as play allows the adults to reconstitute their own play as reality." The relationship of play to reality here described is central not only to the ending but also to *The Treasure Seekers* as a whole: it occurs partly because Albert's Uncle enjoys playing up to the children's sense of wonder, for example, by popping a half crown into the hole they have dug for treasure; but also because on more than one occasion the children's intervention unexpectedly solves an adult problem in ways that could not have been expected or foreseen—as when the Generous Benefactor lives up to his title and extends Father's loan, when Noël finds a real princess (though she is not in the least their idea of one), or when, in the final chapters, the children's mistaken assumption about their Uncle's poverty enables him to recognize theirs.

The interplay between imagination and reality is inevitably a favorite theme in writing for children, but one crucial model for *The Story of the Treasure Seekers* was Frances Hodgson Burnett's *Sara Crewe, or What Happened at Miss Minchin's* (1887), the earlier version of *A Little Princess* (1905). Nesbit's attitude to Burnett mingles admiration with an edge of resentment. Albert-next-door in his frilly collars and velvet knickerbockers registers her irritation with Fauntleroy as spoiled only child and "muff" (as Rothwell notices), whereas chapter 13, "The Robber and the Burglar," blatantly reworks Burnett's *Editha's Burglar* (1888). The whole framework of *The Story of the Treasure Seekers,* that of a family come down in the world, bearing up bravely in reduced circumstances and later recovering its lost status and fortunes, has many parallels with the story of Sara Crewe, demoted from parlor boarder to slavey. Sara sustains herself during her trials through acts of the imagination, through her "supposings," much as the Bastables sustain themselves through their imaginative games, and her dreams finally come true through the intervention of another "poor, broken-down" Indian benefactor—in this case her father's lost business partner, who showers her with the accumulated wealth of the East. As Reimer observes, imperial wealth had a special significance at this period, and parallels between the oppression of colonial peoples, of children, and of the working class are sharply underscored in Burnett's text, which also introduces a colonial servant, the Lascar, and a sad little monkey to emphasize the point.

Nesbit reworks Burnett's ending, creating a series of misunderstandings around the word "poor," as Reimer shows: the Indian Uncle describes himself as "a poor, broken-down man" to excuse himself from drinking any more of Father's cheap wine, which the Bastables understand as a reference to his financial state. Their mistake establishes links between the final chapter and a discourse of "genteel" (that is, shameful and concealed) poverty that runs through the whole book but is set out in detail in the opening chapter. Although the precise significance of dunning letters and the long blue paper brought by a policeman is hidden from the children, they are not altogether deceived by the polite fictions offered to them: the silver "all went away to the shop to have the dents and scratches taken out of it and never came back. We think Father hadn't enough money to pay the silver man for taking out the dents and scratches" (5–6). The realism with which middle-class poverty is presented inhibits sentimentality, though by invoking Dickens in the final chapter Oswald seems to acknowledge that his narrative belongs ultimately to the mode of fairy tale rather than to a world of strict moral consequence, in which one person's gain is another's loss. Although "Lord Tottenham" in chapter 10 makes fun of Oswald's assumption "that the best way to restore fallen fortunes was to rescue an old gentleman in distress" (153), this turns out, in effect, to be what happens: the Bastables' sympathy for their Uncle's supposed poverty and their determination to give him a really good dinner function on one level as the good deed in the fairy tale, while on another, the children's involvement gives the Uncle the chance to recognize the hardship Father has so carefully concealed and thus to become the ultimate Generous Benefactor. Play becomes reality for the last time as Oswald announces his arrival: "Here comes the coach of the Fairy Godmother. It'll stop here, you see if it doesn't" (283). Such a transformation confers the illusion of power, but no more than that.

Both Reimer and Rothwell take up the crucial question of how much power or independence the Bastables actually achieve, only to be struck by its absence. For Reimer, the construction of the child is bound up with that of the colonial subject, and *The Story of the Treasure Seekers* aims to create "a domination that also manufactures consent," in a process that will allow the adult to make literal what has been metaphorical—that is, in terms of the book's final chapter, to convert fantasy and play into reality. Rothwell also finds the Bastables' lack of power, their constant subjection to adult wishes and to adult interpretation, to be debilitating, in contrast to earlier accounts that tend to represent the Bastables as free and emancipated, and thus as the forerunners of Ransom's Swallows and Amazons or Blyton's Famous Five.

Nesbit's continual mockery of earlier children's books, including those written in the evangelical tradition, exposes the means to spiritual or moral power that they appear to offer. Instead, her own texts generally focus upon the possibilities of imaginative power, usually figured as magic, in a tradition that had flourished since the midcentury. Oswald himself accepts economic dependence and the arbitrary rules imposed by parents, servants, and other authorities, although at the same time he resists their implications by adopting condescending attitudes toward them whenever possible. The Bastables' sense of disempowerment is sharply focused in the opening events of *The Story of the Treasure Seekers*: a parent dies, and a loss of financial security and status follows. One of the worst consequences is that "we left off going to school, and Father said we should go to a good school as soon as he could manage it. He said a holiday would do us all good. We thought he was right, but we wished he had told us he couldn't afford it. For of course we knew" (6). The Bastables must find their own amusements because they do not have lessons or go to school, and they cannot attend the free Board Schools because that would have involved an open acknowledgement that they had lost their middle-class status. The search for a solution or a means of recovery or restoration from such a comedown is probably the commonest element in Nesbit's plots. The plight of Sara Crewe thus becomes a paradigm of what loss of social status involves, one that reveals the depths to which a once pampered and protected child might fall through no fault of her own.

If the Bastables' power is no more than an illusion, it may in part be a necessary illusion, acting as compensation for the increasingly infantilized and protected middle-class child. Nesbit's work was thought of as emancipating because within it the urban middle-class child was released from the oppressive safety of the nursery, schoolroom, or garden to have "adventures." The Bastables' games and excursions brought them into situations of danger, conflict, and risk largely because they *were* children and thus lacked sufficient experience or authority to anticipate or deal with the problems they might encounter. For them, the world of adventure, so often located in an "elsewhere," is imaginatively entered from any park or street, but it is always liable to disruption by "reality" as an irate adult breaks in. As Rothwell explains, they enjoy freedom (within limits), but not power, and it is precisely their lack of power which turns their urban environment into an adventure playground, a place of excitement not unmixed with anxiety.

Part of the process of disempowerment paradoxically involved a changing conception of what constituted subversive behavior in children. One reaction against the romantic and evangelical ideas of the child took the form of a revaluation of childish high spirits, notoriously celebrated in Catherine Sinclair's *Holiday House* (1839), but also strongly present in the May family in Charlotte M. Yonge's *The Daisy Chain* (1856), and later degenerating into sentimental pictures of scamps, scallywags, and lovable pickles. High spirits in the form of elaborate practical jokes or booby traps (such as those which Dicky Bastable favored) became fashionable among schoolboys and young men, and childish bad temper became an occasion for humor rather than punishment as Kipling's "the camelious hump" or Edward Abbott Parry's *Katawampus* (1895) indicate. Naughtiness might acquire a sinister aspect from the adult desire to punish, but it was increasingly accepted as part of childhood and might even be regarded as a virtue in the right circumstances: at the end of *The Wouldbegoods* we learn that Daisy and Denny, nicknamed "the white mice," "have thought of several quite new naughty things entirely on their own—and done them too—since they came back from the Moat House" (330). Once naughtiness came to be regarded as a manifestation of the energies natural to childhood, the Bastables could display it with impunity. A new and rather different code of behavior began to influence the up-bringing and conduct of middle-class children in the second half of the nineteenth century, a code influenced by Thomas Arnold and the new public schools. It is this that the Bastables subscribe to, accord-ing to Albert's Uncle: "I have known you all for four years—and you know as well as I do how many scrapes I've seen you in and out of—but I've never known one of you tell a lie, and I've never known one of you do a mean or dishonourable action. And when you have done wrong you are always sorry. Now this is something to stand firm on. You'll learn to be good in other ways some day" (*Wouldbegoods,* 116). This is the code that Oswald himself upholds and that Nesbit's books seek to instill in her readers.

The active high spirits that welcome adventure and all too often lead to "naughtiness" were not unrelated to the qualities of courage and daring promoted in fiction for boys and were more often encour-aged in boys than in girls. Both *The Story of the Treasure Seekers* and *The Red House* employ male narrators, but Oswald's narrative consis-tently celebrates masculine values at the expense of girls' interests and games, whereas the main claim to originality of *The Red House* lies in its use of a male narrator to valorize domestic life, love, and mother-hood. As the girls stereotypically crowd around the cradle on the final page, Dicky asks if "they might not go and see the pig." Oswald's impatience with baby worship is voiced in his own later relation of events in *The New Treasure Seekers* (160), where his view that "babies are far more trouble than rabbits" strikes a welcome, if predictably "masculine," note. As he explains in *The Wouldbegoods,* he prefers love stories "where the hero parts with the girl at the garden-gate in the gloaming and goes off and has adventures, and you don't see her any more until he comes home to marry her at the end of the book" (329). The Bastables introduce a necessary astringency into *The Red House,* though they do so by means of a construction of masculinity that is now rightly suspect. Nesbit's cross-writing here negotiates not only the adult-child divide, but also the polarities of male and female values.

Works Cited

Burnett, Mrs. Frances Hodgson. *Sara Crewe, or What Happened at Miss Minchin's* and *Editha's Burglar.* London and New York: Frederick Warne, 1888.
———. *A Little Princess.* London: Frederick Warne, 1905.

Carroll, Lewis. *Alice's Adventures in Wonderland.* London: Macmillan, 1865.
———. *Through the Looking Glass and What Alice Found There.* London: Macmillan, 1872.
De la Motte Fouque. *Sintram and His Companions* and *Undine.* [1814]. London: Gardner, Darton and Co., 1896.
Dickens, Charles. *Holiday Romance,* in *Reprinted Pieces.* [1868]. Oxford: Oxford University Press, 1958.
Garnett, Edward. Reader's reports in the Berg Collection of the New York Public Library.
Grahame, Kenneth. *The Golden Age.* London: John Lane, 1895.
———. *Dream Days.* London: John Lane, The Bodley Head, 1898.
James, Henry. *What Maisie Knew.* New York: Charles Scribner, 1897.
———. *The Two Magics: The Turn of the Screw, Covering End.* New York: Macmillan, 1898.
Jefferies, Richard. *Bevis: The Story of a Boy.* London: Sampson Low, 1882.
Kipling, Rudyard. *Just So Stories.* London: Macmillan, 1902.
Lewis, C. S. "On Three Ways of Writing for Children." *Of This and Other Worlds.* Ed. Walter Hooper. London: Collins, 1982.
Nesbit, E. *The Story of the Treasure Seekers: Being the Adventures of the Bastable Children in Search of a Fortune.* London: T. Fisher Unwin, 1899.
———. *The Wouldbegoods: Being the Further Adventures of the Treasure Seekers.* London: T. Fisher Unwin, 1901.
———. *Thirteen Ways Home.* London: Anthony Treherne, 1901.
———. *The Red House.* London: Methuen, 1902; 6th ed. 1913.
———. *The New Treasure Seekers.* London: T. Fisher Unwin, 1904.
Parry, Edward Abbott. *Katawampus, Its Treatment and Cure.* London: David Nutt, 1902.
Sinclair, Catherine. *Holiday House.* Edinburgh: William Whyte, 1839.
Stevenson, Robert Louis. "Child's Play" in *Virginibus Puerisque.* [1881]. London: Chatto and Windus, 1921.
Wordsworth, William. *Lyrical Ballads.* Ed. R. L. Brett and A. R. Jones. [1798]. London: Methuen, 1971.
Yonge, Charlotte Mary. *The Daisy Chain.* London: Parker & Son, 1856.

The Periodical Publication of the Bastables

The Story of the Treasure Seekers (1899)

Material used in chapter 8 ("Being Editors") appeared as "The Play Times" in *Nister's Holiday Annual* for 1894, 1895, and 1896. Chapters 1, 2, and 7, "miserably mutilated," according to Nesbit, appeared as "The Treasure Seekers" by Ethel Mortimer in "Father Christmas," Dec. 1897, a special number of the *Illustrated London News.* During 1898 the *Pall Mall Magazine* published chapters 4 and 5 (together) in April, chapter 10 in May, chapter 6 in June, chapter 14 in July, and chapters 15 and 16 (together) in August. Chapter 9 appeared in the *Windsor Magazine*'s September 1898 issue. The *Pall Mall Magazine* featured in 1899 chapter 3 in May, chapter 11 in August, and chapter 13 in September. Chapter 12 appeared in the *Windsor Magazine* in October 1899, and the book was published at the end of 1899.

The Wouldbegoods (1901)

Four stories appeared in the *Pall Mall Magazine* during 1900: chapter 3 in July, chapter 1 in August, chapter 5 in October, and chapter 6 in November. The rest were published in 1900 in the *Illustrated London News:* chapter 2 on 18 August, chapter 4 on 17 November, and chapter 7 on 22 December. In 1901, chapter 9 appeared on 19 January, chapter 8 on 23 February, chapter 10 on 23 March, chapter 11 on 20 April, chapter 12 on 18 May, chapter 13 on 29 June, and chapter 14 on 20 July.

The New Treasure Seekers (1904)

The first chapter appeared in the Christmas number of *Black and White,* 1901, and the
second in the *Illustrated London News* for Christmas 1900. The rest appeared in the
London Magazine—chapter 3 appearing in December 1903, and the rest following at
monthly intervals thereafter until chapter 11 was published in Aug. 1904. Chapter 12
appeared in November 1904, and no previous publication has been found for the
final chapter. (The serialization of *The Railway Children* ran in the *London Magazine*
from January 1905 to January 1906.)

Oswald Bastable—and Others (1905)

"An Object of Value and Virtue" appeared in *Crampton's Magazine* for February 1902
and "The Arsenicators" in the *London Magazine* for September 1904. Earlier publication of "The Runaways" and "The Enchanceried House" has not been found.

SOCIAL TRAFFIC

Benevolent Brothers and Supervising Mothers: Ideology in the Children's Verses of Mary and Charles Lamb and Charlotte Smith

Donelle R. Ruwe

We can assert two indisputable truths: one is that there were not mere dozens, nor even hundreds, but actually thousands, of women whose writing was published in Great Britain in the half century between 1780 and 1830 that subsumes the Romantic period; and the other is that until very recently we have known very little about it. What that says about the sociology of literary criticism is obvious to any reader and therefore need not occupy us any further.

Curran, "Women Readers," 179

Although the current recovery of thousands of British women who published in the Romantic period has exposed the gendered politics of past literary criticism, we still participate in a hierarchical gendering of genres. Thus, while republishing women's novels, women's poetry, and women's feminist and pedagogical tracts, Romantic scholars have not directed sustained attention to women's verses for children.[1] That such verses seem incongruous in relation to a Romantic discourse suggests that we have not carried forward far enough our revisionings of what constitutes British Romanticism. Studying women's verses for children as cross-writing—as works that transgress the divisions between adult and children's literature—reveals the inadequacy of the interpretive conventions that we apply to children's texts. Even though we acknowledge that Romantic ideologies construct poetry as a privileged discourse restricted by class, education, and gender, we still discuss women's poetry for children as if it were

Children's Literature 25, ed. Francelia Butler, R. H. W. Dillard, and Elizabeth Lennox Keyser, guest ed. Mitzi Myers and U. C. Knoepflmacher (Yale University Press, © 1997 Hollins College).

only a historical artifact—not art that engages ongoing aesthetic and poetic debates.

By contrast, this essay argues that children's verses critique a Romantic ideology that privileges aesthetics over social concerns, and do so by representing patriarchal literary authority in terms of symbolic family dynamics. More precisely, I will demonstrate that Mary and Charles Lamb's *Poetry for Children* uses brother and sister figures to expose the patriarchal structure of poetics—but stops short of radically subverting these structures or positing an alternative, feminine poetics. Charlotte Smith also uses representations of siblings to critique aesthetics, but, as I will demonstrate, her project is far more subversive. Unlike the Lambs, Smith encourages women to enter into and then transform poetics. Ostensibly written for "young persons," Smith's *Conversations Introducing Poetry* is actually a mother's manual on teaching children to become poets. Smith places brothers and sisters under the supervision of a powerful mother-poet who insists that girls as well as boys must be educated in the fundamental skills of poetry creation, reading, and analysis. Poetic authority, in Smith's *Conversations,* resides with the matriarch.

As recent work by Alan Richardson and Mitzi Myers has shown, children's literature can be a vehicle for women writers' self-expression, "a conceptual space where politics, social history, ideology, and literary representations of all kinds meet, interpenetrate, and collide" (Richardson, *Literature,* 2). Children's literature is also an "inherently transgressive genre" that insists that readers play both child and adult (Myers, "De-Romanticizing," 92). Yet studies of Romantic aesthetics have presented women's verses for children as uncomplicated texts written at a child's reading level, overlooking the ways in which works overtly written for children hide covert messages intended for adult readers. Our critical biases valorize either a masculine high Romanticism, or, more recently, women who seem to represent early feminists. Neither tradition of criticism has much room for didactic children's verses.[2] This devaluation of women's children's verses is rooted in the aesthetic politics of the Romantic era itself. The canonical writers mythologized the child, turning pedagogy into a poetic "master narrative—the Romantic story of the emergent male self" (Myers, "De-Romanticizing," 89). Further, in the Romantic era, poetry as a genre was constructed through the categorization of popular texts as nonpoetry (the feminized, the sentimental, the ephemeral) and of high art as real poetry (the classical, the philosophical, the muscular epic). It is at this historical moment—when the poetic canon is being created and poetry is being defined in a closing of the ranks *against* the massive incursion of women's poetic texts—that Mary and Charles Lamb wrote *Poetry for Children,* which insistently genders art and education, and Charlotte Smith wrote *Conversations Introducing Poetry,* a pedagogical text that teaches little girls to become poets not in the feminine sentimental mode, but in the classical tradition. In contrast to masculine Romantic views of the child as a supernatural being "trailing clouds of glory," women poets depict children as susceptible to influence and steer boys and girls toward surprisingly feminine, even feminist, behaviors. I suggest that the Lambs and Smith use their children's poetry as a vehicle for critiquing the patriarchal ordering of literary and social culture. Their texts represent cross-writing: they write about children and ostensibly to children, but they also use their representations of children to send a message about the gendering of culture to adults. In particular, they trope the gendering of literary authority as a big brother and use this trope both to reveal and to alleviate the debilitating effects of a patriarchal poetic discourse.

In reading children's poems about siblings, I am not focusing on biographical brother and sister relationships in which the big brothers within poems refer back to actual brothers. Rather, I trace fictional representations of brothers and sisters in which the brother is a trope for patriarchy in general and for the patriarchal tradition of poetry in particular. As I will argue, this trope (patriarchy represented as a less-threatening brother figure) allows women to negotiate a place within patriarchal structures without being overwhelmed by or locked within a fruitless struggle against patriarchy. Sisters need not overthrow their brothers—they just need to negotiate a space that is relational yet allows for some independence. In these texts, "brothers" are taught to educate their sisters in classical languages, in poetry, and in mathematics and science, and "sisters" are taught to demand a literary education. At their finest, these poems teach boys and girls that dutiful brothers not only support their little sisters but also support their literary efforts and education. Unfortunately, such poems also potentially reinforce patriarchy, for by encouraging the benevolence of brothers, they ultimately support the brother's position as the sibling with control over knowledge and education.

Indeed, the Lambs' poetry, in contrast to Smith's more radical transformations of society, often presents the brother-sister dynamic as damaging to the sister. Even if the brother figure in the Lambs' poems can be positively influenced, conciliating the brother to gain concessions is not without risk. For example, in Mary Lamb's "The Broken Doll," a selfish baby brother breaks his sister's new wax doll, but she is told to remain kind and loving:

> A sister's discipline is this,
> By studied kindness to effect
> A little brother's young respect.
>
> . . . .
>
> For thus the broken doll may prove
> Foundation to fraternal love.   (371)

As the "may" implies, the sister has no guarantee that after her self-sacrifice the little boy will not become a petty dictator. Gender difference so far outstrips age difference in representing society's imbalance of power that even a physically helpless infant brother can break his sister's possessions with impunity and can regulate, through his presence alone, his older sister's behavior. The Lambs show that the stability of the patriarchal family depends upon the sister's suffering, but the Lambs' critique does not extend to suggesting a systemic change. By contrast, Smith's *Conversations Introducing Poetry* not only critiques patriarchy but also promotes an enlightened society that supports the aspirations of women. Smith presents the brother and sister pair under the guidance of an authoritative mother who is teacher, poet, naturalist, and literary critic. Smith's mother not only structures the education of her children, but she also teaches her son to teach his sister poetry. Rather than break his sister's dolls, Smith's brother is required to create poetic versions of dolls for his sister's pleasure and edification.

After I sketch the role of sibling relationships in the early nineteenth century, I will shift my discussion to poetry about brothers and sisters by Mary and Charles Lamb and Charlotte Smith. There I will detail the effect such poems should have on our understanding of children's literature within British Romanticism when they are considered seriously in light of their poetic structures and not only as didactic texts. In describing middle-class, sibling relationships in the Romantic to mid-Victorian eras, Leonore Davidoff and Catherine Hall suggest that the brother-sister relationship is not only an important literary and social construction, but also can be compared to other male-female relationships such as that between fathers and daughters:

> The brother-sister tie was idealized in literature and had a strong basis in everyday life. Brothers and sisters shared economic resources as well as family origins. . . . The relationship gained in intensity from the nostalgia surrounding common childhood experience when that stage in life was held as the key to innocence and happiness. . . . As with fathers and daughters, brothers and sisters approached the model masculine-feminine relationship without the explicit sexuality of marriage. (348)

The father-daughter dynamic is reflected in brother-sister relationships: the brother becomes an "indulgent monitor" of his sister's behavior. Further, an unmarried sister potentially shifts from being her father's dependent to being a ward of her brother and, if he is married with children, to living on his sufferance as a de facto servant in his household.

Nevertheless, the lines of power between sisters and brothers are far more fluid than those between a father and his daughter. Thus, invoking a brother figure instead of a father figure is a more accessible strategy for women to use in critiquing patriarchal structures. Sisters and brothers are raised together in the nursery and are dressed and taught alike until the boy is considered old enough to wear breeches. After this point, however, sisters and brothers eventually receive different educations. Boys learn intellectual subjects; girls gain accomplishments such as sewing, watercoloring, and music. Wollstonecraft, the Edgeworths, Hannah More, Catharine Macaulay, and other early critics of female education condemned this education's substandard and haphazard quality:[3] "All those vices and imperfections which have been generally regarded as inseparable from the female character, do not in any manner proceed from sexual causes, but are entirely the effects of situation and education" (Macaulay 402). One proposed solution was for girls to be educated at home, with their studies guided by benevolent brothers. This education would allow young girls to remain within the sheltering bosom of the family. Such an arrangement had economic advantages as well: instead of the expense of educating two siblings, the boy, whose education was of more importance, could in some fashion share his learning with his sisters.[4] Although men and women were perhaps equally able to ac-

quire new learning, men and women did not have an equal need for
such learning. As Anna Letitia Barbauld—a late eighteenth-century
poet, critic, and education reformer—writes,

> Young gentlemen, who are to display their knowledge to the
> world, should have every motive of emulation, should be formed
> into regular classes, should read and dispute together, should
> have all the honors, and, if one may say so, the pomp of learning
> set before them, to call up their ardor. It is their business, and
> they should apply to it as such. But young ladies, who ought only
> to have such a general tincture of knowledge as to make them
> agreeable companions to a man of sense, and to enable them to
> find rational amusement for a solitary hour, should gain these
> accomplishments in a more quiet and unobserved manner. . . .
> The best way for women to acquire knowledge is from conver-
> sation with a father, a brother, or a friend, in the way of family
> intercourse and easy conversation, and by such a course of read-
> ing as they may recommend. (Ellis 57) [5]

Although she clearly displays her own knowledge by publishing popular and not "carefully concealed" texts, the erudite Barbauld's pedagogical reforms support the culturally defined differences between
the educational needs of women and those of men. Ironically, the
"classical" education given to young men was often training in Latin
and Greek, except at radical academies like Warrington where Barbauld's father taught. By contrast, a woman's education involved
modern languages and, as such, was more immediately useful.

Given the importance of brothers to their sisters' educations, it
is not surprising that poetry discussing brother-sister dynamics frequently explores the gendering of education and literature. The concluding stanzas of "The Duty of a Brother," a poem written by Mary
Lamb and later amended by her brother, sums up the way in which
the gendering of nineteenth-century literary discourse is represented
in poems about siblings:

> Leave not your sister to another;
>   As long as both of you reside
> In the same house, who but her brother
>   Should point her books, her studies guide?
>
> .   .   .   .

> It is the law that Hand [of Nature] intends,
>   Which fram'd diversity of sex;
> The man the woman still defends,
>   The manly boy the girl protects.   (372)

Within the context of the Lamb family history of poverty, dementia, matricide, and literary achievement, this is not a simple didactic poem about brothers and sisters. In terms of textual composition, Mary Lamb wrote "The Duty of a Brother." Her brother Charles amended it. In real life, Mary, who was ten years older than Charles, raised her younger brother, although in the poem the brother appears older. As an adult, Charles did become Mary's caretaker and protected her from the consequences of her insanity. To read this poem as nothing more than a poetic discussion of the Lambs' biographical interaction, however, is to commit the error of underreading. Its broader cultural and poetic implications must be considered as well, for "The Duty of a Brother" encapsulates the relationship between siblinghood and literary authority. The Lambs represent, biographically and literarily, my argument that the brother-sister relationship can be interpreted as critiquing patriarchal structures. Although the Lambs do not intend to critique patriarchy through their brother figures, the ambiguity of this figure invites contemporary critics to read against the grain, to find embedded within their poems subversive alternatives. In writing "the man the woman still defends,/the manly boy the girl protects," Mary and Charles leave the subject of the sentence ambiguous. Is it that "the man, the woman still defends" or "the man, the woman, still defends"? Is the woman the subject or the object? The point is that although the content of the poem suggests that the brother, through "diversity of sex," is the defender, the syntactic structure suggests that the subject is constructed through language, through cultural systems. And how the poem is read—the practice of culture—is subject to change.

Nineteenth-century brothers and sisters were complexly intertwined; they were close in childhood, split by gendered education and opportunities, but never entirely independent from mutual love, resentment, and obligation. The two-volume *Poetry for Children,* co-written by Charles and Mary Lamb and published without any success by the Godwins in 1809, exemplifies the complexities of siblinghood both in its textual representation and in its authorial history.[6] Although two-thirds of the poems in *Poetry for Children* have been attributed to Mary, the poems were unsigned, and the books were published anonymously as by the author of *Mrs. Leicester's School,* another cowritten Lamb text. Ironically, although writing anonymously protected Mary Lamb from her public notoriety as a woman who had murdered her mother with a kitchen knife, it also meant that her coauthor, Charles, in writing anonymously, was necessarily writing from a woman author's position. Readers would expect a woman author to write fictions such as *Mrs. Leicester's School,* fictions that follow the pattern of narration established by Sarah Fielding's *The Governess, or, Little Female Academy* (1749). Publishing *Poetry for Children* as if it were by the author of *Mrs. Leicester's School* thus made it appear that Mary and Charles Lamb were a single, female author.[7] The convoluted and intertwined sibling authorship of *Poetry for Children* makes it the ideal place to begin my discussion of how women poets and their cross-writings reinscribe patriarchy as a less disabling brother figure within their children's texts and how this reinscription is intended for both children and adults.

Poetry for Children invokes a key moment in nineteenth-century brother-sister interaction: the masculine rite-of-passage called, for want a better term, "going into breeches," when a boy matures enough to move from wearing nursery skirts to wearing breeches. In children's poems, authors invariably connect this moment to a boy's advancement into greater learning and maturity.[8] Although this masculine rite of passage distances the boy from the gynocentric nursery, it does not prove the inherent superiority of the male child. Rather, it proves that brothers are given advantages through artificial means. Both boys and girls are given new clothes as they outgrow the nursery, but only boys are allowed to move beyond skirts into the greater freedom of breeches. The gender differences in physical freedom of movement extend to modes of literature production. Men are not naturally superior in the arts; rather, they have the advantage of breeches: superior text-iles that correspond to superior text-ual advantages.[9]

In *Poetry for Children,* Charles's "Going into Breeches" shows the freedom the young boy assumes along with his grown-up clothing. Charles also foregrounds the social conditioning that accompanies the clothes:

> Joy to Philip, he this day
> Has his long coats cast away,
> And (the childish season gone)
> Puts the manly breeches on.
> Officer on gay parade,
> Red-coat in his first cockade,
>
> .   .   .   .
>
> Sashes, frocks, to those that need 'em—
> Philip's limbs have got their freedom—
> He can run, or he can ride,
> And do twenty things besides,
> Which his petticoats forbad:
> Is he not a happy lad?
> Now he's under other banners,
> He must leave his former manners;
> Bid adieu to female games,
> And forget their very names,
> Puss in Corners, Hide and Seek,
> Sports for girls and punies weak!
> Baste the Bear he now may play at,
> Leap-frog, Foot-ball, sport away at.   (365–66)

Immediately upon donning his breeches, the young boy moves beyond the feminine—feminine clothing, games, manners, and language (names). The boy's maturity is also written in slyly sexual language: the boy escapes the feminine "puss" in order to fill out his own breeches. In portraying the turn from the mother toward the masculine, this poem notes that boys are allowed superior forms of activity and play.[10] It also notes that once a boy child becomes a "little MANIKIN," he must also take on the serious and grim responsibilities of masculinity:

> He must have his courage ready,
> Keep his voice and visage steady,
> Brace his eye-balls stiff as drum,
> That a tear may never come.   (366)

The downside of playing adult male roles is that adult men are required to act in ways contrary to their emotions. "Going into Breeches" suggests that mental and emotional behaviors are learned:

in what is surely a deliberate pun, "Smart," a term for intellectual
prowess, is here used to represent an emotional and physical hurt—
"to smart"—and is rhymed with "heart":

> If he get a hurt or bruise,
> To complain he must refuse,
> Though the anguish and the smart
> Go unto his little heart.   (366)

As if to emphasize that gendered behavior is not biological, this
poem is immediately followed by Mary's "Nursing," in which mothering is depicted as a learned phenomenon. An elder sister, upon the
death of their mother, nurses her sleeping, ten-week-old, orphaned
brother. Whereas Charles's brother celebrates new freedom and maturity in his breeches and accepts masculine stoicism, Mary's sister matures by accepting domestic burdens. Masculine detachment and its
converse, feminine empathy, are both learned responses. Although
Philip's stiff-as-a-drum manhood requires him to deny his outer emotions, the sister's femininity requires that she act upon her emotion.
These poems do not challenge the constructions of femininity and
masculinity. Individually and even more so in conjunction, however,
they do insist that sex-specific spheres of women and men be socially
defined.

The Lambs' poetry for children continually links problems of
women's becoming authors, artists, and musicians to problems with
female education. In "The Sister's Expostulation on the Brother's
Learning Latin" and its companion poem, "The Brother's Reply," the
brother-sister dialogue shows a second rite of passage—the learning of classical languages—that has been denied to this particular
little girl:

> Shut these odious books up, brother—
> They have made you quite another
> Thing from what you us'd to be—
> Once you lik'd to play with me—
>
> . . . .
>
> Now believe me, dearest brother,
> I would give my finest frock,
> And my cabinet, and stock
> Of new playthings, every toy,
> I would give them all with joy,

> Could I you returning see
> Back to English and to me.

In "The Sister's Expostulation on the Brother's Learning Latin" (attributed to Charles), the sister is well aware that education, in this case represented by the brother's new knowledge of "Latin," has split her brother from herself. To obtain her brother's attention and the formal education he supplies, this sister would happily drop the playthings of her life. Perhaps ominously, however, the anticipation of her brother's return "back to English and to me" is heralded by garbled grammar: "Could I you returning see" is the most awkward of all of this poem's lines. The "I" who would willingly give up her toys must in turn subordinate herself to her brother, the "you" whose return signifies a return to grammatical order in the final line of this poem. The return of the brother also signifies the sister's last word: she is no longer the speaking subject, "I," but the object, "me."

In "The Brother's Reply" to "The Sister's Expostulation," the brother calls her complaint "ignorant babble." He belittles her for scorning Latin, and then explains how easy it is to learn. Like wearing breeches and controlling emotion, Latin just requires practice. It is not an inherent ability given to one sex and not the other, but it is essential to understanding the classics and the foundations of contemporary language. Finally, the brother confesses that it is miserly to keep his learning to himself and "(if our parents will agree)/You shall Latin learn with me" (402). In the end, the Lambs' poetry reaffirms that girls as well as boys can learn. The Lambs' answer to educational inequity, however, does not threaten patriarchal control of knowledge. Girls can and should learn, but only under the supervision of their brother and parents.[11]

These poems on the first wearing of breeches, the girls' first nursing, and the boys' first learning of Latin all describe childhood rites of passage in which the unity of the nursery is broken by the gender differentiations of culture. Sisters know that they have been their brothers' equals or betters in the nursery. Thus they know the masculine mind is not inherently superior in the creative arts, but it does have the advantage of superior social freedom and education. Through the trope of the brother, children's poetry potentially can critique patriarchy by insisting on a cultural rather than an inherent, biological superiority of men. Unfortunately, although the Lambs attempt to create enlightened patriarchy through representations of benevolent brothers, their project ultimately reinforces masculine authority. After all, even an enlightened patriarchy is still a patriarchy. In these poems, big brothers are still powerful—no matter how benevolent. Thus, the Lambs' poetry for children alters neither poetic nor educational structures.

I would like to reread Charles Lamb's often-quoted condemnation of women didacticists in light of my critique of the ultimately conservative ideology of the Lambs' children's verses. Like *Poetry for Children,* which does not fully utilize the subversive potential of the brother figure, Charles's diatribe in this letter to Samuel Taylor Coleridge defends only that imaginative literature associated with the master narrative of the boy becoming a man. It is this emergent male self that he defends from the threat of the phallic mothers, the female pedagogues:

> Mrs. Barbauld['s] stuff has banished all the old classics of the nursery; . . . Mrs. B's & Mrs. Trimmer's nonsense lay in piles about. Knowledge insignificant & vapid as Mrs. B's books convey, it seems, must come to a child in the *shape* of *knowledge* . . . instead of that beautiful Interest in wild tales, which made the child a man. . . . Is there no possibility of averting this sore evil? Think what you would have been now, if instead of being fed with Tales and old wives fables in childhood, you had been crammed with Geography & Natural History.? [sic] **Damn them.** I mean the cursed Barbauld Crew, those **Blights & Blasts** of all that is **Human** in man & child. (*Letters* 2:81–82)

Charles's rhetoric against "the cursed Barbauld Crew" privileges imaginative literature over other forms of knowledge while it undercuts the authoritative voices of strong women pedagogues such as Barbauld and Trimmer. Charles associates the classics and other "imaginative" texts with the process of the boy's becoming a man. In what today would seem an ironic reversal of the typical gendering of discourses, Charles links masculine knowledge to "old wives fables" and feminine knowledge to the sciences. This maneuver forms part of a more general Romantic trend in which male Romantics colonize feminine knowledges such as emotional sensitivity and folk literature while simultaneously denigrating other, more threatening knowledges (such as science's threat to the preeminence of literature) by feminizing them. In fact, Romantic-era glorifications of pure and natural folk literature are revisionist misreadings of "tales and old wives fables." Such tales are often literary in origin as well as predominantly conservative in form; they are intended to frighten children into being obedient.

Charles's diatribe usefully reveals the less than objective nature of his own claims to objectivity. In describing his contributions to *Poetry for Children*, Charles insists that his poems for children are "humble" (and thus not authoritative or didactic), and that they are on a large "number of subjects, all children, pick'd out by an old Bachelor and an old Maid" (*Letters* 3:14). In claiming to be non-didactic and nonauthoritative (a bachelor and a maid are, by implication, childless), Charles is participating in the backlash against the strong women writing pedagogical works for children. In the same way that Charles ignores the literary and conservative background of "old wives fables," he also denies the literary and conservative project underlying *Poetry for Children*. One inevitable aspect of children's writing is the cross-perspective of the author who, although an adult, attempts to write from a child's perspective: however much adults attempt to regress into the child's innocent, magical thinking, they still are "compelled, in varying degrees, to hold on to the grown-up's circumscribed notions about reality" (Knoepflmacher 499). Authors often address this mixture of perspectives by providing their texts with narrative frames and prefatory material acknowledging that the author as well as the buyer of the book is an adult. Charles's description of *Poetry for Children* suggests that he refuses to recognize his own position as an adult, that he intends to present children as speaking, thinking, and feeling on their own without adult intervention. But these children cannot be "natural"; they are representations of children within which an adult's own views of childhood and child education are naturalized. In effect, the didacticism that Charles rails against in the "cursed Barbauld crew" is present in his own work — but more ominously disguised. In representing sibling relationships in their poems, Mary and Charles conceal their own authorial position and adult perspective by presenting these interactions as uncomplicated and natural. *Poetry for Children*, which I have suggested uses the trope of the big brother to represent patriarchy, and which often shows sisters conciliating big brothers for educational concessions, presents this depressing dynamic as natural. As such, the style of the poetry undermines the content of the poems themselves, which often portray authority being given to the brother through cultural, not natural, causes.

When Mary Lamb writes, under her own brother's protection, poems for children about how to create protective brothers and about the masculine biases of poetics, the results are arguably limited. Because Mary was a female murderer convicted of criminal insanity and was under the court-approved supervision of her generous and forgiving brother, it is not surprising that Mary's as well as Charles's representations of sisters promote women's self-control and subordination to others. Neither Mary nor Charles develop a gynocentric literary discourse, but they do provide contemporary critics with an important case study delineating the range of thematic content and ideological positions that can be held by writers who choose to work from a woman's position—as that position (the maternal, the domestic, the dependent, the emotional, the object) is defined within masculine poetics. Both Charles and Mary call for women's access to education, for a recognition of women's abilities to write, for an understanding that the gender separations of literary discourse are cultural rather than biological. Other writers, however, are more aggressive in using brother figures to negotiate for an influential position within poetics. Charlotte Smith (1749–1806) is a poet and novelist who is now considered one of the first British poets whom we, as Stuart Curran suggests, would call "Romantic." Wordsworth himself acknowledges her importance to his own project when he writes prophetically that she is a poet "to whom English verse is under greater obligations than are likely to be either acknowledged or remembered" (Curran, "Introduction," xix). Whereas Mary and Charles Lamb's prose writings have overshadowed their children's poetry, Smith's recovery as a poet and novelist has overshadowed her children's books.

Smith's two-volume set, *Conversations Introducing Poetry: Chiefly on Subjects of Natural History. For the Use of Children and Young Persons* (1804), is written in a fascinating cross of genres and voices that are linked by the important structural device of a mother—a representation of Smith herself—who guides the conversations introducing poetry to her son, George, and younger daughter Emily. Smith is here an ideal example of the cross-writer: she provides a teaching model to her audience of mothers, as well as a teaching text intended for an audience of children. Curran, in editing the first modern edition of Smith's collected poetry (1993), prints the poetry from *Conversa-*

tions but none of the prose, none of the "conversations." Although
Curran's edition acknowledges that Smith is qualified "to sit among
the most select poets of this age" (xxvii), he overlooks the significance of the generic mixings within such volumes as *Conversations*.
Smith's poetry, in the context of its framing narrative, is far more
polyvalent than a reading of the poetry alone implies. The poetry in
isolation often fits the stereotypical, feminine mode of straightfor-
ward lyrical meditations on nature—what Angela Leighton has called
the Sapphic version of feminine, emotive writing in contrast to the
Corinne style of public, political feminine texts. In context, however,
the prose surrounding each poem provides the poetry with social,
domestic, naturalist, theological, and literary implications. Such mixings of poetry with other genres suggest that this poetry was not a
pure form meant to express the sublime or the growth of the mind of
man: as *Conversations* demonstrates, poetry can be mixed with prose
and, if necessary, even the supposedly sacrosanct Milton can have his
poems altered in order to make him suitable for young readers.

Smith, like Mary and Charles Lamb, uses the trope of a benevolent
big brother to represent literary authority. This brother, however, is
less powerful and less destructive than are the brothers in the Lambs'
Poetry for Children. This brother is not only being trained to educate his
sister, but he is also doing so under the watchful eye of an all-knowing
mother, the Georgian era's version of a heroic mother: the rational dame or the morally commanding governess. Whereas the Lambs
present sibling negotiations in which the big brother usually has the
advantages of age and gender, Smith presents the brother-sister duo
under a mother's supervision. Most importantly, Mrs. Talbot's lessons
function as model lesson plans. Smith's *Conversations* is ostensibly written for "the use of children and young persons," but as cross-writing
its more important audience is mothers. Smith teaches mothers how
to teach their children—and in particular, how to teach their sons to
teach their sisters.

As in her earlier two-volume *Rural Walks: In Dialogues. Intended for the
Use of Young Persons* (1795), *Conversations* presents an idealized family:
a highly educated mother who teaches her children how to care for
each other. In this later book, however, an essential part of this caring
includes learning how to share and encourage each other's poetic
efforts. In contrast to our critical debates about the "egotistical sublime" and "a leveling Romanticism," Smith stresses collaboration and
the importance of building the community and family in a way not

unlike Carol Gilligan's description of a feminine ethic of care. Smith notes that the text itself is a collaboration: she includes (and often rewrites) poetry by Ovid, Mrs. Barbauld, Mr. Crowe, Mr. Cowley, Mr. Gifford, and Smith's own sister (who later becomes a children's author). Her lessons are always student centered: when Emily expresses interest in glowworms, Mrs. Talbot prepares a natural history lesson on the subject. She even teaches Emily to place George under feminine surveillance lest he become arrogant; his moral health is a family concern.

Smith's text, unlike the Lambs' poetry, consistently presents the elder brother as under the control of his female relations and, at this moment, has the mother teaching the sister the skills to use in controlling a brother. Smith stresses that brothers must be inspired to become lifelong supporters of women's education while they are still young and accessible. She argues that art requires knowledge— not inherent, natural abilities—in her words, "Education formed the perfect Rose!" (1: 160). In a very pragmatic way, if women writers can influence the educations of boys and girls, brothers who are taught to be benevolent as boys might well grow into benevolent fathers. As Smith's text makes absolutely clear, it is up to mothers to intervene aggressively in the educations of their sons so that they have been trained to consider the literary and educational needs of women.

In *Conversations*, Mrs. Talbot, George, and Emily walk in the woods and visit the beach. Along the way, Mrs. Talbot takes every available opportunity to lecture about the history of insects, plants, and birds in which the children show an interest. She moralizes about the importance of education, poetry, family, and class consciousness. She also writes and recites poetry and teaches the children to write and recite poetry as well. The following exchange is a typical passage:

> EMILY. Mama, I touched a very light pretty plant that is like an acacia, only much smaller and with finer leaves, and instantly it withered away.
>
> GEORGE. I could have told you what that is—It is the sensitive plant—I saw them, you know, Mamma, at a nursery gardener's.
>
> MRS. TALBOT. And perhaps you may remember that I then told you, it is called the emblem of excessive sensibility; and a great many fine things have been said of persons whose delicate nerves make them resemble this plant; of which, however, there are several sorts, some with more and others with less of this ex-

traordinary quality; while the more robust of the genera do not possess it at all. . . . Your aunt compared this singular species of the mimosa, to persons who yield to an excess of sensibility, or what is termed so; which arises much oftener than is generally imagined, from their having too much feeling for themselves, and too little for others. While we sit in this recess, . . . I will endeavor to recollect and repeat the lines she addressed to

THE MIMOSA.

Softly blow the western breezes,
Sweetly shines the evening sun;
But you, mimosa! nothing pleases,
You, what delights your comrade teizes,
What they enjoy you try to shun.   (1:69–71)[12]

In this passage, Mrs. Talbot gently deflates the pretensions of George, who is eager to display his mastery of knowledge and overwhelm his little sister's observation of a "very light pretty plant." Myers has discussed this pattern of sibling rivalry within Maria Edgeworth's children's books.[13] A domineering, self-important brother "acts the universalist knower who thinks that there is a single valid meaning and that he owns it," a braggadocio only exacerbated by the sister's more honest ignorance, which allows him to conceal better his own shaky learning and disembodied logic (Myers, "Reading Rosamond," 66). The brother "dramatizes language and literature as dominance and control, knowledge to be brandished over others" (67). Mrs. Talbot, throughout *Conversations,* discourages George's self-aggrandizement even as she encourages the less confident Emily. On this occasion, Mrs. Talbot suggests that George's volunteered information is incomplete: he has not remembered that on a previous occasion she had already taught him about the plant. George has not learned his lessons as thoroughly as he should have.

As is typical in her conversations, the naturalist lesson is accompanied by a moral lesson. Smith's Mrs. Talbot cautions her children, through the example of the sensitive plant, not to succumb to excesses of sensibility—a particular concern for Romantic-era women writing about female education. An education focusing on women's sensibilities would "exercise [women's] imagination and feeling, till the understanding, grown rigid by disuse, is unable to exercise itself —and the superfluous nourishment the imagination and feeling have received, render the former romantic, and the latter weak" (Wollstonecraft, *Hints*, 382).[14] Sarah Trimmer, whose review of *Conversations* reprints the above passages containing "The Mimosa," approved of Smith's fusion of moral lessons and imaginative literature and recommended her text as an invaluable addition to any child's Christian education: "We have often heard it remarked by those who are employed in the business of education, that there is very little poetry fit for children to commit to memory. This complaint will be in a great measure removed by the publication of these elegant and engaging volumes, which contain a considerable number of beautiful pieces that cannot fail of giving delight both to those who learn and to those who teach; and they are rendered still more interesting by the instructive conversations with which they are intermixed" (177–78). Trimmer was the author of countless children's pedagogical books and the education polemic *An Essay on Christian Education* (1812), as well as being the watchdog editor of *The Guardian of Education* (1802–6), the first journal to review children's books for parents, readers, and buyers. That Trimmer did not object to the subversive underlying project of Smith's volumes—that boys as well as girls should be educated at home under a woman's authority—is to Smith's credit, and perhaps to Trimmer's as well (Trimmer educated six boys herself). Smith skillfully negotiates her desire to encourage women's classical education and potential literary achievements while writing a pedagogical text that would appeal to the conservative audience represented by the readers of Trimmer's journal.

Under the guise of providing moral children's literature, Smith encourages women's literary aspirations and demonstrates how to develop writing skills. Mrs. Talbot teaches her children—and the book's female readers—to keep commonplace books as writing tools: to collect poetry, images, and information about nature that is then turned into new poems. Smith defuses the anxiety of authorship by having Mrs. Talbot correct, for children's special needs, the poems of literary patriarchs. She also discusses the importance of professionalism, including writing for money, not self-glorification, and the wise management of income. Finally, Mrs. Talbot requires George to assist her in writing the closing long poem of *Conversations,* in which all the plants and flowers of the garden are turned into mythological beings. The purpose of this tour de force is for the brother to help the sister accept mythology as "natural" rather than paganistic, for, as Smith asserts throughout the two volumes, without an understanding of mythology the daughter will not be able to write or read great literature: "You cannot . . . understand poetry without knowing the heathen mythology" (2:36).[15] Smith denounces the flaws in contemporary education of boys as regards mythology: "In the present system of education, boys learn at school the heathen mythology; and Ovid, the most fanciful, and by no means the most proper among the Roman poets, for the perusal of youth, is almost the first book put into their hands. Your elder brother, therefore, became acquainted with all these fabulous people . . . he used to give me, while we looked over his lessons together, very clear accounts of their genealogy and exploits; but mingled with such remarks, as determined me to introduce these imaginary beings to George's acquaintance in another manner" (2:161). *Conversations* now becomes an exploration of how to teach the reluctant Emily who, in "the purity of [her] natural taste, and [her] perception of what is most beautiful," resists learning the Pantheon. The good and moral Emily mistakenly believes the Pantheon to be patently untrue, potentially immoral, and without any practical use. Mrs. Talbot enlists the aid of George to create a horticultural goddess named Flora to awaken Emily's imaginative powers. In "Flora," the flowers and plants of the family garden are transformed into mythological creatures, demigods of the garden, so that the little girl's resistance to "heathen" mythology will be bridged by her love of botany and all of God's creation.

Stuart Curran and Judith Pascoe both present "Flora" as a breakthrough text for Smith in which she blends fantasy literature, botanical science, and Erasmus Darwin's *The Botanic Garden* to create a hybrid poetic that is fully realized in her later, posthumous "Beachy Head."[16] Neither critic mentions the important context of "Flora" as the magnum opus of *Conversations Introducing Poetry*. Smith's two volumes of conversations on nature, poetry, and morality build up to "Flora" and prepare its defense. "Flora," however botanically exciting, is expressly intended to make mythology palatable and noncorrupting for young girls and boys.

Mrs. Talbot insists that mythology is essential for understanding great literature. Without it, Talbot fears that Emily will never be able to appreciate what she has determined to be the essential great books of the culturally literate: the epics of Homer, Ovid, Fenelon, Virgil, and Milton; the "mock heroics" of Pope and Hayley; and the great poems by Shakespeare and Erasmus Darwin. The fairy tales that Mrs. Talbot had loved as a child, "The Royal Ram" and "The Yellow Dwarf," cannot bend Emily's resistance to imaginative literature.

Even Darwin's *Botanic Garden* fails to reach Emily, despite its emphasis on nature and botany. Mrs. Talbot, in desperation, creates Flora: "I am so desirous you should acquire a taste for these agreeable fictions, that I enlisted George in my service, while you were out on your visit to your friends on Thursday evening; and we fancied we could dress to please you an ideal being" (*Conversations,* 2:169). Mrs. Talbot compels the brother to work for the benefit of his sister. In one of Smith's most startling gender and genre crosses, this boy coauthors with his mother children's literature for a girl, in order to enable her to write and read "masculine" texts informed by the classics.

George's and Mrs. Talbot's ideal being, Flora, is a miniature Titania whom Mrs. Talbot compares to Shakespeare's elfin queen. To entice Emily to love Flora, Mrs. Talbot depicts Flora as if she were a doll to be dressed. She and George appropriate plant names for "the wardrobe" of the creature, intending "to inspire [Emily] with something like a taste for these children of imagination; just as it was formerly the idea, that girls should be encouraged to understand dress by ornamenting their dolls" (*Conversations,* 2:182). Manipulating little girls into learning through their pleasure in dressing dolls appears in other pedagogical texts—but with less altruistic motives. Jean-Jacques Rousseau's influential book on child education, *Emile,* recommends that girls play with dolls in order to develop their sense of taste in clothing: "The doll is the girl's special plaything; this shows her instinctive bent towards her life's work. The art of pleasing finds its physical basis in personal adornment, and this physical side of the art is the only one which the child can cultivate" (396). Rousseau's little girl spends all day dressing and undressing her doll, until even her meals are forgotten. Rousseau suggests that this excessive desire to adorn dolls is to be encouraged, for it is the earliest moment at which little girls express their natural inclinations to make themselves pleasing. Though the little girl is too young to engage in coquetry herself, "in due time she will be her own doll" (396).

Sophy, Rousseau's ideal girl, has emotional abilities but limited faculties of imagination and reason. Rousseau suggests using girls' pleasure in dressing dolls to entice them into learning to sew. By contrast, Smith joins other women pedagogical writers in attacking this view as outdated, and she uses dolls to inspire Emily to use her imagination.[17] "Flora" is a radical revision of Rousseau's project. This poem is also a more radical use of dolls to effect cultural change than Mary Lamb's "The Broken Doll," in which girls are urged to turn the other cheek in the hope that boys—grown into men—will no longer break either dolls or their adult counterpart, women. Smith's powerful mother insists upon the brother's behaving with respect. She requires him to create (rather than mutilate) a doll for his sister in order to expand her knowledge, not her "art of pleasing." In effect, Mrs. Talbot is feminizing the brother, teaching him how to play dolls—for George is the one who originally dresses Flora, and he is the one who is expected to turn garden plants into dolls and doll dresses.

   Most radical of all, however, is the garden itself. Smith's "Flora" is not the saccharine paean one might expect in a nineteenth-century children's poem about flowers and dolls. Flora is a warrior queen. These horticultural dolls are not playing houses—they are playing war. All of the flowers and plants of the garden—traditionally feminine symbols—are dressed in armor and waging battle against encroaching insects.[18] In a strange gender reversal, the rose becomes the warrior that attacks the worm:

> For conquest arm'd the pigmy warriors wield
> The thorny lance, and spread the hollow shield
> Of Lichen tough; or bear, as silver bright,
> Lunaria's pearly circlet, firm and light.
> On the helm'd head the crimson Foxglove glows,
> Or Scutellaria guards the martial brows,
>
> . . . .
>
> With stern undaunted eye, one warlike Chief
> Grasps the tall club from Arum's blood-dropp'd leaf,
> *This* with the Burdock's hooks annoys his foes,
> The purple Thorn, *that* borrows from the Rose.
> In honeyed nectaries couched, some drive away
> The forked insidious Earwig from his prey,
> Fearless the scaled Libellula assail,
> Dart their keen lances at the encroaching Snail,
> Arrest the winged Ant, on pinions light,
> And strike the headlong Beetle in his flight.   (2:185–86)

In the overheated rhetoric of the sexual life of garden plants, Smith's feminine flowers are not passive—they come alive and attack. Unlike the sexual violence in Blake's "The Sick Rose," in which the "crimson joy" of the passive rose has been poisoned by the secret love of the invisible worm, these flowers attack their attackers. In a series of masculine assaults by the phallic snail, ant, earwig, and beetle, the honeyed plants pull out their thorns and drive away the men. In yet another moment of genre-gender crossing, these feminine flowers, the minions of Flora, are armed with lances and thorns. The wardrobe that George and Mrs. Talbot have created to feminize mythology is, ironically, war-dress.

Flora's weapons—the thorns of the pygmy warriors and the lances of the Libellula—are examples of Smith's mythology and are symbolic of the classical education that hones the mind. Smith's cross-writing encourages girls to arm themselves with knowledge—and more importantly, teaches mothers not only how to educate their children, but also how to educate themselves through nature and through reading the many books she recommends and interprets for Emily. *Conversations*, in fact, is best read as a mother's manual on how to keep a commonplace book, how to turn botanical observations into poetic texts, and how to read and interpret the poetry of other authors. Throughout the book, Mrs. Talbot discusses things that are clearly beyond the understanding of most children, such as Robert Burns's opinion of money's importance. Further, Mrs. Talbot continually alludes to the role of parents in creating poets: Pope only becomes a poet because his father is willing to "encourage his son to make verses; correct and recorrect them, and . . . exclaim with great appearance of satisfaction, 'these are good rhymes' " (2:97). *Conversations* is metapoetic and metapedagogic: it is poetry about poetry, and children's literature about teaching literature to children. To emphasize that these poems and conversations were written for adults as well as children, the last two poems of *Conversations*, "Studies by the Sea" and "Flora," were both republished in Smith's final collection of poems for adults, *Beachy Head, Fables, and Other Poems* (1807).

Perhaps Smith's greatest achievement is that *Conversations*, in encouraging women to become authors, succeeded in fostering the writing career of her youngest sister, Catherine Ann Dorset. As Smith writes in her preface to *Conversations:* "A near relation sent me several [poems] which she had composed on purpose, and one or two which had long lain in her port folio. Thus encouraged, my collection insensibly increased. . . . There are seven pieces not my own, some of them a little altered, to answer my first purpose of teaching a child to repeat them; and five of my own reprinted. Of the remainder, though the Relation to whom I am obliged objected to my distinguishing them by any acknowledgment, it is necessary to say, that where my interlocutors *praise* any Poem, the whole or the greater part of it is *hers* (2:i–iii)." Smith's generosity in welcoming her young sister into professional publishing is an extension of the project of *Conversations* to introduce poetry to mothers and children. Not surprisingly, Dorset's first published collection of poetry, *The Peacock "At Home"* (1807), shows her indebtedness to her sister and *Conversations*. Like "Flora" and its joy in the specificity of Linnean botanical terms, Dorset's *The Peacock* presents an extravaganza of personified bird species that behave like Smith's animated insects and plants — in this case, social climbers attempting to throw a party that will outdo the grasshopper's fete.[19] Most significantly, Dorset's first anonymous publication in Smith's *Conversations* gives her the courage to begin her extensive career as a children's author.

The final message of Smith's book is a call to arms urging women to educate their sons, daughters, and themselves so that they will be prepared to fend for themselves in an unjust and masculine world. Smith herself knew the value of literature as a defense and a livelihood. She was wed before her sixteenth birthday in an arranged marriage to a man who ran through her dowry and his fortune, dragged her into debtor's prison, and finally — after several separations — fled permanently to France, leaving her to support their eight surviving children. If her husband was her greatest misfortune, her writing was her livelihood and gave public voice to her oppression. In fact, the emotional despondency of her appropriately named *Elegiac Sonnets* (1784) was so stirring that its multiple reprints and numerous expanded editions inspired the Romantic-era revival of the sonnet and its characteristic mode of psychological and emotional soul-searching. Ironically, it is when Smith moves outside those poetic genres that we associate with canonical Romanticism and into children's verses that her poetry becomes optimistic and ends on an emotional upswing. The continuing sense of being under siege that is debilitating in her sonnets becomes a galvanizing force in "Flora." Her children's verses encourage women's authority as literary and moral educators. And so, when the queen's garden of *Conversations* is embattled, its occupants are prepared to fight back using the weapons gained through the lessons of *Conversations*. Emily, we assume, will now understand poetry; and the brother, through Mrs. Talbot's pedagogical undertaking, is reading their coauthored poem to his little sister, attempting to educate her in the tools necessary to the criticism and creation of art.

Notes

1. See Linkin's "Taking Stock of the British Romantic Marketplace" for information about the academic impact of new publications featuring women's texts. Myers's forthcoming edition of Jane Taylor's poetry should redress some of the current neglect of women's poetry for children in scholarly editions of Romantic-era poetry.

2. The reception of Mary Lamb's children's verses is a case in point: the reconsiderations of women poets by Curran and Ross do not mention Lamb (see "The 'I' Altered" and *Contours of Masculine Desire*). Aaron's *A Double Singleness* and Mellor's *Romanticism and Gender* recognize Mary Lamb as an interesting prose essayist but do not discuss her poetry. Likewise, Richardson's *Literature, Education, and Romanticism*, winner of the 1995 American Conference on Romanticism book prize, mentions only her prose fiction. In giving women's poetry for children superficial attention, we uncritically participate in Romantic ideologies that dismiss their work as not worthy of sustained attention. Ezell has discussed the problems with our contemporary creation of a women's literary history based on the desires of feminist scholars to find literary ancestors. Such a prioritizing of feminist writers relegates to the margins those women authors who do not fit modern feminist expectations.

3. These critical works include Maria Edgeworth (with Richard Lovell Edgeworth), *Practical Education* (1798); Maria Edgeworth, *Letters for Literary Ladies* (1795; 1799); Catharine Macaulay, *Letters on Education* (1790); Hannah More, *Strictures on the Modern System of Female Education* (1799); Mary Wollstonecraft, *Thoughts on the Education of Daughters* (1787) and *A Vindication of the Rights of Woman* (1792); and Sarah Trimmer, *An Essay On Christian Education* (1812).

4. The practice of educating brothers to the detriment of their sisters is explored most famously in Woolf's *Three Guineas* (1938). Woolf's feminist polemic explains her resentment of her brothers' easy access to a university education—an access she was denied.

5. Barbauld, as this passage suggests, was well aware of the importance of brothers to the education of young women. She coauthored pedagogical books with her younger brother John Aikin, including the influential *Evenings at Home*. Having no children of her own, she asked to raise one of her brother's sons, Charles Aikin, and then used her experience in teaching him reading to publish yet another popular text for children, *Lessons for Children* (1778–79). McCarthy argues that the overly reactionary sentiments of this passage, in its suggestion that young gentlemen need "the pomp of learning" whereas young girls need only "a general tincture of knowledge," is not primarily about the gendering of education. Instead, McCarthy argues that Barbauld (who was educated in and taught at a dissenting academy) is reacting to Anglican education rather than defining her own pedagogical position on girls' education ("Sending a Riddle"). For a history of the reception of Barbauld's *Lessons*, see Myers's "Of Mice and Mothers." For information on Barbauld's pedagogical writings in the context of women's education debates, see Robbins, " 'Women's Studies' Debates in Eighteenth-Century England." For discussion of Barbauld's educational writings as they arise from "the dissenters' unitarian concept of life," see Ross's "Configurations of Feminine Reform: The Woman Writer and the Tradition of Dissent."

6. The dismissal of the Lambs' poetry begins with the ill-fated Godwin printing house. Although Godwin's press specialized in what would seem the innocuous field of children's literature, this marketplace was increasingly politicized and contentious. Godwin's reputation as a radical ensured that he would run afoul of influential critical organs such as Sarah Trimmer's *The Guardian of Education* and *The Anti-Jacobin Review*. Financially overextended, forced to author texts under a variety of pseudonyms (William Scolfield, Edward Baldwin, Theophilus Marcliffe), and the victim of an em-

ployee's embezzlement, Godwin as a juvenile publisher was doomed. Although there was a later American edition of *Poetry for Children* with some omissions (1812), and individual poems were reprinted in a variety of anthologies, so few copies of *Poetry for Children* were printed in this 1809 first edition that Charles himself wrote in 1829, that he was unable to find a copy (Lucas 3:491). Lucas, editor of the Lambs' compiled works, could only track down three or four extant copies. For full information on the Godwin's publishing efforts, see St. Clair's "William Godwin as Children's Bookseller."

7. Critics of the Lambs' poetry as well as Charles himself have been careful to distance him from the perceived stigma of publishing in the feminized genre of children's literature. Summerfield's idiosyncratic *Fantasy and Reason* suggests that children's literature "was an ideal way of keeping Mary quietly occupied, even though for [Charles] Lamb it was 'task work' coming on top of his work at East India House" (274). Lucas suggests that *Poetry for Children* was undertaken for financial reasons and quotes a letter from Robert Lloyd to his wife (1809): "It is *task* work to them, they are writing for money, and a Book of Poetry for Children being likely to sell has induced them to compose one." Charles, in a letter to Coleridge, also describes the volume as "task work": "Our little poems are but humble, but they have no name, You must read them remembering they were task-work" (*Letters*, 3:14).

8. William Upton's books of children's poems, *The School-Boy* and *The School-Girl* (modeled after Ann Taylor's popular "My Mother"), provide a typical example of a "going-into-breeches" poem. In Upton's opening poem, "Just Breeched," the accompanying illustration shows a young boy being pushed outdoors—away from the domestic home—to join the other, older boys and their active outdoor sports:

> Just Breech'd, and proud to show his cloaths [sic]
> (His mind sweet budding like the Rose,)
> To join his little Play-mates, goes
>   THE SCHOOL-BOY!
>
> With Juvenile pride he's seen to tell
> (While flatt'ring hopes his bosom swell,)
> He's learnt to Cipher, Read and Spell
>   THE SCHOOL-BOY!   (166)

Upton connects the wearing of breeches to the schoolboy's academic achievement, his ability to "Cipher, Read and Spell." The closing poem and illustration, "At College," shows the schoolboy dressed in mortarboard and dark robe, ready to study science at the glowing, Parthenon-like temple in the background. A boy's education stretches in one natural continuum from wearing breeches to attending college. Upton's schoolgirl, however, goes to school in new clothes that emphasize her sweet innocence, not her maturing mind: "THE darling Child sweet Pledge of Love! / Playful, and innocent as the dove, / With fine new shoes, sets out to prove / THE SCHOOL-GIRL!" (170). At the seminary for young ladies she learns sewing, needlework, dancing, drawing, music, and geography. Her final triumph is "Quitting School": "ACCOMPLISH'D, vers'd in ev'ry rule, / . . . Retires at length, complete from school / THE SCHOOL-GIRL!" (171).

9. Barrett Browning's mid-nineteenth-century epic about the rise of a female poet, *Aurora Leigh*, sums up the pervasive connection between gendered clothing and the gendering of literature: "This vile woman's way / of trailing garments, shall not trip me up, / . . . in art's pure temple" (159).

10. Richardson also makes this point about the significance of nineteenth-century children's fiction that emphasizes the rough-and-tumble nature of boys' play. He suggests that the nineteenth century defined masculinity in negative terms: that which is not feminine. Maturing boys are thus depicted as playing sports, wrestling, and

pulling off pranks as indications of their distance from maternal influence and their willingness to enter the refined aggression of adult masculinity (see Richardson, "Reluctant Lords").

11. In many ways, these texts reflect the literal education of the Lambs: Charles went to Christ Church Hospital, whereas Mary learned at home from Charles and books.

12. Smith's cautions to Emily and George not to touch the sensitive plant, or the mimosa, might also be warning young persons to avoid the dangers of sexual excitation. Eighteenth-century pornography, as Bewell notes, had a popular sub-genre of "botanical pornography," and the most notable of these texts was "James Perry's *Mimosa or The Sensitive Plant* (1799), which drew upon the analogy between plants and sexual organs" (87). Bewell suggests that the field of botanical writing, which was so dominated by women authors in the Romantic era, was often adapted by women "in order to talk discreetly about sexuality" (92).

13. Myers suggests, as I do here, that by dramatizing a particular kind of sibling rivalry in which masculinist forms of knowledge are enacted, Edgeworth interrogates the canon and masculine authority ("Reading Rosamond"). A similar argument is presented by Jacobus about George Eliot's writing in "The Question of Language." See also my discussion of Mary Lamb's "What Is Fancy?" in which a brother jealously defends his position as an authority by undercutting his sister ("Gendering Subjectivity").

14. Smith's *Conversations* is clearly in the same mode as Sarah Fielding's *The Governess, or, Little Female Academy* (1749); Mary Wollstonecraft's *Original Stories from Real Life; with Conversations* (1788; 1791); and John Aikin and Anna Letitia (Aikin) Barbauld's *Evenings at Home* (1792–96). These texts advocate new pedagogic techniques as well as a new mode of female heroism—the educating mother figure who excels in rationality, self-command, and moral autonomy (Myers, "Impeccable Governesses," 34–35). For information about how these children's texts with strong female mentors played a part in developing writing as a professional yet socially acceptable occupation for women, see Briggs 221–50.

15. Smith's careful denunciation of "heathen" mythology and her own Christianized version might not express her own views of mythology, but instead might be a reflection of market pressures. The rationalists of the turn of the century—Lucy Aikin, Anna Letitia Barbauld, Richard and Maria Edgeworth, even the radical Mary Wollstonecraft—engaged the pedagogical advice of Rousseau and Locke, sometimes finding "imaginative" literature detrimental to children's developing minds. For quasi-theological reasons, the religious right also disapproved of non-didactic children's literature. On the extreme right, Sarah Trimmer attacks even retellings of biblical stories because "we are told by GOD himself, that *the imagination of the heart of man is evil from his youth*" (*Guardian* 1:248). For analysis of Trimmer's position on imaginative literature, see Watson's "Coleridge and the Fairy Tale Controversy" and Richardson's "Wordsworth, Fairy Tales, and the Politics of Reading."

16. Schiebinger's *The Mind Has No Sex?* explores the importance of botany to women in the eighteenth and nineteenth centuries. Schiebinger suggests that botany, of all the sciences, was the one most approved of for women. For Charlotte Smith's poetic use of eighteenth-century botanical writings, see Pascoe's "Female Botanists and the Poetry of Charlotte Smith" and Curran's "Charlotte Smith and British Romanticism," esp. 74–77.

17. For information on the response of nineteenth-century French authors to Rousseau, women's education, and the cultural significance of dolls, see Lastinger's "Of Dolls and Girls."

18. Poetic gardens often invoke the Spenserian bower of bliss: gardens represent a feminized space that tempts and subsequently emasculates the knight on his quest. The eighteenth century also had a cultural and economic tradition of feminine gardens: the kitchen garden. Further, while the eighteenth-century invention of the great landscape park (with the careful placement of lakes, hills, ruins and trees requir-

ing several generations to mature) was associated with the patrilineal heritage of the gentleman's estate, and its concomitant assumption of political and cultural authority achieved through possession of property, the "gardening" elements within these landscapes, such as shrubs, flowers, and walks, were often the province of women. See Bell for information on gender in the eighteenth-century landscape garden.

19. Like her sister's children's poetry, which responds to the poems of others, Dorset's wildly popular *The Peacock "At Home"* (1807) is a response to William Roscoe's *The Butterfly's Ball and the Grasshopper's Feast* (1807); the two poems were frequently paired in one volume (Demers 249–55; Jackson 208–13).

Works Cited

Aaron, Jane. *A Double Singleness: Gender and the Writings of Charles and Mary Lamb.* Oxford: Clarendon, 1991.

Barbauld, Anna Letitia [Published as John Aikin and Anna Letitia Barbauld]. *Evenings at Home; Or, the Juvenile Budget Opened.* 6 vols. London: J. Johnson, 1792–96.

———. *Lessons for Children: In Four Parts.* 1778–1779. London: J. Johnson, 1808.

Bell, Susan Groag. "Women Create Gardens in Male Landscapes: A Revisionist Approach to Eighteenth-Century English Garden History." *Feminist Studies* 18 (1990): 471–91.

Bewell, Alan. "Keats's 'Realm of Flora.'" *Studies in Romanticism* 31 (1992): 71–98.

Blake, William. *The Complete Poetry and Prose of William Blake.* Ed. David V. Erdman. New York: Doubleday, 1988.

Briggs, Julia. "Women Writers and Writing for Children: From Sarah Fielding to E. Nesbit." *Children and Their Books: A Celebration of the Work of Iona and Peter Opie.* Ed. Gillian Avery and Julia Briggs. Oxford: Clarendon, 1989. 221–50.

Browning, Elizabeth Barrett. *Aurora Leigh: A Poem by Elizabeth Barrett Browning.* Chicago: Academy Chicago, 1979.

Curran, Stuart. "Charlotte Smith and British Romanticism." *South Central Review* 11.2 (1994): 66–78.

———. "Introduction." *The Poems of Charlotte Smith.* Ed. Stuart Curran. New York: Oxford University Press, 1993. xix–xxix.

———. "Romantic Poetry: The I Altered." *Romanticism and Feminism.* Ed. Anne K. Mellor. Bloomington: Indiana University Press, 1988. 185–207.

———. "Women Readers, Women Writers." *The Cambridge Companion to British Romanticism.* Ed. Stuart Curran. Cambridge: Cambridge University Press, 1993. 177–95.

Darwin, Erasmus. *The Botanic Garden.* London: Jones, 1824.

Davidoff, Leonore, and Catherine Hall. *Family Fortunes: Men and Women of the English Middle Class, 1780–1850.* Chicago: University of Chicago Press, 1987.

Demers, Patricia, and Gordon Moyles, eds. *From Instruction to Delight: An Anthology of Children's Literature to 1850.* Toronto: Oxford University Press, 1982.

Dorset, Catherine Ann. *The Peacock "At Home": A Sequel to the Butterfly's Ball.* London: J. Harris, 1807.

Edgeworth, Maria. *Letters for Literary Ladies.* 1795. London: J. Johnson, 1799.

Edgeworth, Maria, and Richard Lovell Edgeworth. *Practical Education.* 1798. New York: Harper, 1855.

Ellis, Grace A. *A Memoir of Mrs. Anna Laetitia Barbauld with Many of Her Letters.* 2 vols. Boston: James Osgood, 1874.

Ezell, Margaret J. M. *Writing Women's Literary History.* Baltimore, Md.: Johns Hopkins University Press, 1993.

Fielding, Sarah. *The Governess; Or, Little Female Academy.* 1749. London: Oxford University Press, 1968.

Jackson, Mary V. *Engines of Instruction, Mischief, and Magic: Children's Literature in England from Its Beginnings to 1839.* Lincoln: University of Nebraska Press, 1989.

Jacobus, Mary. "The Question of Language: Men of Maxims and *The Mill on the Floss.*" *Writing and Sexual Difference.* Ed. Elizabeth Abel. Chicago: University of Chicago Press, 1980. 37–52.

Knoepflmacher, U. C. "The Balancing of Child and Adult: An Approach to Victorian Fantasies for Children." *Nineteenth-Century Fiction* 37 (1983): 497–530.

Lamb, Mary, and Charles Lamb. *The Letters of Charles and Mary Lamb.* Ed. Edwin W. Marrs, Jr. 3 vols. Ithaca: Cornell University Press, 1975–78.

———. *Poetry for Children.* Ed. E. V. Lucas. 1903. *The Works of Charles and Mary Lamb.* Vol. 3 of 6 vols. New York: AMS, 1968.

Lastinger, Valérie C. "Of Dolls and Girls in Nineteenth-Century France." *Children's Literature.* Ed. Francelia Butler, et al. Vol. 21. New Haven: Yale University Press, 1993. 20–42.

Leighton, Angela. *Victorian Women Poets: Writing Against the Heart.* Charlottesville: University Press of Virginia, 1992.

Linkin, Harriet Kramer. "Taking Stock of the British Romantics Marketplace: Teaching New Canons Through New Editions?" *Nineteenth-Century Contexts* 19 (1995): 111–23.

Lucas, E. V., ed. *The Works of Charles and Mary Lamb.* Vol. 3. 1903. New York: AMS Press, 1968.

Macaulay, [Graham], Catharine Sawbridge. *Letters on Education.* In *First Feminists: British Women Writers, 1578–1799.* Ed. Moira Ferguson. Bloomington: Indiana University Press, 1985. 400–411.

McCarthy, William. "Sending a Riddle: Problems of Anna Letitia Barbauld's Autobiography." Fifth Annual Conference on Eighteenth- and Nineteenth-Century British Women Writers. South Carolina, Columbia. 21 Mar. 1996.

McCarthy, William, and Elizabeth Kraft, eds. *The Poems of Anna Letitia Barbauld.* Athens: University of Georgia Press, 1994.

Mellor, Anne K. *Romanticism and Gender.* New York: Routledge, 1992.

More, Hannah. *Strictures on the Modern System of Female Education.* 1799. *The Works of Hannah More.* Vol. 6. New York: Harper, 1855.

Myers, Mitzi. "De-Romanticizing the Subject: Maria Edgeworth's 'The Bracelets,' Mythologies of Origin, and the Daughter's Coming to Writing." *Romantic Women Writers: Voices and Countervoices.* Ed. Paula R. Feldman and Theresa M. Kelley. Hanover, N.H.: University Press of New England, 1995. 88–110.

———. "Impeccable Governesses, Rational Dames, and Moral Mothers: Mary Wollstonecraft and the Female Tradition in Georgian Children's Books." *Children's Literature.* Ed. Francelia Butler, Margaret Higonnet, and Barbara Rosen. Vol. 14. New Haven: Yale University Press, 1986: 31–59.

———. "Of Mice and Mothers: Mrs. Barbauld's 'New Walk' and Gendered Codes in Children's Literature." *Feminine Principles and Women's Experience in American Composition and Rhetoric.* Ed. Louise Wetherbee Phelps and Janet Emig. Pittsburgh: University of Pittsburgh Press, 1995. 255–88.

———. "Reading Rosamond Reading: Maria Edgeworth's 'Wee-Wee Stories' Interrogate the Canon." *Infant Tongues: The Voice of the Child in Literature.* Eds. Elizabeth Goodenough, Mark A. Heberle, and Naomi Sokoloff. Detroit: Wayne State University Press, 1994. 57–79.

Myers, Mitzi, ed. *The Poems of Jane Taylor.* New York: Oxford University Press. In progress.

Pascoe, Judith. "Female Botanists and the Poetry of Charlotte Smith." *Re-Visioning Romanticism: British Women Writers, 1776–1837.* Ed. Carol Shiner Wilson and Joel Haefner. Philadelphia: University of Pennsylvania Press, 1994. 193–209.

Richardson, Alan. *Literature, Education, and Romanticism: Reading as Social Practice, 1780–1832.* New York: Cambridge University Press, 1994.

———. "Reluctant Lords and Lame Princes: Engendering the Male Child in Nineteenth-Century Juvenile Fiction." *Children's Literature.* Ed. Francelia Butler et al. Vol. 21. New Haven: Yale University Press, 1993. 3–19.

———. "Wordsworth, Fairy Tales, and the Politics of Children's Reading." *Romanticism and Children's Literature in Nineteenth-Century England.* Ed. James Holt McGavran, Jr. Athens: University of Georgia Press, 1991. 34–44.

Robbins, Sara. " 'Women's Studies' Debates in Eighteenth-Century England: Mrs. Barbauld's Program for Feminine Learning and Maternal Pedagogy." *Michigan Feminist Studies* 7 (1992–93): 53–82.

Roscoe, William. *The Butterfly's Ball and The Grasshopper's Feast.* London: J. Harris, 1806.

Ross, Marlin. "Configurations of Feminine Reform: The Woman Writer and the Tradition of Dissent." *Re-Visioning Romanticism: British Women Writers, 1776–1837.* Ed. Carol Shiner Wilson and Joel Haefner. Philadelphia: U. of Pennsylvania P., 1994. 91–110.

———. *The Contours of Masculine Desire: Romanticism and the Rise of Women's Poetry.* New York: Oxford University Press, 1989.

Rousseau, Jean-Jacques. *Emile.* Trans. Barbara Foxley. London: J. M. Dent, 1993.

Ruwe, Donelle R. "Gendering Subjectivity: Woman Romantics In a Poetry Survey." *MLA Approaches to Teaching British Women Poets of the Romantic Era.* Ed. Stephen Behrendt and Harriet Kramer Linkin. New York: MLA. Forthcoming.

Schiebinger, Londa. *The Mind Has No Sex? Women in the Origins of Modern Science.* Cambridge, Mass.: Harvard University Press, 1989.

Smith, Charlotte. *Beachy Head: With Other Poems.* London: J. Johnson, 1807.

———. *Conversations Introducing Poetry: Chiefly on Subjects of Natural History. For the Use of Children and Young Persons.* 2 vols. London: J. Johnson, 1804.

———. *Rural Walks: In Dialogues. Intended for the Use of Young Persons.* 2 vols. London: T. Cadell, Jr. and W. Davies, 1795.

St. Clair, William. "William Godwin as Children's Bookseller." *Children and Their Books: A Celebration of the Work of Iona and Peter Opie.* Ed. Gillian Avery and Julia Briggs. Oxford: Clarendon, 1989. 165–79.

Summerfield, Geoffrey. *Fantasy and Reason: Children's Literature in the Eighteenth Century.* Athens: University of Georgia Press, 1984.

Taylor, Ann. *My Mother: A Poem Embellished with Designs.* London: Tomkins, 1807.

Trimmer, Sarah. *An Essay on Christian Education.* London: Rivington & Hatchard, 1812.

———. Review of *Bible Stories, Memorable Acts of the Ancient Patriarchs, Judges, and Kings, Extracted from Their Original Historians, for the Use of Children,* by William Scolfield [William Godwin]. *The Guardian of Education* 1 (1802): 244–64.

———. Review of *Conversations Introducing Poetry, Chiefly on Subjects of Natural History,* by Charlotte Smith. *The Guardian of Education* 4 (1805): 177–85, 299–301.

Upton, William. *The School Boy* and *The School Girl. A Treasury of Illustrated Children's Books: Early Nineteenth-Century Classics from the Osborne Collection.* Ed. Leonard De Vries. New York: Abbeville, 1989. 166–71.

Watson, Jeanie. " 'The Raven: A Christmas Poem': Coleridge and the Fairy Tale Controversy." *Romanticism and Children's Literature in Nineteenth-Century England.* Ed. James Holt McGavran, Jr. Athens: University of Georgia Press, 1991. 14–53.

Wollstonecraft, Mary. "Hints." *The Other Eighteenth Century: English Women of Letters, 1660–1800.* Ed. Robert W. Uphaus and Gretchen M. Foster. East Lansing, Mich.: Colleagues Press, 1991. 382–84.

———. *Original Stories from Real Life; with Conversations.* London: J. Johnson, 1788.

———. *Thoughts on the Education of Daughters.* 1787. Bristol: Thoemmes, 1995.

Woolf, Virginia. *Three Guineas.* 1938. New York: Harcourt, 1966.

Canonical "Orphans" and Critical Ennui: Rereading Edgeworth's Cross-Writing

Mitzi Myers

Jane Austen demonstrably learned much from the Anglo-Irish author Maria Edgeworth (1768–1849) and highly praises her predecessor's tales in both *Northanger Abbey* and personal letters, but Edgeworth would never have given a novel-aspiring niece Austen's advice: "You are but *now* coming to the heart & beauty of your book; till the heroine grows up, the fun must be imperfect" (Le Faye 275).[1] Far from it: Edgeworth revels in children, and they figure prominently in all her work, often playing pivotal roles in stories marketed primarily for adult readers. But, as this volume's introduction notes, it is not just the traffic between child and adult inside and outside her tales that identifies Edgeworth as a cross-writer, for she negotiates numerous borders—national, historical, and generic, as well as generational. She enjoys literary crossdressing as a male narrator in addition to cross-writing for hybrid audiences, and virtually everything she produced is highly intertextual with literary, cultural, and Revolutionary political history, as well as with the events of her own life.

The 1989 French Revolution bicentenary witnessed an extraordinary outpouring of scholarship and criticism, significantly challenging and revising our thinking about the meaning of that event for literary, historical, and cultural studies. Far more than the American Revolution, the French Revolution has provided the model for what we think of *as* revolution. Issues of gender surfaced repeatedly in this body of revisionary scholarship, often in troubling ways. It has been argued, for example, that French Revolutionary rhetoric quickly contained and erased the universalistic implications of citizenship—that it relegated women to a "private" and domestic sphere of noncitizenship and thus underwrote the binary opposition of public and private that still organizes our thinking about men, women, and social life.

The approaching bicentenary of the 1798 Irish Rising is unlikely to receive anything like the scholarly attention lavished on French

Children's Literature 25, ed. Francelia Butler, R. H. W. Dillard, and Elizabeth Lennox Keyser, guest ed. Mitzi Myers and U. C. Knoepflmacher (Yale University Press, © 1997 Hollins College).

events, although it will certainly be commemorated and debated. Because Irish historiography, like Irish studies in general, remains unusually masculinist and adultist, it is unlikely that even heated discussions among historians and literary critics will devote much attention to issues of war and gender in representing and interpreting the "year of the French" invasion. Women's and children's wartime experiences have elicited little scholarly attention until very recently, yet in civil turmoil there is no boundary between battlefront and home front. Even more than in most internal strife, Irish women of all classes and ages had a strong sense of war's realities, not just in 1798, but also in the years that produced and succeeded that traumatic summer. The disciplinary measure of "free quarters," for example, meant that women would be intimately involved with soldiers stationed in or pillaging from their homes; they saw the house burnings and torture that led to the outbreak, and they wrote about the politics that produced those measures in letters and journals.

Women lived with the war's results as well, extending their significant social commentary into the decades following 1798, during which Ireland was effectively governed by martial law. The "protected" domestic space of family homes was fortified like a military outpost for many of those years, yet the patriarchal tradition that women have nothing to say on war persists, rendering invisible what women did say. Political, social, and literary histories typically erase women's war and peace work because they limit what counts as "war" to combat experience and political decision-making alone. Because the 1798 Rising so quickly became a site of masculine mythology and romantic martyrology, women's participation in and representations of 1798 have scarcely been noticed, yet women (and children), as both early accounts and more recent histories emphasize, were everywhere present. They traveled with the insurgents, they often fought, many died by fire or pike, quite a few were raped or robbed, many witnessed murder and searing brutality, hundreds grieved, and a good number wrote personal accounts—some factual, some fictionalized.

The best known and probably the first woman writer to consider the events of the 1798 Irish Rebellion and the politics of the decades which produced that tragic year is Maria Edgeworth. Her multilayered and multidisciplinary accounts and recyclings in letters, memoirs, legal documents, and fictions for both children and adults reflect, refract, and gender war and Revolution repeatedly and obliquely. All are highly, and often covertly, political; they provide fresh insight into how women write war and violence, and they raise tantalizing questions about the interplay of fictional narrative and factual document, gender and genre. They are "intertextual" not only with one another, but also with the historical records (of prior Irish rebellions as well as the 1798 Rising) and with the narrative accounts of other participants. Here I want first to notice hitherto unremarked intertextualities among Edgeworth's multiple rebellion narratives: the interplay between "Anglo" and "Irish" voices, between children and adults both within and between the two tales cited, and between the "romantic" and "realistic" narrative strategies informing Edgeworth's reformist rewriting of the "tale" as genre.

The canonical "Orphans" of the title refer to the young Irish and Anglo-Irish protagonists of a multi-audience tale and by extension to the occlusion of children's literature from the adult canon; *Ennui* is italicized because it is one of Edgeworth's most popular adult fictions from the first series of *Tales of Fashionable Life* (1809). "Fashionable" here refers to what is current and modern, not to high life—another generic label, like her favorite "moral tales," whose shifting connotations have skewed critical interpretation toward tedium. Rather than bracketing off Edgeworth's children's stories from her adult tales or partitioning her Irish from her English work, more adequate accounts of Edgeworth's family romances and scenes of instruction need to mix tales for juveniles and adults. In doing so, this essay follows Edgeworth's own literary practice. She published a second three-volume set of *Tales of Fashionable Life* in 1812, again, as is typical of her work, interweaving tales of the Irish, the English, and the Continental, juxtaposing the juvenile with the adult, and aligning conventionally "feminine" alongside conventionally "masculine" concerns.

In effect, Edgeworth's authorial packaging of these six volumes, perhaps her most critically acclaimed works in her own day and probably the biggest money makers, embodies my argument for her as a paradigmatic "border crosser," a resonant term for the intellectual author as cultural worker that I borrow from postcolonial criticism. Concerned with authorial positionalities which construe homelessness as home, with border crossers who reinvent traditions not within a discourse of submissive repetition but as critique and transformation, Abdul R. JanMohamed's formulation is especially useful with juvenile and "Anglo-Irish" texts. If adult texts for child readers proverbially exemplify the need to be "at home," what we conventionally call for want of a better term "Ascendancy" or "Anglo-Irish" authors

2 opposing melodies

as often exhibit the contrapuntal awareness of reformist intellectuals situated on cultural borders.[2] All "Anglo-Irish" writers are not Sir Richard Musgrave, notorious for his horrific demonization of Irish Rebellions as one big Catholic conspiracy bent on Protestant genocide; no "Anglo-Irish" woman writer inhabits quite the same intellectual space as her father, her brother, or her husband.

narrow

We might productively consider Edgeworth as a gendered border intellectual, positioned between cultures, analytically scrutinizing them, and employing her interstitial cultural locale to represent, overtly and covertly—by both authorial statement and symbolic form—utopian possibilities of group formation and communal living. We can read her displaced and sometimes distanciated Rebellion narratives as deterritorializations which rewrite and thus reterritorialize home and exile within an Enlightened protofeminist discourse, which typically imagines the child's body and voice as crucial to affective renewal and to cultural and political regeneration. Two highly intertextual tales about Ireland exemplify these complex issues: a children's story called "The Orphans," circulated in 1799 right after the savage—and savagely repressed—Irish Rebellion of 1798 and first published in the revised and enlarged *Parent's Assistant* of 1800, and *Ennui*, the Irish tale for adults that Edgeworth started writing some years before its 1809 appearance: the latter's absentee masculine narrator leaves his English estate to visit the ancestral castle in his native Ireland, only to become enmeshed in the nightmares of Gaelic history, domestic insurrection, and French invasion. In their different yet interrelated ways, both tales constitute a woman's way of representing Revolution. Perhaps, therefore, they can help push us toward a revisionary, if not revolutionary, rethinking of what Edgeworth embodies and this volume conceptualizes as cross-writing—a transgressive and creative miscegenation of public and private spaces, gender and generational issues, and domestic and national politics. Children's literature and the imperialist expansion of colonial empire are by no means so simply related as some literary histories suggest, nor can tales for young and old, for mass and elite audiences, and for Irish and Anglo publics be so tidily segregated as much comment on multiaudience authors takes for granted.

marriage between races

The paper call which initiated the Modern Language Association division session that eventuated in this thematic issue of *Children's Literature* suggests that considering cross-writing—the authors and works which transgress the usual demarcations separating children's from adult literature—can help critics address key issues in contemporary critical theory and cultural studies, from the notions of ethnicity, class, and gender inscribed within fictions to the interpretive conventions and generic schema readers bring to printed forms. For example, what continuities or divergences mark the writings of those who create separate works for child and adult? How do we know which literature is for children and which is for adults? How does writing for children or imagining a dual readership for a text influence authorial decisions and / or the author's rank in literary history? How does including children impinge upon canonical standing? How do the romance conventions that underwrite most children's literary forms lend themselves as readily to reformist political aims as to the wish-fulfillment and ideological imposition that twentieth-century critics more typically expect? How might recontextualizing a work simultaneously reconceptualize how we think about it, or even change what we see when we consider its visual representations as well?

Using Maria Edgeworth to exemplify the writer who is, multiply, a border crosser, this essay specifically addresses a few of these very hard questions. Edgeworth's investment in the juvenile can be and often has been interpreted as a case of arrested development, the sign of the daddy's girl who never quite grew up, the woman writer who is at best complicit with patriarchy, at worst the girlish victim of parental abuse and intellectual incest. In this narrativizing of Edgeworth's authoriality, the daughter shuns mature sexuality to wield her father's pen: her paternal partner Richard Lovell Edgeworth dictates; the good little girl just writes. (However disingenuously, Edgeworth herself often fancies this ventriloquial account, although a more accurate version would show that the supposedly dutiful daughter's stories brought into being the loving father-mentor that the once neglected little girl desired: the "Richard Lovell Edgeworth" who plays a starring role in literary histories' summations of his daughter's career is also a character in one of his daughter's most successful narratives.) Alternatively, of course, masculinist Romantics like Charles Lamb sidestep the scenario of Edgeworth as victim to figure her (along with Anna Letitia Barbauld, Mary Wollstonecraft, and other Enlightened women writers for the young) not as perpetual child, but as wicked witch: maternal educators are construed as petrifying Medusas, grinches who kidnap boys of feeling for nefarious rational purposes. We need only, in Lamb's memorable phrase, "**Damn** them . . . the cursed Barbauld Crew, those **Blights & Blasts** of all that is **Human** in man & child" (*The Letters of Charles and Mary Anne Lamb*, 2:82).[3]

As a feminist historical critic rather than a hysterical male competitor in the literary marketplace, I am especially interested in the political uses of the child figure for the woman writer. How come Edgeworth so persistently takes the child's part—and why has her identification with the child been interpreted so diversely and often deleteriously? The first tales she wrote as a teenager in the 1780s were for a little brother, and the last tale she published in 1848, when she was in her eighties, is a juvenile fiction too. Throughout her career she mixes writing for juveniles with adult novels, most of her grown-up tales feature children in important roles and imagine life as educational process, and all her stories, including those for adults, were first read to and critiqued by a domestic audience that always included the family youngsters. Indeed, the Edgeworths were philosophically committed to living with their children: the youngsters were acquainted with family business and finances, they took part in the Edgeworths' sophisticated domestic conversation, and Maria did her writing on a little desk in the big family library where the estate business and the children's lessons also took place. If these details conjure up specters of wizened premature adults victimized by Enlightened philosophy, I should point out that the adult Edgeworths were addicted to storytelling, charades, play acting, bizarre inventions, and delightfully messy chemical experiments, as well as to serious thinkers such as the Scottish philosophers Dugald Stewart and Adam Smith. They were also, by nineteenth-century standards, shockingly free of piety; Edgeworth's reviewers' biggest complaint was that her little people never said their prayers. Edgeworth's correspondence shows that many of her adult works were read by children outside her own family as well, just as her juvenile tales were appreciated by cosmopolitan men of letters like Sir Walter Scott and John Gibson Lockhart. (But that is another story, one that raises important questions about the sources and strategic uses of our contemporary bifurcations—or rather, multiplicities—of readership.)

Actually, Edgeworth had three—maybe even four—concomitant careers and several overlapping audiences when she was the leading British woman writer in the early years of the nineteenth century: she was a storyteller for the young (and a pioneer education writer also, a precursor of Pestalozzi and Froebel); she was a feminocentric novelist with a predilection for strong women (as in her *Belinda* of 1801 and *Helen* of 1834) and for "masculine" subjects like politics (as in her ambitious 1814 analysis of British culture, *Patronage*); and she was the pioneer regional novelist of Irish life who inspired Walter Scott (as in *Castle Rackrent* [1800], *Ennui* [1809], *The Absentee* [1812], and *Ormond* [1817]). Edgeworth's closest competitor for literary pre-eminence was Madame de Staël on the continent; no other British woman writer even came close. (Jane Austen's reputation came many years later, and is indeed close to being a twentieth-century phenomenon.) Edgeworth made more money and was more widely read than any other woman novelist of her day. She was also reviewed in major journals when no other novelist was, and she effectively founded the family novel (for which Louisa May Alcott gets credit) as well as the regional tale (for which Scott gets credit). She was taken seriously as an artist and a thinker when competitors like Lady Morgan were not. Just about every nineteenth-century children's writer and Irish novelist went to school to Edgeworth, but the writer who once seemed assured of canonical status on multiple grounds has since been multiply displaced. If the woman who *should* be there *isn't*, then why not? What happened?

Exploring Edgeworth's cross-writing suggests why. If writing for, to, about, and as a child, however brilliantly successful in its day, hasn't proved good for Edgeworth's long-term canonical health, what does that say about the construction of the literary canon and about the methods of literary interpretation that have prevailed until recently? Even feminist criticism (despite women's historical and biological implication in childhood) looks askance at the child text: it's nobody's baby. Gender has long since been in; generation (except when it has to do with adult sexuality) remains out. Crossdressing is hot; cross-writing is not. Rather than the closet pedophiles James R. Kincaid's *Child-Loving: The Erotic Child and Victorian Culture* has discovered us to be, we seem to be pedophobes, at least when the text in question displays no overt sexuality. Unlike many nineteenth-century male writers (and twentieth-century male critics), Edgeworth never gazes on the child with prurient longings, but she does have a lot to say about children as politicized citizens. Far from the stuffy, didactic realist entombed in conventional literary histories—volumes apparently produced by people who have not read her work—she is a lively storyteller with a taste for the metafictional and a dizzying disregard for the boundaries that mark off child and adult, romance and realism, masculine and feminine, and, in the case of my exemplary texts, the short story of "The Orphans" and the novelette called *Ennui*, with a transgressive disregard for the bloody divisions between Catholic Gaelic culture and the Anglo-Irish Protestant Ascendancy as well.

Formally, Edgeworth's work is as suspect as is its author's cultural and canonical positioning. The tale—the term Edgeworth uses for all her fictions throughout her life, from early dialogues for tots to triple-deckers like her last adult novel, *Helen* (1834)—the tale looks suspiciously like a bastard. She genders, juvenilizes, and obliquely politicizes those "two qualities for which there are no precise English words—*naïveté* and *finesse*" that she admires in Marmontel's *contes* (*Ormond*, ch. 29, 356). Not exactly the historical romance of Scott (whose *Waverley* [1814] credits Edgeworth as inspiration), not exactly the classic realist courtship novel of Austen (whose fictions both overtly cite and covertly echo her predecessor), but something betwixt and between, Edgeworth's literary panoramas veer disconcertingly from sociological and linguistic accuracy to what one critic terms "unnatural incident."[4] Edgeworth's fondness for coincidences, freaky plots, and creaky conclusions jars against her naturalized characters and settings, as well as against the shrewd social critique and witty, revelatory dialogue of her adult fiction. Viewing Edgeworth's authoriality through the lens of cross-writing shakes up current assumptions about literary reputation, representational content (I consider the child as a political figure who counts), and narrative form (I locate the tale as an ambiguously crossdressed genre—a cross-genre, as it were, which links dual genders, generations, genres, and authorial programs). Ultimately, I argue, the child Edgeworth recurrently embodies and the trajectory of cross-writing she recurrently traverses mark not the author's regression, but her ambition. A woman's way of representing Revolution, they unite the writer's psychic needs as feeling private subjectivity with the Enlightened educator's reformist public political agenda. A perspective that is feminist and postcolonially (or messily) pluralist reveals the interdependence of Edgeworth's child and adult literature; that interdependence is her signature theme; and, via retellings and intertextuality, that generic interdependence is her signature technique as well.

The determining cliché in postcolonial criticism is that the imperialist oppressor objectifies and controls the ethnic other through feminization and juvenilization: the colonist always sees the colonized as a deficient child. What could be worse than thinking of the native as a kid? Probably to the surprise of most feminist critics, Kincaid announces that "[g]ender . . . is of very little importance to child-loving" (13). Perhaps who is gendering the native as child is not highly important in the totalizing schema of postcolonial or Orientalist criticism, but the adultist critic's "childish" and the juvenile literature specialist's "childist" connote quite differently. And in the case of Edgeworth's cross-writing, gender and historical locale matter very much indeed. As Enlightened landlords—and Maria was trained to administer the family estate as a teenager—the Edgeworths made no distinction between Anglican and Catholic. They thought of themselves as proponents of a regenerated cultural community, as mediators between native Catholics oppressed by the Penal Laws and the ultra-Protestant Orange element among the Anglo-Irish. When the Irish Rebellion broke out in 1798, the Edgeworths found themselves fleeing from advancing rebel armies only to be nearly lynched by a reactionary Orange mob that suspected their progressivism and assumed they were conspiring with the French invaders. When they returned to Edgeworthstown, they found that the rebels, grateful for family favors, had left their house unharmed among the smoking ruins of their neighbors' estates—a situation that further fueled suspicions about their allegiance.

The literary analogue to her ambiguous physical positioning in the Irish midlands of County Longford, Edgeworth's so-called "Unionist" fiction, was not written as simpleminded propaganda for the 1800 Act of Union that followed the Rebellion and that ended Ireland's semi-autonomous status, as some critics have concluded. Instead, tales like "The Orphans" for youngsters and *Ennui* for adults similarly embody the notion of ethnic harmony in the bodies and minds of the child. When John Ruskin, who was extraordinarily fond of Edgeworth (he called her tales the most "re-readable books in existence"), faults her juvenile family in "The Orphans" because they aren't obtrusively and distinctively stereotyped as Irish, he rather misses the point.[5] In the volatile political atmosphere of post-Rebellion paranoia, when the normative repressive attitude is to claim that the Gael is intrinsically, essentially different, irremediable and ineducable, Edgeworth's little orphan children—so ably directed by their big sister Mary in their progress from a precarious existence living in the rocks to communal popularity, entrepreneurial success, and a solid house of their own—look rather different. While the adults are offstage, the Catho-

[margin annotation: ethnic harmony]

[bottom margin annotation: having a disposition to impose oneself or one's opinions on others]

lic orphans and the Anglo-Irish girls who turn up as fairy godmothers enact a reconciliatory agenda that is coded juvenile and feminine. Similarly, the supposedly Anglo hero of *Ennui* is precipitously cured of the fashionable malady that has made his life a misery when he discovers that he is, as it were, his own foster brother: Edgeworth makes the old romance cliché of the babies switched at nurse a marvelous political intervention. It is education, not blood, that makes the man, and the apathetic anti-hero Glenthorn can only grow up by becoming an Irish child and learning feeling from his Gaelic mother, old Ellinor, the supposed foster-nurse who is simultaneously a story-telling Mother Goose figure and the embodiment of Ireland's past.[6] As with Mary's dead mother in "The Orphans," the maternal Ellinor is the big love object in Edgeworth's adult fiction *Ennui*—and a surrogate for the author as storyteller too—the behind-the-scenes manager who secretly engineers the interpenetration and rejuvenation of England and Ireland.

"The Orphans" and *Ennui* share magical endings, reconciliatory cultural agendas, and heavily overdetermined parent-child and sororal relations. Both theatricalize realistic, documented stories through fairy-tale events and conclusions, and these dual codings and generic indeterminacies help us to define the tale as transgressive prose fiction genre, the literary homologue of ideational cross-writing. Mixing feminist cultural studies and narratology, I have noted how Edgeworth's Irish locale (as well as her own family life) leads her to turn to the child as a focus in her tales for both juveniles and adults. In each, the tale as utopian genre unites realism and romance and the politicized body of the child bridges the gap between hostile cultures: the Anglo-Irish and the native Gaelic. At once predictive fairy tales and pragmatically detailed sociology (a manual for everything from making rush candles to managing an estate), Edgeworth's magical narratives formally convey a socio-symbolic message. They may begin (as does "The Orphans") with invoking what was—"Near the ruins of the castle of Rossmore, in Ireland, is a small cabin, in which there once lived a widow, and her four children"—but they end by mapping a different future (71). Their form constitutes an ideology in its own right: in each, the author uses a transformative romance, constructed from ordinary realities, to defiantly reject Musgrave's nightmare of Irish commonality as mass murder in favor of an alternative community that rewrites Rebellion as rejuvenation. Mary gets not merely Virginia Woolf's proverbial room of one's own, but a whole house

exhausted of vigor or energy

and a thriving female-managed business as well; the effete Glenthorn matures, thinks rationally, and achieves lawyerly success only after he sheds his Anglo shell and regresses to the feeling Gaelic child.[7]

Figuring her political and cultural answers within child characters and within the childlike genre of the tale, Edgeworth embodies a revisionist political agenda. In cross-writing similar themes and genres for child and grown-up and thus transgressing the usual demarcations between children's and adults' literature, Edgeworth simultaneously satisfies personal psychological needs, posits utopian political answers to her war-torn homeland's radical divisions, and pioneers the cross-dressed genre of the tale, a mix of the desiring daughter's family romance and the masculinist Enlightenment's rationally realistic history. Ironically, it is just these daring transgressions that—misread and misvalued—have done in the author's literary standing today. In recovering the child and the cross-writing that figure so largely in Edgeworth's achievement, we not only begin to recover Edgeworth for the canon, but we also gain some ways of thinking about the political and cultural relevance of cross-writing for other women writers and for some men as well. In taking child-centered texts seriously *politically,* as reformist spaces intertextual with grown-up works and lives and perhaps more radical than adultist conformities permit, we add an important dimension to current psychoanalytic or pedophiliac theorizing about the role of the juvenile in both our cultural construction of ourselves and our historical reconstruction of the past. *sexual desire for child by adult*

Having sketched some generic and thematic continuities in Edgeworth's Irish tales for two audiences, I now turn to look more closely at the cross-writing between historical fact and fictional structure within "The Orphans" and between this verbal representation and two visualizations, one contemporary with the story's initial appearance, one more recent. The first illustrated edition of *Parent's Assistant* (originally published in 1796) was the revised and expanded version of 1800 in six little volumes: this new third edition appeared in two forms, the upscale format with a frontispiece to each volume, and a pictureless printing that was much less expensive. Because Edgeworth père had four wives and twenty-two children, the household provided both a domestic laboratory for educational experiments and an always eager audience. Like many writers of children's books, Maria Edgeworth began writing for children whom she knew, telling her siblings the stories orally from notes on a slate and producing finished text only when the child auditors approved. It is noteworthy that the children heard adult novels read aloud and pronounced critical judgment on what their sister had written for grown-ups as well. The children did not inhabit a separate nursery world. Instead, just as the Edgeworths' published educational ideology promoted, they lived in the midst of the family: the daughter's writing, the estate business, and the children's lessons and play were conducted in the roomy library, as many visitors and the family letters and observational records recount. It is this cross-generational representational space that makes the Edgeworths so fascinating to study, for the household itself physically embodies cross-writing. The Edgeworths' menage and program constitute cross-writing politically as well as materially, for they imagine children's "private" domestic activities in relationship to a "public" political world.

Maria Edgeworth's stories, like many children's tales, hence sustain textured readings and operate at multiple levels, depending not merely on whether the reader is child or adult, but on gender and national affiliation as well. The rare illustrations add yet another intertextual dimension to this layering. First, it is worth recalling that despite John Newbery's earlier wealth of illustrations and later Victorian sumptuousness, most late-eighteenth-century stories are *not* illustrated, so any frontispiece is highlighted by its rarity. Take, for example, the frontispiece for the fifth volume of the 1800 *Parent's Assistant,* the one featuring the new story of "The Orphans," just one of several new tales about Ireland appearing shortly after the bloody Rising of 1798. Provocatively, the revised edition came out the same year that the semi-autonomous Irish Parliament was bribed to vote itself out of existence and the same year that Edgeworth's much more famous adult tale, the notoriously ambiguous *Castle Rackrent,* was published. (The Union of Great Britain and Ireland legally took effect in 1801 on 1 January, which happens also to be Maria Edgeworth's birthday.) "The Orphans" imagines a complex and multiple audience, and, as we've noted, Edgeworth had her reasons for modifying what typical English readers thought of as "Irish." Young Mary and her siblings are energetic, forward-looking, and successful. When the mother dies early in the story and the children find themselves homeless, having been evicted from their cottage by the money-grubbing agent who cannot wait for the rent, they do not despair. They take up residence in a barely habitable part of a decaying castle (the ruins of Irish history) and busily set to work to repair their fortunes—and metonymically, their homeland's as well. Without melodrama or overstatement, the agent comes across as heartless, dishonest, and stupid; the children, of course, are far from passive recipients of grown-up wisdom. Many adults in Edgeworth's children's tales are, like the agent, satirized as petty and mean-minded, or like the beggar Goody Grope, the domesticated witch of this story, as incapable of dealing with life. Benefactors usually show up, as do the adolescent Anglo-Irish sisters here, but not until the children have already resolved daunting dilemmas on their own.

The children in the *Parent's Assistant* are miniature heroes and heroines domesticated from quest-romance. They nurture and counsel ailing or inept parents, they pay the bills, they help out siblings and rescue their pets from slaughter or sale. Brave, ingenious, and strong on character and determination, they are never at a loss for long. These tales of everyday heroism offer the child of the late eighteenth century far more than behavioral rules. They give child readers—boys and girls alike—confidence in themselves and in their abilities to solve problems and to achieve a more satisfying material, intellectual, and emotional life. The characters can think as well as feel, work as well as play. Edgeworth's romance conventions grant them agency, and her realistic sociology locates that agency in a historical political economy. It is this heroic quality, depicted with dramatic flair and a seemingly transparent vernacular realism, that makes the stories still so appealing, once we cease to expect exercises in Romantic nostalgia and sentimentality. Edgeworth's tales are also, if one thinks back to Puritan moralizing or forward to Evangelicalism, refreshingly secular. The children depend on themselves, without recourse to God or prayers. With its stress on the children's inventive ways to advance financially and to shape a cozy home for themselves through mutual cooperation, "The Orphans" is in many ways yet another variation on the Robinson Crusoe routine, always a favorite in children's books, of reconstructing a world from the ground up. How *does* one set up housekeeping in a tumbledown castle? How do the children survive and ultimately triumph by reclaiming their good name from gossip, founding a little business, and becoming householders on their own?

Clearly, the story is ideologically charged—English readers are being shown that the Irish aren't inherently ineducable and lazy, as many contemporary conservative thinkers insisted. Similarly, the lively cooperation and family harmony that the young orphans display in their relations with the neighboring Anglo-Irish sisters, as well as among themselves, contravene propagandistic images of the Irish as Papist plotters—bloodthirsty bearers of pikes—as in Sir Richard Musgrave's notorious history of Rebellion atrocities, much reprinted around this time. The script that the story offers for Irish child readers is meant as an enabling and empowering one—one that enlists authorial literacy to demonstrate that the orphans' literacy and skills (they have been educated by their mother and a good schoolmistress) assure their success. Not only smart, but also affectively gifted, the orphans embody the familial affection Edgeworth so highly valued in the native Irish and in her own relationships as well. Edgeworth's child's tale is a woman's war story: Edgeworth herself had fled for her life from invading rebel armies, only to find her family in more danger from loyalist Orange mobs. Her father narrowly escaped being stoned to death by rioting conservatives for his supposed pro-French sympathies. Ballinamuck, the final battle of the Rebellion concluding "the year of the French," was fought only a few miles from Edgeworthstown, and apprehensions ran high. Like the insurgents' gesture of protecting the Edgeworths' estate from damage because of the family's good relations with the villagers and tenantry, "The Orphans" is a symbolic act, a constitutive movement toward a new reality for the writer and her readers alike. It is a peacemaking, cross-writing effort that thematizes the union of hearts that the liberal-minded author hopes will replace contemporary sectarianism.

With this plot structure in mind, we can look freshly at the illustration for "The Orphans," which assumes a complex and ironic meaning when we connect it intertextually to the accompanying narrative and contextually to the environing historical trauma from which it emerged. The later 1790s had been marked by extraordinary violence and upheaval. Warlike events on the homefront neither began nor ended in 1798. Even in relatively quiet County Longford, the site of Edgeworthstown, house burnings and murders by maurauding loyalist yeomanry were common, as were retaliatory raids for arms by the largely Catholic secret society called the "Defenders." Houses were forts, yet the optimistic children's stories Edgeworth was writing are far from escapist. The drawing for "The Orphans" published in 1800 was probably sketched in early 1797 by Frances Beaufort, daughter of clergyman-cartographer D. A. Beaufort, at the request of Mrs. Ruxton, Richard Lovell Edgeworth's favorite sister and Maria Edgeworth's favorite aunt. By the time Joseph Johnson's project of an illustrated *Parent's Assistant* was realized, Edgeworth's third wife was dead, and

Figure 1. Like Edgeworth's tale, the 1800 illustration is multilayered; the scene looks idyllic, but the decayed historical castle is about to fall. The pictured child workers (who are not the orphans) will flee in terror, whereas the orphans will cope and eventually triumph.

[handwritten: Fourth wife of Edgeworth's father a year younger than Edgeworth herself.]

Frances, a year younger than Maria, was his fourth and last wife. The wedding took place at the very start of the Rebellion in May 1798, and Maria's continuation of her father's *Memoirs* for this period skillfully and revealingly interweaves both her private upset and that of the Irish public, as well as the dual restorations of peace, a cross-writing of political and domestic worlds that plays throughout her work.

A talented artist, Frances Beaufort Edgeworth illustrated most of the stories, some under her maiden and some under her married name. Her choice for "The Orphans" illuminates the multiple cross-writings of child and adult, public and private, Anglo and native, that inform the written tale (fig. 1). The representation was ready to be shown to the youngest Edgeworth child, little William, born in 1794 and three years old in 1797: "When we showed Miss Beaufort's beautiful drawing to little William," Maria writes, "he asked immediately if those little boys were not blowing soap bubbles."[8] Out of context, several children blowing bubbles in front of a ruined castle will surely conjure up the *vanitas* references so dear to the hearts of art historians confronted with pictures of children at play. The decayed turrets (which the story tells us go all the way back to the time of Henry VII), in conjunction with the evanescent bubbles and the *[handwritten: vanishing]* playmates' rounded limbs, surely say that youth is fleeting, buildings fall, and all life fails: the charmingly clad youngsters (notice the Enlightened child's clothes, which were novel in that they were made for carefree play) will one day be just like the castle. So much for the universalizing and the emblematizing. Observed more closely and situationally, the frontispiece exists in ironic relation to what is going on in the story. First, these are not the orphans themselves, but their village playmates taking a recreational break from their participation in the orphans' thriving domestic "manufactory" (97). At the very moment when the pictured bubbles swell and drift upward, another part of the castle is crumbling with a tremendous crash. The nicely clad village youngsters will be scared to death and run away, rather to the brave orphans' scorn. The family's naughty pet goat has butted a dangerous rock once too often, and the rubble of the dislodgement brings to light a cache of rare antique coins. But the long buried treasure, the hidden other of the vanishing bubbles, does not mark the orphans' salvation. The pot of gold—thanks to the dishonest rent agent for the absentee English landlord and to the treasure-hunting Goody Grope, who quickly appears on the scene ready to tear down the rest of the orphans' precarious dwelling for more loot—produces no magical happy ending.

Like so much else in Edgeworth's writing, the treasure is invested with political implications. The agent steals the gold, so the orphans are ostracized as thieves for a time—their good name dissipates, perhaps like the bubbles and certainly like the post-Rebellion image of Ireland and the Irish. Solving the mystery and clearing of the orphans' good name depend on intelligence, as well as the cooperation of both the Anglo-Irish and native Irish. The reputational commodity that the orphans eventually capitalize into solid gains (for they anticipate Jeremy Bentham's notion of reputation as negotiable property, just they emblematize the successful small entrepreneurship of political economy's palmy youth) must be, so to speak, refictionalized.[9] The naive fairy-tale structure is reconstituted as Enlightened fable. The buried treasure of the mythopoeic romance quest, which Frye reminds us "means wealth in its ideal forms, power and wisdom," is displaced from a mysterious given to ongoing human agency (*Anatomy* 193). Luckily, the smart, friendly sisters have chemically marked the valuable coins so that they can be identified scientifically. The story, like Edgeworth's adult Irish novels, especially *Ennui* (which deals directly with the 1798 Rising), is obsessively interested in rumor and reputation, in how what people say determines what happens. After all, many historians attribute much of the slaughter which marked the Rebellion on both sides to rampant genocidal rumors. Protestants and Catholics alike recurrently expected to be butchered by the other, and the elder Edgeworth himself, as both his daughter's continuation of his *Memoirs* and *Ennui* develop, almost lost his life because of gossip—the stories people tell and mistell.

The ironized illustration for "The Orphans," like the tale and like the contemporary politics implicit within the romance plot structure, demands nuanced interpretation. But if the bubble-blowing children are ambiguously and amusingly intertextual, a wry comment on the ways in which historical juvenile tales can be transformed into charmingly innocuous Romantic representations when uprooted from their context, the illustration that accompanies a twentieth-century reprint works another way. It implies a reading as referentially unlayered and baldly adultist as the stark modern sketch itself. Like the environs of Edgeworth's Enlightened tale, now retitled "The Orphans' Reward" and reprinted in Gillian Avery's 1965 collection, *In the Window Seat: A Selection of Victorian Stories,* the graphic representation transforms our expectations of the story from experiential process and child agency to benefits bestowed by adults (fig. 2). Foregrounded are the Anglo-

MARIA EDGEWORTH

The Orphans' Reward

Figure 2. The 1965 reprint of Edgeworth's story Victorianizes the title; the illustration solicits the reader's pity rather than emphasizing the children's agency. Reproduced from "The Orphans' Reward," in *In the Window Seat: A Selection of Victorian Stories,* ed. Gillian Avery (Princeton, N.J.: Van Nostrand, 1965). Illustration copyright © 1965, Susan Einzig.

Irish sisters, mysteriously grown much older and distanced from twelve-year-old Mary and her younger siblings, Edmund and the little sisters, who all grieve pathetically over their mother's grave in the background. As J. Hillis Miller notes in his account of the intertextual traffic between illustrations and "literature," here redefined as "cultural studies," as is often the case nowadays, the word "illustration" means bringing to light, thus opening out fictions as multimedia collaborative productions, continually being relabeled and recreated as alternative stories (61). Revealingly, the modern illustrator of Edgeworth's politicized fairy tale for its time shuts down the author's cross-writing with an unambiguous stop sign—no cross traffic here. But Enlightened authors and postmodern readers nevertheless negotiate borders: they know how to jaywalk.

Notes

1. Austen's letter to her niece Anna, an embryo writer, is no. 107 in Deirdre Le Faye's 1995 update of R. W. Chapman's earlier Oxford editions [hereafter RWC] (no. 100 in the older editions, because this third edition includes new material). Dated 9–18 Sept. 1814, it is one of Austen's most cited because it is full of novelist-to-novelist advice. This letter is immediately followed in the collection by a tribute to Edgeworth,

the epistolary equivalent to Austen's high praise in the fifth chapter of *Northanger Abbey* (pp. 37–38 in the Oxford ed.): "I have made up my mind to like no Novels really, but Miss Edgeworth's, Yours & my own" (278, no. 108, 28 Sept. 1814; RWC no. 101).

2. Postcolonial studies I draw on here include Caren Kaplan's suggestions toward a feminist poetics of location, Abdul R. JanMohamed's overview of Edward Said's achievement, and Henry A. Giroux's analysis of Paulo Freire's reformist pedagogy. Said himself has been notably uninterested in gender issues and prone to polarizations of "us" and "them," but his work is nevertheless helpful in reconceptualizing the issues of gender, generation, and nationality that Edgeworth's hybrid tales make visible.

3. Lamb's letter to Coleridge is dated 23 Oct. 1802; despite his curses, Lamb's own juvenile works are much indebted to the women's tradition he deplores.

4. This phrase comes from the Irish Chief Justice Charles Kendal Bushe, one of the many contemporary readers who pronounces *Ennui* "very good, but wou'd be better if the unnatural incident of the change at Nurse was not forc'd unnecessarily into it" (Somerville and Ross 200). Bushe was a family friend—his astute observations on the interplay between father and daughter are among the best, and he is also the original for a character in *Patronage*, Maria Edgeworth's 1814 political tale. Although he was not a professional literary critic, his response is very similar to that of the masculine reviewers who ruled the journals. Men of the time tend to be especially sticky about violations of probability for two reasons. First, their professional training valorizes rule, precedent, logic, and reason. Second, transgressing probability undercuts the moral effect, and they make the didactic aim paramount. To fault Edgeworth in these terms is to fault her for being *insufficiently* didactic. Twentieth-century aesthetic critique has of course a different rationale, though it is also implicitly masculinist.

5. Ruskin began his career by imitating Edgeworth in childhood, and he enthusiastically recommended her fictions to a variety of audiences. In his mid-nineteenth-century letter to Henry Acland he also claims to have read Edgeworth's tales and *Patronage* "oftener than any other books in the world, except the Bible" (cited from Henry Acland [1855?] Bodleian MS. Acland d. 72 in Butler 2). The Cook and Wedderburn edition of *The Works of John Ruskin* contains an extraordinary number of references to Edgeworth; for the critique of "The Orphans," see *Works* 29: 431n, May 1883.

6. For more about Ellinor as Mother Goose and Mother Ireland, see my " 'Completing the Union': Critical *Ennui*, the Politics of Narrative, and the Reformation of Irish Cultural Identity."

7. Postmodern work on mixed generic forms that constitute an ideology in their own right, a symbolic answer to a sociocultural problem, goes back to Northrop Frye's groundbreaking recognition of the "perennially childlike quality of romance," its ability to meld the nostalgic and the revisionist proletarian. Frye's quest-romance (which we can domesticate as well as masculinize) desires "a fulfillment that will deliver it from the anxieties of reality but will still contain that reality" (*Anatomy of Criticism* 187, 193). In *The Secular Scripture: A Study of the Structure of Romance*, Frye further discusses this demotic utopianism: the "element of social protest is inherent in romance" (77). The generic indeterminacy or dual generic coding in Edgeworth's tales (and the French *contes moraux* from which she formally derives) readily assimilates with what Fredric Jameson terms "magical narratives" and Peter Hulme names "colonial romance." Revealingly, both are concerned only with men's forms—Hulme's discussion centers on *Robinson Crusoe*—and with adult works: see Jameson's ch. 2, "Magical Narratives: On the Dialectical Use of Genre Criticism," in *The Political Unconscious: Narrative As A Socially Symbolic Act;* and Hulme 208–22. For a similar erasure of the woman writer (and reader), the young heroine, and the domestic quest-romance, see Martin Green's two studies dichotomizing the "domestic" novel and the guy tale: *Dreams of Adventure, Deeds of Empire* and *The Robinson Crusoe Story*.

8. Maria Edgeworth's letter in her *Memoirs* is probably misdated October for April, judging from other internal and external evidence (1:77).

9. Edgeworth thought Bentham pompous and a bad stylist, but like many other Enlightenment thinkers, she valued early utilitarianism and political economy as liberatory for their secularization and democratization of pleasure, pain, and social good, a positive perspective that we have to read back through many layers of later history and interpretation to rediscover. For Bentham's account of reputation as "a kind of fictitious object of property . . . constituted in your favour," the loss of which deprives you of "happiness or security," see *An Introduction to the Principles of Morals and Legislation* (ch. 16, 193). Edgeworth read Adam Smith and later carried on a lively correspondence with David Ricardo (which anticipated by several years the potato Famine of the 1840s). The Edgeworths were much concerned with bettering the lot of the Irish poor.

Works Cited

Austen, Jane. *Northanger Abbey and Persuasion.* 1818. Vol. 5 of *The Novels of Jane Austen.* Ed. R. W. Chapman. 3d ed. 5 vols. London: Oxford University Press, 1959.

Bentham, Jeremy. *An Introduction to the Principles of Morals and Legislation.* Ed. J. H. Burns and H. L. A. Hart. London: Methuen, 1982.

Butler, Marilyn. *Maria Edgeworth: A Literary Biography.* Oxford: Clarendon, 1972.

Edgeworth, Maria. *The Absentee.* In *Tales of Fashionable Life.* 3 vols. London: J. Johnson, 1812. (Occupies the end of vol. 5 and all of vol. 6 in the original 6 vol. format.)

————. *Belinda.* Intro. Eva Figes. 1801. Rev. 3d ed. London: Pandora, 1986.

————. *Castle Rackrent: An Hibernian Tale Taken from Facts, and from the Manners of the Irish Squires, Before the Year 1782.* Ed. George Watson. 1800. The World's Classics. Oxford: Oxford University Press, 1981.

————. *Ennui.* In *Tales of Fashionable Life.* 3d ed. Vol. 1 of 3 vols. London: J. Johnson, 1809.

————. *Helen: A Tale.* 3 vols. London: Richard Bentley, 1834.

————. *A Memoir of Maria Edgeworth, with A Selection from Her Letters by the Late Mrs. [Frances] Edgeworth.* Ed. Her Children. 3 vols. London: Privately printed by Joseph Masters and Son, 1867.

————. *Ormond: A Tale.* 1817. Shannon: Irish University Press, 1972.

————. "The Orphans." In *The Parent's Assistant.* 1800. 6 vols. in 2 books. Classics of Children's Literature, 1621–1932. New York: Garland, 1976. In vol. 5, bk. 2.

————. "The Orphans' Reward." In *In the Window Seat: A Selection of Victorian Stories.* Ed. Gillian Avery. Princeton, N.J.: Van Nostrand, 1965. 99–122.

————. *The Parent's Assistant.* 6 vols. London: J. Johnson, 1800.

————. *Patronage.* 4 vols. 2d ed. London: J. Johnson, 1814.

————. *Tales of Fashionable Life.* 1809; 1812. 6 vols. London: J. Johnson, 1812.

Frye, Northrop. *Anatomy of Criticism: Four Essays.* Princeton, N.J.: Princeton University Press, 1957.

————. *The Secular Scripture: A Study of the Structure of Romance.* Cambridge, Mass.: Harvard University Press, 1976.

Giroux, Henry A. "Paulo Freire and the Politics of Postcolonialism." In *Composition Theory for the Postmodern Classroom.* Ed. Gary A. Olson and Sidney I. Dobrin. Albany: State University of New York Press, 1994. 193–204.

Green, Martin. *Dreams of Adventure, Deeds of Empire.* New York: Basic Books, 1979.

————. *The Robinson Crusoe Story.* University Park: Pennsylvania State University Press, 1990.

Hulme, Peter. *Colonial Encounters: Europe and the Native Caribbean, 1492–1797.* London: Methuen, 1986.

Jameson, Fredric. *The Political Unconscious: Narrative as a Socially Symbolic Act.* Ithaca, N.Y.: Cornell University Press, 1981.

JanMohamed, Abdul R. "Worldliness-Without-World, Homelessness-as-Home: Toward a Definition of the Specular Border Intellectual." In *Edward Said: A Critical Reader.* Ed. Michael Sprinker. Oxford: Blackwell, 1992. 96–120.

Kaplan, Caren. "Deterritorializations: The Rewriting of Home and Exile in Western Feminist Discourse." *Cultural Critique* 6 (spring 1987): 187–98.

Kincaid, James R. *Child-Loving: The Erotic Child and Victorian Culture.* New York: Routledge, 1992.

Lamb, Charles. *The Letters of Charles and Mary Anne Lamb.* Ed. Edwin W. Marrs, Jr. Vol. 2: 1801–9. Ithaca, N.Y.: Cornell University Press, 1976.

Le Faye, Deirdre, ed. *Jane Austen's Letters.* 3d ed. Oxford: Oxford University Press, 1995.

Miller, J. Hillis. *Illustration.* Cambridge, Mass.: Harvard University Press, 1992.

Musgrave, Sir Richard. *Memoirs of the Different Rebellions in Ireland.* . . . 2d ed. Dublin: Milliken; London: Stockdale, 1801.

Myers, Mitzi. "'Completing the Union': Critical *Ennui*, the Politics of Narrative, and the Reformation of Irish Cultural Identity." *The Intersections of the Public and Private Spheres.* Ed. Paula R. Backscheider and Timothy Dykstal. *Prose Studies: History, Theory, Criticism* 18.3 (Dec. 1995): 41–77.

Ruskin, John. *The Works of John Ruskin.* Ed. E. T. Cook and Alexander Wedderburn. 39 vols. London: George Allen, 1903–12.

Scott, Sir Walter. *Waverley: Or, 'Tis Sixty Years Since.* Ed. Claire Lamont. The World's Classics. 1814. Oxford: Oxford University Press, 1986.

Somerville, E[dith] OE[none], and Martin Ross [Violet Martin]. *An Incorruptible Irishman: Being an Account of Chief Justice Charles Kendal Bushe . . . , 1767–1843.* London: Ivor Nicholson and Watson, 1932.

Parables and Parodies: Margaret Gatty's Audiences in the Parables from Nature

Alan Rauch

Born in 1809, six months after Charles Darwin, Margaret Scott Gatty is a name now in some danger of disappearing from the annals of both literature and science.[1] Although a prominent and early writer of literature for children, including *The Fairy-Godmothers* (1851), she is frequently lost in the shadow of her successful and now more popular daughter Juliana Horatia Ewing. And even though her advocacy of scientific pursuits, particularly for women, was ahead of its time, cultural historians of science regard her mainly as a quaint example of Victorian botanizers. Both views, I think, sell Margaret Gatty short, and they do so in at least two ways: first, because they insist on a formulaic separation between her work in "science" and her work in "literature"; and second, because Gatty's status as a writer for children and as a scientific amateur diminishes the current critical sense of her potential impact. In the following pages I want to argue that Gatty's influence was far more significant than we have been led to believe, and that her work, falsely divided between literature and science, involved a focused effort to use children's literature as a means of confronting one of the most serious issues in Victorian scientific culture. That this effort is expressed in a series of stories for children, her *Parables from Nature,* should not diminish its significance at all; Gatty, as I will argue, understood that in writing for children she would reach across audiences and, she hoped, across generations. Gatty's accomplishment as a writer with multiple audiences reminds us that the idea of audience, particularly in children's literature, is still not well defined. The readership of the *Parables,* like most works for children, included not merely the conventional notion of "adults" and "children," but also—among other categories—children being read to, adults reading for themselves, and adults rereading the literature of their childhoods.

I would like to express my appreciation to Susan Drain of Mount Saint Vincent University in Halifax, Nova Scotia, for generously providing archival materials and background information that were helpful in the writing of this essay.
Children's Literature 25, ed. Francelia Butler, R. H. W. Dillard, and Elizabeth Lennox Keyser, guest ed. Mitzi Myers and U. C. Knoepflmacher (Yale University Press, © 1997 Hollins College).

The enduringly successful *Parables from Nature,* a collection of wonderful stories drawn from natural history and published in various "series" from 1856 to 1861,[2] could be found on the reading list of virtually every middle-class child in the latter part of the nineteenth century. Although Gatty continued to write for children, she also published the *History of British Sea-Weeds* (1863), perhaps in an effort to stake a claim in the elevated discourse of serious scientific amateurs. Her *Sea-Weeds* is a staid, serious, and thorough work that extols the virtues of scientific knowledge and recommends algology as an appropriate pastime for both men and women who were interested in learning, as she writes in the introduction, about the "goodness of God." The remainder of the text is, for the most part, free of references to God or even natural theology; having made her point at the outset, Gatty recognizes that her readers have come to the text for facts and not for natural theology. Her willingness to set religious arguments aside may owe something to the *Parables,* in which she had already insisted on the necessary connection between God and nature. What Gatty's *Sea-Weeds* and the *Parables* have in common is a dedication to the notion that scientific curiosity is an essential part of the human intellect; both depend, the latter more explicitly than the former, on Gatty's strong belief that curiosity about nature can satisfy both the intellect and the soul.

The scientific curiosity that Gatty encourages in the *Parables from Nature* extends to both adults and children alike. Gatty, as U. C. Knoepflmacher has noted, found "adult sanction and adult purpose for the childlike wonder she extracted from nature" and in doing so was able to balance the audiences she knew would be drawn to her book (503). Recent scholars, including Knoepflmacher, Jacqueline Rose, and Peter Hunt, have reminded us that we need to tease out the complicated nexus of readers who come to children's literature. The endurance of "classics" may often be generated by the devotion of children, but it is guaranteed by the active assent of adults. And the willingness of adults to purchase and read children's books (both to themselves and to their offspring) may be only tangentially related to child-driven preferences. Indeed, this possibility became increasingly likely as children's literature grew more popular and as more writers of note began to try their hand at the genre. Thus although the prior reputation of an author (say, of Ruskin) or the professional status of an author (of a Kingsley) may have meant nothing to a child, it was of enormous importance to the adults who bought the works.

The dynamics of reading are worth pursuing briefly here in order to suggest how complex the notion of an "implied" reader in children's literature can be. Although recent criticism in children's literature has become more responsive to critical theory, it still has not undertaken a fully nuanced approach to the multiple audiences in children's literature or to the complicated intersections between children's authors and their many readers. The dominant paradigm for understanding the reading dynamics of children's literature posits a simple dyad, that between adult author and child reader, without going much further. Aidan Chambers, for example, who draws heavily on the work of Wolfgang Iser, does not address the conceptual shifts that adult readers surely undergo as they read children's literature together with children and separately on their own. Hugh Crago acknowledges this dynamic to a point, but aside from acknowledging that both children and adults derive comfort from the experience of joint reading, he claims that the adult ceases to have a role as an active reader.

The process of reading children's literature involves highly complicated scenarios. Adults are not merely coreaders with children; they are active readers on their own who may find themselves deeply engaged in material that they are ostensibly reading for others. And even when adults do read together with children, their status is anything but unproblematic. After all, although adults may have a clear sense of authorial status (as I have just suggested), children—especially preliterate children—do not. The reader, when reading aloud, may, in a child's eyes, *become* the author. That unspoken sense of empowerment—of authorial responsibility—surely complicates the reader's sense of responsibility and of self. What's more, the process of reading texts aloud involves interpretive gestures that must necessarily reconfigure the text at each reading. No doubt countless readers of this paper have, in the process of reading a children's story aloud, sensed, and perhaps responded to, the layering of the text.

The many states of readership in "adult" narrative increase significantly when adults actually collaborate with children in the process of reading.[3] Jacqueline Rose's argument, that children's literature always has an adult agenda, can be extended further if we remember that children will often recruit nearby adults to explain and rationalize the text in front of them. Yet even without prompting, adult readers may find the nicely laid-out arguments in children's books useful for their own consideration of the issues at hand. My purpose in underscoring these complexities is to open the range of possibilities of "reader response" in children's literature. This range is crucial for our understanding of Margaret Gatty's purpose and influence in the middle of the nineteenth century. Gatty's stories reveal a very sophisticated sense of "audience" at work. She clearly understood that by writing for children she gained a set of audiences that would give her work lasting significance. And the point is not simply that as a woman her potential audiences were limited; it is that by writing for children she felt that she could influence both present and future readers. Conscripted by the act of reading, adults would both absorb and transmit Gatty's views on religion and science while the audience of children were themselves amused and taught by the *Parables*.

What then was Gatty's ideological project in her *Parables*? Gatty's commitment to science was both sincere and rigorous, but her contribution to the culture of science is too often measured by her modest success with the publication of *British Sea-Weeds*. Yet the purpose of the *Sea-Weeds* was to advance science, not to change it. The *Parables*, on the other hand, map out an entirely different, and a more scientifically engaged, topic. Gatty created the *Parables* to cultivate a new generation of biologists who would find in her stories the strength to resist the growing materialist explanations.

Gatty knew, from her broad understanding of both recent scientific developments and instructional works for children, that children would absorb scientific knowledge from texts intended to bridge the nursery and the laboratory. That bridge, if left to the devices of secular popularizers of science, was fraught with danger. If the progress of knowledge could also be interpreted as a transition from viewing nature as divinely inspired to a completely materialist enterprise, someone had to intercede in order to restore nature's sacred foundation. To accomplish this goal, Gatty not only resisted interpretations of nature that were not grounded in the divine; she also argued forcefully against the very use of scientific theory, which distanced the role of God in nature, if it didn't eliminate it entirely. Her position was intensified after the publication of Darwin's *Origin of Species* in 1859, but it was always firmly rooted in the tradition of natural theology. Never shrill or strident, Gatty found a way to resist evolutionary and materialist thought by writing for an ostensibly young audience that would not yet have taken sides, as well as for an older audience, for whom the issues were neither resolved nor clear. Thus although her "parables" were amusing and pleasant to read, Victorian children were also learning from them that God and nature could never be treated separately. At the same time, their parents were being gently persuaded to take sides in a debate that, for many, was very much unresolved in their own minds. Although seldom referred to in "serious" histories of evolutionary debate,[4] Gatty undoubtedly helped shape popular attitudes about evolution in the latter part of the century. Having found a way to participate in that debate without calling attention to either herself or her purpose, she wrote a work that was "one of the most famous and highly praised Victorian books for children," according to Diane Johnson (v). There has rarely been a time when *The Parables*, in one form or another, have been out of print.[5]

The charm of Gatty's *Parables* belies the fact that they also formed an important critique of evolutionary theory just at the point of its emergence. Wendy Katz, in her discussion of Gatty's later *Book of Emblems*, notes that both the *Parables* and the *Emblems* were "attempts to counter the assault on religion from science" (47). Although this observation is undoubtedly true, it stops short of recognizing a more ambitious project. Like Charles Kingsley, whose *Glaucus* (1855) must surely have influenced her,[6] Gatty was still interested in preserving science as an acceptable and edifying expression of religious belief without allowing the more pernicious explanatory elements of science to replace abiding faith in the divine. Slipped into her tales of personified animals, plants, and scientific specimens are narratives that seek to undermine the kind of presumption that Gatty associated with the speculation and theory behind evolutionary thought. Gatty, as Gillian Beer has pointed out, attacks "the assumption of full explanation within the natural order, and also on that vastly extended time-scale which makes everything possible" (140–41). Beer's reading of Gatty, though brief, recognizes the way that Gatty exploits and satirizes Darwin's own methods of argumentation. By accentuating Darwin's broad generalities and his "concealed" anthropocentrism (which is more arrogant from a religious perspective), Gatty finds a way to use Darwin's own rhetoric not only against him, but also for her own purposes.

Published in several different series, Gatty's *Parables* undertake the modest but purposeful enterprise of training children to think about science in moral terms. Part of Gatty's effort was to have readers focus on the real rather than the imagined. "Observation and Revelation," observes the Bookworm, a character in "Knowledge Not the Limit of Belief," "are the sole means of acquiring knowledge." Thus although her stories—which include talking plants and animals—use fancy, they avoid fantasy. *The Parables,* however whimsical, are always grounded in the observable and the empirical.[7] In later series of *The Parables,* Gatty included detailed notes that contextualized the natural history of the characters in her stories. The impatient House Cricket in "Waiting," who considers himself imperfect within the scheme of nature, learns that he must wait for his true purpose to be realized. What drives the story is a teleological lesson that grounds virtually all of Gatty's work. In Gatty's preordained world, it is essential to know the facts. We therefore learn in the published endnotes to "Waiting" that "*Gryllus domesticus,* the House Cricket, belongs to the same order as *Stenobothrus viridulus,* the common grass-hopper of our meadows and grassy hill-sides. Nay, it even belongs to the same section of the Order, viz. to the *Saltatoria,* or 'jumpers;' but to a different family or tribe, the *Gryllodea;* whereas *Stenobothrus viridulus* is of the family *Acridiodea*" (444).[8]

For many readers these are, as Gatty understood, "hard words," but she insists on using them nonetheless. Her notes remind us that the subject at hand is real and that part of our function is to classify and learn about the "real." Nevertheless, although scientific explanations such as those found in the notes are salutary, our attempts to go beyond mere classification are a useless—if not defiant—effort. And, not unlike the cricket who doubts that God has a design for his particular species, humans who interpret their existence on materialist grounds alone come perilously close to a similar lack of faith. In the chirp of the cricket, we can contemplate and interpret the meaning of our own existence: "They sing a song of hope fulfilled; and though in that glad music there be neither speech nor language which we can recognise as such, there is yet a voice to be heard among them by all who love to listen, with reverent delight, to the sweet harmonies and deep analogies of nature."[9] Gatty's comprehensive notes to her parables and her own interest in science are, for her, analogous to the song of the cricket. To suppress the intellectual capacity for scientific inquiry would be to deny a uniquely human characteristic that must clearly be part of a greater plan for the understanding of God.

The tension between the importance of scientific research and the impertinence of theoretical speculation is central to any reading of Gatty. Her stories, not to mention her *British Sea-Weeds,* emphasize the need for clear, methodical, and focused collection and analysis. She insists to the reader that interpretation beyond the intense work of classification and description is an undertaking for which the human mind is inadequate. "Only let natural history be pursued with 'reverence,'" she warns aspiring algologists, "so that we may not become conceited with our beautiful but imperfect 'broken lights'" (xx). The amateur pursuit of algology can be, she continues, "a fountain of perpetual enjoyment, and a resource against thousands of lesser and often foolish disturbances of life, which are otherwise so apt to lay too keen a hold upon the mind, especially of those who lead quiet uneventful lives." As a strategy to limit the digressions of idle minds, Gatty's prescription gives fair warning to armchair naturalists who might be swayed by reading scientific theory without even having gotten their feet wet.[10]

But scientists themselves, as Gatty well knows, are not immune to the attractions of speculation and theory. Gatty mocks, for example, scientific arrogance in "Knowledge Not the Limit of Belief," a story that places her readers within earshot of a discussion between the specimens in a Naturalist's study. All of the specimens are impressed by the remarkable powers demonstrated by science—represented by two naturalists whose studies of a seaweed reveal it to be a form of plant life. A zoophyte, "observing" their meticulous work, is convinced that "there are no powers beyond those that man possesses." ("First Series," 22) The zoophyte is restricted, she reminds us, to a very narrow range of sense capabilities and is easily impressed by things beyond the realm of mere sense. The analogy is clear and owes a great deal to traditional natural theology: we are to God as the zoophyte is to the naturalist. In Gatty's story, "Inferior Animals," human presumption to "be as God in knowledge" forms the basis of her most savage critique of theory in general, and of evolutionary theory in particular (see fig. 1). It is a witty parody that turns the logic of evolutionary theory around on itself. The reader learns from an assembled council of scholarly rooks, who have gathered at their equivalent of the Linnean Society (or perhaps the British Association for the Advancement of Science), that the "inferior animals" in question are human beings, "the thin-skinned, clothes-wearing creatures" who "still hop lop-sided on the ground." ("Second Series," 35–36) The dominant speaker is a rook who has taken on the troubling question of the origin of mankind.[11] The answer, according to the speaker, is clear: "My friends, man is not our superior, was never so, for he is neither more nor less than a degenerated brother of our own race! Yes, I venture confidently to look back thousands of generations, and I see that *men* were once *rooks!* Like us they were covered with

Figure 1. William Paton Burton's (1828–83) illustration for "Inferior Animals" (*Parables from Nature*, 2d ser. [London: George Bell and Sons, 1897], 29). Burton was only one of many distinguished artists, including E. Burne-Jones, W. Holman Hunt, and John Tenniel, who illustrated Gatty's *Parables*.

feathers, like us lived in trees, flew instead of walking, roosted instead of squatting in stone boxes, and were happy and contented as we are now!" ("Second Series," 30). The description of the degeneration of rooks into human beings is Gatty's attempt to ridicule the possibility of the evolutionary development of species in general. Gatty gathers "scientific" evidence of humans trying to regain their rooklike features by living in brick highrises and by smearing the landscape in soot in what might be called atavistic impulses. Her approach relies on a clear understanding of the theoretical arguments behind the development of species and her target—Darwin's evolutionary theory—was from a text that would resonate with adult readers only. Her exaggerations are familiar because she is drawing on a rhetorical style adopted by contemporary theoretical discourse, which many of her adult readers surely found appealing, if not fully persuasive. Parodies thrive, to a great extent, not merely on their ability to mimic a form, but on the rhetorical strength of the form they mimic. A strong parodist, Gatty teased out an imitative approach that offered the broadest comic possibilities for the greatest number of readers. Evolutionary development, which relied heavily on the logic of inference, could easily be parodied in a way that would be instructive for adults and amusing to children, and thus could function as a corrective for both. George Levine has noted that Darwin "could not avoid the fictions of hypothesis" (101), and that the stylistic roots of *The Origin* can be found in Paley's *Natural Theology*. Gatty almost certainly felt the rhetorical force of Darwin's secular adaptation of Paley and understood that her critique of evolutionary theory could not simply dismiss it on the basis of logic. She needed, as she explained to William Henry Harvey, to use Darwin's logic as a tool against him: "Of course Darwin's theories are the moving cause of my attempting the subject but with his theory I have not meddled at all. I have only shown that other fools may build up other theories & prove them by facts, & be in the dark at the end. The rook's argument is very fair and conclusive for a rook. Man's arguments (whether Darwin's or Lamarck's or anybody else's) to show how God created the world & its various creatures may be very fair & conclusive—for a man—But the one may be as great & utter bosh & misconception as the other."[12]

However amusing Gatty's tale of the rooks is, it presupposes an understanding, if not an appreciation of, evolutionary development and thus, in a sense, invites the possibility of undermining itself as a parody. In other words, the effectiveness of Gatty's parody of evolutionary thought relies on the persuasiveness and perhaps even the effectiveness of the original argument. The following passage, which explains (in Lamarckian terms) how the human arm developed— from a prototypical rook's wing—is a case in point. Calculated to ridicule the notion of descent with modification, it is actually more suggestive and provocative than Gatty could have ever anticipated:

> Now it is well known to you all, by observation of our young ones, that wings grow by use. After the young brood make efforts at flying, those necessary appendages increase. Thus much, therefore, is clear. Practice brings power, and power brings on growth and enlargement. And, in a similar manner, want of practice brings a falling away of strength, and diminution in size. Why, then, should there be any insuperable difficulty in further believing it

possible that the never-used and consequently constantly dimin-
ishing wings of generation after generation, should disappear at
last entirely as wings, leaving only the outer bone remaining, as
a sort of claw whereby to lay hold on what was wanted—bared of
all its beauty and ornament,—in fact, the long uncouth arm of
the present man? ("Second Series," 32)

Gatty's juxtaposition of arm and wing poses the very question that
troubled or at least hounded comparative anatomists, including Darwin's foe, Richard Owen, for years: how is it that two such radically
different structures, could—in the final analysis—be so remarkably
similar?

Gatty's emphasis on the effects of "use and disuse" seems more
than accidental. Darwin, in the first edition of *The Origin,* places a
great deal of emphasis on "habit," or use and disuse. Having noticed
that the wing bones of domestic ducks are lighter than those of their
wild counterparts, Darwin concludes that the "change may be safely
attributed to the domestic duck flying much less, and walking more,
than its wild parent" (11). Darwin pursues a similar theme much later
in the work when, using a generalized genus of birds, he speculates
that the forelimbs might, by "a long course of modification," become
"adapted in one descendant to act as hands, in another as paddles, in
another as wings" (447). Gatty, perhaps recognizing the weaknesses
in an argument based on use and disuse (weaknesses that Darwin
himself was intensely aware of), creates a text that, with humor and
wit, echoes some striking images from *The Origin.* Through her inversion of Darwin's argument, Gatty suggests that the existence of
individual species has less to do with phylogenetic commonality, or
with the habits of use and disuse, than with divine will. To accept the
logic behind Darwin's flexible protobird is to accept the very same
logic argued by her philosophical rook.

But although "Inferior Animals" may have struck many readers as
a powerful critique of evolution, it must also have provoked others to
speculate—quite seriously—not about degeneration but "generation"
or evolution. The parody actually puts the very question that Gatty
wanted her readers to avoid in sharper focus. Like so many writers
before her, and like many who followed, Gatty is finally caught in
the inevitable dilemma faced by writers who want to accept science
but reject science's logic and method. Though intended to quell the
overreaching curiosity of young minds, *The Parables,* which endured

at children's bedsides for decades, may well have prompted as many questions as it answered. Gatty understood that the only role that she could play in the fight against evolutionary theory—a task that she understood as daunting—was as a writer for children. To attempt a broader polemic was too complicated for any single author or any one approach: "The human mind is so variously constituted in different people that Mr. Darwin may not derive as much poison from his own book as other people do. He may have some curious muddle-headed confusion of brain which enables him to believe in a great Creator & a great creative "Natural Selection" (capitals of course) at the same time. I confess I am unable to do so. Indeed if you have really read 'Inferior Animals' in the Red Snow volume, you must see that I have combated the Darwin presumption as far as I could in a small way, & without entering lists which I was not qualified for." [13]

Gatty's sense of the battles for which she was qualified had less to do with the extent of her scientific knowledge than it did with her sense of the proper social order. One only has to read Gatty's "Law of Authority and Obedience" to appreciate how deeply she respected the divisions between class, social position, and, of course, gender (fig. 2).[14] In order to critique the scientific establishment of Darwin, Owen, or even Chambers, Gatty would have to have challenged those who already excluded women and amateurs from the formal practice of science. Her effort, as the wife of a cleric and a mother, is grounded in the moral consequences of scientific theory on the intellectual lives of children and their guardians. "I am not such a fool," she wrote to William Harvey, "to be tussling with Darwin's or any body's theories. I cannot suppose that I can quiz their specialties: &, between Darwin and the Vestiges how am I qualified to distinguish and decide?" [15]

Far from being foolish, Gatty understood that *The Parables* would serve her purpose without breaching the prevailing rules of social standing. What is more, she knew that by choosing to write for children, she was not necessarily losing an adult audience. The parents, governesses, teachers, and guardians who either read to children or were read to by children formed a considerable part of her audience. They, no less than the children, were the target of the challenging teleological questions posed in *The Parables*. Gatty's "drift," as she described it, "to show that there may be, in the limited faculties of the investigator, an insuperable bar to his coming to just conclusions," almost seems to presume that her logic will find adult sympathizers.

Figure 2. Margaret Gatty herself chose to illustrate "Training and Restraining" (*Parables from Nature*, 2d ser. [London: Bell and Daldy, 1861?], 80), by depicting a child and an adult reading together, rather than portraying the events of the story (although a climbing plant can be seen on the window sill). In the parable itself, a group of garden flowers is persuaded to abandon the "unnatural" supports provided by the gardener, only to be beaten down by wind and rain. A young girl, comparable in age to the child depicted in the illustration, observes the scene of destruction and realizes "the necessity of training, restraint, and culture, for us as well as for flowers, in a fallen world" (93).

It's difficult to gauge Gatty's effect on the generations that followed. Her stories clearly had lasting appeal, and Gatty's resistance to evolution and her rejection of theory were not exceptional. One of Gatty's most famous readers was the young Rudyard Kipling who acknowledges his debt to the *Parables* in his autobiography, *Something of Myself* (22). Gatty's influence is unmistakable in the parable-like collection known as the *Just So Stories*, which uses animal narratives to suggest that the world can't be understood on the basis of organic or systematic laws. Kipling turns what might be considered Darwinian adaptations—the camel's hump, the rhinoceros's skin, and the elephant's nose—into moral fables about irascibility, gluttony, and insatiable curiosity. Like Gatty, Kipling is interested in shaping the behavior of his child readers and, following Gatty's lead, he does so by turning science on its ear in a way that was sure to intrigue adults. Kipling also shares and extends Gatty's interest in preserving a strong social order in England. "Mother Hive," a story published as part of *Actions and Reactions* (91–116), not only reiterates Gatty's earlier themes of proper social order, mapped out through the hierarchy of bees in "The Law of Authority and Obedience," but intensifies their urgency by adding the threat of unwanted parasites, the Wax-moths, who seek to infiltrate and erode the very structures of bee life.[16] It is a political fable that all but leaves child readers behind, and in doing so recognizes that the audience for moral parables need not be juvenile. Stories such as "Mother Hive" suggest not only the extent of Gatty's influence (something she hoped for), but also an understanding of Gatty's methodological strategy. Kipling, once the child reader, is now the adult writer, and it is clear that his early reading experience informs the strategy of his mature ideological project.

The effect of children's literature on its many readers is remarkable indeed. Contemporary readers who enjoyed Kipling's "How the Alphabet Was Made" as children may, as adults, find the deterministic ascendancy of English (*the* alphabet in question), full of disturbing colonial implications. As both Gatty and Kipling knew, however, it is equally likely that unreconstructed versions of children's literature continue to influence us in ways of which we are unaware. The "enchantment" of children's literature may be more than a simple cliché, because it does serve to charm and instruct critical and uncritical readers alike by narratives that are amusing and beguiling. That the very same narratives set up ideological structures that are easily absorbed and often repeated is something that is only rarely considered by the readers themselves. The effect of children's narrative can be powerful indeed, especially when the "balance" between the appeal to children and the appeal to adults is handled delicately.

Margaret Gatty, as U. C. Knoepflmacher has argued persuasively, handled that balance remarkably well. Gatty knew that her most important and most enduring contribution to science was tucked neatly inside her *Parables from Nature*. It was, she hoped, through the *Parables* that readers would reformulate their conception of scientific practice and their estimation of scientific "fact." Gatty found a way to enter the major controversy of her day—a debate from which most women were excluded—and to make an important contribution to its development. Gatty's concluding story in her *Parables*, "A Vision" ("Second Series," 121–26), almost seems to reflect on her project as a whole. It is an autobiographical narrative that describes a Sunday morning walk that leads the distracted narrator into a rustic church "disfigured by 'daubings' " and "hideous straight lines," instead of into her own "aesthetically restored church." But in the "simple yet majestic Service that followed," the narrator comes to understand the powerful meaning of a passage "so often heard without emotion." Gatty suggests that the "vision" of the narrator is an experience open to all readers who are willing to glean simple truths even in the most humble narrative settings. This final story can thus be taken as a parable on the very act of reading the *Parables*. It is a message intended to recruit all of her audience, whether they had been charmed by her stories or not, and it implicitly recognizes that every one of the many readers of children's literature is worth the writer's attention.

Notes

1. For biographical details about Margaret Gatty, see Juliana Horatia Ewing's "Memoir of Margaret Gatty," Christabel Maxwell's somewhat erratic biography, and Gillian Avery's biography of Ewing. Susan Drain provides an interesting discussion of Gatty's work on seaweeds, as well as of the tension between amateurs and professionals.

2. The publishing history of *The Parables* is somewhat complex. There were five "series," each of which included additional stories, although each individual series was reprinted. The stories themselves had often appeared in separate publications such as *The Monthly Packet*. The notes and illustrations to *The Parables* appear in an 1861 illustrated edition that included the first and second series.

3. In addition to the important work by Iser, Stanley Fish's *Is There a Text in This Class?* is useful in suggesting the possible range of "interpretive communities," particularly when we keep in mind the fact that Fish relies on the idea of the class text as a main trope. And although Fredric Jameson essentially ignores works for children, his arguments about the political nature of narrative are essential to the criticism of seemingly apolitical children's literature.

4. The otherwise thorough works by recent scholars such as Peter Bowler, Adrian Desmond, and James Moore pay scant attention to critics of evolutionary theory outside of the traditional forums for discussion.

5. Recently, a number of parables have been "retold" as predominantly Christian fables in books by Pat Wynnejones. Wynnejones's retellings are meant to reach a younger audience, and although they retain some of the charm of Gatty's stories, they are compromised, in my view, both by a mawkish piety and by the loss of intriguing scientific detail.

6. Kingsley's *Water Babies*, which like Gatty's works conveys an interest in scientific parables for children, was not published until 1863. For a discussion of the *Water Babies* in the context of Kingsley's fiction, see my essay on *Alton Locke*.

7. Gatty's work appeared during a period that Michael Hearn has called a "golden age for the literary British fairy tale" (xix). It was also a time when science, as a subject of popular interest for young and old, was pervasive.

8. The endnotes can be found in the Garland reprint edition of the *Parables*, which has a preface by Diane Johnson.

9. This citation and all remaining citations are from the 1899 edition of *The Parables*, which is split into "First Series" and "Second Series." *Parables*, "First Series," 35.

10. In an interesting digression in her *British Sea-Weeds*, Gatty considers the influence of climate on the distribution of marine plants and specifically addresses the difference in vegetations between two locations sharing the same latitude. The prevailing theory, "with a diagram in its favour" Gatty notes sarcastically, is that the changes are due to "Gulfstream influence." Gatty dismisses such speculation as "rather a mythical idea" and directs the reader instead to the experiential evidence provided by Captain Maury. "People may adopt which theory they like best," she warns her theoretically disposed readers, "but those of have seen the coast of County Clare, the Isle of Man, and the northeast shores of England, will have a strong leaning towards Maury's creed" (xvi).

11. Gatty's decision to make rooks the protagonists of her story may owe something to the status they are given in Robert Chambers's *Vestiges of Creation* (1844). "The corvidae," Chambers argues with a nod toward William Swainson's work in ornithology, are "our parallel in aves" (275); "the superior organization and character of the corvidae" is reflected in the fact that, like humans, "they are adapted for all climates, and accordingly found all over the world" (270–71).

12. HAS 48:149–50. Gatty to William Henry Harvey, 4 May 1861. In the Sheffield City Archives.

13. HAS 52:12–14. Gatty to Mrs. Carter (George Johnston's daughter). 13 Mar. 1862. In the Sheffield City Archives.

14. Moderation and respect for social order is also the dominant theme of "Out of the Way" in Gatty's *Aunt Judy's Tales*. Franz, the central character, learns from experience that he must neither aspire too low nor too high. At the conclusion of the story, secure in a bourgeois ideology, he returns home to join in his "old partner's prosperous business" (138).

15. HAS 48:149–50. Gatty to William Henry Harvey, 4 May 1861. In the Sheffield City Archives.

16. It is perhaps worth noting that "The Law of Authority and Obedience" is one of the stories retold by Pat Wynnejones in her "Story of Benjamin the Bee" in an effort to promote "contentment and a willingness to use the particular gifts God has given us, so that the whole 'body' . . . works together" (endpaper). Given that this piece is part of a religious series, the interest in conformity and submission to social and institutional hierarchies is not surprising.

Works Cited

Avery, Gillian. *Mrs. Ewing.* London: Bodley Head, 1961.

Beer, Gillian. *Darwin's Plots: Evolutionary Narrative in Darwin, George Eliot and Nineteenth-Century Fiction.* Boston: Ark Paperbacks, 1983.

Bowler, Peter. *Theories of Human Evolution: A Century of Debate, 1844–1944.* Baltimore, Md.: Johns Hopkins University Press, 1986.

Chambers, Aidan. "The Reader in the Book." Repr. in *Children's Literature: The Development of Criticism.* Ed. Peter Hunt. New York: Routledge, 1990. 91–114.

Chambers, Robert. *Vestiges of the Natural History of Creation and Other Evolutionary Writings.* 1844. Ed. James A. Secord. Chicago: University of Chicago Press, 1994.

Crago, Hugh. "The Roots of Response." Repr. in *Children's Literature: The Development of Criticism*. Ed. Peter Hunt. New York: Routledge, 1990. 118–31.

Darwin, Charles. *On the Origin of Species*. 1859. Introduction by Ernst Mayer. Cambridge, Mass.: Harvard University Press, 1964.

Desmond, Adrian. *The Politics of Evolution*. Chicago: University of Chicago Press, 1989.

Drain, Susan. "Marine Botany in the Nineteenth Century: Margaret Gatty, the Lady Amateurs and the Professionals." *Victorian Studies Association Newsletter* (Ontario, Canada) 53 (1994): 6–11.

Ewing, Juliana Horatia. "Memoir of Margaret Gatty." In Gatty, *Parables of Nature*. London: George Bell, 1899.

Fish, Stanley. *Is There a Text in This Class?* Cambridge, Mass.: Harvard University Press, 1987.

Gatty, Margaret. *Aunt Judy's Tales*. London: Bell and Daldy, 1863.

———. *British Sea-Weeds*. 1863. London: Bell and Daldy, 1872.

———. *Parables from Nature*. "First Series" and "Second Series." London: George Bell and Sons, 1899.

Hearn, Michael. *The Victorian Fairy Tale Book*. New York: Pantheon, 1988.

Hunt, Peter. "Poetics and Practicality: Children's Literature and Theory in Britain." *The Lion and the Unicorn* 19.1 (June 1995): 41–49.

Iser, Wolfgang. *The Implied Reader*. Baltimore, Md.: Johns Hopkins University Press, 1974.

Jameson, Fredric. *The Political Unconscious: Narrative as a Socially Symbolic Act*. Ithaca, N.Y.: Cornell University Press, 1981.

Johnson, Diane. "Preface." Garland reprint of *Parables of Nature*. New York: Garland, 1976.

Katz, Wendy R. *The Emblems of Margaret Gatty: A Study of Allegory in Nineteenth-Century Children's Literature*. New York: AMS Press, 1993.

Kingsley, Charles. *Glaucus, or Wonders of the Shore*. Cambridge: MacMillan, 1855.

Kipling, Rudyard. *Actions and Reactions*. 1909. In *The Writings in Prose and Verse of Rudyard Kipling*. New York: Charles Scribner's Sons, 1925.

———. *Something of Myself and Other Autobiographical Writings*. 1937. Ed. Thomas Pinney. Cambridge: Cambridge University Press, 1990.

———. *Just So Stories*. 1912. Harmondsworth, Eng.: Signet Classic, 1974.

Knoepflmacher, U. C. "The Balancing of Child and Adult: An Approach to Victorian Fantasies for Children." *Nineteenth-Century Fiction* 37.4 (Mar. 1983): 497–530.

Levine, George. *Darwin Among the Novelists*. Cambridge, Mass.: Harvard University Press, 1987.

Maxwell, Christabel. *Mrs. Gatty and Mrs. Ewing*. London: Constable, 1949.

Merrill, Lynn. *The Romance of Victorian Natural History*. Oxford: Oxford University Press, 1989.

Moore, James. *The Post-Darwinian Controversies*. Cambridge: Cambridge University Press, 1979.

Rauch, Alan. "The Tailor Transformed: Kingsley's *Alton Locke*." *Studies in the Novel* 25.2 (summer 1993): 196–213.

Rose, Jacqueline. *The Case of Peter Pan; or The Impossibility of Children's Fiction*. 1984. Philadelphia: University of Pennsylvania Press, 1993.

Wynnejones, Pat. *The Story of Benjamin Bee*. Belleville, Mich.: Lion, 1984.

———. *The Story of Charlotte Caterpillar*. Belleville, Mich.: Lion, 1984.

———. *The Story of Jeremy Cricket*. Belleville, Mich.: Lion, 1984.

———. *The Story of Robin Redbreast*. Belleville, Mich.: Lion, 1984.

"The Best Magazine for Children of All Ages": Cross-Editing St. Nicholas Magazine (1873–1905)

Susan R. Gannon

The Children's Magazine: A "Space in Between"

In its "golden age" under the guidance of founding editor Mary Mapes Dodge, *St. Nicholas Magazine* was considered the finest literary magazine for children ever produced.[1] Many would say it has yet to be surpassed. In her celebrated article "Children's Magazines," written for Roswell Smith of *Scribner's Monthly* just before she undertook her editorial duties on *St. Nicholas,* Dodge stressed the importance of measuring the contents of a publication to the child's needs. "A child's magazine is its pleasure-ground," she said. "Let there be no sermonizing . . . no wearisome spinning out of facts, no rattling of the dry bones of history." She expressed concern that "the little magazine-readers find what they look for and be able to pick up what they find." "Boulders," she said, "will not go into tiny baskets" (353). Yet there was always a fair amount of discreet sermonizing in *St. Nicholas,* and the magazine was, in fact, addressed not only to children but to a very important audience of adults.

This significant secondary audience of adults—a key factor in the success of any literary magazine for children—raises a number of problems. For one, the "adult" implied in the diverse fictions, features, and editorial projects of the magazine is as elusive an abstraction as the "child" to be found there. Such constructs conceal as much as they reveal of the complex motivations, ideological assumptions, and lived experience from which they arise. Jacqueline Rose has spoken eloquently about the way the enterprise of children's fiction "hangs on" "the impossible relation between adult and child," "setting up a world in which the adult comes first (author, maker, giver) and the child comes after (reader, product, receiver), but where neither of them enter the space in between" (1–2). The children's periodical—exemplified here by *St. Nicholas*—certainly

Children's Literature 25, ed. Francelia Butler, R. H. W. Dillard, and Elizabeth Lennox Keyser, guest ed. Mitzi Myers and U. C. Knoepflmacher (Yale University Press, © 1997 Hollins College).

shares that "impossibility" in the sense of being written and produced by adults for a primary and defining audience of children. But
St. Nicholas was also for adults. And I think the magazine did offer its
readers something of a "space in between," where differing—sometimes age-specific—visions of child-adult relations could be figured,
tested, and vigorously discussed.

The care with which the magazine addressed its primary audience
of children has been documented elsewhere.[2] This paper explores
less familiar territory: the way *St. Nicholas* catered to its significant
secondary audience of adults and the importance of this audience
as a presence in the magazine's reading environment. One popular
strain of formula fiction that appears often in *St. Nicholas*—the fiction
of benevolent intervention in which a caring adult rescues a dependent or needy child—will exemplify the way fiction in the magazine
allowed adult and child readers to reflect on the issues of power and
dependency so central to their relations. In terms of vocabulary, the
presence of child role-models, illustration, and even many details of
address, such stories look child-oriented. Yet they were constructed
to offer the possibility of an alternative kind of reading for adults. I
will examine a sampling of such stories, looking in some detail at two
pieces written by Lucy G. Morse, whose work Dodge particularly admired. Frances Hodgson Burnett's *Little Lord Fauntleroy* became a best-
selling novel perhaps in part because of the enthusiasm with which
Dodge used her "pulpit" in *St. Nicholas* to promote it and to encourage
a particular way of reading it. A study of Dodge's editorial handling of
this novel will suggest the way young and old were drawn into a community of readers whose vivid responses to Burnett's novel raise compelling questions about the image of childhood it presented to them.

Editing St. Nicholas *for the Adult Reader*

In November 1873 the innovative magazine for adults, *Scribner's
Monthly,* proclaimed the arrival of Scribner and Company's new magazine for children, *St. Nicholas:* "Whether we shall lead the little child,
or the little child shall lead us, remains to be seen; but it will be pleasant to have him at our side, to watch his growth and development,
and to minister, as we may, to his prosperity. . . . Wherever 'SCRIB-
NER' goes, 'ST. NICHOLAS' ought to go. They will be harmonious companions in the family, and the helpers of each other in the work of
instruction, culture and entertainment" (Erisman 378). Having made

clear that they envisioned America's premier magazine for children as family fare, the publishers sought testimonials from prominent educators, ministers, and men of letters endorsing the magazine as fine family reading, with something for everyone. Bayard Taylor reported that all the members of his "old homestead were charmed with the volume." Dr. R. Shelton MacKenzie, of the Philadelphia *Press,* admitted he had "found heaps of things in ST. NICHOLAS" that he "had forgotten, had imperfectly known, *or had been wholly ignorant of,*" so, he conceded, "I too, sit at the feet of Gamaliel." And Charles Dudley Warner vowed that "the best magazine for children of all ages" was actually even more entertaining for grown people than some of the quarterlies ("What Some Eminent Men Think of *St. Nicholas*" 1).

Adults were addressed unmistakably in much of the commercial and editorial advertising for the magazine. The ads for clothing, services, medicines, self-help projects, reading matter, and games suggest a readership presumed to be ambitious, hard-working, concerned about its health, interested in the liberal Christian press, well traveled, and often in a position to make decisions about the furnishing of schools, churches, and other institutions. The editorial advertising assumes adult readers will be civilized, literate, pious in a general way, and anxious to do all that might be possible to place children in their care in the best position to achieve security and success in a difficult world. "A Word to Subscribers" in one early issue proclaims the magazine's *"necessity"* "to every home-circle," noting the *"healthy, earnest, and inspiriting occupation, the practical and hopeful views of life, the lessons in correct taste, the habits of inquiry and investigation, the awakening of new interest—*in short, the *varied instruction and pleasure* afforded by ST. NICHOLAS, all tending toward a *thorough and general improvement"* (2). Parents were told that the magazine presented the work of the finest authors and illustrators money could buy, and that its volumes represented the core of a fine home library. Editorial ads boasted of the "galaxy of eminent men and women" that *St. Nicholas* "by some hook or crook beguiled into writing for its lucky children" ("True Story," 7), including such luminaries of the adult literary world as Alcott, Twain, Burnett, Longfellow, Kipling, Whittier, Tennyson, and certainly a great many of the most popular writers for *Scribner's Monthly* (later the *Century*). And prominent illustrators of the day were said to have contributed pictures that were "often works of real art, not only as engravings, but as compositions of original design" ("True Story," 8).

Editorial comment in *St. Nicholas,* whether in Dodge's "Jack-in-the-Pulpit" column, the "Letter-Box," later book reviews, or the occasional note to readers, appeals to the adult, either directly, or "over the shoulder of" the child reader. When Dodge's son, James M. Dodge, spoke at commencement exercises of a school in Philadelphia, his address, "The Money Value of Training," was printed in *St. Nicholas* with an editorial commendation to the attention of "the older boy readers . . . and their parents" (57). Everywhere in the editorial departments there are humorous asides, jokes, and solemn nonsense that only an adult would be likely to "get." One hellishly hot August, for example, Dodge produced a solemn parody of her usually earnest "Jack-in-the-Pulpit" column for those who could enjoy it (the parents), and dismissed her young readers to run and play rather than bother to read it (*St. Nicholas,* Aug. 1875, 648–49). Often, information about books and services for children or about deserving charities would be directed to parents. If letters printed in the "Letter-Box" provided a group self-image for the juvenile readers (Gannon and Thompson 117–18), adults could share the contributions of like-minded parents and guardians who encouraged their children's critical thinking by discussing with them the magazine's contents. The letters from such ordinary caretakers were supplemented by communications from celebrities and experts in different fields, all written in the *St. Nicholas* mode—which was friendly, uncondescending, intelligent, and positive.

Dodge was aware that few editors succeeded at editing for parents and their children. She thought that most children's magazines were, if anything, too timidly edited "for the approval of fathers and mothers," the result being "a milk-and-water variety of the adult's periodical" (352). Dodge eliminated material she thought might be sectarian, politically divisive, or morally offensive to her readership (Gannon and Thompson 138–50). But her editorial policies were less stodgy than those of her editorial colleague at the *Century,* Richard Gilder, who was notorious as the editor who trimmed and polished *Huckleberry Finn* for his readers. Dodge was not prudish, and she often praised books she had cut for her own pages when they appeared, without those cuts, in hard covers. Like other magazine editors of her time and place, Dodge seemed to feel that she had entered into a sort of unspoken contract with her subscribers that whatever appeared under her aegis would be wholesome and improving. And she appreciated the risk that purchasers of *St. Nicholas* took when they bought a whole package of readings because it had her imprimatur. As another well-known editor of the period put it, "The buyer of a magazine buys a variety of literature. He may buy it for one thing, yet have another, for which he also pays, thrust upon him. The buyer of a book on the other hand knows—or should know—what he is getting in for" (Burlingame 83).

There is evidence that many contributors expected their work to be read by the young and the old. While writing *Jack and Jill* for Dodge, Louisa May Alcott confided to her, "Fathers & Mothers tell me they use my books as helps for themselves, so now & then I like to slip in a page for them, fresh from the experience of some other parent" (Alcott 237). John T. Trowbridge noted that he "was sometimes amused by hearing of a parent carrying home the periodical containing an installment of one of . . . [his] serials, and hiding it from the younger members of the household until he had enjoyed the first reading of the chapters." In fact, Trowbridge thought that "one secret of their success" was that his stories, "written ostensibly for the young, were intended for older readers as well" (*My Own Story*, 331). Realistic fiction like Trowbridge's sometimes needed to be cut in order to pass muster with the more censorious segment of the adult audience. Dodge's friend Lucy Morse felt it necessary to address the adult readership's possible alarm at their children's being exposed to the speech of the New York streets in her story "The Ash-Girl." She opened the story by telling young readers they were about to read a painful and possibly disturbing story about a girl who "saw a kind of life from which your parents would shield you with loving tenderness." Morse added, "I shall have to repeat the language she used, and perhaps, tell you of some of the things she saw and heard; but if you will read my story carefully to the end, I do not believe it will hurt you" (386). Working-class speech, immigrants' accented speech, or regional speech appear in much of the magazine's realistic fiction, and it is pretty clear that house standards simply required that such effects be toned down to a tolerable level. More problematic was colorful slang of the sort children might pick up and quote. This tended to be cut, when possible.[3]

Behavior that might offer a bad example to children was also censored. In the magazine's illustrations, Gellett Burgess's goops were not allowed to stick their tongues out, Twain's Huck and Tom could not go barefoot, and a maiden's skirts could not swirl immodestly above her ankles (Gannon and Thompson 138–41). Indeed, Dodge,

like other editors of the period, was adept at deflecting attention
from risky material by providing innocuous illustrations for it. For
one Trowbridge serial she refused to allow a drunk scene to be illustrated and—over the author's protests—had his rough-and-tumble
heroes depicted as fresh-faced innocents.⁴ Titles that might attract
the wrong sort of attention from adult readers became anathema at
St. Nick. When Frank Stockton offered her a series with the word *pirate*
in its title, Dodge sweetly replied, "You will probably suggest a better
title. You see we don't mind telling about Pirates . . . but to say 'Pirate'
in one's title provokes the wrath of parents and guardians at the very
outset of a serial's career. We *have* done it—but it is . . . hardly safe to
do it again."⁵ A number of Dodge's letters from contributors explore
alternatives to plot situations she had indicated might draw the wrath
of parents. Thomas Nelson Page expressed concern that an incident
in a story could be considered "contra bonos mores" by Dodge, and
he offered to omit a potentially offensive word and have a character
remove the bullets from a gun if that would mend matters.⁶

In a lightly fictionalized sermon on reading by S. S. Pratt called "A
'Diet of Candy' by the Mother of a 'Devouring Reader,'" a boy who
skims his monthly issue of *St. Nick,* reading only the "candy" or immediately appealing selections, is reminded of the excellent things
he has skipped in the issue he has just "finished." The piece shows
mothers how to guide their children's reading while subtly suggesting
that an intelligent woman might also profit from reading *St. Nicholas*
herself. Little Arthur's mother is "one of that army of busy mothers
who spend the whole day working for home and children, and in the
evening snatch a brief hour in which to feed their own hungry minds"
(557). She reads history in her spare time and asks him to read a historical serial aloud to her, insisting, "I am as much interested in it
as you" (557). She concludes her homily with a warning that "if you
allow your love for stories full sway, it may entirely destroy your taste
for anything else" (559) and compares Arthur's literary preferences
to those of a woman she'd heard of who sent her daughter to the public library each week, telling her "to look into the book" and "if there
are lots of 'ohs' and 'ahs,' I shall be sure to like it." The lesson on taste
here is, as the crucial comparison suggests, not limited to children.
But Dodge preferred to teach by indirection, and she advised readers
that "it is by the subtle something which we call *atmosphere,* rather
than by direct teaching, that the home molds a child. The chief business of a mother is to surround a child with beautiful influences."⁷

And how better to do that than by sharing the best of children's magazines with her offspring? In 1875, Mrs. J. G. Burnett offered mothers a Dickensian Christmas reverie in which, drowsing over her issue of *St. Nick,* the narrator is shown how a series of parents and parent-surrogates from various social backgrounds read the magazine with their charges. Like "A 'Diet of Candy,' " this article is a kind of sermon for parents and caretakers on the importance of their role in mediating the cultural message of *St. Nicholas.* It is clear that the editors of the magazine saw the scene of its reception as an interaction between children and the significant nurturers in their lives—an interaction that replicated the lively multivoiced conversation about the contents of the journal found in its editorial departments and Letter-Box columns. The adult reader in pieces like those by Pratt and Burnett is offered an idealized self-image as a cultural gatekeeper on the model of Dodge herself. To borrow a phrase from Jacqueline Rose in which she describes the positioning of the child, this sort of article "draws in" the adult reader; it "secures, places, and frames" that reader as an enlightened agent of the magazine's editorial program (2).

When, at one point, little Arthur in "A 'Diet of Candy' " reminded his mother of how she had sneaked off to enjoy *St. Nicholas* by herself, she laughed and said, "It was *not* generous I know, but that very act proves my high opinion of stories. They have their place in literature, and a noble one it is; not a serial in *St. Nicholas* but has some strong and true lesson within it; something that should make one better and purer" (559). But how exactly did *St. Nicholas's* fiction try to make its adult readers "better and purer"? Obviously, parents were urged "to feed their own hungry minds," to procure the best reading for their children and share it intelligently with them, but a major editorial aim in the selection of fiction, art, and poetry directed toward the adult audience in *St. Nicholas* was to stimulate in them attitudes toward children the editors thought desirable. Dodge used her pulpit in *St. Nicholas* effectively to publicize organized charities, but she looked to individual charity to provide much relief to marginal, dependent, and powerless children. So she put special stress on presenting children in a way that would appeal to adult sympathy. Very often, especially in the early days of the magazine, Dodge would supply a frontispiece with a picture of an attractive child together with an essay that would set the picture in heart-tugging context.[8] And she published a great many poems and stories that seem to exist only to describe children as innocently touching parental sensibilities because of their weakness, tininess, and inability to speak correctly. Infants were described fondly as naughty little darlings, bewitching in a baby way (*"Lolly Dinks's Doings"* 190), who could give "a zest and charm" to life "beyond the power of any caterer" (Johnson 604) if they were allowed to lisp and dimple their ways into grown-up hearts. Dodge knew such saccharine material had limited appeal to other children, but she believed that adults wanted it and that it would motivate them to do good. In an unpublished letter Dodge wrote to Louise Chandler Moulton, which notes that Moulton's "Prince Oric"—a poem of pure, unadulterated baby worship—would soon be introduced to *St. Nick*'s young readers, she assured Moulton that "if they do not quite understand the situation I feel sure their elders will."[9]

Formula Fiction Addressed to Adults

The great bulk of the short fiction in *St. Nicholas* was formulaic—repetitive in character, plot, and thematics. As R. Gordon Kelly has pointed out, such fiction expressed the anxieties of adults in a time of rapid social, technological, economic, and cultural change, and offered a variety of scenarios for resolving tension and reaffirming "the values, expectations, assumptions, hero types, and needs" of the genteel elite who made up the pool of contributors, editors, and many of the subscribers of the magazine (*Mother*, 35). Formula fiction in *St. Nicholas* often addressed the passing on of values thematically, particularly in the form of stories in which an adult intervenes benevolently in a needy child's affairs. And many of these stories seem to have been addressed primarily to adults, though they were accessible to children.

Adult readers, as Peter Hunt has noted, "can never share the same background (in terms of reading and life experience) as children" and often have different purposes in reading (Hunt 46). Innocent and experienced readers are likely to understand these stories differently for "perceptions of narrative patterns, and much else, are based on an appeal to a common culture, and the culture of the primary readers of children's literature" is not the adult's (74). Reading such a formulaic story can be like looking at one of those pictures of duck / rabbit, old woman / young girl whose meaning depends on selective attention to certain visual signals and repression of others. Such a picture is susceptible to three quite different kinds of reading: either "trick image" may be seen as dominant, or the viewer may choose to look at the whole as a set of shapes, colors, and lines capable of being construed variously. An adult might be programmed by reading and life experience to see one of these stories as describing a benevolent "colonizing" project—what Kelly calls a "gentry mission"—in which a character effects the conversion of others to elite values, often with significant cultural consequences for both readers and those who were the objects of the gentry mission. A child, coming to the same reading, might recognize it as a familiar "Cinderella" story in which the protagonist's intrinsic merit is recognized and rewarded by those in power.

Of course, the critic who stands back from the formulaic story, resolutely determined to see neither duck nor rabbit, child nor crone, may be troubled by the flickering return of images that embody hidden and painful contradictions: children rescued miraculously from need are inducted into the very establishment that created their problems; the young learn to leverage their neediness into a powerful claim on their elders by a calculated presentation of their own "innocence." The critical viewer might even, for the briefest of moments, get a hint of the secret on which both versions of the story turn: that if children need adults, adults also need children—their cooperation, docility, and innocence, as well as their resistance, awkward questions, and waywardness.

Fred Erisman has quite properly described certain character "traits deemed important" in the great bulk of *St. Nicholas*'s fiction. As he sees them, the youngsters in *St. Nicholas* "respect duty, keep an open mind, are unquestionably honest, are thrifty and industrious, and above all are unwaveringly self-reliant" (386). But in stories designed to arouse the humanitarian sympathies of the adult reader, such qualities may be more a matter of demonstrated potential than achievement. In order to make adult readers feel the urge to help, support, and reward young people, such stories tend to stress the helplessness of these promising children in the face of overwhelming problems. And the ante is raised by the children's innocent inability to understand the darker side of experience. There are a number of signals that such tales are directed primarily to adults and only secondarily to children. Children tend not to be the focal characters, and they do not say much. They are primarily acted upon rather than acting, and they don't determine the outcome of their experience. They are sometimes strikingly limited, babyish in their speech, and so forth. The adult response to the child's appeal is elaborated upon and carefully modeled for the reader. Frequently, such pieces use fairly adult vocabulary and sophisticated narrative techniques. And it is common that the stories turn on or end in a deliberate attempt to evoke a response (often tears) by an adult.

St. Nicholas had its own variation on the familiar Victorian "waif" story in which a poor child is rescued from cold, starvation, and exploitation. In these stories the child's support system has been lost or badly compromised. The child is often isolated, dirty, tired or ill, and barely able to communicate. Though religious motives are sometimes cited by the benefactors, the rescue that takes place is more likely to center on assimilation into a middle-class family than on a religious conversion. When the child is asked the inevitable question "What is your name?" the answer is often, "They call me . . . [an epithet, or ugly nickname]." At a key moment in the story, the child is often given a new or more presentable name.

"Patches" by Rosa Graham shows this sort of story in its simplest form. Here a little girl is peddling strawberries door to door. The woman of the house notices the child is starving, although the girl carries boxes of delicious berries. When Aunt Ruth realizes the child has resisted the tempting berries because to eat them would be dishonest, "a fountain" swells in her "kind heart" (774). She wastes no time, but bathes, feeds, reclothes, and adopts the child, pledging to teach and love her. Aunt Ruth is rewarded eventually as little "Patches," rechristened "Mamie," grows up to be "an industrious little body" who tries "her best to lighten the labors of the good woman to whom she owed so much" (774).

In "The Kind Turkey-Man" by Sergent Flint, a little girl is walking along toward the city on a cold evening. She is picked up by a man taking his turkeys to market. She touches his heart with her story: she had been rejected by those to whose care her father had abandoned her and now was vaguely seeking a "cousin" in the city somewhere. The farmer leaves her at a marketplace and later sees her tempted to steal an apple, resisting the temptation, and collapsing from hunger. He takes her home to his wife, and in a move common in such stories, they adopt her to replace a little girl they have lost named, like the waif, Mary.

Two stories by Dodge's good friend, Lucy G. Morse, demonstrate the way the basic waif story could be elaborated upon. In "The Ash-Girl," an orphaned little beggar-girl—a real-life Cinderella who makes her living by picking over the ashes set out in the New York streets

—decides to conduct a house-to-house search for a real mother. "Cathern" is turned away from door after door, but she finally sees a small coffin being carried out of a house, pushes her way past the servant at the door, and begs the grieving mother to adopt her. The first part of the story addresses child readers forcefully using Cathern as a focal character, and it develops in agonizing detail the thoughts, hopes, and fears of the little girl throughout her search, which is full of disappointments and dead ends. In the latter stages of the story, however, the "mother" she chooses, Mrs. Percy, becomes the focal character. Though she drew away and turned her face to the wall as the child's meaning dawned upon her, "when she turned again and saw the weak little frame trembling from head to foot, and heard her desolate cry, she suddenly knelt down, spread wide her arms, and cried: 'Come, come to me! It is as if my child cried out to me from heaven! Put your little head, so, upon my breast, and I will be as true —as true a mother to you as I can' " (392). The major illustration for this story is of "Cathern and the Lady," but Cathern stands in shadow and the lady in the foreground, her face turned to the light, not yet able to look at the little girl. She seems just roused from her grief. The ragged child looks quite out of place in the gracious parlor filled with plants and flowers, lace curtains and fine carpets. She stares intently at Mrs. Percy, who seems still dazed and numb. Though Morse specifically addressed the story to children at the outset, its moral is perhaps as much aimed at mothers like Mrs. Percy as toward younger readers: "I hope rather it will make you think, when you see the little streetsweepers, beggars, or poor children, that there may be hidden away under all their rough exterior, tender, warm feelings, and hearts that are taught through suffering to be pure and true" (386).

But the sequel to "The Ash-Girl," "Cathern," seems predominantly addressed to mothers, especially at first, and thematically it is concerned with problematizing the process of mothering itself, as Mrs. Percy, for all her good intentions, proves to be not the perfect mother Cathern had dreamed of after all. "Cathern," published a year after the first story, shows that washing, feeding, clothing, and renaming a little vagrant is easier than teaching her to be a gracious, motherly person herself. Having impulsively promised to be a mother to the little girl, Mrs. Percy is unwilling to go back on her word, but for a time the child keeps opening up old wounds. A full appreciation of the story requires that the adult reader understand and sympathize with Mrs. Percy's feelings and see matters from her point of view. A now well-dressed and rosy "Kathleen" assumes she has indeed found a "real" mother who feels toward her as she had toward her own child, but the reader is meant to see clearly how poor a substitute she is for angelic little Mabel Percy. When Kathleen, still very much the street urchin, goes out for a walk with Mrs. Percy, she evens old scores with the neighborhood children, jostles a passerby, and pushes an innocent baby into the gutter. Mrs. Percy realizes that civilizing and educating Kathleen in her religious and social responsibilities will not be easy, but she commits herself to this transformative task.

In the latter stages of this story, the focus shifts to the child's perspective. By the end of the story, Kathleen, her conscience having been awakened, has taken on the toddler she had pushed as her own special charge and has committed herself to becoming the little girl's "mother." But her epiphany comes in the bittersweet moment when she realizes that Mrs. Percy is only "playing" mother to her in much the same way that Kathleen is "playing" mother to baby Trudy. The stubborn self-reliance and enterprise that had sent "Cathern" out onto the streets to search for a mother comes to "Kathleen's" aid as she tells herself that if worst comes to worst, and she ends up on the streets again, she can support "her" baby by going back to begging. She is sobered by her new understanding of her relation to Mrs. Percy, but she gains the strength to find both her place in the world and her mission, which will be to mother as many of the lost and homeless as she can. This sequel critiques and interprets the simplicities of the earlier story. Just as "The Ash-Girl" offered young readers a story of enterprise rewarded, an updated kind of Cinderella story, this one demonstrates and approves the change of heart experienced by a maturing Kathleen. But it also offers adults a feeling picture of both the appeal and the cost of undertaking the sort of gentry mission that seemed in the first story to be proposed as a simple solution to a child's problems. In particular, "Cathern" suggests the real difficulties such an acculturation project may face because "mother" and "child" must yet learn to speak a common language, and it recognizes the existence of some perhaps unresolvable tensions between them.

Sometimes the appealing qualities displayed by hapless children in *St. Nicholas*'s stories are simply a readiness and ability to profit from cultural education, with the adult merely intervening to reward a display of taste or talent. In Washington Gladden's "Angel in an Ulster," a kindly gentleman observes two children wistfully standing in front of a poster advertising an oratorio they wish they could hear.

Attracted by their display of aesthetic interest, he finds that their family has fallen on hard times, and they have had to give up concerts and even their monthly *St. Nicholas* magazine. Needless to say, he sees that they have a merry Christmas, showering them with gifts and goodies, including a subscription to their favorite magazine. In Charles Barnard's "Tommy the Soprano," the young hero wakes up one cold Christmas morning to find the fire out and his mother ill. He faints while singing a beautiful solo at church, and his talent and self-discipline draw the kind attention of the organist's wife. The outcome for him is a career, an income, and a new life (5).

As these stories and "The Ash-Girl" suggest, *St. Nicholas*'s waif stories often implied that children who were helped to join the middle class would in turn benefit their kindly helpers and become part of the gentry mission themselves. And indeed, many of these stories are so constructed that although adults might be primarily addressed with a sentimental sermon on the need for reform and social intervention, children might find appealing the story itself, which is centered on the rise to happiness and power of a little, downtrodden victim who manages to manipulate the adult world by demonstrating just the right mixture of innocence, dependence, and aptness to learn appropriate cultural lessons. These children might particularly enjoy the frequent final hint that the assisted waif could one day become an adult empowered to help others.

The Case of Little Lord Fauntleroy

Frances Hodgson Burnett's *Little Lord Fauntleroy* presented a telling picture of the empowerment of the innocent child by a proper gentry upbringing. The story was popular with both adults and children, though it was perhaps primarily addressed to adults.[10] But its picture of parent-child relations appealed very much to Dodge, a widow whose emotional life had long centered around her sons, and she saw the piece as sending an important and uplifting message to her child readers and their parents. She gave Burnett twice as much per printed page as other authors, saying "my heart goes out to the staunch, true-souled little fellow & I expect to have lots of fun with him."[11] Against her principles, Dodge even extended the space she gave the serial when its author ran over her allotted limit because she found the little lord "so altogether charming that we shall not have the heart to 'cut' him appreciably. He is a child to love and remember all one's life."[12] Dodge avidly promoted the serial, the novel when it appeared in hardcover, and the stageplay based on it, and she put her own editorial spin on the image of parent-child relations represented in all of them.

In the autumn of 1884, Burnett wrote to Dodge mentioning that she had been "possessed by a child's story" suggested by her intimate acquaintance with "a very beautiful engaging and ingenuous little American boy of English descent." She "kept thinking of the kind of charm his simple, quite graceful and unconscious little American freedoms would have for a certain class of magnificent but kindly potentates in England."[13] Though she terms her novel "a child's story," it seems clear that even when describing its first conception Burnett consciously considered the way her situation would appeal to a certain adult audience. She says of the little boy, "He has great beauty and bravest affectionate little heart & the most bewitching gallant little way." "He is a child," she adds, "who has a gift for being adored." His appeal comes in part because he "knows of no barrier between himself and anything human."[14] The point of the matter, confided Burnett to Dodge, was that Fauntleroy "does not know the subtle difference between dukes and corner groceryman but he is just as sweet & sympathetic and courteous in his small confiding way to one as to the other—It makes many pretty situations—he is so ignorant of grandeur but he has such a kind little heart."[15]

There is an appealing Cinderella story for children here, but though the vocabulary and syntax remain within the grasp of a younger reader, Cedric is rarely allowed to be a focal character for long, and Barbara Wall suggests that "one factor in the popularity of *Little Lord Fauntleroy* was undoubtedly that, although it could be called a children's story, it was not a story overtly addressed to children" (169). Cedric is usually seen from without, and he is doted upon incessantly by the narrative voice, as well as by almost all the adult characters in the story. There is also a subtler situation for adults to savor: the Earl of Dorincourt's gradual capitulation to his little grandson's goodness, innocence, and charm, and his reluctant acknowledgement that his daughter-in-law is, though American, a perfect lady and the admirable mother who has nurtured this paragon of a child. "The end is of course . . . ," said Burnett, "that everyone is just a trifle kinder and happier for having known him—& his mother is as much appreciated as himself."[16] That Cedric's mother also triumphs is in many ways a key element in the story, for her successful gentry mission makes her an idealized role model for mothers. Little Ceddie, as the reader is often told, has his mother's "great, clear, innocent eyes," eyes he uses to pressure the old Earl into doing what he innocently thinks is right (110).[17] When the old Earl's sister, Lady Lorridaile, hears about Ceddie, she worries that he will be ruined, spoiled as his uncles had been "unless his mother is good enough and has a will of her own to help her take care of him" (148). Minna Tipton, the mother of the rival claimant to the title of Lord Fauntleroy, is, as the family lawyer observes, "evidently" "a person from the lower walks of life" (181). The rival mother has a "handsome, common face, a passionate temper, and a coarse, insolent manner." But Dearest, as Cedric calls her, and as even the Earl's servants observe, is "one o' the right sort, as any gentlemen 'ud reckinize with 'alf a heye" (180). Her "voice was very sweet, and her manner was very simple and dignified" (182). She was "unafraid of the Earl, and though she knew it a 'magnificent thing to be the Earl of Dorincourt,' she cared most that . . . [Cedric] should be what his father was—brave and just and true always" (183). Dearest is discreet and generous. She tells the Earl she knows Cedric loves him, and the Earl respects her for not telling the boy why she was not received at the castle. (The old Earl has refused to see her.) In the final analysis the real secret of Ceddie's success is shown to be "that he had lived near a kind and gentle heart, and had been taught to think kind thoughts always and to care for others. It is a very little thing, perhaps, but it is the best thing of all. He knew nothing of earls and castles. He was quite ignorant of all grand and splendid things. But he was always lovable because he was simple and loving. To be so is like being born a king" (204).

Jacqueline Rose sees children's literature as setting up "the child as an outsider to its own process," aiming, "unashamedly, to take the child *in*" (2), in order, Nodelman puts it, to persuade the child of an adult version of childhood (34). For Rose it is important to this project that "none of this appears explicitly inside the book itself, which works precisely to the extent that any question of who is talking to whom and why is totally erased" (2). But the children's literary periodical as an institution foregrounds the whole question of who is speaking to whom and why, and it frames episodes of a serial for its readers as contributions to an extended and multidirectional conversation. Reader responses selected for publication in a children's periodical may be part of a didactic project to "turn children from acceptable versions of childhood into the right sort of adults"

(Nodelman 34), but as young writers to Dodge's "Letter-Box" complain, share creative misreadings, express starry-eyed admiration, ask blunt questions, and echo the grown-ups they respect, we are given a privileged look into the process by which young and old make and remake images of themselves and each other.

No sooner had *Little Lord Fauntleroy* begun to appear in *St. Nicholas* than letters began turning up in the "The Letter-Box" agonizing over how the serial would end, and begging Mrs. Burnett to be good to Cedric, let all go well, and make the story as long as possible. A child from Bangor, Maine, was sure that "when the grandpa sees Lord Fauntleroy's mother, he will like her, and have her come up and live with them" (L. C. B., *SN* 13.11 [Sept. 1886]: 877). Mary G., a more practical reader from Washington, D.C., thought the story *St. Nick's* best of the year, "only I did not like to have the new Lord Fauntleroy coming in to take his place. I hope Mrs. Burnett will have the Earl buy the new Lord Fauntleroy out" (*SN* 13.11 [Sept. 1886]: 876). Children and their parents were represented in the "Letter-Box" as reading the story and discussing it together: the children often took a proprietary interest in Cedric's pony and expressed concern about his mother's welfare, whereas the parents saw him as almost too good to live long. A family in Omaha agreed it was the most beautiful story they had ever read, and young Menie C. W. reported: Mother "thinks Cédric will die before the end, but I hope not" (*SN* 13.11 [Sept. 1886]: 876). Marguerite H., a well-read fourteen-year-old reader from Greenville, South Carolina, said she thought Cedric "seems to be a second Paul Dombey, with his quaint, old-fashioned sayings. I hope he will not die shut up in the gloomy castle, with his cross old grandfather, away from the companionship of 'Dearest'" (*SN* 13.9 [July 1886]: 715). And an eleven-year-old from Memphis gives us a picture of the way the reading of the story might have been moderated for young readers by the active forum of the whole family circle: E. P. P. writes, "I think Lord Fauntleroy is the sweetest little fellow I ever read about. Every time I get a new number of ST. NICHOLAS, I sit down on the rug by mamma and read 'Little Lord Fauntleroy' out loud for mamma and my little sister to hear. Mamma and papa both like it ever so much" (*SN* 13.12 [Oct. 1886]: 954). Cedric's affection for his mother seems to have been understood sympathetically by the readers whose letters were selected for publication, who often expressed concern that she would be accepted and the family brought together. One twelve-year-old boy wrote, "I am so fond of my mother;

so I must tell you how much we are pleased with 'Little Lord Fauntleroy' and his 'Dearest' mother" (*SN* 13.11 [Sept. 1886]: 877). The "we" here suggests that both mother and son saw their relationship in terms Burnett and Dodge would have understood.

Most of the enthusiasts for Cedric who wrote to *St. Nicholas's* "Letter-Box" were girls, some of whom—perhaps in response to the "adult" message in the story and the editorial support Dodge gave it—took a precociously maternal attitude toward Ceddie. A girl from California wrote, "Cedric reminds me of my little cousin Birdie (that is his pet name). One day his aunt (who is an artist) asked him if he did not want her to paint him. He said: 'I had rather be as I are.' He is nearly four years old" (*SN* 13.7 [May 1886]: 554). Though Cedric did have noble qualities that made him mature for his age (his honesty, courtesy, sense of social responsibility, and courage), it is not so much these that draw the approbation of the narrative voice in the novel, but rather his appearance, innocence, diminutiveness, and pert charm. The reader is told insistently about his "cheerful, fearless, quaint little way of making friends with people" (10), "his darling little face" (9), "his honest, simple little mind" (46), "the simple, natural kindliness in the little lad which made any words he uttered, however quaint and unexpected, sound pleasant and sincere" (102). It is not surprising that older teenagers enjoyed getting sentimental about Cedric. And Burnett had modeled this process for them within the story when the flirtatious Miss Vivian Herbert succumbs to Fauntleroy's charm (to the despair of all her grown-up beaux) at a party late in the book.

Eighteen-year-old "Yum Yum" of New York wrote in June 1886 (*SN* 13.8: 635) that she had "just fallen in love with 'Little Lord Fauntleroy,'" adding, "I wish the 'small boy' of the present day would copy after him, but I fear that would be too 'pretty a state of things'" (635). But of course a scruffy, ordinary little American boy's easy democratic manner with everyone would be no great matter. The poignancy of the circumstance depends on the narrator's convincing the reader that the child *is* actually superior to certain other humans, however adorably unaware of the fact he may be. Ceddie's innocent inability to understand the possible malice or self-interest of his elders might present "a pretty situation," but it offers a curious lesson to his agemates, for few of them old enough to read the book for themselves can have failed to grasp that to know as much as they already do about the wickedness of the world is to be situated, in Burnett's terms, firmly on the other side of innocence. A child might reasonably see the determination of "Cathern," the honesty of "Patches," or the commitment to high culture of the children in "Angel in an Ulster" as behavior to emulate, but neither the stunning beauty nor the unfeigned innocence of Ceddie are to be acquired by choice or effort.

Still, Dodge and many of her readers, both young and old, were convinced Fauntleroy was a perfect model for children and that his relationship with his mother offered a wonderful example to parents and children who read *St. Nicholas* together. Dodge commented in an editorial note in the "Letter-Box": "During the last few months, many of those who have been so deeply interested in 'Little Lord Fauntleroy' have formed their own eager opinions of just how that beautiful story could, would, or should end. But all such readers . . . will agree that in the concluding chapters, printed this month, Mrs. Burnett has anticipated or fully satisfied their desires" (*SN* 13.12 [Oct. 1886]: 954). In that same issue, in her "Jack-in-the-Pulpit" column, Dodge felt impelled for once to preach a sermon and announced that "the dear little Lord" would be her text. "In fact," she said, "he is the sermon, too. So I need say no more except to publicly announce from my pulpit, with all due solemnity, that he is a boy after your Jack's own heart. And to every youngster among you, dearly beloved, I say, 'Earl or no Earl,—go thou and be like him!'" (*SN* 13.12 [Oct. 1886]: 954).

So eager was she to encourage what she saw as the missionary work Cedric Errol might do among the young that when the novel was adapted for the stage, Dodge went out of her way to include publicity pieces on the play as well as several articles on Elsie Leslie Lyde, the little girl who played Fauntleroy on the New York stage. She also printed numerous letters from children detailing the delights of the stage productions. A child from London who understood the importance of Dearest's ladylike restraint explained that there was an unauthorized stage adaptation "which was not at all nice, for it was not a bit like Mrs. Burnett's pretty story; for instance, in this play Mrs. Errol dresses up as a nurse and goes to the castle to see her boy in disguise. Isn't it horrid?" She saw the "proper" play, however, which Mrs. Burnett called "The Real Little Lord Fauntleroy" (*SN* 16.3 [Jan. 1889]: 238). When that play came to Boston, one young critic who had read the novel three times commented coolly: "I did not like it so well as the story. They left out the dinner party and Little Lord Fauntleroy didn't sit on a crackerbarrel, and didn't ride the pony, and there wasn't any dog" (*SN* 16.3 [Jan. 1889]: 237). But the little Bostonian was unusual; most writers were effusive in their praise and admiration, and some children even mentioned seeing the play more than once. Dodge herself saw the play at least twice, once when the young actor Tommy Russell played the part, and once when Elsie Lyde had the lead role.[18] Like most commentators, Dodge preferred the ringleted, golden-haired Elsie, whose performance was thought to be more sensitive and moving than Tommy's.

St. Nicholas published a puff piece by Lucy C. Lillie on little Elsie Leslie Lyde, drawing upon materials supplied by Dodge. Elsie had been invited to Dodge's evening "at homes" on Central Park South, where she had met many writers and artists, including Reginald Birch, who illustrated *Little Lord Fauntleroy*. Elsie seems to have had an Alice Liddell–like charm for literary and artistic gentlemen. Among her admirers were such "trustable" grown-ups as the actor William Gillette, who wrote sentimental verse to her, and Mark Twain (407). Lillie's article is addressed to both children and parents because "many people in Elsie's audience—'grown-ups' as well as children—would like to know something of the home life and the surroundings of the dear little girl who is helping to make 'Fauntleroy' a classic with us" (408). The piece depicts Elsie as a sheltered, well brought-up, and unspoiled child who shared many of the virtues of Cedric Errol, and it suggests that she, too, might be seen as a role model by America's children. Several months after the piece was printed, Dodge printed a letter from a little southern girl named "Heatherbell," one of many letters Dodge said had been received in response to the article: "Dear ST. NICHOLAS: Elsie Leslie Lyde's picture in the April number, 1889, was perfectly lovely! I looked at it and studied it for a long while. The expression is so gentle and child-like. She looks like a sweet dear little girl; and from what I have read of her, I think she would be a fair and true example for other children to follow. If we children could all be as simple, earnest, unaffected, and loving as Elsie is described to be, what a blissful and sweet little world the 'child-world' would be! Don't you think so, ST. NICHOLAS? I have named my large French doll with long bright curly hair, Elsie Leslie Lyde" (*SN* 13.9 [July 1889]: 717).

This letter seems to have assimilated a sentimental adult attitude so completely as to sound very unchildlike, but if indeed it is a child's letter, Heatherbell seems to be recommending to other children what sounds strangely like the learning of a stage part. The engravings made from publicity photos of little Elsie Lyde to which Heatherbell gave such studied attention are indeed remarkable. Elsie was a pretty child, but the expression on her face is enigmatic. She looks slightly bored, guarded, yet fiercely attentive. Her eyes are those of a child "used to being watched," and to being the object of "someone else's contemplation" (Steedman 136). She is aware of her own power to compel admiring attention and perhaps just a little contemptuous of it.

Carolyn Steedman has suggested that "the movements, gestures, demeanour and voice of childhood were taught to generations of child performers" in the period, "who became liable to rejection and dismissal if their repertoire appeared studied or forced." The "charming artlessness" that so appealed to Dodge's set in little Elsie "could be learned too, and child stars of the second half of the nineteenth century were the ones who had studied the 'quaint and pretty ways of childhood' most assiduously" (147). The appeal of Elsie to intelligent, artistic adults emerges especially in a curious follow-up piece some time after her run as Fauntleroy was over. Elsie was playing in a dramatization of Twain's *The Prince and the Pauper* when her "trustable" admirers William Gillette and Mark Twain decided to embroider a pair of slippers for her. Twain wrote an amusing letter to Elsie for *St. Nicholas* about this project full of wisecracks and puns only an adult would be likely to understand. In reply, Elsie, who appears to have been a shrewd and funny little girl, wrote him a note asking him to sit down with her the next time he came to visit and please explain the big words. (Though *St. Nicholas* as a matter of policy corrected spelling and punctuation in children's letters to the "Letter-Box," they left Elsie's atrocious spelling alone, apparently considering it part of her charm.) [19]

There were no doubt some very young children who heard Cedric Errol's story without attending much to the insistent praise of his adorable ingenuousness because they were more interested in the pony, the dog, and the crackerbarrel. But Cedric's seems to have been a role many parents wanted their children to play, and *St. Nicholas* actively encouraged imitation of that "sweet child" whose life brought "to many who doubtless have battled more with the pride and evil and hard-heartedness of their own natures than they might care to admit" a "message of peace and good-will" (Lillie 403). Dodge herself told Burnett after seeing the play on New Year's Day, 1889: "The Play is doing a great missionary work, and I am delighted to see hosts of little folk attending the Sat. matinees. No intelligent child can see the play without being materially helped and elevated by it—It is one of the most wholesome and best influences of the day."[20] It is apparent from their letters that some slightly older children responded to Cedric like fond and affectionately amused adults, whereas others seem to have been dazzled by his glamour and the success and approval he won from all and sundry. This latter group probably included some children sharp enough to notice that the appearance of innocence might be used to charm and please adults and to gain a good deal of interesting attention from them. But "conscious innocence" is always problematic, and the "knowing" ingenuousness of the child actor, while acceptable onstage, can be painful to contemplate in real life. Moreover, the pose can evoke suspicion and hostility when it does not ring true with a particular audience. When Burnett's novel became a best-seller, a "culture text" known in its outlines to many who never read it, and hence became subject to popular reinterpretation,[21] the assessment of Fauntleroy's image was not invariably positive, especially among the young male population of America (though you would not have known this from the carefully managed contents of the "Letter-Box"). Many boys who had not read the story—and thus missed the chance to admire Cedric's democratic ways and solid "manly" virtues[22]—assumed he was soft and delicate, the foppish, wishy-washy "mama's boy" they thought they saw in Birch's illustrations. Popular cultural history of the period is rife with tales of misery endured by little American boys forced by well-meaning, sentimental mothers to wear long curls and velvet and lace suits in imitation of Fauntleroy as drawn by Birch and impersonated by Elsie Leslie Lyde. There is an archetypal story about a little New York boy togged out in the full gear and set upon by toughs who asked him, mockingly, who gave him the haircut. His answer apparently was a heartfelt, "My mother, *God damn her!*" (Downs 176).

Of course, some adults might have agreed with those hooligans. One adult reader of the novel in *St. Nicholas* was Robert Louis Stevenson, who wrote to Dodge that he had read *Fauntleroy* with "indescribable amusement and delight" but added: "It is the most pickthank business to find fault with anything so daintily humorous and prettily pathetic; and yet I could wish the author had conceived the tale one touch more humanly: by making Fauntleroy this piece of sheer perfection she has missed the delicious scene-à-faire: the scene when the boy misbehaves, and our wicked earl becomes in turn his teacher in goodness. If you think the authoress would value the appreciation of a brother craftsman, it would be kind in you to communicate the news of my pleasure."[23]

Stevenson's faintly scornful description of the piece as "daintily humorous and prettily pathetic" perhaps expresses the same uneasiness those New York urchins felt at the idea of a boy set up to be such a "piece of sheer perfection." It is not surprising to see the creator of Alan Breck and Long John Silver suggest a more "human" reading of the situation in which an adult who is both good and bad intervenes to teach virtue to a realistically flawed child. But it is hard not to notice that Stevenson's adult experience of life and art prepare him as an experienced "craftsman" to shape *his* alternative plot along the lines of the formula fiction of benevolent adult intervention—the kind of fiction we have seen to be so appealing to adult readers of the magazine—albeit with his own twist.

The vogue for Elsie Lyde and for Fauntleroy in *St. Nicholas* shows with unusual clarity the extraordinary appeal to many adults—members of the editorial staff, contributors, and readers—of the image of the innocent child. James Kincaid has recently made some provocative suggestions about why and how adults of the Victorian period admired children, responded to them, and made major emotional investments in them. His comments on the way "the child" can be made to carry a wide variety of different meanings for adult audiences are particularly interesting. He argues that the "emptiness of the figure" lays particular claim to adult attention, and that "the vacuity of the child makes it available for centerings we do not want to announce openly" (79). (It is interesting to notice the tendency of adults as well as children to somehow want to rewrite Fauntleroy to their own tastes, and intriguing that the stage production offered in effect two Fauntleroys—one played by a husky boy, the other by a dainty girl.) Even for readers unwilling to follow Kincaid to conclusions he draws from these observations, the mass of his evidentiary detail raises questions about the purposes Elsie Lyde served in the imaginative lives of the older readers of *St. Nicholas,* questions that are not likely to have simple or unitary answers. Readers of Carolyn Steedman's *Strange Dislocations: Childhood and the Idea of Human Interiority, 1790–1930* may be persuaded to see *St. Nick*'s golden-haired Elsie as an interesting example of popular personification, "that kind of active making of something out of ideas, information heard about or read, stories, realisations . . . summed up in the living child . . . there before your very eyes" to offer an emblem of the self and its history (170). What might adults entranced with child performers like Elsie have been seeking in their own pasts? Steedman sees in such behavior "a bid for recurrence, eternity, sameness" in the face of the evanescence of childhood, though this way of looking at the phenomenon also opens up more interesting questions than it answers (171).

Exploring the "Space in Between"

In the light of Jacqueline Rose's discussion of the "impossibility of children's fiction," Perry Nodelman suggests that these important questions be asked about children's literature: "What claims do specific texts make on the children who read them? How do they represent childhood for children, and *why* might they be representing it that way? What interest of adults might the representation be serving?" (34). I would add a few questions to the list, particularly with regard to the children's periodical: What claims do specific "children's" texts make on the *adults* who read them? How do they represent childhood for *adults*, and *why*? How do *adults* figure in the reading environment of the children's periodical?

This exploratory discussion suggests how some sources might begin to yield useful information about the claims *St. Nicholas* made on its adult readers. Editorial and commercial advertising, testimonials, reviews, and editorial correspondence have identified interests the magazine served for adults. Details of address, illustration practice, and articles directed toward making adults instruments of editorial policy reveal the ways in which the magazine tried to position its adult audience. My inquiry into the way childhood was represented for adults in *St. Nicholas* focuses on fictions of benevolent intervention and on the magazine's handling of the whole Fauntleroy phenomenon. But I have been able to scrutinize just *one* strain of formula fiction, *one* long serial together with its readers' response, and the way the magazine turned *one* living child into an icon of childhood. Alternative lines of inquiry might well have produced different insights. What do fictions of transgression and punishment say about the power relation between child and adult? What questions are raised by a serial about failed parenting? Elsie Lyde was not the only young protege of Dodge to be made into a personification of childhood for adults: What does the case of Helen Keller tell us?

Pursuing the question of how childhood was represented for adults in *St. Nicholas* is a fascinating but vexing business: fascinating because of the sheer abundance of data presented and the wide spectrum of attitudes reflected in it; vexing because so much of the basic groundwork on which modern scholarship relies—analytical bibliography, adequate indexing, effective content analysis—remains to be done on *St. Nicholas*. So much of the information we would like to have has yet to be accumulated, assimilated, and organized, let alone defined and subjected to "rising levels of generalization" (Wolff 127). Further, if Steedman and Kincaid are correct in suggesting that the reasons why childhood is represented as it is in children's literature lie in adults' unspoken needs, the evidence to be gathered from *St. Nicholas* needs to be set in a variety of appropriate psychological and historical contexts. How did real adult readers fill the "vacuity of the child," and why? What particular losses in their own lives might they have tried to recover by idealizing exemplary children? If we are to understand the role adults played in the reading environment offered by *St. Nicholas,* the reading history of the magazine needs to be investigated much more vigorously than it has been to date, and the adult role in it must be carefully theoretized.[24] How did read-aloud sessions and intergenerational discussion affect the way children and adults read periodical fiction? How did "script" preferences of young and old reflect—and shape—editorial choices? Answering such questions is not an individual endeavor. Exploring the fascinating "space in between" that Dodge's "pleasure ground" offered children and adults clearly needs the organized, collaborative effort of many scholars. But though there is much to be done, as one pioneer investigator has put it, "the possibilities are tantalizing" (Myers 43).

Notes

Unpublished library holdings are quoted here with the kind permission of The Library of Congress (LC); the Donald and Robert M. Dodge Collection, Princeton University Library (D&RMD PUL); and the Wilkinson Collection, Princeton University Library (W PUL).

1. Until July 1881, the magazine's full title was *St. Nicholas: Scribner's Illustrated Magazine for Girls and Boys;* for the rest of Dodge's editorship, it was titled *St. Nicholas: An Illustrated Magazine for Young Folks.* For convenience the magazine will be referred to as *St. Nicholas* and abbreviated in citations as *SN.*
2. See Gannon and Thompson, and Erisman.
3. For a detailed examination of an office memorandum concerning the need to cut improprieties in John Townsend Trowbridge's *His One Fault* and the cuts made

when the novel was serialized, see Gannon and Thompson 142–45. For cuts made in *Tom Sawyer Abroad* see Firkins. But see also Gannon and Thompson 145–50.

4. John Townsend Trowbridge to Mary Mapes Dodge, 31 Mar. 1874, D&RMD PUL.

5. Mary Mapes Dodge to Stockton, 28 May 1897, D&RMD PUL, box 2, folder 73.

6. Thomas Nelson Page to Mary Mapes Dodge, 13 Oct. 1887, W PUL, box 2, folder 64.

7. "True Story," editorial advertising supplement bound in *SN* 10.2 (Dec. 1882), 1–8 numbered separately following 160. Bodleian Library, Oxford, per. 2714, d. 27.

8. Were the editors of *St. Nicholas* aware of the sexual subtext of much Victorian portraiture of children? That they might have had an inkling—at least about the sweetly submissive pictures of little girls in mob caps so popular in the 1870s—is suggested by their handling of a reproduction of Joshua Reynolds's portrait of Miss Penelope Boothby. This picture inspired Millais to paint "Cherry Ripe" (1879) and Lewis Carroll to produce a photograph of Xie Kitchin as Penelope Boothby, "anything but pure" (Mavor 165). Dodge used the picture as the frontispiece for the third volume and presented it with a commentary by Rebecca Harding Davis that frankly assumed adult readers would wonder how the "brilliant, wicked world" into which she had come had used the little girl. "Was she among the famous dazzling beauties whose history no child could read?" asked Davis. But she salvaged the picture's innocence for adult readers by a firm assurance that the real Penelope died at seven and "went home just as we see her, to the land where there are so many children, and where He who loves them best of all never leaves them" (1). See also Polhemus and Williams on the interpretation of such pictures.

9. Mary Mapes Dodge to Louise Chandler Moulton, 24 Jan. 1890, LC.

10. Barbara Wall notes that Burnett's earlier story for *St. Nicholas*, "Editha's Burglar," showed the author so "very aware of a potential adult audience that she is unable to adjust her tone for children or to direct address to them" (167). Wall sees *Little Lord Fauntleroy*, on the other hand, as "a book which fulfilled all the requirements for being popular with both children and adults" (167).

11. Mary Mapes Dodge to Frances Hodgson Burnett, 2 Apr. 1885, repr. Wright 145.

12. Mary Mapes Dodge to Frances Hodgson Burnett, 12 June 1885, repr. Wright 149.

13. Frances Hodgson Burnett to Mary Mapes Dodge, [autumn] 1884, repr. Wright 141.

14. Frances Hodgson Burnett to Mary Mapes Dodge, [autumn] 1884, repr. Wright 141.

15. Frances Hodgson Burnett to Mary Mapes Dodge, [autumn] 1884, repr. Wright 142.

16. Frances Hodgson Burnett to Mary Mapes Dodge, [autumn] 1884, repr. Wright 142.

17. Hollywood's casting of Mary Pickford in the roles of both mother and son in a 1921 silent film seems strangely apt, given the way the two characters are identified in the book. Claudia Nelson notes the way in which Fauntleroy's unspoken but effective criticism of his grandfather's values "as the criticism of male values from the standpoint of the woman—made *Little Lord Fauntleroy* . . . a best-seller" (19).

18. According to Elsie Lyde in an interview with Spencer Mapes, The Society for the Prevention of Cruelty to Children insisted that there be another actor to spell her on certain matinee days. She did not seem convinced it was necessary.

19. "Writing," said Lucy C. Lillie, "is to her just what it was to dear Pet Marjorie [*sic*]: The 'thoughts come, but the pen won't always work'" (410).

20. Mary Mapes Dodge to Frances Hodgson Burnett, 5 Jan. 1889, repr. Wright 167.

21. The concept of the culture text has been elaborated in Paul Davis's recent book on Dickens's *A Christmas Carol*. See also Paul B. Armstrong's treatment of the text as the creation of its readers.

22. See Claudia Nelson on the "manliness" of the idealized androgynous boy (1–5).

23. Robert Louis Stevenson to Mary Mapes Dodge, 5 Apr. 1887, repr. Wright 156.

24. Theoretical approaches to periodical writing suggesting some of the complexities of the genre and the many ways it eludes editorial control include work by Beetham, Brake, and Pykett. See bibliographies in Drotner; Kelly, *Children's Periodicals;* Gannon and Thompson; and Myers. Work in this area is covered in *Victorian Periodicals Review* and *American Periodicals. The Golden Age of* St. Nicholas, *1873–1905,* which is currently in preparation by Susan Gannon, Suzanne Rahn, and Ruth Anne Thompson, will cover reader interaction with the magazine, editing problems, and the magazine's handling of a number of contemporary issues.

Works Cited

Alcott, Louisa May. *Selected Letters of Louisa May Alcott.* Ed. Joel Myerson and Daniel Shealy. Athens: University of Georgia Press, 1995.

Armstrong, Paul B. "The Conflict of Interpretations and the Limits of Pluralism." *PMLA* 98.3 (May 1983): 341–51.

"A Word to Subscribers." Editorial Advertising Supplement. *SN* 2.3 (Jan. 1875): 2.

Barnard, Charles. "Tommy the Soprano." *SN* 2.3 (Jan. 1875): 148–50.

Beetham, Margaret. "Open and Closed: The Periodical as Publishing Genre." *Victorian Periodicals Review* 22.3 (fall 1989): 96–100.

Brake, Laurel. *Subjugated Knowledges: Journalism, Gender & Literature in the Nineteenth Century.* Houndmills, Eng.: Macmillan, 1994.

Burlingame, Roger. *Of Making Many Books: A Hundred Years of Reading, Writing, and Publishing.* New York: Charles Scribner's Sons, 1946.

Burnett, Frances Hodgson. *Little Lord Fauntleroy.* Afterword by Phyllis Bixler. New York: Signet/Penguin, 1992.

Burnett, Mrs. J. G. "Some Young Readers of *St. Nicholas.*" *SN* 2.12 (Oct. 1875): 761–63.

Christ, Carol T., and John Jordan, eds. *Victorian Literature and the Victorian Visual Imagination.* Berkeley: University of California Press, 1995.

Clarke, William Fayal. "Fifty Years of ST. NICHOLAS: A Brief Anniversary Compilation of Chronicle and Comment." *SN* 14.1 (Nov. 1876): 16–28.

Davis, Paul. *The Lives and Times of Ebenezer Scrooge.* New Haven: Yale University Press, 1990.

Davis, Rebecca Harding. "About the Painter of Little Penelope." *SN* 3.1 (Nov. 1875): 1–3.

Dodge, James M. "The Money Value of Training." *SN* 31.1 (Jan. 1903): 57–65.

Dodge, Mary Mapes. "Children's Magazines." *Scribner's Monthly* (July 1873): 352–54.

Downs, Robert B. *Famous American Books.* New York: McGraw-Hill, 1971.

Drotner, Kirsten. *English Children and Their Magazines, 1751–1945.* New Haven: Yale University Press, 1988.

Erisman, Fred. *"St. Nicholas." Children's Periodicals of the United States.* Ed. R. Gordon Kelly. Westport, Conn.: Greenwood, 1984. 377–88.

Firkins, Terry. "Textual Introduction." In *Tom Sawyer: Tom Sawyer Abroad; Tom Sawyer, Detective,* Vol. 4 of *The Works of Mark Twain,* ed. John C. Gerber, Paul Baender, and Terry Firkins. Berkeley: University of California Press, 1980.

Flint, Sergent. "The Kind Turkey-Man." *SN* 3.5 (Mar. 1875): 14–16.

Gannon, Susan R., and Ruth Anne Thompson. *Mary Mapes Dodge.* New York: Twayne, 1992.

Gladden, Washington. "Angel in an Ulster." *SN* 9.2 (Dec. 1881): 106–14.

Graham, Rosa. "Patches." *SN* 4.12 (Oct. 1876): 774–76.

Hunt, Peter. *Criticism, Theory, and Children's Literature.* Oxford: Basil Blackwell, 1991.

John, Arthur. *The Best Years of the "Century": Richard Watson Gilder, "Scribner's Monthly," and the "Century Magazine," 1870–1901.* Urbana: University of Illinois Press, 1981.

Johnson, Rossiter. "Little To-Bo." *SN* 16.8 (June 1889): 604.

Kelly, R. Gordon, ed. *Children's Periodicals of the United States.* Westport, Conn.: Greenwood, 1974.

———. *Mother Was a Lady: Self and Society in Selected American Children's Periodicals, 1865–1890.* Westport, Conn.: Greenwood, 1974.

Kincaid, James. *Child-Loving: The Erotic Child and Victorian Culture.* 1992. New York: Routledge, 1994.

Lillie, Lucy C. "'Fauntleroy' and Elsie Leslie Lyde." *SN* 16.6 (Apr. 1889): 403–13.

"Lolly Dinks's Doings." Review of *Lolly Dinks's Doings* by Elizabeth Stoddard. *SN* 2.3 (Jan. 1875): 190.

Mavor, Carol. "Dream Rushes: Lewis Carroll's Photographs of the Little Girl." In Nelson and Vallone.

Milliken, Elsie Leslie Lyde. Interview with Spencer Mapes, Jan. [1935?]. Donald and Robert M. Dodge Collection, Princeton University Library.

Morse, Lucy. "Cathern." *SN* 4.5 (Mar. 1877): 302–10.

———. "The Ash-Girl." *SN* 3.6 (Apr. 1876): 386–92.

Myers, Mitzi. "Sociologizing Juvenile Ephemera: Periodical Contradictions, Popular Literacy, Transhistorical Readers." Review of Kirsten Drotner, *English Children and Their Magazines, 1751–1945. Children's Literature Association Quarterly* 17.1 (spring 1992): 41–45.

Nelson, Claudia. *Boys Will Be Girls: The Feminine Ethic and British Children's Fiction, 1817–1917.* New Brunswick, N.J.: Rutgers University Press, 1991.

Nelson, Claudia, and Lynn Vallone. *The Girl's Own: Cultural Histories of the American Girl, 1830–1915.* Athens: University of Georgia Press, 1994.

Nodelman, Perry. "The Other: Orientalism, Colonialism, and Children's Literature." *Children's Literature Association Quarterly* 17.1 (spring 1992): 29–35.

Polhemus, Robert M. "John Millais's Children." In Christ and Jordan.

Pratt, S. S. "A 'Diet of Candy' by the Mother of a 'Devouring Reader.'" *SN* 18.7 (May 1891): 557–59.

Pykett, Lyn. "Reading the Periodical Press: Text and Context." *Victorian Periodicals Review* 22.3 (fall 1989): 101–8.

Rose, Jacqueline. *The Case of Peter Pan: Or The Impossibility of Children's Fiction.* Rev. ed. Houndmills, Eng.: Macmillan, 1994.

Steedman, Carolyn. *Strange Dislocations: Childhood and the Idea of Human Interiority, 1780–1930.* Cambridge, Mass.: Harvard University Press, 1995.

Trowbridge, John Townsend. *His One Fault.* SN 12:4–10, 133–35, 187–91, 272–78, 352–58, 413–18, 501–7, 590–96, 669–75, 767–[771,] 821–26, 905–9 (Nov. 1884–Oct. 1885).

———. *My Own Story: With Recollections of Noted Persons.* Boston: Houghton Mifflin, 1903.

"The True Story of *St. Nicholas.*" Editorial Advertising Supplement bound in *St. Nicholas Editorial Supplement. SN* 10.2 (1882–83), paginated 1–8 following p. 160. This supplement was located in the Bodleian Library copy of an edition specially prepared for the English market. Per. 2714 d. 27.

Twain, Mark, and Elsie Leslie Lyde. "A Wonderful Pair of Slippers." *SN* 17.4 (Feb. 1890): 309–13.

Wall, Barbara. *The Narrator's Voice: The Dilemma of Children's Fiction.* Houndmills, Eng.: Macmillan, 1991.

"What Some Eminent Men Think of *St. Nicholas.*" Advertising Supplement bound in *SN* 2.3 (Jan. 1875): 1.

Williams, Leslie. "The Look of Little Girls: John Everett Millais and the Victorian Art Market." In Nelson and Vallone.

Wolff, Michael. "Damning the Golden Stream: Latest Thoughts on a Directory of Victorian Periodicals." *Victorian Periodicals Review* 22.3 (fall 1989): 126–29.

Wright, Catharine Morris. *Lady of the Silver Skates: The Life and Correspondence of Mary Mapes Dodge.* Jamestown, R.I.: Clingstone, 1979.

DUBIOUS BOUNDARIES

Goblin Market *as a Cross-Audienced Poem: Children's Fairy Tale, Adult Erotic Fantasy*

Lorraine Janzen Kooistra

Writing about the *Alice* books, W. H. Auden articulated a commonly held critical position: "There are good books which are only for adults, because their comprehension presupposes adult experiences, but there are no good books which are only for children" (Auden 11). This point of view is implicit in our categorization of many "classics" that are cross-audienced either because, like *Robinson Crusoe* and *Gulliver's Travels,* they began as adult books and were later adapted for children; or because, like *Alice* and *The Rose and the Ring* (and indeed like many Victorian fantasies), they began as children's books but are now read almost exclusively by adults. The idea seems to be that "classics" are those works that are not only simple enough, adventurous enough, and fantastic enough to appeal to children, but also have an underlying depth of meaning that is satisfying to a mature sensibility. Although cross-audience prose classics may originate in either the adult or the juvenile literary system, this is much less true for poetry. Most anthologies of children's poetry are in fact composed of poems written for adults but later thought suitable for children—such as Scott's "Proud Maisie," Arnold's "The Forsaken Merman," and Yeats's "The Song of Wandering Aengus."[1]

I wish to thank the Social Sciences and Humanities Research Council of Canada for its generous support, which made possible my research for this paper. I am also indebted to Jan Marsh, Jill Shefrin, Catherine Thompson, Nick Hedges, John Bolton, and John P. Kooistra for their interest and assistance. Every effort has been made to ensure that all necessary permissions have been obtained for the reproductions in this paper, which have been made possible by the generous assistance of Nipissing University. Special thanks are due to The Osborne Collection of Early Children's Books, Toronto Public Library, for permission to reproduce from its collection Warwick Goble's illustration in Dora Owen's *Book of Fairy Poetry.*

Children's Literature 25, ed. Francelia Butler, R. H. W. Dillard, and Elizabeth Lennox Keyser, guest ed. Mitzi Myers and U. C. Knoepflmacher (Yale University Press, © 1997 Hollins College).

Figure 1. Poster for Nick Hedges's production of *Goblin Market* (Battersea Arts Center, London, 1995). Photograph by Nobby Clark, depicting Laura (Zoe Waites) and Lizzie (Polly Wiseman).

Christina Rossetti's *Goblin Market* is one such poem for grown-ups that has been appropriated for a juvenile audience in anthologies, school texts, plays, and picture books. It has also been commandeered for "adults only" in magazines and books, as well as on the stage. For this reason, *Goblin Market* is not only a cross-audienced poem; it also dramatically enacts the truism that good children's literature has no age restrictions, whereas some adult literature is accessible only to mature readers. In the course of *Goblin Market*'s long history of production, the children's fairy tale has remained open to dual readerships, but the textual boundaries of the erotic adult fantasy have been actively policed. Thus a typical blurb on a juvenile picture book claims that "Christina Rossetti's narrative poem can be read with pleasure by youngsters and adults alike" (*Goblin Market,* 1981). On the other hand, the poster advertising a recent Battersea Arts Center production of *Goblin Market* describes the work as "an erotic, adult fairytale" and warns: "This performance contains nudity and is unsuitable for children"[2] (fig. 1).

As both a children's fairy tale and an adult erotic fantasy, *Goblin Market* has managed to invoke particularly polarized audiences. Yet there are perhaps more similarities between juvenile literature and sexual fantasy than there might at first appear. Both rely on contextual constraints—modes of production and distribution as well as nonverbal visual signs—to construct their implied audiences. And each takes its definition from implicit assumptions about sexuality. Because childhood is often defined as that period of life before sexual maturation, the topic of sexuality is generally deemed either inappropriate or incomprehensible to child readers. Erotic fantasy, on the other hand, designates its "adults only" readership precisely by featuring explicit sexual content. Christina Rossetti's poem offers a fascinating study in the politics of audience formation, for *Goblin Market* crossed all these boundaries from the outset: it was written for adults; it used the form of the children's fairy tale; and it was about sex.

Although *Goblin Market*'s internal audience is indeed "the little ones" to whom Laura tells her story,[3] it is important to remember that the poem's first known public audience was not children but adults. In October 1861, publisher Alexander Macmillan read Rossetti's manuscript to a working-men's society in Cambridge. The workers' reception suggests that they recognized that *Goblin Market*'s simple style was actually a vehicle for its mature content: "They seemed at first to wonder whether I was making fun of them," Macmillan wrote the poet's brother Gabriel: "by degrees they got as still as death, and when I finished there was a tremendous burst of applause" (95). The men's suspicion that Macmillan was "making fun of them" suggests that their immediate reaction to the poem's nursery rhyme meters and skipping rhymes was that they were being patronized by a fairy tale meant for children. Their subsequent silence and appreciation indicates their final approbation of the poem's subject matter and its appropriateness for grown-ups. Although it is impossible to know for certain at this late date, it seems likely that Rossetti deliberately used the fairy-tale form—suitable for oral readings and hence accessible to wider audiences—to convey an important story to a specific group of adults. As Jan Marsh's research indicates, the writing of *Goblin Market* in 1859 coincided with Rossetti's initial employment as a lay sister at Highgate Penitentiary, a home for the reclamation of "fallen women." According to Marsh, this poem may not have been "written explicitly for the girls or Sisters at Highgate," but it is highly likely that it was inspired by Rossetti's work here. Moreover, because Rossetti probably worked at Highgate from 1859 to 1864 (Marsh, "Christina Rossetti's Vocation," 244–45), there may have been later opportunities to share the poem's emphasis on sexual sin and on sororal redemption with the audience who evoked it.

Although the precise relationship between Rossetti's poem and its potential listeners at Highgate may never be known, *Goblin Market*'s original print public is clear: the poem was produced for adults in Rossetti's first volume of poetry, *Goblin Market and Other Poems* (1862).[4] Even in its first production as an adult-directed work, however, *Goblin Market*'s richness as a cross-audienced poem was immediately discerned. Mrs. Charles Eliot Norton, one of the poem's first reviewers, recognized *Goblin Market*'s potentially dual audience when she observed that it was a poem "which children will con with delight, and which riper minds may ponder over" (402). Despite this early recognition of the poem's availability to a readership of children as well as adults, however, the evidence suggests that the poem remained the predominant property of "riper minds" in Christina Rossetti's lifetime. Although Victorian children doubtless read *Goblin Market* (or had it read to them), neither personal memoirs nor accounts of nineteenth-century children's reading habits make any mention of the poem, which only later became a "children's classic."[5]

I

The first evidence we have of children "conning" *Goblin Market* is its appearance in school textbooks in the late nineteenth and early twentieth centuries. As Richard Altick indicates in his social history of the nineteenth-century's mass reading public, Matthew Arnold's campaign to develop culture and taste by introducing British literature into the curriculum resulted in the publication of anthologies specifically designed for elementary school pupils. The children's task was to memorize passages of poetry and explain the allusions (Altick 159–61). How much "delight" there was in this process is open to conjecture. What is much more certain is that this kind of institutional production went a long way toward establishing *Goblin Market* as a children's classic.

A school textbook defines not only a general audience (children), but also a specific sector of the juvenile population—for example, eleven- to fourteen-year-olds. For this reason, *Goblin Market* was constructed as a poem for children at precisely the same time—and by the same set of discursive practices—that "the child" was being differentiated according to age, sex, and class. Thus the issue of what is children's literature always brings with it the accompanying problematic of what is "the child." And, as Jacqueline Rose observes, "there is no language for children which can be described independently of divisions in the institution of schooling, the institution out of which modern childhood has more or less been produced" (7). The construction of the child, and of a literature for her, will always be overwritten by "grown-up" economic and educational institutions, as well as by the historical contexts and material conditions out of which these ideologies have developed. The questions, "what is good for the child?" and "what can we produce for the child?" are closely connected.

Practically speaking, a school textbook necessarily has a dual readership: the teacher and the student. Mary A. Woods, headmistress of the Clifton High School for girls, drew on her teaching experience as well as on her own favorite reading matter when she published her anthologies of poetry for the classroom. Justly praised for the originality of her selections, Woods must also be credited for the insight that led her to select *Goblin Market* as a poem adolescent girls—as opposed to the seven- to eleven-year-olds targeted in her *First School Poetry Book* (1886)—would enjoy. She originally included the poem in *A Second School Poetry Book* (1887) for use in "the Middle Forms of High Schools, *i.e.* . . . girls from eleven to fourteen or fifteen" (Woods v), and years later, when she divided her *Second Poetry Book* into two parts, the first for the Lower Middle Forms (girls eleven to thirteen), and the second for Upper Middle Forms of High Schools (girls thirteen to fifteen), Woods reserved *Goblin Market* for her oldest students. It seems a reasonable conjecture that practical classroom experience motivated Woods to present Rossetti's poem to the more mature pupils as the group who would most appreciate it. Although this appearance in a school textbook marks *Goblin Market*'s debut as children's literature, it is equally clear that a definite sector of the juvenile population has been targeted: those on the threshold of sexual maturation and womanhood.

A similar age distinction for the implied child reader is apparent in the three-part *Children's Rossetti*, which Macmillan published in 1914. Designed for use in the classroom, each volume of poetry is directed to a different age level. *Goblin Market* appears in the third volume, which is designated for senior students. Like Woods's anthology—and like the *Goblin Market* edited by schoolteacher Edith Fry in 1912 for Blackie's Library for Senior Pupils—the *Children's Rossetti* indicates its school-text status by its glosses on hard or unusual words and its elucidations of allusions and abstruse meanings. At the same time, Macmillan's *Children's Rossetti* and Blackie's *Goblin Market* designate the child reader in another, nonverbal way: by the presence of illustrations.[6] Their inclusion raises the issue of the material ways by which a juvenile audience is written into a book. Size of type, margins, and spacing are some of the visual signs used to designate readerships. The dimensions of the book, the sturdiness of the paper, and the style of jacket design are also important. But no single visual sign proclaims "children's book" with the same compelling authority as do pictures. In children's books as in other forms of literary production, "readers are made by what makes the book" (Macherey 70).

Economic factors are inextricably linked to the business of moving adult poetry into the children's literary system. Poetry anthologies directed at the young, whether for use as school textbooks or to be given as gifts or prizes, were a reliable source of income in the turn-of-the-century book trade (Feather 159). Publishers were quick to capitalize on two guaranteed sellers in the rapidly developing children's market: fairy lore and colored prints. The gift book became "big business" as "the illustrators cast their particular vision on time-honored fairy tales, nursery rhymes, and fables" (Meyer 26, 14). As Christine Chaundler confides in *The Children's Author: A Writer's Guide to the Juvenile Market* (1934), "the easiest kind of story to sell" to publishers in this period was the imaginative fairy tale (19, 13). I cite Chaundler here because she was also, in fact, one of the first editors to seize on *Goblin Market* as an appropriate fairy tale for an illustrated children's anthology, *My Book of Stories from the Poets* (1919). Dora Owen was quick to follow with her *Book of Fairy Poetry* (1920). Owen's anthology makes explicit the artificiality of the notion of "children's poetry" by drawing attention to the gift book's dual readership: "This anthology is designed primarily for children but also for all lovers of poetry and fairy-lore" (preface). The table of contents confirms that almost all the poems included in this collection—from Shakespeare's "Ariel's

Figure 2. Warwick Goble, "Buy from us with a Golden Curl," in Dora Owen, *Book of Fairy Poetry,* p. 42.

Song" to Gerard Manley Hopkins's "A Vision of Mermaids" and W. B. Yeats's "The Host of the Air"—were written for adults. But as one of Warwick Goble's popular gift books, this lavish publication, with sixteen tipped-in colored plates mounted on dull-olive art paper and protected by tissue guards, was calculated to appeal to adult buyers who wanted the best for their children—and themselves (fig. 2).

If gift books like the *Book of Fairy Poetry* seem designed for both the drawing room and the nursery, others had a more age-specific appeal. Like Owen's anthology, Chaundler's *My Book of Stories from the Poets* is illustrated with glossy color pictures. Chaundler's collection differs from Owen's, however, in that she translates the poems in her collection into prose in order to make the stories more "natural" and hence more accessible to her child reader (Chaundler, *My Book,* ix). Chaundler's intervention suggests how inappropriate *Goblin Market* might seem to certain children's publishers and editors. In the process of converting Rossetti's poetry to prose, Chaundler inculcates a moral at every opportunity, lest Rossetti's fairy tale seem to celebrate rather than forbid pleasure. For example, the child reader is warned at the outset of the story that "though the goblin fruit was so beautiful to look at, the village people did not dare to buy it. . . . For the goblin fruit was poisonous and brought terrible grief and harm to the unwary person who ate of it" (1–2). It is only *after* this meaning is established that the protagonists, Lizzie and Laura, are introduced. These golden-haired, rosy-cheeked sisters are clearly divided into naughty and nice categories. And when Laura tastes the antidote on her sister's face, the real cure is not, as it is in Rossetti's poem, the fruit juice itself, but rather contrition for her naughtiness: "And overcome with grief and remorse she pressed Lizzie to her, and kissed her again and again, while for the first time since she had eaten of the forbidden fruit, tears of penitent sorrow fell from her eyes." As her lips touch the "magic juices," Laura suddenly realizes "how foolish and wrong she had been to taste goblins' fruit, and with cries and tears she paced up and down the room, until at last she fell unconscious to the floor" (10). Suitably punished and remorseful, Laura is allowed full recovery, but the moral of Rossetti's epilogue—"For there is no friend like a sister"—is displaced in Chaundler's adaptation by warnings against curiosity and disobedience, the misdemeanors of childhood.

Not all gift books, of course, were anthologies. Many were single works published in newly illustrated separate volumes. One of the reasons that the "Golden Age" of illustrated books for children reached its peak between 1905 and 1914 (Dalby 7) was that many Victorian classics went out of copyright in this period. When the copyright on *Alice's Adventures in Wonderland* expired in 1907, for instance, eight newly illustrated versions were published in the first year alone (Felmingham 29). Even Rossetti's *Goblin Market,* which never achieved the almost cult status of *Alice,* inspired six newly illustrated editions in the first three decades of the century. The development of the three-color process and the relatively cheap costs of paper and printing at this time provided the economic base for an expanding industry that was institutionally supported by schools and libraries, as well as by a growing middle-class audience with changing attitudes toward both children and books. The development of the industry and the establishment of its market were also assisted by magazines such as *The Bookman* and *The Studio*. In 1896, *The Bookman* added a new section on children's books to its annual survey of illustrated books in its Christmas supplement (Rose 105). In 1897, *The Studio* devoted its entire special winter issue to "Children's Books and their Illustrators." In his article, art critic Gleeson White candidly admits that the illustrated children's books of the day are in fact produced by, and for, adults: "As a rule it is the 'grown-ups' who buy; therefore with no wish to belittle the advance in nursery taste, one must own that at present its improvement is chiefly owing to the active energies of those who give, and is only passively tolerated by those who accept" (5).

White's tacit admission of the dual adult-child audience for illustrated books is in line with much recent writing on books produced in what has been called the new "Golden Age" of children's literature. Treld Pelkey Bicknell credits this renaissance to such factors as "the interest of excellent writers and artists in the children's book field, great technical advances in printing (especially the opportunities offered by offset lithography), marketing techniques to expand sales, full-blown awareness of the importance of children's books among publishers, teachers, librarians, and parents" (in Kingman 58). Trading in what Brian Alderson calls "the international nostalgia market" (in Kingman 23), artists and publishers have seized on Victorian fantasy classics as vehicles for their work. Illustrated fairy tales, in other words, are once again "big business." Two notions that have remained constant since White's fin-de-siècle article on illustrated children's books are first, that picture books both give pleasure to the child and educate her aesthetic sensibilities; and second, that picture books are too good for children alone: adults, especially collectors, are also important consumers.

Three newly illustrated editions of *Goblin Market* produced in this most recent "Golden Age" confirm these picture-book principles. Two of them—one published by Victor Gollancz in 1980, the other by David R. Godine in 1981—self-consciously write in their dual readership by their picture-book-as-art-book approach to the form. These books represent the new, post-modern gift book, which is calculated to appeal to children, collectors, and prize-giving juries. The other publication was brought out in 1970 by E. P. Dutton in America and in 1971 by Macmillan in the United Kingdom. Illustrated and adapted by Ellen Raskin, this book is more specifically targeted at a child reader—and, of course, the parents, librarians, and teachers who buy books for her. For this reason, this *Goblin Market* is, like Chaundler's earlier adaptation, an interesting text to study, for it tells us much about how contemporary attitudes to children simultaneously produce "the child" and the book. As with Chaundler's version, it is not only the addition of pictures, but also the active censorship and emendation of the text, that enables Ellen Raskin to represent Rossetti's poem for modern children.

According to Zohar Shavit, the business of translating adult texts into children's books involves "an adjustment of the text to make it appropriate and useful to the child, in accordance with what society regards (at a certain point in time) as educationally 'good for the child' and an adjustment of plot, characterization, and language to prevailing society's perceptions of the child's ability to read and comprehend" (Shavit 113). As we have seen, Christine Chaundler translated Rossetti's poem for a postwar child audience by converting the putatively difficult poetry into comprehensible prose. At the same time, she altered the plot and characterization to inculcate contemporary ideologies of sin and remorse, using the tale as an appropriate apparatus for behavior modification in disobedient children. The fairy tale contained a pill. Half a century later, no such bitter pill must be swallowed in Ellen Raskin's adaptation of *Goblin Market*. Rather, Raskin presents modern children with a carefully censored version of the poem, omitting all references to death and muting any suggestion of sex and violence. What is educationally "good" for the modern child is, apparently, not a cautionary tale, but rather a happy experience in a fairy-tale world where nobody really dies or gets hurt.

In Raskin's updated version of the poem, the goblins are mischievous but not downright evil. Gone is the moral universe of Christine Chaundler's fairy-tale world. Instead, Raskin set out to make the goblins "appealing" in order to render "Laura's temptation more plausible" (Raskin, "Afterword"). Making the goblins visually appealing, of course, is also a means of downplaying any sense of danger or fear that the language of the poem might evoke; as Raskin notes, the goblins "had always been drawn as frightening creatures" ("Afterword"). Thus Raskin's illustrations write the child reader into the scene in two ways: first, by the visual code of the picture book, which features brightly colored watercolors splashed across all the page openings; and second, by the visual censorship of violence and danger through the representation of "appealing" goblins. Raskin's goblins are funny

Laughed every goblin
When they spied her peeping:
Came towards her hobbling,
Flying, running, leaping,

Figure 3. "Laughed every goblin." From *Goblin Market* by Ellen Raskin. Copyright ©
1970 by Ellen Raskin. Used by permission of Dutton Signet, a division of Penguin
Books USA Inc.

little men and animals in bizarre, faintly medieval costumes whose
antics appear comic rather than abusive or threatening (fig. 3).

This visual framing of the meaning of Rossetti's poem is combined
with an active intervention with regard to its plot and language, one
designed to make it suitable for "the contemporary reader." Although
Raskin claims her emendations are all in the interest of eliminating
"outdated Victorian proprieties" ("Afterword"), in fact the 1970s version seems considerably more squeamish than the poem published
in 1862. The cautionary story of Jeanie,

> Who should have been a bride;
> But who for joys brides hope to have
> Fell sick and died
> In her gay prime

is erased, as are other suggestions that encountering goblin men
might be fatal. When Laura tastes the fruit a second time, there is no
suggestion that sense might fail "in the mortal strife," and the question "Is it death or is it life?" is similarly silenced. Although represen-

27   Or like the mane of horses in their flight,
          Or like an eagle when she stems the light
          Straight toward the sun,
          Or like a caged thing freed,
          Or like a flying flag when armies run.

Figure 4. "Or like the mane of horses in their flight." From *Goblin Market* by Ellen Raskin. Copyright © 1970 by Ellen Raskin. Used by permission of Dutton Signet, a division
of Penguin Books USA Inc.

tations of death were not only tolerated, but also positively endorsed
in Victorian and Edwardian children's books (Peppin 12; Smith 91),
such images are apparently no longer appropriate for the modern
child—on the printed page, at least (screen adaptations are a different matter).

Sexuality, on the other hand, has always been a more or less taboo
area in the realm of representation for children. But notions of what
is sexy are both historically contingent and subject to the different
restrictions of verbal and visual media. In 1919 Christine Chaundler,
for instance, had no difficulty in verbally representing the two sisters
lying "side by side in their little white bed, their golden heads close
together on the pillow" (5), whereas in 1970 Ellen Raskin clearly
finds such sexual resonances disturbing and deletes the passage. Both
adapters find Rossetti's language beyond the comprehension of children in the scene where Lizzie calls upon Laura to "Eat me, drink
me, love me." Chaundler has Lizzie say "never mind my bruises—
kiss me and taste the goblins' fruit once more!" (9–10). Raskin omits
this passage altogether, and alters Rossetti's "Hug me, kiss me, suck

my juices" to "Hug me, kiss me, *taste the* juices / Squeezed from goblin fruits for you" (26; italics added). The accompanying illustration shows an unconscious Laura lying in her sister's arms as the fruit juices drip off Lizzie's face into her open mouth (fig. 4; p. 27). Such a visual representation displaces any sexual resonances evoked by the sisters' embrace by eliminating the kisses altogether. A theatrical version of Rossetti's poem, first arranged for acting by E. Hynes in the *Girls' Realm Annual* for 1913 and later rearranged by the Rev. Maurice Bell in 1921, similarly omits the embrace between the sisters. After Lizzie triumphs over the goblins in the last scene, Laura simply re-enters the wood, fully restored to her former youthful beauty (15). Presumably Laura's cure had to be effected off-stage because the passionate encounter between the sisters was deemed inappropriate or beyond the understanding of a young audience.

II

If, as Peter Hunt argues, the study of children's literature "presents unique challenges of interpretation and production" because it "necessarily involves language acquisition, censorship, and the whole issue of sexuality" (21), the same is true—with the exception of language acquisition—for the study of adult erotica. Like children's literature, adult fantasy material produces its audience under conditions of censorship and defines itself in terms of sexuality. Moreover, it uses specific visual signs, connected to its specialized methods of production and distribution, to designate its target audience. And when it comes to establishing meanings and audiences, images can be as important in the production of erotic fantasy as they are in material for children. At the same time, of course, erotic fantasy defines itself by its obsessive concern with precisely what children's representations disguise or displace. Far from omitting passages like "Hug me, kiss me, suck my juices" and "Eat me, drink me, love me," restricted productions of *Goblin Market* make the sexual possibilities of such images central to their representations.

Adapted versions of Rossetti's poem have been produced explicitly for grown-ups in *Playboy* in 1973, in *Pacific Comics* in 1984, and on the stage in 1995. Erotic representations present images of sexual fantasy in forms that deliberately restrict audiences by age and, often, by sex. Thus, the cover of *Playboy* inscribes its audience with the words "Entertainment for Men"; *Pacific Comics* warns that its contents are

for "Mature Readers"; and the posters and programs by the Battersea Arts Center (BAC) caution that the performance "is unsuitable
for children." This is, of course, a long-established marketing ploy.
The king in *Huckleberry Finn*, for instance, knows that in staging the
Royal Nonesuch, the key to a sell-out crowd is not the representation itself, but rather the promise of titillation and the expression of
the forbidden by signals like "LADIES AND CHILDREN NOT ADMITTED"
(Twain 136). Similar advertising labels for *Goblin Market* distinguish
between the children's fairy tale and the erotic adult fantasy by sig-
naling the explicit portrayal of nudity and sexuality. In contemporary
productions of *Goblin Market*, mature content is defined by images of
heterosexual gang rape and lesbian love.

Because all three versions that present *Goblin Market* as an erotic
fantasy for adults include images of naked women touching each
other, it seems worthwhile to focus on their differences. Although
all the audiences are restricted, *Playboy*, with its international circulation, has a large readership—whereas the BAC production, with its
three-week run of performances in a seventy-five-seat theater,[7] and
Pacific Comics, with its narrow distribution to the direct sales marketplace of the specialist comics store, both have relatively small audiences. In addition, *Playboy* belongs to that category of erotic fantasy
whose specialized marketing and production methods give it the des-
ignation "pornography" (Caughie and Kuhn 156). Although context
and mode of consumption also place *Pacific Comics* on the fringes of
the pornography industry, the BAC's *Goblin Market*, which played to a
mixed public audience, belongs to a different tradition altogether—
the avant-garde tradition of fringe theater. There are also important
differences in production and representation. Neither *Pacific Comics*
nor the BAC evoke the child in their representation of the poem.
Playboy, on the other hand, deliberately presents *Goblin Market* as children's literature in order to make its "Ribald Classic" especially provocative. The editor invites his readers to be "turned on" by what "the
kids have been reading for the past 114 years" (Rossetti, "*Goblin Market:* Ribald Classic," 115). As if deliberately duplicating the verbal text
as a work for children, moreover, *Playboy* abridges Rossetti's poem in
much the same way for the adult sexual fantasist as Ellen Raskin did
for the contemporary child:[8] by deleting about a third of the lines
and omitting the stories of the kernel stone and Jeanie. Thus, the
displacement of the textual language by the accompanying graphics
allows *Goblin Market* to be transformed into adult erotica. Predictably,

Figure 5. "Eat me, drink me, love me." Reproduced by Special Permission of *Playboy* magazine. Copyright © 1973 by *Playboy* magazine. Illustration by Kinuko Craft.

Playboy celebrates the very moment that Raskin's text omits and her picture revises; a full-page glossy spread now gives a sexually explicit representation of the sisters' final embrace (fig. 5).

On the other hand, both the *Pacific Comics* "Pathways to Fantasy" version of *Goblin Market* and the BAC's dramatic production include Jeanie's story. In fact, Jeanie is central to Nick Hedges's dramatization of Rossetti's poem. Hedges wanted to convey the poem in a theatrical language as rich and sensuous as the literary language and included only two passages from the text: the story of Jeanie and the epilogue. The ghost of Jeanie, like some grotesque bride—a decrepit Miss Havisham in a tatty veil—appears in the opening scene and intermittently haunts the stage. The play opens with Lizzie and Laura raking away a pile of decaying autumn leaves, and uncovering sheets and pillows, which they use to make up a bed. When Jeanie flits in to lay her dead bridal bouquet on the girls' bed, the idea that "twilight is not good for maidens" is visually enforced at the same time that the sexual implications are underscored. Interestingly, the story of the kernel stone is also central to Hedges's conception of the poem: from her first encounter with the goblins, Laura keeps the kernel stone in her locked fist, despite all Lizzie's attempts to loosen her hold. It is not until Lizzie redeems her with the antidote that Laura can open her hand and release the poisonous stone.[9] Far from being censored, images of death and disappointment are thus foregrounded in this "erotic, adult fairytale" (BAC program notes). Perhaps this is because, in the realm of the erotic imaginary, sex and death have always been bed partners.

The stories of Jeanie and the kernel stone are also left intact in *Pacific Comics*'s version of the poem. In fact, only eighty-three lines of Rossetti's text are omitted in this comic book for grown-ups. Omissions include repetitions and similes rather than plot-related material. The most significant textual alteration is actually a visual effect: the running-on of the lines of Rossetti's verse into regular chunks of prose, so that the poetic form of the language is disguised. Because the verse is not otherwise altered, this emendation seems motivated by the limited space a comic-book frame allows for lettering, rather than by the consideration of audience accessibility (as in Chaundler's conversion of verse to prose). Unlike children's books, the adult fantasy comic is not concerned with either language competency or the censorship of sex, death, and violence. On the other hand, there is an obvious similarity between children's books and comics: the necessary addition of colored illustrations. Indeed, comic-book convention demands multiple pictures on every page, so that John Bolton's artwork for the poem probably represents the most lavishly illustrated *Goblin Market* ever produced—which is likely why TV Ontario relied on this visual source in a recent production of *Goblin Market* for its *Introduction to Literature* series. Despite these similarities of production, the pictures in *Pacific Comics* are not, of course, designed for a juvenile audience. A specialist in the fantasy and erotic horror genre, Bolton evokes both the sensuous and the scary in his series of frames for the final encounter between the sisters (fig. 6).

Comics are often associated with children, but the production and distribution of *Pacific Comics* as a work "For Mature Readers"—sold in what Roger Sabin calls "the 'locker-room' atmosphere" of specialist shops that are "unwelcoming to women" (228)—establishes a very specific male audience for this production of *Goblin Market*. Indeed, adult comics inhabit a no-woman's land between pornography and juvenile literature; newsagents who stock them, for instance, usually place them "above the bottom shelf and the children's comics, but below the top shelf and the porn magazines" (106). There are historical reasons for this. Adult comics evolved in America as part of the

Figure 6. John Bolton, "She cried, 'Laura,' up the garden." *Goblin Market* in *Pacific Comics* (1984), p. 17. By courtesy of the artist.

counterculture of the sixties and seventies in reaction to the restrictions of the Comics Code. Established in 1954 in response to lobbyists like psychiatrist Fredric Wertham, who wanted "to re-establish the line between what was acceptable for children, and for adults,"[10] the code banned material relating to sex and violence (158, 161). Adult comics developed out of these conditions of censorship, and were at first an underground phenomenon. Then, with the emergence of "fandom" and the direct sales market, specialist shops appeared, initiating the "adult comics revolution" of the eighties in both Britain and North America (175–76). *Pacific Comics* was one of the new independents to focus on the "sword and sorcery" or fantasy genre for the direct sales marketplace. As editor Bruce Jones writes in his introductory letter to the reader, the "Pathways to Fantasy" title sets out to "define a new meaning for the word [fantasy] and with it reach a whole new generation of readers"—with the help of the fans who are "to share in the job of shaping and molding the look of our new book" by writing letters outlining their fantasy preferences.

The fantasies in this particular issue of *Pacific Comics* range from a story of a Neanderthal superhero fighting aliens and predators ("Stalking"), to a ghost story with erotic nuances ("A Night to Remember"), to a tale of an illicit encounter between a golden-haired virgin and a handsome prince who is married to a green-haired witch ("Hunger"), to an ironic retelling of the Medusa story ("Oh What a Lovely Estate Have We"). In the midst of these fantasies, *Goblin Market* is both the most artistically interesting and the most subtle in its sensuousness. The focus is on the relationship between the sisters—their beauty, love, and strength—more than it is on their relations with the goblins. Thus, both the power and the sexiness of women, rather than their victimization, are the theme of Bolton's artwork. Coming from an artist who worked for a year producing *Bionic Woman* strips for Marvel, and whose personal artistic interest has always been female subjects, particularly nude female subjects, this emphasis is not surprising.[11] The artistic excellence, coupled with the portrayal of lesbian love in a fantasy world, makes this version of *Goblin Market* highly collectable. In fact, it is probably a prime candidate for the label "GGA," or "Good Girl Art," which is used in collectors' price guides. As Roger Sabin explains in *Adult Comics,* the development of superheroes for girls (such as Wonder Woman and Sheena) also opened up a new market of older boys and men who liked "their undisguised erotic charge" and who valued "an artist's ability to draw sexy women" (223 and 288, n. 8). Thus the demand of collectors has established a market for high-quality glossy productions of erotic, adult fantasies like *Pacific Comics*'s *Goblin Market.*

III

Clearly, the different strategies that go into the formation of age- and sex-specific audiences at particular moments in history depend on the material means of production and distribution, and on the ideologies produced out of these bases. But there is still room for a fair amount of overlap and blurred boundaries because the categories of "child" and "adult" are not fixed. The target audience for adult comics, for instance, is males aged sixteen to twenty-four (Sabin 3). This was precisely the age of the reclaimed prostitutes at Highgate Penitentiary (Marsh, *Christina Rossetti,* 224), who may have inspired Rossetti's poem and heard it read aloud. "Adult" in these very different contexts seems defined by those over sixteen who have a certain amount of sexual awareness, for whether it is received as an erotic fantasy or as a sexual parable, the poem in these instances requires a sexually sophisticated audience.

But sexual knowingness is a slippery term by which to discriminate between children and adults. *Goblin Market's* first targeted child
audience, after all, hovers right at the edge of this great divide between innocence and experience, for Headmistress Woods included
the poem in her anthology for fifteen-year-old schoolgirls. In fact,
almost all productions of *Goblin Market* for children (with the exception of Ellen Raskin's picture book) target the oldest "child" category
available to juvenile literature: those aged eleven to fourteen.¹² In
thinking of *Goblin Market* as a children's fairy tale and an erotic adult
fantasy, then, it is important to keep the boundaries fluid rather than
distinct: it is not a question of "either or," but of "both." This was
brought home to me when I gave my own eleven-year-old daughter,
Alison, an unillustrated copy of *Goblin Market* to read. She enthused
about the poem: how much the sisters loved each other, and how one
sister saved the other from the wicked goblins. Then I asked if she
had found it at all frightening. There was a long pause before she admitted, "Well, mummy, I think I would have, *if I had understood it.*" In
her reading she had focused, as perhaps other children have done,
on the comprehensible fairy-tale plot of the poem, while at the same
time she both sensed and submerged the sexual undertones of its
imagery and themes. As Auden suggests, some "comprehension presupposes adult experiences" (11); but the act of reading may include
unconscious strategies of self-censorship as well.

Because *Goblin Market* for children has been produced primarily
for adolescents, it is worth asking how young people in this age group
might represent the poem themselves. A recent production of *Goblin
Market* as a dance drama put on by a ninth-grade class from the Lincoln County School of Performing Arts for the Sears Niagara District
Drama Festival in 1993 provided me with a unique opportunity to see
how some contemporary thirteen- and fourteen-year-olds read Rossetti's poem (fig. 7). The students in Catherine M. Thompson's Grade
Nine Comprehensive Arts Class produced their own script, set, costumes, soundtrack, and choreography for their performance. The
play was also overseen by a student director, and so it can be fairly
called a youth production. Their source material was Anita Moss and
Jon C. Stott's *The Family of Stories: An Anthology of Children's Literature,*
but despite this context for the poem, these "children" clearly did
not read *Goblin Market* as a juvenile fairy tale. Instead, they produced
a drama of violence, abuse, and death, whose main message seems
to be "just say no to fruit." Their *Goblin Market* is the story of drug

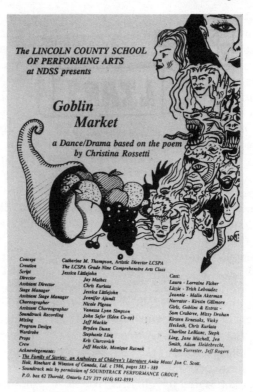

Figure 7. Poster for the Lincoln County School of Performing Arts production of *Goblin Market* for the Sears Ontario Drama Festival (St. Catharines, 1993).

pushers whose traffic means certain death for the unwary. This fate is reinforced by the visual imagery: Jeanie's coffin dominates the stage at center back throughout the entire performance, and twice Jeanie rises from the grave to dance in a dream sequence as a warning to the addicted Laura. At one point, the goblins insinuate that Laura must trade sexual favors for fruit or risk a beating.

What was most interesting to me as I watched this production was not the teenagers' inclusion of sex, violence, and death, or even their interpretation of Rossetti's story of unquenchable desire as a tale of drug addiction.[13] Rather, I was astounded by their alteration of the relationship between the sisters. Like the Reverend Bell's dramatic adaptation, this student performance omits Lizzie and Laura's healing embrace. In this production, however, the omission seems to reflect squeamishness about feminism rather than sexuality, and it results in a story of female victimization rather than female power and sisterhood. In fact, the close relationship between the sisters is entirely lost: Lizzie is whiny and Laura self-centered. Instead of coming home with her face dripping with juices that Laura must kiss away, Lizzie brings her sister actual pieces of fruit, thereby eliminating the need for the recuperative embrace. Moreover, far from thinking first of Lizzie's danger as in Rossetti's text,

> Must your light like mine be hidden,
> Your young life like mine be wasted,
> Undone in mine undoing
> And ruined in my ruin

the Laura of this student production simply snatches the fruit and begins to eat voraciously. For her part, Lizzie is not motivated to brave the goblin men primarily out of fear for her sister's life, but rather because Laura hits her and yells at her (in fact, calls her a bitch) to force her to bring her more fruit. Indeed, the entire performance focuses on individual needs rather than altruistic actions. Although the play ends with a narrator reading Rossetti's epilogue, the message that "there is no friend like a sister" is ironically contradicted by the preceding performance.

It is perhaps not fair to look for consistency and acumen in a performance of ninth-grade students, but I think the production does suggest that this group of contemporary adolescents, at least, had no trouble incorporating the thematics of sex, death, and violence into their understanding of *Goblin Market*. Moreover, the students reproduced the generic dualities of the poem—its combination of fairy story and cautionary tale—with some skill. In other words, they certainly seemed to have some comprehension of the sexual experiences that Rossetti's poem invokes—but not its religious or redemptive ones. If any censorship is operating here, it is not the kind of active policing that "tones down" adult material for children either by eliminating references to sex or death or by suppressing immoral content. On the contrary, by a curious inversion, these fin-de-siècle adolescents suppress the moral precisely by enacting scenarios of sexuality and violence on a stage where selfishness is substituted for selflessness. The production is a timely reminder that our constructions of childhood innocence are, indeed, constructions. At the same time, the students' production dramatizes the degree to which historical time and place shape both narratives and interpretive strategies.

Goblin Market's richness depends upon the tension between its simple language, nursery-rhyme meters, and fairy-tale form, as well as its serious commentary on sexual politics and sacrificial, sisterly love—whether that love is seen as spiritual, feminist, or both. By playing with the shifting nuances of innocence and experience in a chain of evocative images, *Goblin Market*'s language inscribes the possibilities of its own production as not only a children's fairy tale and a piece of adult erotica, but also as a religious allegory, a feminist fantasy, a moral tale, and more. At the same time, *Goblin Market*'s other producers—its adapters, illustrators, directors, and performers—remind us of the many ways in which texts operate within a network of institutional, economic, and ideological forces that produce audiences and meanings with each representation. The ongoing dialectic between language and readers produces *Goblin Market*s whose forms of communication are indeed determined by the conditions that determine their production.[14]

Notes

1. The poems are taken from the *Oxford Book of Poetry for Children* (1982), ed. Edward Blishen, but these selections are typical of many children's anthologies.

2. Battersea Arts Center, England's "National Theatre of the Fringe," produced a stage version of *Goblin Market,* adapted and directed by Nick Hedges, 4–29 Apr. 1995.

3. Unless otherwise noted, all citations of *Goblin Market* are taken from *The Complete Poems of Christina Rossetti*, vol. 1, 11–26.

4. For a history of this work's production and reception in the Victorian and modern periods, see Lorraine Janzen Kooistra, "Modern Markets for *Goblin Market,*" *Victorian Poetry* 32, nos. 3–4 (1994): 249–77.

5. See, for example, Annabel Huth Jackson, *A Victorian Childhood;* E. M. Field, *The Child and His Book;* Edward Salmon, *Juvenile Literature as It Is;* Amy Cruse, *The Victorians and Their Books;* Lance Salway, *A Peculiar Gift: Nineteenth-Century Writings on Books for Children;* and Richard Altick, *An English Common Reader.*

6. *Goblin Market* is illustrated in Macmillan's *Children's Rossetti* with Gabriel Rossetti's original two plates for the poem. Blackie's *Goblin Market* is illustrated with two full-page black-and-white plates and a frontispiece by Florence Harrison, who illustrated *Poems of Christina Rossetti* as a Blackie gift book in 1910.

7. The BAC *Goblin Market*'s audience had, however, a wider international audience than its London debut would suggest: the production also toured Prague and Jerusalem.

8. Raskin abridges the poem by 197 lines and *Playboy* by 199 lines. Except for the story deletions mentioned above, most of the omissions (repetitions, similes, and the like) relate to matters of linguistic richness rather than plot.

9. Information in this paragraph is taken from a telephone interview with Nick Hedges, 9 May 1995.

10. Wertham wrote *The Seduction of the Innocent* (1954) in which he argued that comics led to delinquency. With his authority as a psychiatrist, Wertham led the crusade against comics that ultimately resulted in the industry's establishment of the Comics Code. See Sabin, esp. chap. 12.

11. Interview with John Bolton, 13 Dec. 1994.

12. Children's literature is usually defined as books for readers under age fifteen. See Darton 1.

13. A similar reading of the poem as a story of drug addiction and sexual abuse was given in the Trestle Theatre Company's production of *Goblin Market,* with original music composed by Aaron Jay Kernis. This production toured England from 12 January to 22 January 1995 with the Birmingham Contemporary Music Group.

14. I am indebted here to Pierre Macherey's theory that books do not produce readers by some mysterious power, but by historical and material conditions (Macherey 70).

Works Cited

Altick, Richard D. *The English Common Reader: A Social History of the Mass Reading Public, 1800–1900.* Chicago: University of Chicago Press, 1967.

Auden, W. H. "Today's 'Wonder-World' Needs *Alice.*" *Aspects of Alice: Lewis Carroll's Dreamchild as Seen Through the Critics' Looking-Glasses, 1865–1971.* Ed. Robert Phillips. New York: Vanguard, 1971.

Blishen, Edward, ed. *Oxford Book of Poetry for Children.* Oxford: Oxford University Press, 1982.

Caughie, John, and Annette Kuhn, eds. *The Sexual Subject: A* Screen *Reader in Sexuality.* London: Routledge, 1992.

Chaundler, Christine. *My Book of Stories from the Poets.* London: Cassell and Co., [1919].
———. *The Children's Author: A Writer's Guide to the Juvenile Market.* London: Pitman & Sons, 1934.

Cruse, Amy. *The Victorians and Their Books.* London: Allen & Unwin, 1962.

Dalby, Richard. *The Golden Age of Children's Book Illustration.* London: Michael O'Mara, 1991.

Darton, F. J. *Children's Books in England: Five Centuries of Social Life.* 3d. ed. Cambridge: Cambridge University Press, 1982.

Feather, John. *A History of British Publishing.* London: Croom Helm, 1988.

Felmingham, Michael. *The Illustrated Gift Book, 1880–1930.* Aldershot, Eng.: Scolar, 1988.

Field, Mrs. E. M. *The Child and His Book: Some Account of the History and Progress of Children's Literature in England.* 2d ed. London: Wells, Gardner, Darton, 1892.

Goblin Market. Dir. Jay Mathes for the Lincoln County School of Performing Arts at the Sears Ontario Drama Festival, Sean O'Sullivan Theater, Brock University, St. Catharines, Ont., 23 Feb. 1993.

Goblin Market. Introduction to Literature Series. Videocassette. TV Ontario, 1994.

Goblin Market. Music Composed by Aaran Jay Kernis. Dir. by Toby Wilsher and Joff Chafer. Performed by the Trestle Theater Company and the Birmingham Contemporary Music Group. On tour in England, 12–22 Jan. 1995.

Goblin Market. Dir. Nick Hedges. Battersea Arts Center, London, 4–29 Apr. 1995.

Hunt, Peter. *Criticism, Theory, and Children's Literature.* Oxford: Basil Blackwell, 1991.

Jackson, Annabel Huth. *A Victorian Childhood.* London: Methuen, 1932.

Kingman, Lee, Grace Allen Hogarth, and Harriet Quimby, eds. *Illustrators of Children's Books, 1967–1976.* Boston: The Horn Book, 1978.

Kooistra, Lorraine Janzen. "Modern Markets for *Goblin Market.*" *Victorian Poetry* 32.3–4 (1994): 249–77.

Macherey, Pierre. *A Theory of Literary Production.* Trans. Geoffrey Wall. London: Routledge & Kegan Paul, 1978.

Macmillan, George A., ed. *Letters of Alexander Macmillan.* Printed for private circulation, 1908.

Marsh, Jan. *Christina Rossetti: A Literary Biography.* London: Jonathan Cape, 1994.

———. "Christina Rossetti's Vocation: The Importance of *Goblin Market.*" *Victorian Poetry* 32.3–4 (1994): 233–48.

Meyer, Susan E. *A Treasury of the Great Children's Book Illustrators.* New York: Abradale, 1987.

Moss, Anita, and Jon C. Stott, eds. *The Family of Stories: An Anthology of Children's Literature.* New York: Holt, Rinehart and Winston, 1986.

Norton, [Mrs. Charles Eliot]. " 'The Angel in the House' and 'The Goblin Market.' " *Macmillan's Magazine* 8 (Sept. 1863): 398–404.

Owen, Dora, ed. *The Book of Fairy Poetry.* Illus. Warwick Goble. London: Longmans, Green, 1920.

Peppin, Brigid. *Fantasy Book Illustration, 1860–1920.* London: Studio Vista, 1975.

Rose, Jacqueline. *The Case of Peter Pan, or the Impossibility of Children's Fiction.* London: Macmillan, 1984.

Rosetti [*sic*], Christina. *Goblin Market.* Illus. John Bolton. *Pacific Comics.* "Pathways to Fantasy" 1.1 (1984): 9–18.

Rossetti, Christina. *Goblin Market.* Illus. Florence Harrison. Ed. Edith Fry. London: Blackie and Son, 1912.

———. *The Children's Rossetti.* Illus. 3 pt. London: Macmillan, 1914.

———. *Goblin Market.* Arranged for acting by Maurice Bell: Maurice Bell, Wheatley Vicarage, Oxon, 1921.

———. *Goblin Market.* Illus. and adapted by Ellen Raskin. New York: E. P. Dutton, 1970.

———. "*Goblin Market:* Ribald Classic." Illus. Kinuko Craft. *Playboy* 20.9 (1973): 115–19.

———. *The Complete Poems of Christina Rossetti.* Ed. R. W. Crump. Variorum ed. Vol. 1. Baton Rouge: Louisiana State University Press, 1979.

———. *Goblin Market.* Illus. Martin Ware. London: Victor Gollancz, 1980.

———. *Goblin Market.* Illus. George Gershinowitz. Boston: David R. Godine, 1981.

Sabin, Roger. *Adult Comics.* London: Routledge, 1993.

Salmon, Edward. *Juvenile Literature as It Is.* London: Henry J. Drane, 1888.

Salway, Lance, ed. *A Peculiar Gift: Nineteenth Century Writings on Books for Children.* Harmondsworth, Eng.: Kestrel, 1976.

Shavit, Zohar. *Poetics of Children's Literature.* Athens: University of Georgia Press, 1986.

Smith, Joanna. *Edwardian Children.* London: Hutchinson, 1983.

Twain, Mark. *The Adventures of Huckleberry Finn.* New York: Airmont Books, 1962.

White, Gleeson. "Children's Books and their Illustrators." *The Studio,* Special Winter Number (1897): 1–68.

Woods, Mary A. *A Second School Poetry Book.* London: Macmillan, 1887.

———. *A Second Poetry Book.* London: Macmillan, 1890.

The Government of Boys: Golding's Lord of the Flies and Ballantyne's Coral Island

Minnie Singh

> *government:* . . . *2. The manner in which one's action is governed. a. In physical sense: Management of the limbs or body; movements, demeanor; also, habits of life, regimen. b. In moral sense: conduct, behaviour; becoming conduct, discretion.* Obs.
>
> Oxford English Dictionary

> *Perhaps in the twentieth century, the sort of fables we must construct are not for children on any level.*
>
> William Golding, 1962[1]

A memorable scene early in William Golding's 1954 *Lord of the Flies* eloquently suggests the ambition of Golding's fabulist intentions. On the island that at this point in the text is still an innocent playground, one of the younger boys, Henry, who is building castles in the sand, is covertly observed by an older boy, Roger:

> Roger stooped, picked up a stone, aimed, and threw it at Henry — threw it to miss. The stone — that token of preposterous time — bounced five yards to the right and fell in the water. Roger gathered a handful of stones and began to throw them. Yet there was a space round Henry, perhaps six yards in diameter, into which he dared not throw. Here, invisible yet strong, was the taboo of the old life. Round the squatting child was the protection of parents and school and policemen and the law. Roger's arm was conditioned by a civilization that knew nothing of him and was in ruins. (Golding, *Lord,* 62)

The "space round Henry, perhaps six yards in diameter," into which Roger dare not throw, is nothing other than the shrunken dimensions of civil society — the restraints taught by parents, school, policemen, and the law. What Roger is unable to disobey is not the ex-

Children's Literature 25, ed. Francelia Butler, R. H. W. Dillard, and Elizabeth Lennox Keyser, guest ed. Mitzi Myers and U. C. Knoepflmacher (Yale University Press, © 1997 Hollins College).

press prohibition of civil society against violence, but an internalized restraint—that is, civility. Significantly, in the penultimate chapter of the book, it is Roger who hurls the mighty rock that sends Piggy crashing to his death (181): more starkly than any other character, he represents the erosion of restraint, the return to a sort of Stone Age. If the project of government may be understood macropolitically as civilization, then its micropolitical counterpart is education, with civility as its project. Golding's text is notable for making explicit this cluster of associations, which has long been the implicit staple of the literature of boyhood.

Lord of the Flies is an overseas adventure story, the self-conscious culmination of a long line of boys' adventure stories. "It's like in a book," Ralph announces after their initial exploration of the island:

> At once there was a clamour.
> "Treasure Island—"
> "Swallows and Amazons—"
> "Coral Island—"
> . . . .
> "This is our island. It's a good island. Until the grownups come to fetch us we'll have fun." (34–35)

Golding's story seeks to dispel this intertextual glamor with grim realism; it both participates in and criticizes the history of the adventure story, whose originating canonical text is *Robinson Crusoe.* But the adventure story that was almost schematically Golding's pre-text was Robert Michael Ballantyne's 1858 *Coral Island,* one of the earliest such stories to have boys, in the absence of adults, for its main characters.

Children's literature has so naturalized this device that we forget how important a narrative innovation it must have been: we may be reminded of its innovative quality by the analogy of an exclusive dogs' club, where pampered pets may watch *101 Dalmatians* and other canine classics starring their own kind. *The Coral Island* is *for* boys and *about* boys, and it is even narrated *by* a boy, or, at least, by a former boy:

> I was a boy when I went through the wonderful adventures herein set down. With the memory of my boyish feelings strong upon me, I present my book specially to boys, in the earnest hope that they may derive valuable information, much pleasure,

great profit, and unbounded amusement from its pages. (Ballantyne, xxx)

The Coral Island preserves the homiletic form of the educational tract, but it delivers the homily in user-friendly terms—and thus inaugurates a dominant tradition in the literature of boyhood. R. L. Stevenson gratefully acknowledged Ballantyne in the verses that preface *Treasure Island* (Stevenson iii); and G. A. Henty, the most prolific boys' writer of the late nineteenth century, is known to have been influenced by Ballantyne's methods (Carpenter and Pritchard 43).

More than a century after Ballantyne's daring and successful experiment in boys' literature, William Golding declared, in his 1962 lecture at Berkeley on the writing of *Lord of the Flies:* "Ballantyne's island was a nineteenth-century island inhabited by English boys; mine was to be a twentieth-century island inhabited by English boys" ("Fable" 89). Written out of the agonized consciousness of England's loss of global power, *Lord of the Flies* may be read with some accuracy as a parodic rewriting of Ballantyne's *Coral Island.* The three central characters of *Lord of the Flies*—Ralph, Piggy, and Jack—are caricatures of Ballantyne's three boy heroes—Ralph, Peterkin, and Jack—who, shipwrecked on an island like Crusoe's (albeit in the South Seas), heroically survive violent encounters with cannibalistic natives and bloodthirsty pirates. The idyllic Coral Island is transformed by Golding into an infernal place: whereas Ballantyne's adventurers master nature, using and developing technology for the purpose, Golding's boy characters are helpless captives whose only hope is rescue.

Indeed, the first part of Ballantyne's text is a protracted meditation on a Rousseauistic education in which the boys learn to gather, hunt, cook, fight, save, and hide not through instruction but from necessity. We may remember that Rousseau suggests that Emile read and mime *Robinson Crusoe* (Rousseau 147–48); in Ballantyne's book, the boys' forced sojourn on the island is both the occasion and the means for their education. They also learn science, or specialized knowledge, from the disinterested study of their surroundings and the inferences they draw from their observations. In this way, they discover that crabs shed their skins and that hydraulic pressure causes water to spout inland. This spirit of rational inquiry distinguishes Ballantyne's boys from Golding's, who forget more than they learn and unresistingly fall prey to their irrational terrors.

Moreover, Ballantyne's boys take a blithely utilitarian view of their material environment, which represents to them the availability of ready-made value. Upon discovering the milk of the coconut, which he takes to calling "lemonade," Peterkin, who is by common consent the jester (and as such is distinct from Golding's Piggy, the butt of all jokes), exclaims, "Meat and drink on the same tree! . . . washing in the sea, lodging on the ground—and all for nothing! My dear boys, we're set up for life; it must be the ancient paradise—hurrah!" (27–28) and, later, "So . . . we seem to have everything ready prepared to our hands in this wonderful island—lemonade ready bottled in nuts, and loaf-bread growing on the trees" (43). The boys' life on the island joyfully conjoins work and pleasure. By studied contrast, in *Lord of the Flies* work and play are absolutely and irrevocably divorced: work is conservative and constructive; play, liberating but destructive.

The thrills of the Coral Island are twofold: they alternate between delight in eating—literally sucking at the bountiful plenitude of the island—and terror of being eaten (if not devoured by cannibals, then swallowed up by the bloody jaws of a shark). *Lord of the Flies* effects a darkly Freudian conversion of this wholesome orality into anal-sadistic pleasure. Here even the consumption of tropical fruit, that richly suggestive marker of paradise regained, causes chronic diarrhea—producing not value but waste. Self-consciously representing a later phase of erotic development, *Lord of the Flies* counts on our willingness to see the pleasures of boyhood as immature and outmoded.

We could continue to list the ways in which *Lord of the Flies* deflates and diminishes the heroic occasion and mode of *The Coral Island*. Yet the two books are overwhelmingly similar in their thematic concern with legitimate authority, leadership, and government. Both texts equate good government with the containment and defeat of savagery (whether the savagery is shown to reside within us or without); and both characterize savagery as the absence of a restraining law. Late in *The Coral Island*, the narrator, Ralph, who is now separated from his comrades, appeals to the pirate Bill, his guide through the South Sea islands:

> "Have these wretched creatures [native islanders] no law among themselves," said I, "which can restrain such wickedness?"
> "None," replied Bill. "The chief's word is law. He might kill

and eat a dozen of his own subjects any day for nothing more than his own pleasure, and nobody would take the least notice of it." (Ballantyne 242)

A cluster of associations equates the pirates with "white savages" (193); and their savagery, like that of the natives, manifests itself in "wanton slaughter" (216). If the restraint of pleasure is the defining characteristic of civilization, then boyhood, Ballantyne appears to suggest, is that state of grace where pleasure is harmless, appetite is healthy, and play is productive. Beyond boyhood, pleasure must be restrained, appetite curbed, and play governed.

Lord of the Flies proposes its own version of irresponsible authority in the terrifying figure of Jack, who "makes things break up like they do" (Golding, *Lord,* 139). The Jack of *The Coral Island* had been a natural leader who ruled by superior knowledge—he had read more adventure stories than had the others—and by playful violence. Golding's Jack, on the other hand, is clearly drawn from contemporary alarms about the totalitarian personality. It must be remembered that *Lord of the Flies* achieves its ominous generality of reference by glossing over the specificity of its Cold War context. The boys suspect that there has been a nuclear explosion (Golding, *Lord,* 14), and, at the end, Ralph's greatest remembered fear is of the "Reds" (162).[2] Golding himself uses the term "totalitarian"—a word that only took on its full negative import after World War II—in his remarks on *Lord of the Flies:*

Before the Second World War I believed in the perfectibility of social man; that a correct structure of society would produce goodwill; and that therefore you could remove all social ills by a reorganization of society. It is possible that today I believe something of the same, but after the war I did not because I was unable to. I had discovered what one man could do to another. . . . I am thinking of the vileness beyond all words that went on, year after year, in the totalitarian states . . . there were things done during that period from which I still have to avert my mind lest I should be physically sick. They were not done by the headhunters of New Guinea, or by some primitive tribe in the Amazon. They were done skilfully, coldly, by educated men, doctors, lawyers, by men with a tradition of civilization behind them, to beings of their own kind. (Golding, "Fable," 86–87)

Golding finally leaves us with the not entirely convincing position
that totalitarianism is a form of savagery, and that not even boyhood
is exempt from its encroachments. In Golding's own formulation,

> Man is a fallen being. He is gripped by original sin. His nature
> is sinful and his state perilous. . . . I looked round me for some
> convenient form in which this thesis might be worked out, and
> found it in the play of children. I was well situated for this,
> since at this time I was teaching them. Moreover, I am a son,
> brother, father. I have lived for many years with small boys, and
> understand and know them with awful precision. I decided to
> take the literary convention of boys on an island, only make
> them real boys instead of paper cutouts with no life in them;
> and try to show how the shape of the society they evolved would
> be conditioned by their diseased, their fallen nature. (Golding,
> "Fable," 88)

Rhetorically and ideologically, the claim of *Lord of the Flies* over *The
Coral Island* is the claim of experience over innocence, realism over
romance, truth over illusion, maturity over naivete, and hardship
over ease. At a crucial narrative moment in *Lord of the Flies,* before the
reversion to savagery is properly under way, Ralph, the good leader,
has an introspective realization: "He found himself understanding
the weariness of this life, where every path was an improvisation and
a considerable part of one's waking life was spent watching one's feet.
He stopped, facing the strip; and remembering that first enthusiastic
exploration as though it were part of a brighter childhood, he smiled
jeeringly" (Golding, *Lord,* 76). *Lord of the Flies* encourages us to locate
the possibility of good government in the irrecoverable brighter
childhood of political thought. At the same time, it makes childhood
itself as archaic as the colonial metaphor of enthusiastic exploration.

Steven Marcus wrote in an introduction to Kipling's *Stalky & Co.* in
1962 (the very year in which the increasing classroom use of *Lord of
the Flies* led Golding to explain to college students how he had come
to write it):

> In no other language does the word for boy have the kind of
> resonance that it does in English. . . . In what other language is
> there such an epithet as "Oh, boy!"—an expression of the very
> essence of spontaneous delight . . . boy is one of the sacred words
> of the English language; boyhood is—or for one hundred and

fifty years was—a priestly state or condition; and the literature of boys and boyhood has had, for a secularized era, something of the aura of doctrinal or holy writ. (Marcus 152)

In part, at least, the doctrine of boyhood relies on the congruence of subject and implied reader; thus, *The Coral Island* is a founding text of the genre. *Lord of the Flies* violently debunks the mythic doctrine: it is a book *about* boys, but evidently is neither *for* boys nor *by* a boy. In disrupting the generic economy of boyhood, it opens its textual portals to *any* reader who is prepared to take pleasure in the sober triumph of modernist truth over heroic illusion. If pleasure is, indeed, a suitable criterion for making cultural and generic distinctions, then *Lord of the Flies*, by consistently and mysteriously pleasing young readers (even those who first encounter it as prescribed reading), has invented the genre of adolescent writing. For the innocent homosocial pleasures of boyhood it substitutes the potent but shameful solitude of adolescence; for the nostalgia of the literature of boyhood it inserts the alienation of the new literature of adolescence.

The substitution of adolescence for boyhood is, of course, a powerful historical phenomenon, not simply a textual one. One way of understanding the shift is by grasping the relation of boyhood to the maternal feminine. Underwriting the pleasure of boyhood is the absent yet authorizing figure of the mother—Ralph Rover's mother who stoically bids her adventurous son adieu in *The Coral Island:* "My mother gave me her blessing and a small Bible; and her last request was that I would never forget to read a chapter every day, and say my prayers; which I promised, with tears in my eyes, that I would certainly do" (Ballantyne 5). Boys will be, and can be, boys only with the complicity and permission of their mothers; an extreme instance of this narrative typology can be found in J. M. Barrie's Peter Pan, the eternal boy who kidnaps two generations of Wendys because he needs a mother.

From the barren emotional landscape of *Lord of the Flies,* the female parent is all but missing. Only once in Ralph's daydreams does she appear, and then she is associated with severe emotional loss: "Once . . . they had lived in a cottage on the edge of the moors. In the succession of houses that Ralph had known, this one stood out with particular clarity because after that house he had been sent away to school. Mummy had still been with them and Daddy had come home every day" (Golding, *Lord,* 112). Had Mummy not abandoned him, would

Ralph's government of the island have succeeded? In fundamental ways *Lord of the Flies* remains tethered to the social discourse of family values. If boyhood is guaranteed by the familiar and forgiving figure of the mother, surely adolescence is betrayed by the unforgivable absence of the mother—an absence that represents simultaneously the terrible failure of civilization and the enabling condition of maturity.

In a recent Film Board of Canada production, a character laughingly recommends that the world be governed by postmenopausal women. The film is *Forbidden Love: The Unashamed Stories of Lesbian Lives;* the character is one of the aging women who were interviewed for the documentary. Men, she explains, are only boys, and, she adds, we know from *Lord of the Flies* what *boys* are like.

Oddly enough, her reading of William Golding's pessimistic fable is clever only in substituting the gendered "men" for the universal "man." In other respects it might well meet with the author's approbation, for *Lord of the Flies* takes considerable pains to establish that at the heart of civilization lurks a persistent savagery, and that men, once stripped of the veneer of adulthood, quickly revert to being wanton boys who kill one another for their sport. Indeed, the book's remarkable success has made the reversion to savagery a cultural byword, and a powerful one because it represents the transformation from the civilized to the savage as simultaneously regression and maturation. To become savage is to regress to the anthropological infancy of mankind, but to recognize one's essential savagery is to be psychologically mature: this is the intriguingly mixed message of Golding's book.

Notes

1. "Fable," 86.
2. Golding's parodic intent—to spoof "redskins," that cliché of boyhood culture—takes a tendentious form in the book, for Reds-as-native-Americans (an obsolete enemy) are made to share features of savagery with Reds-as-Communists (the real enemy). Thus, Jack and his troop, the enemies of civilization, appropriate Native American cultural practices (warpaint and ululation) to mark their association with bad government.

Works Cited

Ballantyne, R. M. *The Coral Island: A Tale of the Pacific Ocean.* Ed. J. S. Bratton. The World's Classics. Oxford: Oxford University Press, 1990.
Carpenter, Humphrey, and Mari Pritchard. *The Oxford Companion to Children's Literature.* Oxford: Oxford University Press, 1984.

Forbidden Love: The Unashamed Stories of Lesbian Lives. Dir. Aerlyn Weissman and Linne Fernie. Film Board of Canada English Programs, Studio D, 1992.

Golding, William. "Fable." In Golding, *The Hot Gates and Other Occasional Pieces.* New York: Harcourt, Brace, & World, 1965.

———. *Lord of the Flies.* New York: Perigee, 1954.

Locke, John. *Locke on Politics, Religion, and Education.* London: Collier Macmillan, 1965.

Marcus, Steven. "Stalky & Co." In *Kipling and the Critics,* ed. Elliot L. Gilbert. New York: New York University Press, 1965. 150–62.

Rousseau, Jean-Jacques. *Emile.* Trans. Barbara Foxley. Everyman's Library. London: J. M. Dent, 1911.

Stevenson, Robert Louis. *Treasure Island.* Medallion Edition. New York: Current Literature, 1909.

Figure 1. Fenn's rational dame in her schoolroom. From Fenn, *A Spelling Book* (London: J. Harris, 1805). Cotsen Children's Collection, Princeton University Library.

Varia

"Mistress of Infantine Language": Lady Ellenor Fenn, Her Set of Toys, and the "Education of Each Moment"

Andrea Immel

Lady Ellenor Fenn (1743–1813), better known during her lifetime under the pseudonyms Mrs. Lovechild and Mrs. Teachwell, is usually characterized in critical histories and reference books on children's literature as a prolific but well-intentioned hack who had little influence on later writers. Some critics allow that Fenn had a lively style, an observant eye, and an ability to write to the level of her intended audience, but everyone agrees that these strengths do not quite compensate for her lack of imagination, her tendency to moralize, and her apparent willingness to produce works conforming to her publisher Marshall's commercial formulas.[1] After reading commentary by modern scholars on Lady Fenn, one comes away with the impression that she has been grudgingly included because she belongs to that group of late eighteenth-century writers for children that Percy Muir dubbed "a monstrous regiment of women" (Muir 82).

Yet their contemporaries writing for the two leading eighteenth-century review journals, the *Monthly* and the *Critical,* present these women's accomplishments in quite a different light. For example, the respected dissenting divine and educator William Enfield observes in his article on Edgeworth's *Parent's Assistant* that writers for children are now considered citizens of the republic of letters: "It is not

I gratefully acknowledge the assistance of James Davis, Rare Books Librarian, UCLA Department of Special Collections, and Jill Shefrin, Osborne Collection of Early Children's Books, Toronto Public Library.
Children's Literature 25, ed. Francelia Butler, R. H. W. Dillard, and Elizabeth Lennox Keyser, guest ed. Mitzi Myers and U. C. Knoepflmacher (Yale University Press, © 1997 Hollins College).

now deemed an unworthy employment for writers of the most distinguished abilities, to draw up instructive and amusing books even for children. . . . At present, writers of the first order do not feel themselves degraded by employing their talents in this way; and the public is well inclined to bestow due praise on such useful exertions" (*MR* 21, ser. 2 [Sept. 1796]: 89). Another reviewer says in a notice of Mrs. Trimmer's *Footsteps* (1786) that the growing body of elementary works for children constitutes "one of the most important, though not the most brilliant, among the literary improvements of the present age. . . . This province, humble as it may seem, requires more than ordinary talents" (*CR* 62 [1786]: 152).

Contemporary reviewers praised Lady Fenn as one of those authors like Anna Letitia Barbauld, Sarah Trimmer, and Maria Edgeworth who had the special gifts needed to write for very young readers.[2] In a thoughtful review of Fenn's *Parsing Lessons* for the *Monthly,* Jabez Hirons writes that she "designs well; her method is amusing; and she has already, we are told, had the satisfaction of finding that her labours have been acceptable" (*MR* 28, ser. 2 [1799]: 334). The reputations of all four women were in eclipse by the end of the nineteenth century, but Fenn is the only major member of the "monstrous regiment" whose work critics have yet to reexamine. The most obvious explanation is that the majority of her works were out of print by the mid-nineteenth century.[3] Another more pertinent reason may be that much of her oeuvre falls outside the purview of children's literature scholarship: Fenn's most successful books were not fiction but readers, grammars, and introductions to natural history for small children. Ironically, modern critics have not judged her by the titles contemporaries valued most highly, but rather by the handful of imaginative works written early in her career—genres to which she never returned.[4]

On the other hand, it may be that Fenn's achievements as a writer for children have been misunderstood rather than underestimated. Her long career coincides with the late eighteenth-century boom in the production of children's books and toys, but scholars have never noticed that by the 1790s she had become quite as interested in designing educational toys as in writing books.[5] Unfortunately, fewer of the era's toys have survived than its books; as a result, it has been difficult to reappraise Fenn's career because almost all of her various "schemes for teaching" are known only from publishers' advertisements or from suggestions for their use in her books addressed to mothers who wished to teach their young children at home.[6]

We can now take a second look at Lady Fenn, because a complete *Set of Toys* (ca. 1780), the first and most ambitious plaything she designed, has been discovered and is now among the treasures in the Cotsen Children's Collection at the Princeton University Library.[7] Because one of her schemes can be examined and evaluated in light of her approach to early childhood education, it becomes much easier to recognize her as an early advocate of child-centered teaching strategies. Fenn realized that if these "schemes" were to succeed, she had to take into consideration both partners in the process of learning, mother and child: "Few know how to teach agreeably; most are at a loss how to communicate that knowledge which they possess, and few will condescend to begin at the beginning . . . fewer still succeed in attempts to tincture the mind with proper ideas; which is the education of each moment. Such is the volatility of childhood, that we must watch opportunities of making impressions; 'catch as you can th'attention of the minute'" (Fenn, *Friend,* 4–5).

As a teacher of teachers, Fenn saw herself as a guide or facilitator rather than a theorist; with characteristic modesty, she claims, "If I have any conceit, it is that I have acquired the knack of communicating the little knowledge which I possess, so as to be intelligible to the capacities, and agreeable to the taste of infantile Pupils" (Fenn, *Parsing,* vii). She also refers to herself as a dame, the widow woman who kept the village school where children learned their ABCs— a rather surprising comparison, because the dame was a figure of fond derision, if William Shenstone's well-known Spenserian parody, "The School Mistress," accurately reflects contemporary attitudes.[8] Shenstone's dame presides over the "fairy throng" assembled in her tumbledown cottage, "learning's little tenement" (Shenstone ll. 16– 18). She conducts class from her spinning wheel, so she is quite explicitly linked with ignorant lower-class women who told stories to children while working by the fire, as well as with characters like the malevolent fairy in "Sleeping Beauty." The dame is also associated with the nurse and her "quaint arts" to exact good behavior: she hints that she enlists the powers of supernatural assistants—here the proverbial little bird who tells her about any naughty tricks the scholars might play (Shenstone ll. 25–27). Although the dame knows the ways of children, she relies on a crude system of rewards and punishments to induce them to work. Like Samuel Johnson's Latin master, she soundly beats the inattentive child, all the better to frighten those who escaped the birch this time into quickly learning the assigned task perfectly. The diligent she rewards with pennies, praise, or gingerbread. An authoritarian who is alternately harsh and loving, Shenstone's dame requires little of her pupils beyond the ability to sit still, memorize, and recite aloud when called upon. Inspiring a love of learning or making lessons interesting or amusing is beyond her powers.

Why would Lady Fenn invite comparison with the dame, whose pedagogy was primitive and whose store of knowledge was scarcely greater than that of her pupils? Certainly Fenn took pride in her attainments, because she mentions putting away "Milton, Gray, and Shakespeare to turn abecedarian to the children of other people" (Fenn, *Art*, 7–8). Certainly she did not disguise her desire to supplant the dame and her joyless, mindless way of teaching. On the other hand, Fenn must have identified with the dame insofar as they both taught the most basic skills to the very youngest learners. But she calls herself a rational dame, a phrase that emphasizes her willingness to condescend: to employ more enlightened, humane teaching methods and to serve as a role model for mothers. First, Fenn tries to give mothers the incentive to play the dame (and nurse) themselves, even though it means taking over a task normally relegated to a social inferior: "If the human mind be a *rasa tabula*,—you to whom it is entrusted, should be cautious what is written upon it. Who would leave their common-place book among fools, to be scrawled upon?" (Fenn, *Cobwebs,* ix). Second, Fenn emphasizes a woman's fitness for teaching very young children. Although she grants that some educated men could stoop to a small child's level, she argues that "a sprightly young Woman, who will condescend to avail herself of the experience of an old one, is the person to initiate young students" (Fenn, *Parsing,* vi). Third, Fenn offers to assist mothers who wish to teach their children but who are not confident of their abilities by generously sharing her considerable teaching experience: "I am the old Woman who offer [*sic*] my service, and flatter myself with the hope of leading the dear little people with ease and satisfaction" (Fenn, *Parsing,* vi). Elsewhere she declares, "I print for the sake of those ladies who have less leisure than myself" (Fenn, *Cobwebs,* vii).

Of all dame Fenn's hints to mothers, perhaps the most important is showing them how to recognize the signs that a child is ready for an impromptu lesson. Fenn reminds mothers how children behave when engaged by something: not only are they eager to explore with their senses, but they also ask a multitude of questions in an animated fashion. She points out that children pick up a great deal of information about the world from their immediate surroundings in this fashion long before the onset of formal education. However, no mother can always predict when something will attract a child's attention, so she must take her cues from him and respond appropriately. When curiosity prompts a child to ask for information, the mother needs to satisfy his hunger: "Curiosity is the inlet to all knowledge . . . the inquisitive disposition which interrupts the repose of the old bachelor must not be repressed; neither must it pine without food, nor languish for want of proper nourishment. . . . Curiosity is innate: it is the gift of Providence; to direct and regulate it, is our province" (Fenn, *Friend*, 6–7).

Apparently Fenn concluded from her teaching experience that little people, like big ones, learn better and retain more when given the opportunity to converse with a sympathetic listener about the things that have captured their attention. Thus she prefers spontaneous conversation to exercises in memorization like catechizing as a way of directing a youngster's curiosity: "Talk to a child of an object which has caught his attention, and fear not, he will 'With greedy ear devour up your discourse'" (Fenn, *Rational*, iii). Her emphasis on conversation as an instructional method is wholly characteristic of the period, and she probably knew Edward Young's impassioned lines on speech in the *Night Thoughts:*

> Speech, thought's canal! speech, thought's criterion too!
> Thought in the mine may come forth gold or dross;
> When coin'd in words, we know its real worth
>
> . . . .
> Thought, too, deliver'd, is the more possess'd;
> Teaching, we learn; and giving, we retain
> The births of intellect; when dumb, forgot.
> Speech ventilates our intellectual fire;
> Speech burnishes our mental magazine,
> Brightens for ornament, and whets for use.   (Young 35)

Of course, Fenn does not pretend that a mother and a child converse as equals. But she points out that a child can enjoy the benefits of conversation as long as the mother can come down to the child's level by simplifying her syntax and vocabulary and talking with him about the things that interest him. In order to help mothers carry on conversations with their children, Fenn writes model dialogues for mothers in prattle inspired by Anna Letitia Barbauld's monologues in *Lessons for Children, from Two to Three Years Old* (1778). By "prattle," Fenn does not mean nonsense or baby talk (shades of the stereotypical nurse), but rather imitations of children's actual speech—"such stuff as my girl or boy themselves would write, if they could make use of a pen" (Fenn, *Cobwebs*, 1:viii). Not only does she show mothers how to respond to a child's initial question, but also how to introduce new or related ideas and put them into context using appropriate, simple, colloquial—but correct—language. Here a mother explains to her son how to interpret the language of the family dog's gestures—a perfect example of what Fenn means about the "education of the moment" (fig. 2):

> BOY. I love the dog. Do not you?
> MAMMA. Yes, sure.
> BOY. Wag! do you love me?
> MAMMA. You see he does; he wags his tail. When he wags his tail, he says, I love you.
> BOY. Does his tail tell me so? . . . When we go out he wags his tail: what does his tail say then?
> MAMMA. Pray let me go; I wish to go with you.
> BOY. I love to have him go with me (Fenn, *Cobwebs*, 1:43–45).

That Fenn's desire to help mothers become better teachers prompted her to invent various educational toys comes as no surprise. But her dissatisfaction with hornbooks, battledores, primers, and spellers used in elementary reading instruction—all of which are predicated upon extensive memorization—was just as strong a motivation: "To neglect beginnings, is the fundamental error into which most parents fall. . . . Our earliest infancy is disregarded; and when we are taken under tuition, what are we taught? To repeat by rote what we neither understand, nor regard" (Fenn, *Rational*, i–ii). Furthermore, she notes that the design of these materials does not take into account the child's developing sense organs. A child whose eyes cannot yet focus easily on individual characters and words within a block of text quickly becomes frustrated and confused, Fenn observes. Few of the reading passages take into account the little pupils' interests. No wonder so many children associate books with the dis-

Figure 2. Other pictures illustrating Fenn's works show children learning outside the schoolroom. Here the mother works while explaining to her son all the things the dog's wagging tail can mean. From Fenn, *Cobwebs to Catch Flies* (London: J. Marshall, 1783). Cotsen Children's Collection, Princeton University Library.

agreeable experience of memorizing from densely printed pages of syllabaries—an impression often too deeply rooted to eradicate.

Fenn sets out to devise a toy that will make learning pleasurable, just like her kindred spirit Cornelius Scriblerus, the father of the fictional pedant Martinus.[9] Such a toy was to be full of games and pastimes to keep children engaged and amused, and mothers would be able to refresh, replace, and customize its contents as necessary. The mother would be in charge of this special plaything, bringing it out at her discretion and putting it away as soon as the child's attention wanes. It needed to be portable, so that the mother could take it anywhere in the house; for instance, she should be able to sew and supervise the child playing beside her. If a child could learn to read by playing with a useful toy, Fenn reasons, then the process would be greatly enlivened, and the child would regard reading from a book as a privilege to be enjoyed as soon as he masters the skill.

Fenn's solution to the complex problem she poses is a cunningly fashioned wooden chest with a sliding top panel (fig. 3). As Fenn well

Figure 3. In "The Useful Play," two sisters lay out words with alphabet cards, presumably one of Fenn's schemes for teaching advertised at the end of the dialogue. From Fenn, *Cobwebs to Catch Flies*, vol. 2 (London: J. Marshall, 1783). Cotsen Children's Collection, Princeton University Library.

knows, few people can resist the temptation of looking in a closed container and examining its contents. Inside the chest are three wooden boxes stacked on top of one another, rather like a Japanese picnic basket. Each of the boxes is devoted to a different subject— spelling, grammar and arithmetic—and its contents identified by an oval label engraved on pink paper. The individual boxes are divided into different-sized compartments, and each compartment filled with cards, Fenn's preferred aid for teaching small children because cards allow them to concentrate on the single letter, word, or image. The card sets include everything from little alphabets of roman, italic, and black letters for spelling out words; tables for ciphering; illustrated and labeled flash cards for the identification of the parts of speech; and cards illustrated with pictures of birds, animals, games, and objects like a knight's helm, a steam engine, or a water pump (for a priced list of the *Set of Toy's* contents, see fig. 4).

Fenn was by no means the first to hit upon the idea of teaching basic skills with cards, and she surely owes a debt to earlier eighteenth-century inventors of educational games. For example, the unidentified compiler of the steady-selling speller *The Child's New Plaything* (London: T. Cooper, 1742) devised alphabet cards that could be removed from the book, cut apart, and played with (by the fourth edition the backs of the cards have stanzas of a jolly alliterative rhyming alphabet). These cards sweeten the pill by giving children engaging material to memorize, and some of Fenn's card sets are similar in intention. Another well-known educational game, the *Set of Squares* (possibly invented by Benjamin Collins, the Salisbury newspaper printer and partner of John Newbery) teaches reading by playing card games modeled after those played for stakes. (The only known copy to survive is also in the Cotsen Collection.)[10] The *Set of Toys* does not feature these sorts of games very prominently, so it may be that Fenn did not much care for cheating children into learning, especially when it involved exploiting their desire to emulate or compete with older siblings or adults.

However, the picture cards—what she called "cuts"—in the *Set of Toys* are its most innovative feature (she continued to design different kinds of cards until the end of her life). Fenn suggests strikingly modern ways in which the cards can be used to channel children's love of play and novelty into constructive activities. Not surprisingly, they require the mother to engage the child in friendly, lively conversations rather than to teach him how to play games according to prescribed rules. The various hints for using the *Set of Toys* in the *Art of Teaching in Sport* indicate that the mother should improvise her own games with the cards, tailoring the day's activities to the child's interests and attention span. A game might begin by naming the various nouns depicted on the cards; certain objects may arouse the child's curiosity and spark a chat about where they can be found, whether mother and child have seen any of them, how they work, who uses them, and so forth. As they talk about the pictures of things, the mother and child are clearly in the process of what modern educators call "negotiating their [that is, words'] meanings by referring to events and terms in their own remembered experience" (Meek 91).

Before Fenn, few educators paid much attention to children before they attained the age of reason and began formal schooling: Fenn is one of the first to focus on the particular needs of this age group and to make the case for engaged adults like mothers talking, playing, and exploring with small children as a way of integrating learning fully with everyday life. Furthermore, Fenn is wise enough to realize that a mother need not wear a forbidding aspect in order to be an

CONTENTS OF THE COMMON SPELLING BOX.

See Pages 5 and 19, of Art of Teaching in Sport.

ONE Alphabet of Roman Small Letters, Reverse a Cut, See Art of teaching in Sport, pages 9 and 19 .... *s. d.*

Three Cubes or Dice, for the Consonants, page 19.......... 0 3

Alphabets for compoling Words, &c. See Long Box, pages 19 and 26 ... 0 1½

Cube or Dice, for Vowels, pages 23 and 39 .... 0 0½

One Alphabet of Roman Capitals, Reverse a Cut, page 19 .... 0 3

   of Italic Small Letters, Reverse a Cut, page 19 .... 0 3

   of Italic Capitals, Reverse a Cut, page 29 .... 0 3

Child's own Box, page 19 .... 0 3

One Alphabet of Black Letter Small Letters, page 27 .... 0 3

   of Black Capitals, page 24 .... 0 3

A Screen 0 3

Six Spelling Tables, numbered I, II, III, IV, V, VI, page 29 .... 1 0

Six Reading Tables, numbered VII, VIII, IX, X, XI, XII, page 12 .... 0 6

An Alphabet to be pasted on the Cubes, page 19,—one Cube to contain the Vowels, a e i o u y, plus three others the following Consonants, viz. b c d f g h—j k l m n p—r s t v w x 0 1

CONTENTS OF THE COMMON GRAMMAR BOX.

See Page 33, of Art of Teaching in Sport.

TWELVE Cards, containing a compendious Set of Grammar Lessons, to be learned by Rote in small Portions: designed for little People to study as they walk, and numbered in order as they should be learned.......... *s. d.* 1 0

The Parts of Speech, in little PACKETS, viz.

Four Packets of Nouns, with a Cut on the Back of each, page 15, 33, 34, &c. 1 0

One Packet of Articles

One Packet of Adjectives, page 43

One Packet of Pronouns, page 44:

Two Packets of Verbs, pages 45 and 46

One Packet of Helping Verbs,

One Packet of Participles,

One Packet of Adverbs,

One Packet of Conjunctions,

One Packet of Prepositions,

One Packet of Interjections,

One Packet of Termination, page 46, together 1 4

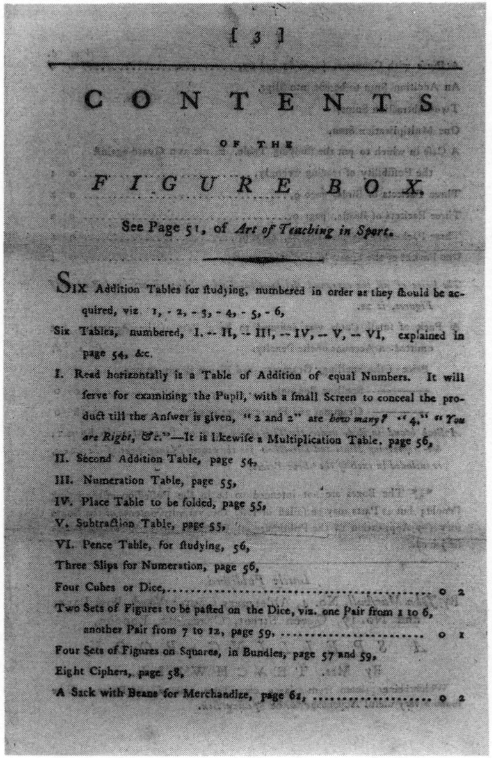

Figure 4. These four illustrations reproduce the leaflet which accompanies the *Set of Toys*. Every item in the boxes is listed and priced, and the entire plaything with a copy of the *Art of Teaching in Sport* cost a guinea—a sum many families must have found prohibitive. From Fenn, *A Set of Toys*. Cotsen Children's Collection, Princeton University Library.

---

[3]

CONTENTS
OF THE
FIGURE BOX.

See Page 51, of *Art of Teaching in Sport.*

Six Addition Tables for studying, numbered in order as they should be acquired, viz. 1, - 2, - 3, - 4, - 5, - 6.

Six Tables, numbered, I. - II, - III, - IV, - V, - VI, explained in page 54, &c.

I. Read horizontally it is a Table of Addition of equal Numbers. It will serve for examining the Pupil, with a small Screen to conceal the product till the Answer is given, "2 and 2" are how many? "4," "You are Right, &c." — It is likewise a Multiplication Table, page 56.

II. Second Addition Table, page 54.

III. Numeration Table, page 55.

IV. Place Table to be folded, page 55.

V. Subtraction Table, page 55.

VI. Pence Table, for studying, 56.

Three Slips for Numeration, 56.

Four Cubes or Dice, ... 0 2

Two Sets of Figures to be pasted on the Dice, viz. one Pair from 1 to 6, another Pair from 7 to 12, page 59 .... 0 1

Four Sets of Figures on Squares, in Bundles, page 57 and 59.

Eight Ciphers, page 58.

A Suit with Beans for Merchandise, page 61, ... 0 2

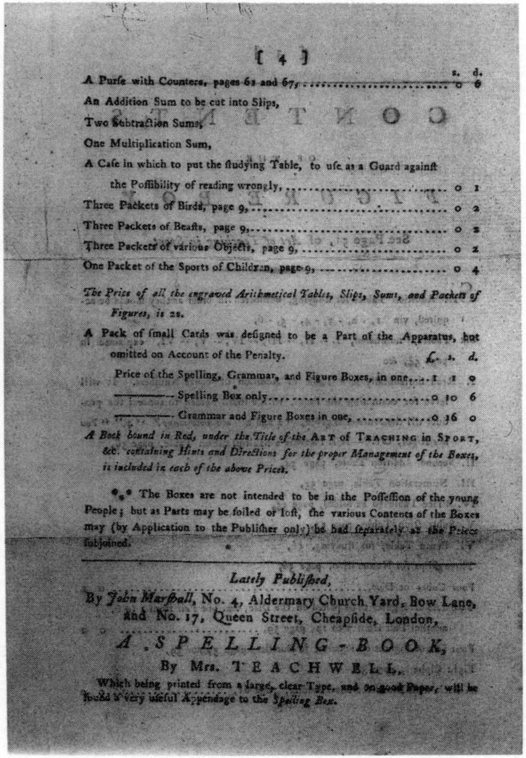

---

[4]

A Purse with Counters, pages 63 and 67,
An Addition Sum to be cast into Slips,
Two Subtraction Sums,
One Multiplication Sum, ... 0 0

A Case in which to put the studying Table, to use as a Guard against the Possibility of reading wrongly.

Three Packets of Beads, page 9, ... 0 2

Three Packets of Beads, page 9, ... 0 3

Three Packets of various Objects, page 9, ... 0 2

One Packet of the Sports of Children, page 9, ... 0 4

The Price of all the engraved Arithmetical Tables, Slips, Sums, and Packet of Figures, is 2s.

A Pack of small Cards was designed to be a Part of the Apparatus, but omitted on Account of the Penalty.

Price of the Spelling, Grammar, and Figure Boxes, in one, ... 1 1 0
— Spelling Box only, ... 0 10 6
— Grammar and Figure Boxes in one, ... 0 16 0

A Book found in Red, under the Title of the Art of Teaching in Sport, &c. containing Hints and Directions for the proper Management of the Boxes, is included in each of the above Prices.

*** The Boxes are not intended to be in the Possession of the young People; but as Parts may be soiled or lost, the various Contents of the Boxes may (by Application to the Publisher only) be had separately at the Prices subjoined.

Lately Published,

By *John Marshall*, No. 4, Aldermary Church Yard, Bow Lane, and No. 17, Queen Street, Cheapside, London,

A SPELLING-BOOK,
By Mrs. TEACHWELL.

Which being printed from a large, clear Type, and on good Paper, will be had as every useful Appendage to the Spelling Box.

effective teacher: like Minerva, who assumed a variety of guises, she can "condescend to wear hanging sleeves and join the dance in the nursery" (Fenn, *School Occurrences*, vi). That Fenn also succeeded in designing and marketing her schemes according to her principles— principles we largely take for granted—is also a considerable achievement: descendants of Fenn's original card sets can be seen in any store that stocks toys for teaching reading to preschoolers.[11] But had she not shown teachers ways in which they could accommodate little children without sacrificing their authority, the kind, sprightly rational dame and her boxes filled with cards would not have triumphed over the ignorant schoolmistress and her hornbook, switches, and sweets. Thanks to the discovery of the *Set of Toys*, we can now acknowledge Lady Fenn as both a pioneer in the development of modern child-centered pedagogy and a designer of educational aids.

Notes

1. Darton may not rate Fenn very high as a children's author, but at least he acknowledges her virtues on pp. 163–64 in *Children's Books of England*. Mary V. Jackson is much more censorious than Darton: categorizing (incorrectly) Fenn as a Puritan, Jackson sees only "oppressive discipline and intense moralizing" in Fenn's *School Occurrences* (1783). However, she overlooks the depictions of spirited girls resisting peer pressure—and the naughty tempters are rather attractive characters, as they frequently are in real life. See p. 147 in *Engines of Instruction*. Somewhere in the middle is Ruth MacDonald, author of the Fenn entry in the *Dictionary of British and American Women Writers, 1660–1800*.

2. Although her work was certainly not above criticism (Jabez Hirons, who regularly reviewed children's books for the *Monthly Review*, raises several substantial objections against *Fables* [1783] and *Fables in Monosyllables* [1783]), Fenn was not reviewed as harshly as Samuel F. Pickering, Jr. suggests on p. 194 of *John Locke and Children's Books in Eighteenth-Century England*. Except for some brief and very flip reviews in the *Critical*, Fenn's books were on the whole well received.

3. Ads appear for some of Fenn's works as late as the 1840s: for example, the forty-first edition of *Child's Grammar*, the twenty-first edition of *The Mother's Grammar*, and the eighth edition of *Parsing Lessons* are listed at the end of *Le Babillard*.

4. For example, Mrs. Trimmer in the *Guardian of Education* and the anonymous compiler of *The Juvenile Review* enthusiastically recommend practically all of Fenn's educational works but none of her early fiction. Likewise, Fenn's publisher, John Harris, regularly lists the grammatical works, noting how many thousands or hundreds of copies had been sold (the catalog at the end of the 1814 edition of *The Ladder to Learning* is a typical example).

5. For a bird's-eye view of late eighteenth-century toy retailing, see pp. 308–12 in J. H. Plumb's "The New World of Children in Eighteenth-Century England" in McKendrick, Brewer, and Plumb, *Birth of a Consumer Society*. I compiled a chronology of Lady Fenn's books and toys for this essay from the online resources of the *Eighteenth-Century Short Title Catalog*, the book catalog of the Osborne Collection, and the revised and enlarged edition of Marjorie Moon's *John Harris's Books for Youth, 1801–1843*.

6. Promotion of the *Set of Toys* was under way as early as 1783, possibly when the set

was in production. In *Cobwebs to Catch Flies* (1783), Fenn puffs the toy in the dialogue "Useful Play," in which the elder sister teaches her younger sister how to devise various spelling games using a box of letters. In the first edition, this dialogue is followed by an ad reading: "Schemes to assist parents in teaching their children, by way of sport, are in the possession of John Marshall and Co., who intend executing them with all possible dispatch. Due notice will be given of their completion." Fenn tinkered with the *Set of Toys* until 1809; she tells how she tried to improve upon her original concept in *The Teacher's Assistant*, a title unknown to Moon that I discovered while researching this essay. Fenn reveals on pp. 6–7 that she was obliged to write *The Friend of Mothers* (1799) because she "had frequently the mortification to perceive that the book, which accompanied the box, had not sufficiently initiated the purchaser in the Art of Teaching in Sport." She also notes that she designed simpler (and less expensive) versions of the *Spelling* and *Grammar* boxes. "Grammatical Amusements in a box," priced at six shillings, and six of Fenn's books appear in Harris's catalogs between 1818 and 1825; one puff says, "the immense sale which they have had, and the continued demand there is for most of them, precludes the necessity of saying any more in their praise" (see items 1018–23 in Moon's *John Harris's Books for Youth*). In addition to the *Set of Toys*, Fenn designed other educational aids, all of which were advertised between 1800 and 1825 by at least three other leading nineteenth-century children's publishers: Darton and Harvey, Benjamin Tabart, and John Harris. For example, around 1809 Harris advertised packs of "curious cards" and boxes of prints with the charming titles *Douceurs, Friendly Whispers*, and *A Secret Worth Knowing*.

7. I know of two other sets: The Osborne Collection has a *Grammar Box* (possibly the second version: its contents differ from those of the Cotsen set) and a private collector has a *Figure* and a *Print Box*.

8. I quote from the 1737 text—the shortest and least sentimental of the three versions—rather than from the final text of 1764. The most readily available text of the first version is reprinted in *The New Oxford Book of Eighteenth-Century Verse*, 305–7.

9. That Fenn compares herself to Cornelius Scriblerus senior is as surprising as her invocation of the dame; few educators would have acknowledged Scriblerus as a source of inspiration because his creators—Arbuthnot, Pope, Swift, and Gay—clearly regarded the character as an addlepated crank and enthusiast for ridiculous, unproven innovations. On the other hand, she may have drawn the parallel as a way of underscoring her willingness to try anything as long as it would improve the quality of elementary instruction; in the *Art* she does express quite strong reservations about most toys.

10. Fenn could well have been familiar with the *Set of Squares;* I have seen ads for it in books issued by Thomas Carnan (J. Newbery's nephew and one of his successors) as late as 1780. For a description of this card game, see Alderson, "Some Notes on 'A Set of Squares.'"

11. Homemade educational toys from the eighteenth century do survive; the most interesting and complete example is the Jane Johnson nursery library from the 1740s in the Ball Collection of Indiana University's Lilly Library. Scholars have not studied these artifacts, nor have they been much collected or valued until quite recently.

Works Cited

Alderson, Brian. "Some Notes on 'A Set of Squares,'" *Children's Books History Society Newsletter*, no. 55 (Sept. 1993): 19–20.

Le Babillard. London: Grant and Griffith, [not before 1842].

Darton, F. J. Harvey. *Children's Books in England.* 3d ed. revised by Brian Alderson. Cambridge: Cambridge University Press, 1982.

[Enfield, William]. Rev. of *The Parent's Assistant* by E. M. [i.e., Maria Edgeworth]. *Monthly Review* 21, ser. 2 (Sept. 1796): 89.

Fenn, Ellenor. *The Art of Teaching in Sport*. London: J. Marshall, 1785.

———. *Cobwebs to Catch Flies*. 2 vols. London: J. Marshall, 1783.

———. *The Friend of Mothers*. London: E. Newbery, 1799.

———. *Parsing Lessons for Young Children*. London: E. Newbery, 1798.

———. *The Rational Dame*. London: J. Marshall, 1783.

———. *School Occurrences*. London: J. Marshall, 1783.

———. *The Teacher's Assistant*. London: J. Harris, 1809.

[Hirons, Jabez]. Rev. of *Parsing Lessons for Young Children* [and] *Parsing Lessons for Elder Pupils* by Mrs. Lovechild [i.e., Lady Ellenor Fenn]. *Monthly Review* 28, ser. 2 (Mar. 1799): 334.

———. Rev. of *The Footstep to Mrs. Trimmer's Sacred History*. *Critical Review* 62 (1786): 152–53.

Jackson, Mary V. *Engines of Instruction, Mischief, and Magic*. Aldershot, Eng.: Scolar, 1989.

Juvenile Review: or, Moral and Critical Observations on Children's Books. 2 pts. London: N. Hailes, 1817.

McKendrick, Neil, John Brewer, and J. H. Plumb. *The Birth of a Consumer Society: The Commercialization of Eighteenth-Century England*. 1982. London: Hutchinson, 1983.

Meek, Margaret. *On Being Literate*. 1988. London: Bodley Head, 1991.

Moon, Marjorie. *John Harris's Books for Youth, 1801–1843*. Revised and enlarged ed. Folkestone, Eng.: Dawson, 1992.

Muir, Percy. *English Children's Books 1600 to 1990*. 1954. London: Batsford, 1985.

Pickering, Samuel F., Jr. *John Locke and Children's Books in Eighteenth-Century England*. Knoxville: University of Tennessee Press, 1981.

Shenstone, William. "The School Mistress." Ed. Roger Lonsdale. *New Oxford Book of Eighteenth-Century Verse*. Oxford: Oxford University Press, 1984.

Todd, Janet, ed. *Dictionary of British and American Women Writers, 1660–1800*. Totowa, N.J.: Rowman & Allenheld, 1985.

Trimmer, Mrs. Sarah. *The Guardian of Education*. 5 vols. London: F. C. and J. Rivington, and J. Hatchard, 1802–6.

Young, Edward. *The Complaint and the Consolation, or Night Thoughts*. London: R. Edwards, 1797.

Reviews

In keeping with the "dialogic" emphasis of this special issue, we offer two rather contrary reviews of a book that concerns itself with the interplay between the voices of adults and children.

Voicing the Unvoiceable

Peter F. Neumeyer

Infant Tongues: The Voice of the Child in Literature. Ed. Elizabeth Goodenough, Mark A. Heberle, and Naomi Sokoloff. Foreword by Robert Coles. Detroit: Wayne State University Press, 1994.

Robert Coles's two-page foreword to this collection dwells on matters that appear to be peripheral to the nineteen essays that follow. Coles's avoidance seems understandable, however, because these contributions are a varied lot, as the introduction by the three editors confirms. Some valuably introduce genres or authors about whom we may know far too little, whereas others helpfully trace the historical representation of children and the adaptation of adult writings for a juvenile readership. And the final offerings, mini-essays in which three contemporary writers look directly at the child language they use or have overheard, provide a refreshing antidote to the academic prose of the other pieces. For even the most original and well-read contributors to this volume all too often undermine their best perceptions by relying on a programmatically voguish language that distracts rather than clarifies.

As a miscellany containing contributions that were solicited to

Children's Literature 25, ed. Francelia Butler, R. H. W. Dillard, and Elizabeth Lennox Keyser, guest ed. Mitzi Myers and U. C. Knoepflmacher (Yale University Press, © 1997 Hollins College).

broaden and enhance four pieces originally delivered at a collo-
quium, *Infant Tongues* is concerned with a great variety of topics, such
as adult authors who impersonate children, the voices of real children, publishers, and the usurpation of power positions. To summarize these diverse strands seems impossible in this space—yet it is fair
to say that a degree of coherence is achieved by the repeated attention paid to the narrative devices authors use to give the illusion that
they are speaking in a child's voice. The reasoning behind the book
thus goes something like this:

1. Children talk; they have "voice."
2. As children become socialized, they modify or self-censor
their language.
3. In trying to render child language, novelists create a host of
mediating devices.
4. Critics write about such novelistic stratagems.
5. Children, novelists, critics, and cultures have conflicting
"interests." The "interests" of novelists and critics may reflect
adult "needs"—as determined by history, sex, or their own sociocultural conditions—rather than the actual conditions of childhood.

A number of the essays in this volume demonstrate both "interests" and "needs" by linguistically and substantively calling attention
to themselves. They thus shuttle between childhood, adult author-
hood, and supervisory critical commentary. Although some contributors manage to limit themselves to their announced topics, rather few
have much to do directly with the "infant tongues" of this confusingly
misnamed collection.

Aside from Darrell H. Y. Lum's fascinating account of his efforts to
capture the pidgin lingo of his youth, it is Gillian Avery's "The Voice
of the Child . . . in Early Modern England" that, by following the
Opies, most directly attends to the actual voices of real children. By
introducing one of the collection's themes, Avery foreshadows a later
contribution in which Maria Tatar argues that children, being unable
to "represent themselves," are obliged to find voice by way of adult
ventriloquism (275). Avery poignantly illustrates one such act of ventriloquism by looking at the example offered by John Evelyn's written
record of his dead little son's life (1659).

Alexandra Johnson considers the self-censorship and modification she detects in the 1810–11 diary of seven- and eight-year-old Marjory Fleming, a vital, imaginative, and literarily impressionable child who wrote directly and with considerable verve. Johnson unfolds for us how even in the course of two years Marjory modulated her natural voice to the subtly felt demands of those she loved; she shows, furthermore, how long after Marjory's death the diary was taken over by well-intentioned nineteenth-century editors who made it consonant with their own orientations and thus, wittingly or unwittingly, colonized what they purported merely to transcribe.

According to Michael Lastinger, the childhood pressures recreated by an adolescent writer, the poet Rimbaud, were hardly unwitting and certainly less subtle or benign. Relying on psychobiography, Lastinger's essay delves into poems such as "Le Bateau ivre" (The drunken boat) in order to recover the "poetic voice [of a] precocious genius [subjected to] the most traumatic forms of emotional, verbal, and sexual contact with the adult world" (144).

The majority of the volume's contributors, however, prefer to look at novelists who give voice to a fictional child rather than consider the accommodated voices of actual children or adolescents. Brian McHale's examination of child talk in John Dos Passos's massive *U.S.A.* trilogy seems paradigmatic in its attention to the totality of the child rendered—from appearance to psychology to language. That totality, according to McHale, is "to a large extent ready-made, . . . pieced together from prefabricated units available in the literary repertoire" (204). Fair enough, and applicable, too, to the adult novelists considered by other contributors: Dickens, Lawrence, and Woolf are perhaps less curious choices than Dos Passos as exemplars of authors who render children.

If child writers are shaped by their culture and novelists who allow children to speak are governed by their own "interests," so, likewise, do publishers respond to external forces that are "ready-made." Suzanne Rahn's fascinating overview of the changing voices of Black characters in American children's books offers an extreme example of McHale's premise about the preconceptions that govern not only the presentation of child language, but also the very idea of childhood. As Rahn shows, Black children were first depicted as speaking in dialect and then became virtually "colorless" in skin hue as well as in their speech; but in the mid-1960s, with the high tides of "Black Pride" and a new "Muslim" consciousness, they once again acquired distinctive voices. These larger social movements, however, went unperceived by publishers until the 1970s, when they marketed the work of authors such as John Steptoe and June Jordan.

The cultural shaping of children also preoccupies Ruth B. Bottigheimer in her study of German children's Bibles. She looks at the stories selected for inclusion, the personages featured, and the diction used in order to assess the cultural transmission of values imposed on child readers. The colonization of childhood, once again, rather than the preservation of actual "infant tongues," seems to be the prime concern of this survey.

The sensations and perceptions of a forgotten child self (like Joyce's invocatory "moocow" at the opening of his *Portrait*) need to be reactivated by anyone writing for or about children, as Darrell H. Y. Lum shows in his story fragment, "Giving Tanks," which he then poignantly discusses in "On Pidgin and Children in Literature." But such "infant voices" cannot survive unmediated. Lum's replication of his Hawaiian Creole English is skilled and touching, but it remains an ingenious writer's crossover between adult and child.

Primarily, then, *Infant Tongues* is best read as a collection of essays in which the editors attempt to document the pressures culture exerts on children or adolescents who write; adult authors who depict the language of fictional children; and the publishers of such authors. Taken as a whole, the nineteen essays suggest a rich area of what is perhaps a subset of rhetoric: the simulation of the language of children and the explication of the forces that shape such a simulation.

The least happy aspect of *Infant Tongues* is, ironically enough, its exemplification of a jargon-ridden critical language that makes the reader long for the less convoluted "tongues," if not of "infants," at least of adults capable of emulating the directness of the child's voice. The book's frequent iteration of academic-political mantras humming about privilegingmajoritariancodifiedandrocentricfictivepassionalvitalistempowerments remains disconcerting because it seems programmatic, factional, and faddish. If such ready-made phrases are merely a thoughtless substitute for precise and nuanced language, then they represent a distinct loss for our understanding and exchange of subtle ideas. And if it reveals (as I feel it does) the authors' palpable design, then it destroys the potential for partnership in a process of inquiry that authors and readers ought to be able to share.

Moving Thresholds, Expanding Genres

Gillian Adams

Infant Tongues: The Voice of the Child in Literature. Ed. Elizabeth Goodenough, Mark A. Heberle, and Naomi Sokoloff. Foreword by
Robert Coles. Detroit: Wayne State University Press, 1994.

*You do not chop off a section of your imaginative substance and make a
book specifically for children for—if you are honest—you have, in fact,
no idea where childhood ends and maturity begins. It's all endless and
all one.*

P. L. Travers

We live in exciting times. Not so long ago, children's literature
seemed a neat and tidy genre, conveniently bounded by Harvey Darton's "commencement" date of 1744 and the idea, based on the
English translation of Philippe Ariès, that children as we construct
them and therefore books specifically for them did not really exist
before the seventeenth century. It was more or less assumed that
the audience for children's books was prepubescent and that one
did not need to bother about literature for adolescents or "young
adults," because, presumably, they were reading either "adult" literature or trash. Moreover, children's literature was largely white,
middle or upper class, and, with the exception of the major fairy-tale
collections, and of a few authors such as Collodi, Jansson, Lindgren,
and Saint-Exupéry, and historical monuments such as *Struwwelpeter,*
Anglophonic. Curiously enough, literature *by* children was not considered children's literature, although the audience for it was as likely
to be a child as an adult. *Touchstones,* the collection edited by Perry
Nodelman and published by the Children's Literature Association in
three volumes (1985–89), perfectly reflects this situation. Aside from
Collodi, *Touchstones* does not even cover the European authors and
works that I have mentioned. Fortunately, our horizons have been expanding. We are learning about the literatures of other times, other
cultures, other ethnic groups within our own culture, and the con-

Children's Literature 25, ed. Francelia Butler, R. H. W. Dillard, and Elizabeth Lennox
Keyser, guest ed. Mitzi Myers and U. C. Knoepflmacher (Yale University Press, © 1997
Hollins College).

cerns of classes other than the well educated and reasonably well-off.

Infant Tongues, a collection of fourteen essays, three short pieces, and an "Afterword," was inspired by four papers given at a 1987 MLA conference on representing the language of the child in literature. The thoughtful introduction by the editors underlines how the essays exemplify not only the expanding boundaries of children's literature but also the instability of the threshold between that literature and literature for adults. Gillian Avery's study of early modern Latin and English conversations for schoolboys leads off with scatological children's rhymes and Aelfric's *Colloquy* (circa 1006) as evidence of early children's voices, but she concentrates on later works of the fifteenth to seventeenth centuries used in England. Observing, after Sir Keith Thomas, that "in spite of the once fashionable theories of such historians as Philippe Ariès, there is plenty of material to show that childhood as a distinctive phase of life was recognized before the eighteenth century" (16), Avery provides generous quotes to picture the early modern English schoolboy as adults of the period may have constructed him and as he may have constructed himself. Avery is on to as yet unexcavated treasures, and the Latin literature of the Middle Ages and Renaissance used in the schools will repay scrutiny by historians of children's literature. The talk of Avery's schoolboys, particularly when it is insolent, will sound very familiar.

Ruth Bottigheimer, on the other hand, in her interesting study of children's Bibles between 1656 and 1753, confirms Ariès's major point that people had a different *sentiment* about children before the eighteenth century than they did later; in modern critical terms, their construction of childhood was "other" than ours. Bottigheimer demonstrates how Bibles reflected a view of children as equivalent to "simple" (uneducated) folk in terms of appropriate reading at the beginning of the period; by the later Bibles, an effort was made to tone down or omit the more lurid stories, although there were differences between Catholic and Protestant Bibles.

Other valuable examinations of juvenile voices in literature for children are offered by Mitzi Myers and Suzanne Rahn. Myers sees Maria Edgeworth's work, which was based on her observations of the many actual children she lived among, as revolutionary. Its realistic portraits and faithfully rendered conversations of children had a significant impact on Edgeworth's contemporaries. Most interesting is Myers's demonstration, through the little story "The Bee and the Cow," of the way Edgeworth illustrates how texts are construed and misconstrued by children and Myers's explanation of the importance of cultural context in these texts' interpretations. It is regrettable, however, that the editors did not include the presumably brief text of "The Bee and the Cow," perhaps in an appendix, as well as the picture of the Edgeworth family that Myers discusses at length. Rahn also considers the influence of cultural context in her important study of the way in which Black speech has been represented in U.S. children's books for the last hundred years. She argues that these representations not only have reflected the racial attitudes of writers, publishers, and award committees, but also helped to "create the racial attitudes that American children absorb and grow up with and unconsciously maintain" (226). The only illustrations in the collection occur in this essay, and they are absolutely essential to Rahn's argument. I also found this essay valuable because it addresses southern children's books, which is a generally neglected subject. Although southern racism is usually more overt, and certainly more repugnant, than the children's books of other areas of the United States, some were widely read and are a part of the cultural constructs of many older southerners.

Fairy tales continue to be given to children as children's literature, and Maria Tatar argues that children's responses to these tales provide a missed opportunity for examining the relationship between children and adults as interpreted by children. As a negative example, Tatar provides Bruno Bettelheim, who never reads fairy tales from the child's point of view: the villains are projections of the child's badness, and the adults can do no wrong. She looks at several revealing studies of children's rewriting of cultural stories that emphasize the tales' malleability in the hands of children; particularly interesting are the examples of the different ways that children regard transgressive behavior.

Further examples of the young speaking directly for themselves are provided by the essays on Marjory Fleming and Arthur Rimbaud. Although Alexandra Johnson's essay on Fleming, the Scottish child prodigy, offers important information on how the drama of Fleming's expression in her story and diaries was toned down to fit the romantic male idea of what was appropriate for a child of the time to do and say, the piece would have profited from some attention to Judith Plotz's essay on the same subject (*Children's Literature Association Quarterly* 17.4 [winter 1992–93]), which perhaps appeared too late to be considered.

On the other hand, Michael Lastinger's rich psychological exploration of the life and poetry of Rimbaud (1854–91), who began producing his greatest work when he was fourteen and ended his literary
career by age twenty, has much to tell us about adolescent genius at
its peak. Although Rimbaud is an important member of the French
literary canon as an adult writer, he is arguably an adolescent as well;
Lastinger notes that Philippe Ariès considers the hero of Wagner's
Siegfried, completed in 1869, when Rimbaud was fifteen, "the earliest
example of a modern adolescent" (160). Moreover, Lastinger argues
that because "nineteenth-century France recognized only ritual passages that led directly from childhood to adulthood, typically such
things as marriage, joining the army, and completing an education or
vocational training" (144), Rimbaud's failure to complete any of these
passages before he briefly joined the Dutch army in 1876 when he was
twenty-two ties his evocative poetry to his childhood. So does, even
more surely, the emotional and probably sexual abuse he suffered
while he was a child, which profoundly affected his view of the adult
world "and indeed language itself" (146) and led him to create a new,
ambiguous, symbolic language as a vehicle for his rage and despair.

The essay by Naomi Sokoloff on Holocaust literature also addresses
children whose tragic childhoods leave them wavering on the threshold between adult and child. She discusses not only the voices of children—in their compositions from the Terezin concentration camp as
presented in *I Never Saw Another Butterfly* (compiled by Hana Volav-
ková) and the voices of children in Uri Orlev's juvenile *The Island
on Bird Street*—but also "adult narratives that imagine the child" with
Louis Begley's *Wartime Lies* as the prime example. Using David Gross-
man's story of "Momik" from *See Under: Love,* Sokoloff points out that
there are fictions "that dramatize interactions among these categories
of writing" (260). Momik must confront something too terrible to be
explained by the literary models he has been using to make sense of
his world, and he is trapped into presenting another reality. In this
sense he is like Edgeworth's working-class child, whose cultural context prevents the expected interpretation of "The Bee and the Cow,"
although her view is perfectly logical.

Cultural context also dominates the essays that address the voices
of children in literature for "adults." I had expected, as a children's
literature scholar, to be least interested in these essays, but I quickly
came to realize the importance of how children are constructed in
such texts: those literary children become part of our construction

of the child, of the child's construction of the self, and of our construction of how children are embedded in a historical period. Thus Mark Heberle's essay on both the child Arthur of Shakespeare's *King John,* who participates in "the longest continuous dialogue involving a child in Shakespeare" (80 lines), and his replacement, the child Henry, tells us much about the importance of the protected child for Shakespeare as a symbol of the maintenance of a just political order. Heberle's essay, which also addresses the Elizabethan view of childhood and touches on the child actors of the period, should provide ideas for further writing and research for those who are scholars of both children's literature and Shakespeare.

Another eye-opener is provided by Andrew Wachtel on childhood and history in Russian literary culture. Although non-Russian speaking readers might wish that he had spent less time on Andrei Belyi's *Kotik Letaev,* which does not appear to be available in English, Wachtel's remarks on Tolstoy's methodology in his "pseudo-autobiography" *Childhood* (1852), the first sustained treatment of a child in Russian literature, do much to illuminate *War and Peace* and its children, as well as later Russian works containing them. Tolstoy develops a three-way interaction between the point of view of the child, the adult narrator, and the implied author, "who can lend his fictional characters as many or as few of his own memories as he chooses" (114). In his explanation of how Russian writers did not see a sharp split between fiction and nonfiction, and thus how their texts must be interpreted simultaneously as fiction and nonfiction, Wachtel uses Gary Saul Morson's term "threshold literature" for works in which it is uncertain which set of mutually exclusive conventions is operable. Because the work can be decoded at least two ways, it has the possibility of becoming two or more different works (see p. 120, n. 3). Indeed the term "threshold literature" is a useful one for looking at most of the works in this collection; Rimbaud's work, for example, can be read as both a cry of adolescent anguish and a sophisticated adult creation of new poetic forms.

Just as Wachtel finds a triple narrative stance in Tolstoy, so does Mary Galbraith locate three narrative positions in the first chapter of *Great Expectations.* In the first section, the narrator "separates himself from the child, but probes deeply" into his experience, sometimes taking an "ironic position"; in the second, the narrator identifies with the child, almost disappearing, "but recounts events from a dramatic position": and in the third the narrator takes Pip's perspective, entering into the child's lived experience. These three positions correspond to the development of "linguistic consciousness" in the child. On the other hand, in Carol Sklenicka's and Mark Spilka's survey of D. H. Lawrence's children, the focus is rather on something like Galbraith's third position, where Lawrence, who conceived of child consciousness as a "vibrating blur," seeks to reproduce how a child might see the world. "The passional consciousness of adult observers like himself," as well as of primitives, is similar to the child's, and the easy movement between ordinary and primitive or childlike consciousness is a characteristic of Lawrence's style. Heberle has already discussed the effect of the silent child standing upon the stage. As Elizabeth Goodenough demonstrates, in Virginia Woolf, Lawrence's "vibrating blur" has become silence; in spite of Woolf's emphasis on the experience of early life in the formation of adult identity, she "calls attention to the interior being of children by her refusal to render their speech" (185). Just as in *Mary Poppins,* although at a later age, the ability to talk (here in extended sentences) is equated in the person of Jacob Flanders with the loss of childhood and "the wonder and marvellous secrecy which children find inherent in life" (200).

I have already mentioned how Rahn's essay demonstrates the effect of cultural stereotypes on the presentation of Black speech. Brian McHale's important essay likewise discusses in theoretical and technical detail how Dos Passos and others of his generation drew upon stereotypical baby talk when representing children's (and often women's and working-class) speech. McHale argues that the novelist does not select from language commonly spoken but from a "prefabricated linguistic stereotype" in a process "generalizable to literary representations . . . of all kinds" (219). The representation of childhood, then, is not an exceptional case because "raw reality is always Other, and that Other is always inaccessible [except] . . . through the repertoires our cultures provide" (219).

The three short pieces from writers of children's and adult literature at first seem dispensable. But they echo the recurrent themes of this collection. Mark Jonathan Harris discusses a formative experience of childhood, when he was five, contrasting the differing accounts of that day by his father and his mother and noting his inability to separate what is a true childhood recollection from his own adult revisions. He speaks of "the conflicts between honesty and hypocrisy, truth and fantasy, reality and magical beliefs, that are at the heart of many coming-of-age novels about twelve- or thirteen-year-olds, the literary age that seems to demarcate childhood and adulthood" (289). Such conflicts are at the heart not only of novels about this age group, but also of writers not far from it, such as Rimbaud. On the other hand, David Shields and Darrell H. Y. Lum address language problems: stuttering and the use of Hawaii Creole English (Pidgin). For these three writers, as for Laurie Ricou in her afterword, it is cultural constructions that governed their ability as children to speak, to be heard, to remain silent, or to indulge in "creative misreadings" (305).

Most children's literature scholars of my acquaintance wear at least two hats; they have received their Ph.D.'s in some dimension of "adult" literature, and they consequently teach children's literature as well as a variety of other texts. When they operate with their children's literature hat, there are certain essays they should not be without: Rahn's essay in general; Myers's and Tatar's pieces for their demonstrations of how children (mis)interpret texts; and, if they are to address the subject of the history of children's literature, the essays by Avery and Bottigheimer. A collection such as this, however, urges us to see not two hats, but the same one with different decorations, because we operate on a movable "threshold" between adult and children's literature—the one literature reaches across and forms the subtext to the other.

Work Cited

Travers, P. L. "I Never Wrote for Children." Quoted in Jonathan Cott, *Pipers at the Gates of Dawn: The Wisdom of Children's Literature*. New York: McGraw-Hill, 1983. 204.

The Culture and Literature of Girlhood: Liberation or Limitation?

Angela E. Hubler

Disciplines of Virtue: Girls' Culture in the Eighteenth and Nineteenth Centuries, by Lynne Vallone. New Haven: Yale University Press, 1995.

The Girl's Own: Cultural Histories of the Anglo-American Girl, 1830–1915, edited by Claudia Nelson and Lynne Vallone. Athens: University of Georgia Press, 1994.

What Katy Read: Feminist Re-Readings of "Classic" Stories for Girls, by Shirley Foster and Judy Simons. Iowa City: University of Iowa Press, 1995.

Karl Marx wrote that "men make their own history, but do not make it just as they please, they do not make it under circumstances chosen by themselves, but under circumstances directly found, given and transmitted from the past" (395). The relationship between agency and structure that he focuses on here is crucial to any criticism, like feminist criticism, originating in and ultimately concerned with political and social change: To what extent are the possibilities for transformation both enabled and limited by the historical and institutional setting? To invoke Marx is thus appropriate in the context of these three provocative works of feminist literary criticism.

Two of these works also situate themselves in terms of cultural studies, an approach to literature and culture that, in its early formulation by Marxist cultural critics like Raymond Williams and E. P. Thompson, stressed the agency of subordinate groups as a corrective to its occlusion (in different ways) in both traditional and orthodox Marxist studies. Paradoxically, although Foster and Simons do not describe their work as cultural studies, their close readings offer perhaps the most sustained and balanced attention to both agency and structure; Their approach is at the same time also the most traditionally literary.

Lynne Vallone's *Disciplines of Virtue: Girls' Culture in the Eighteenth*

Children's Literature 25, ed. Francelia Butler, R. H. W. Dillard, and Elizabeth Lennox Keyser, guest ed. Mitzi Myers and U. C. Knoepflmacher (Yale University Press, © 1997 Hollins College).

and Nineteenth Centuries stresses structure. Vallone focuses on Foucauldian disciplinary practices in the culture of girlhood: "The successful girl internalizes the implicit or explicit ideological messages communicated by her reading, her family, her community, her social class, her sexuality, and finds, ultimately, that happiness and virtue lie within her self-control. . . . Each girl must decide how to conquer and then change her girlish nature—characterized by desire, hunger, anger, ignorance and aggression—into beautiful womanly conduct. The means by which this aestheticized conquest can occur . . . is communicated by girls' culture" (5). Vallone examines the ways in which the values and practices of historical institutions—including England's Magdalen Hospital for penitent prostitutes, dower practices, the Evangelical Movement, and the domestic science movement —were communicated in literature for girls, in canonical texts as well as in less well-known novels, conduct manuals and novels, and tracts.

Vallone's method, bringing historical, nonliterary material and scholarship to bear on literary texts, leads to some brilliant analyses. For example, she discusses the bluntly economic character of marriage—epitomized by the inclusion of dowry amounts in marriage announcements in the *Gentleman's Magazine*—and goes on to note the economic factors behind the reluctance of the blushing female characters in *Evelina, Pamela,* and *Sir Charles Grandison* to sign a marriage settlement or even to agree upon a marriage date: "Harriet Byron's inability to sign proceeds not from fear, but marks her modesty; she is ashamed to be thought 'too' aware of the legal arrangements of marriage, Grandison's wealth and generosity to her, and their impending sexual union, lest she be considered 'forward,' 'knowing,' or 'grasping.' She must literally sign herself into Grandison's hands, and what embarrasses her is the knowledge and awareness of the voluntary act of relinquishment and public avowal of sexual maturity" (61). In this way, Vallone illustrates the effects on the apparently personal experience of the body of the economic relations structuring the social institution of marriage.

Vallone's Foucauldian approach is well suited to her study of the sermons and the conduct literature, which demanded from the penitent prostitute and the charitable girl a similar sacrifice: the relinquishment of desire, and of time and money, respectively. The narration of this relinquishment results in "the pleasure of the act" (the title of the chapter), which is in effect the discipline of female sexuality. Vallone quotes a conduct book by Sarah Green (1793) in which the author, in order to instill chastity in the young female reader, discusses the practice of opening chapel services to the public at the Magdalen Hospital. Her contemporary says of the spectacle: "Nay, the *public* are themselves, in some measure, judges, by seeing their [the penitents'] decent and commendable deportment in the *Chapel* which has dispelled the doubts, and dissipated the scruples of many hesitating objectors to this design" (20). Vallone continues to stress the repressive scrutiny of young women's behavior in discussing the abridgement of *Pamela* for children. This version, which omits the epistolary structure as well as Pamela's voice, thus "truncates her 'transformation' so that she attains not artistry in self-creation, but a kind of static symbolic and iconographic state considered fit for a moral children's book (and conduct discourse as well)" (39).

Interestingly, Vallone describes the agency that women do possess as exercised primarily in self-control and in the repressive control of others, especially children, other women, and the working class. Vallone discusses writers influenced by "religious enthusiasm and re- form" (Anna Letitia Barbauld, Hannah More, Mary Brunton, Mary Martha Sherwood, and Jane Austen) as participating in a conserva- tive project: "images of the child or of childishness . . . are necessarily the projection of the adult reformer's perception of a lack in the child and fear *of* the child: the child is, in effect, a potential revolu- tionary, or, conversely, once provided with appropriate (Evangelical) reformative education and guidance, a well-mannered and content subject" (182, 70). Despite her overgeneralized grouping of these di- verse writers, Vallone's discussion of individual texts in this chapter is nuanced and particular.

Repressive female agency is also discussed in Vallone's final chapter on the National Florence Crittenton Mission for "bad (read 'sexual') girls" (136). (This chapter also appears as an essay in *The Girls' Own*.) Vallone argues that "a rescue home is like a juvenile reformatory, is like a women's prison, is like a penitent prostitute's penitentiary, is like a lock hospital (for venereally diseased prostitutes . . .), is like a female seminary where domestic science is taught" (150). Linking each of these is the influence of the domestic science movement, whose proponents believed that by putting "dirt" or "matter out of place" (in the words of one contemporary reformer) (136) where it belongs, order can be restored. Vallone, almost certainly indebted to Mary Douglas's *Purity and Danger* (1966), concludes that the Mission "swept turn-of-the-century 'dirty' girls into its own place (its 'Home') and renamed them as its own daughters: inheritors of a reformed feminine ideology that both accepted them as ladies and continued to keep them in their place" (152). Here, Vallone's Foucauldian approach turns the world into one monstrous and inescapable panopticon. These reform institutions certainly have many disturbing qualities, yet equating them obscures differences between them and the fact that, even though such institutions may have acquired a life of their own, individuals within them may have been motivated by a less repressive concern for women. Institutions rarely achieve precisely the ends they desire, because they rely upon the agency of individuals, who are not wholly reducible to their regimes. A closer look at the complexities of the relationships between structure and agency, and between the institution and the individual, might have more adequately represented the reality of a culture that both limited and empowered girls.

Essays in *The Girl's Own* address this dual effect of culture. In their introduction, Vallone and Nelson say that the "institutions, practices, and literatures discussed in these essays reveal the ways in which the Girl expressed her independence, as well as the ways in which she was imagined, presented, manufactured and controlled" (2).

Two essays read disturbing cultural attitudes about girlhood sexuality as they are represented visually. Leslie Williams analyzes John Everett Millais's many and popular paintings of little girls, arguing that in the "subordinate, upward glancing images" of the girls he painted, Millais created images of his own subordination to dominant tastes (150). These tastes, which governed the marketplace, grew out of a "culture that valued girlish chastity but left it at the mercy of male sexual and social dominance" (128). In an essay that also opens her *Pleasures Taken: Performances of Sexuality and Loss in Victorian Photographs* (1995), Carol Mavor discusses the influence of this culture on Lewis Carroll's photographs of little girls. Mavor criticizes those who insist that the girls depicted "have no sexuality" and announces that she will "acknowledge the sexuality of children" (158, 159). This claim presumably informs her assertion of Carroll's ability, which seems lacking in other photographers of children, to "capture the performances of *his* child-subjects" (176). For example, in a photograph of Agnes Grace Weld as Little Red Riding Hood, Mavor argues that "her gaze, not unlike Evelyn Hatch's [Hatch was photographed nude by Carroll], confronts us and draws us with a seductive charm reminiscent of Greta Garbo's sultry, wounding eyes" (176). Although Mavor

surely intends to defend Carroll, at least to some extent, against the
child pornographers' annihilation of the subjectivity of his subject,
her comparison to Greta Garbo, an adult with adult sexuality, clearly
illustrates how difficult this task is. Perhaps she would argue that
the Victorian girl's sexuality was, even in prepubescent girls, already
male-directed and expressed in self-objectification. Problematically,
however, Mavor does not elaborate on the character of childhood
sexuality. As a parent and a former girl, my own observations are
that childhood sexuality is quite different from Greta Garbo's. But I
should not have to rely upon personal experience.

Female sexuality is also the focus of Christina Boufis's essay about
newspaper writer Eliza Lynn Linton's attack on "The Girl of the
Period." Anxiety about female sexual desire, fed by sensational fiction like Rhoda Broughton's and linked in the popular imagination
to an increasingly consumerist society, informed her attack. Women's
association with consumption is central also to Judith Pascoe's discussion of the depiction of girlhood by the prolific T. S. Arthur (most
famous for *Ten Nights in a Barroom*). Arthur presents girlhood as a virtuous state that stands in opposition to adult female materialism—a
construction that reflects Arthur's own insecurity as a writer, because
writing is an occupation both subject to the marketplace and "feminized."

Although these essays reveal the way girls were represented, a number of essays, especially those focusing on "cultures of girlhood,"
reveal a struggle for female agency. Claudia Nelson explores the
potentially empowering moment of domesticity in "Care in Feeding:
Vegetarianism and Social Reform in Alcott's America." Nelson argues that a struggle between Bronson and Abba Alcott for control of
the domestic sphere is reflected in Louisa May Alcott's thematic emphasis on gastronomy. Whereas in life Bronson seems to have "stolen
the symbols" of domesticity and female value from his wife, in Louisa
May's "fictional families she restores the centrality of women" (30).

Sally Mitchell discusses the representation of girls' work in career
novels, magazines, and halfpenny papers to determine "how the idea
of paid work affect[s] the culture of girlhood" (243). Joyce Pedersen analyzes liberal feminists' views on education for girls, arguing
in favor of their progressive nature in light of the fact that they, like
liberals in general, asserted the identity of private and public virtue.
Thus, liberal feminists created an androgynous ideal that coexisted,
in seeming harmony, with a continuing insistence on women's domes-

tic obligations. Pedersen is perhaps too easy on the female educators she discusses, whom she notes saw no conflict between domesticity and "women's individual well-being" (210). Although Pedersen mentions Harriet Taylor Mill, it would have been useful to have included a discussion of Mill's challenge to the sentimental ideology informing these views.

Sherrie Inness's wonderful " 'It is Pluck, But—Is It Sense?': Athletic Student Culture in Progressive-era Girl's College Fiction" argues that girls' sports fiction undermines the connection between physical education and the preparation for "efficient motherhood" characteristic of gymnastics in favor of a "revolutionary" depiction of female muscularity, competitiveness, cheering, stoicism, and most important, camaraderie (219). Inness concludes, "The athlete who has experienced the support of her female classmates might realize she does not have to be dependent upon men for support" (236). Although Inness's conclusions may be somewhat optimistic, her analysis is supported by the American Association of University Women survey *Shortchanging Girls, Shortchanging America* (1991), which associates boys' high self-esteem with athletic competence and suggests that athletics might also be an important source of self-esteem for girls. (The liberatory aspects of a school-based girls' culture are also discussed by Foster and Simons in a chapter on Angela Brazil's *The Madcap of the School.*) In her discussion of "*The Barnacle*, a Manuscript Magazine of the 1860s," Julia Courtney argues that the construction of "a culture of girlhood . . . was not inevitably dependent on the institution of girls' schools" (95). The "Goslings," the contributor-readers of the magazine, were influenced by their "Mother Goose," Charlotte Mary Yonge, who had a significant role in both the production and writing of the magazine. Yonge and her Goslings shared the values of the "upper-middle-class Tractarians" (95). Courtney's analysis of the works appearing in the magazine reveal that despite Yonge's "internalized conception of women as subordinate or even inferior," a view shared by many of her contributors, authorship offered them a socially sanctioned area of fulfillment and empowerment (81). The adult lives of the contributors, some of whom continued as writers and teachers, reflect this contradiction: "Their subsequent careers illustrate the common dilemma of late-nineteenth-century middle-class women: the plight of the home daughter, the struggles of those who sought autonomous lives, the need to adjust to spinsterhood" (95).

Martha Vicinus identifies a possible source of empowerment for girls in her fascinating "Models for Public Life: Biographies of 'Noble Women' for Girls." Focusing on biographies of Florence Nightingale, Vicinus notes that although many omitted aspects of Nightingale's life incompatible with traditional femininity (for example, "political manipulation" [57]), some omissions of fact actually functioned to produce a text more encouraging of female achievement:

> If formulaic biographies were to work successfully, they had to permit the reader imaginative escape into the life of the heroine. . . . A shadowy Nightingale could be invested with desirable characteristics more easily than one encumbered with complex motivations. . . . Even though the overt message was often womanly obedience, symbolic moments, such as Nightingale's nightly vigil, permitted an imaginative identification with independent action. Fiction—created by the reader and not just the author—was an essential part of the factual biography. (62)

Essays like those of Vicinus and Courtney are perhaps more successful than is Vallone's book in teasing out the enormously contradictory and complex nature of the "culture of girlhood." Although Vallone acknowledges factors such as Hannah Wooley's periodic expression of "feminist thought" (30) that might require her to temper her analysis, in general she does not adequately identify the effect of contradictory ideologies and practices. This is not to say that Vallone's depiction of women's oppression is false, but that it is not the whole story—it includes one side of the argument rather than the other, and synthesis is not yet in sight.

In contrast, Foster's and Simons's *What Katy Read* represents both sides of the argument in an explicit attempt to understand the role of girls' fiction in both perpetuating and transforming female gender roles and girls' fiction as a category. They identify these concerns in the preface:

> What exactly *is* girl's fiction? What makes it distinctive? Do "classic" books for girls promote significant aspects of women's culture in an attempt to bridge the divide between patriarchal realities and the appeal to female individualism? How do they modify or continue the familiar narrative motifs and patterns of their age in the address to a juvenile audience, and why should such motifs continue to exert an attraction for girls who are products

of a very different cultural climate and consciousness? To what extent can questioning of the age's gender ideologies operate in such literature and would a contemporary juvenile leadership have picked this up? What problems do they raise for the twentieth-century critic intent on recognizing the influential part played by such works in providing model behaviour and value systems for impressionable readers attracted by the thought of, in Elaine Showalter's phrase, "a literature of their own"? (x)

In seeking to answer these questions, the authors examine eight novels "directed at a predominantly female readership" and "engage[d] directly with the conceptualization of girlhood and the development of a gendered identity" (xii). The contradictory nature of these novels is clearly one source of their fascination for the authors, who note that "our views on thinking about those works from a more mature perspective had in some cases radically altered their meanings. . . . we had completely failed to register Mary Lennox's exclusion from the inheritance of Misselthwaite Manor in *The Secret Garden*, so caught up were we in the sense of power and enabling fantasy that the central action of the story generated" (ix).

Although they focus on contradiction, Foster and Simons suggest that some of the common features of the texts they discuss function to empower women. Many of those features are shared with "a female literary tradition," as articulated by Elaine Showalter, and in particular, with sentimental and domestic fiction. Foster and Simons note that the pervasive importance of motherhood, which derives from those traditions, sometimes maintains traditional gender norms—as in Yonge's *The Daisy Chain*, in which a letter written to the children by their dead mother "posits codes of self-forgetfulness, self-control, and gender-appropriate behavior" (68). At the same time that the mother encourages these values, as she also does in *The Wide, Wide, World* and in *Little Women*, the figure of the mother or mother-figure is an empowering one in novels that "emphasi[ze] . . . the marked practical ability of women, or . . . their effectiveness as moral and spiritual teachers" (26). Thus, Foster and Simons identify as subversive the conflict in *The Wide, Wide World* between ideology and desire: Ellen's secular need for the "pre-Oedipal phase of identification with the mother" and the "surface orthodoxy" of the need to reject earthly for divine love (44).

"The notion of a secret place of autonomy and freedom from adult control" (15) appears in *What Katy Did, The Secret Garden,* and in fiction by Edith Nesbit and Angela Brazil. As in *What Katy Did,* such utopias are often natural, Edenic, and the site of female imaginative creativity. Female characters' authorship is another factor that enables female control:

> Female authority is foregrounded in the ability to name, considered a male prerogative in patriarchal theories of language. Like women in the alternative system proposed by feminist critics, the children in these stories produce their own world of meaning by ordering and naming, creating identities opposed to the pre-existing ones offered them in the Symbolic order and in whose establishment they play no part. . . . Mary Lennox weaves her magic narrative to hold Colin and Dickon spellbound in *The Secret Garden;* Jo March and Katy Carr are authors in their own right, with written texts to prove their effectiveness as producers of meaning. Anne Shirley's fantasies recreate her self image in resistance to the reality of her identity as unwanted orphan child; and Mother in *The Railway Children* literally sustains her family through her imaginative invention, her stories' success resulting in buns for tea. (30)

Foster and Simons take up—and complicate—some of the same texts, authors, and issues that Vallone discusses in *Disciplines of Virtue.* For example, Vallone's discussion of Coolidge's *What Katy Did* and Alcott's *Little Women* appears in her treatment of play and humor in American children's literature for both boys and girls. In a confusing introductory section that moves from games in *Alice in Wonderland,* to American economic ideology, to humor in girls' fiction, to drama— a progression based on the word "play"—Vallone acknowledges the potentially subversive and empowering quality of wit and of "theatrical play" but concludes that the " 'rules and regulations' of the new republic allow for both the careful creation and ultimate destruction of the funny girl, the tomboy" (111). Thus, Vallone points out that humor in these texts comes at the expense of Jo and Katy and functions to highlight some internal weakness that must be overcome (133).

Whereas Vallone regards the repressively humorous overcoming of tomboyism as a consciously crafted object lesson for readers, Foster and Simons suggest that Jo's tomboyism and her final relinquishment of the self-assertion and ambition it entails is a reflection of Alcott's own "frustration and self-division. . . . It is this refusal to be easily codified or to be reduced to any single or simple interpretation that forms a significant factor in understanding why *Little Women* has acquired its 'classic status' " (92). Foster and Simons identify the comic character of *Little Women* as a significant shift away from the sentimentality of much nineteenth-century fiction—significant in that the comic often appears in representations of the difficult achievement of a properly gendered identity and thus challenges the assumed status of femininity as "instinctual or natural" (87). For example, the authors note that "At the smart New Year's Eve party at the Gardiners' house, Meg sprains her ankle dancing in high heeled shoes that are too tight, and Jo spills coffee on a dress that she has already ruined with a scorch mark. The incidents offer a striking contrast to Ellen Montgomery's Christmas visit to Ventnor in *The Wide, Wide World,* where the heroine functions as an exemplar of decorum and moral superiority" (90).

This last passage indicates the difficulty of capturing the synthetic moment in the relations of structure and agency, of institutions and individuals. The structures with which the authors discussed above are concerned have most certainly persisted, but at the same time they have also been radically transformed: although Alcott pokes fun at too-tight high heels as symbols of a debilitatingly restrictive notion of femininity, the relations of power that those high heels enforced continue to be reproduced. Yet the ability to view this situation from a comic distance reveals the essentially artificial and hence alterable nature of these relations. And so back and forth we go from one pole to the other, with momentary glimpses of the synthetic whole. Whatever their limitations, each of the books under review offers a substantial if partial reconsideration of this vision of the whole.

Work Cited

Marx, Karl. *The Eighteenth Brumaire of Louis Bonaparte.* In *The Marx-Engels Reader.* Ed. Robert C. Tucker. 2d ed. New York: Norton, 1978.

Beholding American Children: A British Perspective

Patricia Craddock

Behold the Child: American Children and Their Books, 1621–1922, by Gillian Avery. Baltimore, M.D.: Johns Hopkins University Press, 1994.

Gillian Avery's *Behold the Child* gives general readers an absorbing narrative of three hundred years of children's books in America. The focus of her story is the divergence between British and American children's books from a common beginning, a divergence that she attributes persuasively to differences between British and American childhoods. In America a morality that insists on work as the highest good leads to books in which salvation takes the form of economic success and children are expected to have responsibilities and freedom of action. British children—of the book-buying classes—experience instead a prolonged and sheltered childhood with little real-world freedom or responsibility. For nonspecialist British readers, the book undoubtedly provides much new information. For American readers, its primary virtue is that it gives us the opportunity to see ourselves from without, an opportunity that is especially valuable for those familiar only with American children's books.

Avery herself acknowledges that the first half of these three hundred years cannot illustrate her thesis, because during this period nearly all the books read by American children were written in England. The lengthy chapter on the seventeenth century is designed to establish the pattern of American children's lives. Understandably the least original chapter in the book, it covers much territory familiar to anyone knowledgeable about early American history or the history of English children's books. It also illustrates a general problem: Avery's generalizations about American children are based principally on information about those of New England (the best documented region). On the other hand, her portrayal of the "children of godly ancestors" preparing for eternity from earliest infancy is an apt and ironic preparation for the theme of secular salvation

Children's Literature 25, ed. Francelia Butler, R. H. W. Dillard, and Elizabeth Lennox Keyser, guest ed. Mitzi Myers and U. C. Knoepflmacher (Yale University Press, © 1997 Hollins College).

that she sees as central to American children's books, as opposed to the British emphasis on virtue rewarded from above (social superiors, parents, or God).

This chapter also illustrates a strength of Avery's book—her ability to recommend "finds" among older children's books. She can make a reader understand why books familiar now only to scholars were once popular with children. In the seventeenth century, for instance, she describes vividly and sympathetically James Janeway's *A Token for Children,* an account of the exemplary deaths of some thirteen children that might seem to the modern parent or teacher to represent an inexplicable taste of our ancestors. Avery has a knack for the child's-eye view of such a book: "It was the first book [children] had encountered that told stories of children. . . . Here in Janeway were thirteen children manifestly more holy than their elders, some of them as young as five years old, gloriously holding the stage. And there was dialogue and domestic detail, too—scanty, no doubt, but enough to clothe the incidents with some sort of reality. . . . They exhorted their peers and their elders, and were not rebuked for it" (33). No wonder even a Tom Sawyer can temporarily enjoy imagining himself as the hero of a pious death scene!

In the eighteenth century, the Newbery books, with "their emphasis on industry and effort and on the material advantages that accrue therefrom . . . were what the new colonies wanted to read." (49) Avery argues that the American antipathy toward fairy tales and even nursery rhymes, and the thirst for practical, factual knowledge, were already apparent then.

Avery's story is centered, however, on the nineteenth century, with which both part 2, "An American Style," and part 3, "Differing Ideals," deal (a brief "postscript" brings the account to a rather abrupt stop in 1922). Part 3 is divided by gender, as nineteenth-century children's fiction often was; part 2 deals with more general developments.

In these sections, some of the materials required by Avery's descriptive purpose and chronological arrangement seem to be presented merely dutifully, interrupting the presentation of the developments related to her thesis. For example, Avery looks first at the American interest in practical education, on the model of the Edgeworths. This point begins a section called "Rational Ideas." Chronology, however, requires that she interrupt this story with a consideration of the "Mother Goose" controversy, a report on American "toys" and illustrated books, and a discussion of early attempts at putting specifically American subject matter into formats borrowed from the English, such as Samuel Wood's *Street Cries of New York* and William Cardell's *The Happy Family; or, Scenes from American Life.* Avery's descriptions of these developments are useful, but there is some strain in incorporating them into a section that opposes a presumably rational American taste to the British development of a taste for fantasy.

Avery's discussion of Samuel Goodrich's Peter Parley, which was extremely popular in America but not well received in England, effectively rejoinders: "It is with Goodrich that the mainstream of English and American writing for children divides. . . . America was in the grip of facts. . . . [Goodrich] brought colour and interest into children's lives and made them curious about distant places. His books were a substitute for fantasy, opening windows for many young Americans" (81). The recognition that exotic "facts" could serve as a cultural substitute for overt fantasy is astute, and it helps modern readers understand how children could survive a "Gradgrind" education without the emotional and imaginative stunting that Dickens deplores in *Hard Times.* On the other hand, Dickens's very concern suggests that English and American trends were not as different as Avery suggests.

Both clear and valid is the excellent discussion of the divergent traditions of "Sunday School books" in the two countries. A major distinction between English and American Sunday Schools caused a significant difference in the content of the stories they provided for children, Avery shows. English Sunday Schools were started by the elites to benefit the poor and deprived; in America, *all* children went to Sunday School. Thus, after the theme of early piety and pious death was exhausted (in the 1840s in America, much later in England), the subject of American Sunday School fiction was the material success of children who were honest, industrious, and eager to learn. This American didactic cliché did not occur in English stories: "though there were plenty of real-life examples of rags to riches, notably among mid-Victorian railway contractors, English Sunday School writers chose to avert their eyes" (105). In this section, Avery also describes briefly and rather unsympathetically the religious erotic tradition epitomized by Warner's *A Wide, Wide World.* She does not refer to recent feminist debate about this and related texts.

The last section of Part 2, called "Liberty of Thought," returns to the problem of fantasy, myth, and folktale. It contains several of Avery's "finds," for example, the admirable American fairy stories by James Kirke Paulding published in 1838 and two almost forgotten stories by Christopher Pearse Cranch. The American resistance to fantasy throughout much of the century seems an admirable explanation for the fate of such books, and its suppressed continuance in the "exotic fact" books perhaps explains their existence. But Avery's thesis seems to lead her astray when she comes to Baum's *Wonderful Wizard of Oz*, which she regards with undisguised dislike. The dislike is certainly defensible, but what is surprising is her preference for the "Kansas portions" of the book (some six pages!), which can hardly have been shared by any other reader. This preference seems to arise from the assumption that what Americans did well in 1900 was write realistic fiction; thus, Baum too would have written better had he spent more time on the realistic portion of his book. This pushes the thesis much too far. Again, one could wish that even in a book for general readers, Avery had at least referred to the large body of interpretive scholarship and debate about the *Wizard of Oz*.

The "Differing Ideals" of Avery's final section refer less to the differences between British and American books than to the differences between books for boys and those for girls. The section on girls' books includes "family" stories. Its study of "one hundred years of American heroines" is almost entirely descriptive and deals with texts familiar not only in living tradition—real little girls still read them and Disney has made movies of many—but also in analytical feminist scholarship. What is new for the American reader is therefore again the contrast with the British tradition, especially in the use of motifs like the preparation of food and the kitchen as center of the home, and the effortless movement between classes possible in American, but not English, happy endings. Not discussed, however, is the relationship between these developments and those in adult fiction, where the English realistic tradition seems much closer to the American children's model. Avery also mentions only in passing the class, race, and ethnic restrictions that limited American children's fiction, albeit to a more inclusive territory than that of British fiction.

The discussion of American boys' books centers on the presence of sex and the absence of organized sports. The American boy, whether he is experiencing something of the extended childhood enjoyed (or suffered) by the British schoolboy or involved early in the quest first for a livelihood and then for wealth, is aware of the opposite sex and

likely to experience puppy love. As today's students note with aston-
ishment, a Tom Brown and his friends and imitators can reach the
age of eighteen or nineteen without so much as a thought of any
female other than their mothers. The Anglo-Indian Kim is only a partial exception. On the other hand, the extended accounts of football
games and cricket matches on which hang the honor of the House or
the School are not to be found in American books. By the end of the
century, however, books about and for boys in both countries treat
preadolescent boyhood as a "golden" time of freedom and leisure,
with a special emphasis on mischief, role-playing (Robin Hood and so
forth), and such activities as swimming and fishing. Like the spunky
heroine, American heroes were full of spirit; unlike her, her male
counterpart was often actually naughty and destructive, with the indulgent forgiveness of his author.

This well-illustrated book would be an excellent textbook for an
undergraduate course in the history of children's literature, because it
would prevent the neglect of the other tradition that typically infects
textbooks originating in either England or America. It can be recommended also to graduate students preparing to teach in elementary
or middle schools. But this narrative, based almost exclusively on
personal responses to the actual children's books themselves, is not
addressed to those with a scholarly knowledge of American children's
literature. For such readers, the works Avery describes will be familiar and the absence of consideration of current scholarly debates will
be disappointing.

It is perhaps unfair, however, to criticize the book for not being
what it did not aim to be. It succeeds admirably in its own terms: it
provides the general reader with a clear, descriptively comprehensive,
and extremely readable account of the cultural history of American
childhood as it became distinct from that of England, even in those
parts of America most closely tied to English roots.

Reflecting on Girls' Series

Sherrie A. Inness

The Girl Sleuth, by Bobbie Ann Mason. Athens: University of Georgia Press, 1995.

Rediscovering Nancy Drew, edited by Carolyn Stewart Dyer and Nancy Tillman Romalov. Iowa City: University of Iowa Press, 1995.

The 1990s are exciting years for scholars interested in girls' series books. An ever increasing number of researchers, many of them influenced by feminism, are studying these popular texts, which have been phenomenally successful throughout the twentieth century. Other critics are turning to these books in order to understand their enduring role in culture and the ways they shape the values of future women. Scholars such as Kathleen Chamberlain, Deidre Johnson, and Nancy Tillman Romalov all have done substantial work in the girls' series field. Johnson's *Edward Stratemeyer and the Stratemeyer Syndicate* (1993) is particularly noteworthy for its thorough scholarship and its chapter on girls' series. Less known than these three critics is Catherine Sheldrick Ross, whose painstakingly researched essay, "If They Read Nancy Drew, So What? Series Book Readers Talk Back" (1995), provides what is probably the most thorough study of series book readers and their motivations. She argues in this essay that "series books do *not* enfeeble readers or render them unfit for reading anything else" (233). Chamberlain, Johnson, Romalov, and Ross, along with some earlier writers such as Carol Billman and Betsy Caprio, have worked to deepen critics' understanding of girls' series. Now, two new works have been added to the growing number of scholarly books addressing girls' series. Actually, Bobbie Ann Mason's *The Girl Sleuth* (1995) cannot technically be considered a "new" book because it was first published in 1975, but its republication in 1995 will certainly attract a new readership to this classic work in the field. Along with Mason's study, Carolyn Stewart Dyer and Nancy Tillman Romalov's carefully edited collection of essays about Nancy Drew

Children's Literature 25, ed. Francelia Butler, R. H. W. Dillard, and Elizabeth Lennox Keyser, guest ed. Mitzi Myers and U. C. Knoepflmacher (Yale University Press, © 1997 Hollins College).

should also interest new scholars in the exploits of Nancy and other series heroines.

Mason's is the less scholarly of the two books, but because she did not revise the book, she has not had the opportunity to benefit from the last two decades of critical work on girls' series, as have the writers included in Dyer and Romalov's collection. I should also caution that Mason's book is *not* intended as a rigorous, definitive text about girls' series. Rather, *The Girl Sleuth* is the award-winning writer's personal reflections about the significance of girls' series for her during her childhood. Although Mason discusses how other girls might read series books, her focus is chiefly on her own reaction to these books when she was growing up on a remote Kentucky farm where she had "to feed the chickens and milk the cows everyday" (4). Because of the personal tone and jargon-free prose, her book, even twenty years later, is still a good starting place for academics and general readers interested in girls' series.

The Girl Sleuth was Mason's first book, and it displays the keen sense of humor so apparent in some of her better known works: *Feather Crowns, In Country, Shiloh and Other Stories,* and *Love Life: Stories. The Girl Sleuth* was the result of its author's attempt to recuperate after a long period immersed in the arcane issues of graduate school. She recovered by turning to beloved books from her childhood: girls' series books featuring heroines like Nancy Drew, Judy Bolton, and similar detectives. *The Girl Sleuth* is Mason's reflection on the profound effect these books had on her childhood and those of countless other girls. As she comments, "I read them all: Nancy Drew, Judy Bolton, Beverly Gray, Kay Tracey, the Dana Girls, Vicki Barr, Cherry Ames. I was an authority on each of them. But they were also my authorities, the source of my dreams" (4). In 1975, her attention to these series books and others marked her as someone ahead of her time, because she pointed out the significance of studying series books when they were still largely disregarded by teachers, librarians, and scholars. Moreover, Mason connected girls' series books to the burgeoning feminist movement and at one point comments, "Where would women's liberation be without Nancy Drew and Judy Bolton and Beverly Gray and Cherry Ames?" (6). Thus, Mason was one of the first critics to recognize the connections between girls' popular reading and their later life experiences, and she was unusual in seeing that connection positively.

The Girl Sleuth begins by discussing briefly the development of juvenile series during the twentieth century's first decades. Mason writes about the dominance of the Stratemeyer Syndicate, which turned the series book into a highly rationalized commodity by standardizing production and by relying on ghostwriters to churn out thousands of different titles. She also discusses early critical reactions to the "fifty-cent juveniles" produced by Stratemeyer and other publishers, mentioning that some of the books' critics condemned them for their sensationalism, which probably only made them sell more rapidly to eager young readers. She also talks about some of the early series that featured girls, such as the Motor Maids, the Motor Girls, the Adventure Girls, the Khaki Girls, and the Blue Grass Seminary Girls. Although this chapter provides a useful historical survey, it is rather sketchy. After reading it, I found myself wishing that Mason had made more connections between the books themselves and the culture that produced them, but this is a topic for a more comprehensive book than hers.

After this historical discussion, the book's chapters focus on different series, each featuring a girl detective. Mason begins with two chapters devoted to Honey Bunch and the Bobbsey Twins. The author describes the nauseating Honey Bunch to a tee: "Her life is perfectly delightful, full of treats and trips, for Honey Bunch's indulgent Mama and Daddy hung the moon up in the sky just for Honey Bunch" (21). Mason's personal reflections on the role Honey Bunch played in her life are amusing, but she does not dwell in great depth on the socioeconomic and historical reasons for the emergence of Honey Bunch and similar idealized heroines, nor does she do so in her next chapter on the Bobbsey Twins. This kind of critical analysis is beyond the book's scope, but it also reveals one of the book's limitations. Because the majority of the chapter focuses on Mason's personal reflections about the series, a broader analysis of series books and their impact on a variety of readers from all classes, ethnicities, and races is not possible.

After addressing books for younger readers, Mason turns her attention to books for slightly older readers. This chapter, which starts off with a discussion of the Nancy Drew books, is the book's most developed, and it offers many thoughtful insights about the most famous girl sleuth's appeal. Mason conveys the ambivalence of Nancy's place in our society perfectly: "She always has it both ways—protected and free. She is an eternal girl, a stage which is a false ideal for women in our time" (75). Like Mason, feminist critic Ellen Brown also emphasizes Nancy's sterility, calling her a figure "doomed forever to be eighteen . . . with avocation but no vocation" (10). Both Mason and Brown point out that although Nancy appears to offer girls—at least upper middle-class white girls—a degree of personal autonomy, she potentially offers them an intensely artificial role that no real girl, who must inevitably grow older, can fill. For those curious about the famous girl detective, this chapter provides essential insights into Nancy's character.

The next chapter discusses another popular sleuth: Judy Bolton, a character who Mason argues is more "satisfying and substantial" than other similar detective heroines (81). As she points out, "Judy is not in the least glamorous or dainty. She is more interested in her intellect than in her looks" (83). Along with Bolton, Mason also briefly discusses Trixie Belden. Although both of these discussions are informative, they lack the development of the author's discussion of Nancy.

The following chapter is also a trifle sketchy, perhaps because the author is discussing a number of characters who are less influential than Nancy. In it Mason focuses on what she calls the "glamour girls"—Cherry Ames, Vicki Barr, Connie Blair, and Beverly Gray—girls with careers of their own "up in the clouds, in the movies, in busy hospitals and ad agencies" (99). Mason does a fine job of interpreting the novels themselves, but she could have made this chapter even more engrossing with a lengthier discussion of the evolving nature of women's careers in the twentieth century.

The concluding chapter addresses Nancy Drew's changing depiction in the late 1960s and early 1970s. One wishes that Mason had taken the time to rewrite this chapter or update it before *The Girl Sleuth* was reissued, because Nancy's image has changed dramatically in the twenty years since Mason's study was originally published. But even with this shortcoming, her book still has too many strengths to be forgotten.

Dyer and Romalov's collection, which includes an impressive range of essays written by professors, librarians, general readers, writers of series books, and collectors of Nancy Drew books and memorabilia, is more scholarly than Mason's book. Many of the essays are versions of works first presented at the University of Iowa's Nancy Drew Conference in 1993, which was inspired by the discovery that Mildred Wirt Benson, the first person and thus the first woman to receive a master's degree in journalism from Iowa, was the writer of several of the original Nancy Drew books. Dyer and Romalov also put together this collection because they believe that "most of what's written and said about American popular culture in both the mass media and academic works has focused on the passions of boys and men, while the memorable childhood experiences of girls have been largely ignored" (5). This collection seeks to redress this imbalance.

Carolyn G. Heilbrun begins the collection with an essay that was originally given as the keynote address at the conference. Here she argues that Drew is a Golden Age detective who should be associated with other detectives from the Golden Age of detective story writing between World War I and World War II, something that other critics, such as Patricia Craig and Mary Cadogan in *The Lady Investigates: Women Detectives and Spies in Fiction* (1981), have argued against. Heilbrun also suggests that Nancy, at least in the early volumes of the series, has been a role model for feminists: "The roadster, the lack of a female trainer in patriarchy, and the sheer gutsiness are what make the original Nancy Drew a moment in feminist history" (18). One admirable feature of the anthology is that readers do not receive only Heilbrun's opinions about the Keene novels: rather, the essays in the collection provide a wide range of views on the girl detective. The audience thereby gains a better understanding of her complexity.

After Heilbrun's introductory essay, the first part of the four major sections that compose the book focuses on "Creating and Publishing Nancy Drew." The eight essays in this section cover a broad range of material about the production and marketing of Carolyn Keene's books, a task made more difficult by the notorious secrecy of the Stratemeyer Syndicate. Particularly notable is Deidre Johnson's essay on the development of the Stratemeyer books. She displays the wide knowledge of series books that has put her at the head of the field. Also praiseworthy is Geoffrey S. Lapin's essay, "Searching for Carolyn Keene." He explains how he "discovered" Mildred Wirt Benson to have been the "mother" of the Drew books and discusses the court battle that raged over the authorship of the Keene novels. I only wish that Lapin's discussion could have been more extensive. An essay by Benson herself provides fascinating information about the career of this feisty woman. Also of interest is a discussion by Anne Greenberg, the editor at Simon & Schuster who oversees the Drew books, about her involvement with the modern Nancy Drew books and how publishers have altered the books in an attempt to make them more appealing to today's audience. The major shortcoming of these chapters and the others in the collection is their brevity: the writers are able to give only terse introductions to their subjects and cannot develop their thoughts in great depth.

The second section of *Rediscovering Nancy Drew* focuses on readers' responses to the novels themselves. Dyer and Romalov are to be commended for attempting to represent the wide variety of people who read the Keene books. Whether it is Bonnie S. Sunstein's essay on how different readers approach the Drew books, Nancy Tillman Romalov's piece on how libraries have historically reacted to the Keene novels, or Barbara Black's and Joel Shoemaker's commentaries on how librarians perceive series books, the selections in this section provide an overview of different interpretive strategies, which result in some readers condemning them as worthless "trash" and others praising them as exciting adventures that appeal to reluctant readers. This section also includes three essays that adopt multicultural perspectives on Nancy, two from an African-American perspective and one from an Asian-American viewpoint. One wishes, however, that the editors could have included even a greater number of essays from readers with different racial, ethnic, and class backgrounds, although they were limited by the papers presented at the conference.

Part three contains a number of essays that address collecting and studying the Drew novels. David Farah and Gil O'Gara, both prominent collectors of series books, discuss the importance of preserving and researching series books. Karen M. Mason and Esther Green Bierbaum reflect on the difficulties confronting the researcher studying series books and the resources available to such scholars. All of these essays are thought-provoking, but they will appeal more to the collector or researcher than the general audience.

The final section contains articles by writers who have studied how Nancy has been transformed in one fashion or another. Unquestionably, the strongest chapters are Diana Beeson and Bonnie Brennen's "Translating Nancy Drew from Print to Film" and Laura Ruby's "Drawing on a Sleuth: The Case of the Nancy Drew Series," in which the artist discusses how Nancy inspired her artwork. These essays show the collection at its best. They reveal the myriad ways that Nancy Drew has been transformed into a cultural icon that is influential far beyond the narrow realm of her series.

These two books should be required reading for the scholar interested in children's literature or series books in particular, but even general readers would find either book enjoyable to peruse. Both books are part of a growing 1990s fascination about girls' culture as feminist-influenced scholars become more aware of the significance of studying how girls mature into women. We are only at the very beginning of recovering a literature that has been disregarded as irrelevant for much of this century because it was associated with young women.

Works Cited

Brown, Ellen. "In Search of Nancy Drew, the Snow Queen, and Room Nineteen: Cruising for Feminine Discourse." *Frontiers* 13.2 (1992): 1–25.
Craig, Patricia, and Mary Cadogan. *The Lady Investigates: Women Detectives and Spies in Fiction.* London: Gollancz, 1981.
Farah, David, and Ilana Nash. *Series Books and the Media; or, This Isn't All: An Annotated Bibliography of Secondary Sources.* Rheem Valley, Calif.: SynSine, 1996.
Nancy Drew Issue. *The Lion and the Unicorn* 18.1 (June 1994).
Ross, Catherine Sheldrick. "If They Read Nancy Drew, So What? Series Book Readers Talk Back." *Library and Information Science Research* 17.3 (1995): 201–36.
TALL: *Teaching and Learning Literature with Children and Young Adults* 5.3. Special Edition on Series Books. (Jan.–Feb. 1996).

In Search of the New Child: 1730–1830

Susan R. Gannon

The New Child: British Art and the Origins of Modern Childhood, 1730–1830, by James Christen Steward. University Art Museum and Pacific Film Archive University of California, Berkeley, in association with University of Washington, 1995.

James Christen Steward's *The New Child: British Art and the Origins of Modern Childhood, 1730–1830* examines the construction of childhood as it was reflected in and shaped by eighteenth- and nineteenth-century British art, and it aims "to place the evolving representation of children and their families in Georgian Britain . . . in the context of their time" (11). The book, magnificently illustrated with fifty-one color plates and over a hundred black and white illustrations, was published to coincide with an exhibition of the same name organized by the University Art Museum and Pacific Film Archive, Berkeley— an archive whose wonderful collection of material supports, queries, and complicates Steward's narrative of juvenile representation in art and literature.

Because the history of childhood is an intellectual minefield, perhaps it was simple prudence for Steward to chart a centrist course. He concedes that Georgian attitudes toward children show considerable continuity with earlier periods, yet he insists that these attitudes did undergo some striking changes from 1730 to 1830. Questioning social historians' reliance on theoretical pronouncements about child-rearing, Steward sensibly assumes a likely gap between theory and practice in this matter, and he looks to private memoirs, letters, and journals for more reliable evidence as to what actually happened between parents and their children. *The New Child* thus contextualizes visual representations of children within "a tapestry woven of letters, diaries, statistical information, and the evidence of other works of art" (12), in order to explore the period's construction and experience of childhood.

Steward offers a marvelous gallery of paintings, sumptuously reproduced in full-page color plates and chosen to reveal "some of

Children's Literature 25, ed. Francelia Butler, R. H. W. Dillard, and Elizabeth Lennox Keyser, guest ed. Mitzi Myers and U. C. Knoepflmacher (Yale University Press, © 1997 Hollins College).

the new questions faced by artists concerning children, the family, and constructs of childhood as well as their coexistence with traditional manners of representation" (19). An introduction preceding the plates identifies assorted "issues in depicting children that are culturally specific to the Georgian period and therefore socially driven," and suggests that the subsequent text, plates and additional pictures show "with what diversity artists addressed these issues" (19). Among the topics Steward notices in the following chapters is a new "interest in candor and the observed 'childlike' nature of children" (19). He documents a novel spontaneity and freedom in the way children are presented and shows how the scale and design of many new paintings focus attention on children. Steward comments shrewdly on the way children could be used to subvert or comment on the pretensions of adult figures. And he shows how themes of childhood play and lessons could be handled in genre paintings to reveal much about an emergent separate sphere of child life. A final section on the boldness with which some artists—especially in "fancy pictures" (portraits of models playacting in some emblematic fashion)—tested propriety in subtly suggesting childhood sexuality opens up an area of discussion so rich as almost to deserve another volume.

Steward makes excellent use of memoirs, letters, and art history to support his reading of pictures. For example, in his discussion of Sir Joshua Reynolds's portrait of *Lady Caroline Scott as Winter,* he explains that contemporary sources indicate Reynolds was known for his empathy with his child sitters. Knowing some of Reynolds's favorite strategies, Steward suggests that the artist used small animals in this picture to focus the viewer's attention on the girl. But because such animals were also used emblematically, he suspects the animal reference may also be intended to reinforce the notion that the child's world shown here is innocent. For Steward, "the artist has caught his child sitter at a single moment in her life, one in which she . . . is both fragile and vibrant, forthright and in need of protection" (21). Any reader is free to test this reading by inspecting the picture itself, reproduced in the text, but he or she might also consider the confirmation presented by a sophisticated connoisseur's response: Horace Walpole apparently called the picture "delicious" and said of the little girl, "overlaid with a long cloak, bonnet and muff, in the midst of the snow" and "perishing blue and red with cold," she "looks so smiling and good-humoured, that one longs to catch her up in one's arms and kiss her till she is in a sweat and squalls" (20).

The New Child is not organized chronologically; chapters anticipate,

overlap, and recapitulate each other and they offer, in a series of suggestive readings of pictures and their cultural contexts, some useful
surmises about the directions toward which the Georgian world might
have been moving. Steward's patient, sensitive analyses of individual
paintings are, on the whole, persuasive. Yet he seems thoroughly
aware of the possible difficulties and contradictions individual works
present. There is no effort to bully the reader into agreement with
his ideas about how the pictures might be read. In each succeeding
chapter he raises questions with which to probe and investigate certain materials: first the Georgian family and the parental role; then—
in turn—the thematizing in art of the child's involvement with play,
learning, charity, and social class. Steward's approach to conceptualiz-
ing the grand sweep of social history is largely to summarize (briefly)
alternative critical positions and then, diffidently, to suggest his own
preference. He considers, for example, how the rise of sensibility and
shifting class lines impinged on the representation of childhood and
family life, but finds more important than these a "rethinking, from
Locke onwards, of the concept of nature: if nature is good, then children must also be good" (193).

Laying out the larger picture of the movement of ideas and attitudes, however, is not really Steward's strong suit. Though he is rightly
concerned to avoid the usual pitfalls besetting projects like his—producing a merely decorative book, or an illustrated social history, or a
social history of art that doesn't care about the differences in the ways
artists have treated adults and children—it might have been better if
Steward had not tried quite so hard to move beyond the complexities
and contradictions that he finds in so many richly observed individual
pictures. His desire to produce a master narrative that clearly charts
the evolution of attitudes toward children during the period and to
account—in some comprehensive way—for the reasons behind these
shifts leads him to surround his brilliant readings of pictures with
uncritical abstracts of predigested secondary material. And when he
deals with literary history, in particular, Steward sometimes assimilates dubious opinions along with the background data.[1]

Anyone interested in the way childhood was represented in Georgian illustrated books will find much to think about in Steward's
provocative analyses of idealized portraits of loving mothers playing
indulgently with their babies and reserved fathers modeling for their
sons what it means to be a scholar, a connoisseur, or a naval officer.
Steward makes such materials speak volumes about the power rela-

tions and affective bonds that characterized families of the upper and middle classes. His comments on familiar topoi treated in children's books as well as in art—the charity visit, the lesson, children at play—will enrich the reading of many a literary text and illustration. But anyone familiar with the children's books Steward introduces as contextual support for his criticism of pictures will be disappointed to find that he has not always taken the time to familiarize himself intimately with the books.[2] For just as the portraits and fancy pictures he discusses mean more when appropriately contextualized, so too are book illustrations best understood in the light of the texts they are meant to serve.

Steward's dependence on sources like Geoffrey Summerfield and Mary V. Jackson probably accounts for his tendency to look through a rather negative, romantic lens at much Georgian children's literature: he finds this writing wanting in "imagination" and reads into it a systematic intent to repress the desire for social mobility in young readers. Though Steward admits that the child's imagination is called upon in, for example, the kind of instructive tale that dealt with the adventures of an inanimate object, he privileges works like Roscoe's *Butterfly's Ball* (1806) that seem to him to arouse imaginative thought "for its own sake . . . as a vitally constructive part of human nature" (198). To Steward, the presence of an obvious didactic agenda renders negligible the imaginative response of the reader to a story. That readers might have been entertained and imaginatively stimulated by stories designed to instruct seems to escape him, despite his appreciation for the depth and complexity sometimes added to paintings by *their* own didactic programs. The open-mindedness and freshness of observation that mark his readings of portraits and genre paintings of children are too often missing from his observations on the work of people like the Kilners, Ellenor Fenn, or Mary Wollstonecraft.

Even his discussions of the import of the illustrations in such children's books are uncharacteristically imperceptive. Steward remarks that the eighteenth century preferred educational books such as Dorothy Kilner's *The Holyday Present,* "where the child reader could identify with the nurturing domestic environment and find reward personified in illustrations such as 'The Unlocking of the Good Child's Box,' " adding, "A proper sort of domesticity suggested its own reward" (198). That all makes the book sound rather cozy, and the elaborate frontispiece reproduced by Steward indeed seems to show a happy family gathered around for the distribution of rewards to the good. Had Steward given the book the kind of nuanced reading he readily accords to paintings, however, he might have noted the way it treats a subject that can be an urgent one for parents and children: childhood transgression and the parental prerogative to punish. For the most remarkable parts of the story concern the contents of the *Naughty* Child's Box also delivered to the Jennet residence. This box contains instruments of punishment to be used by the parents on the children: medals announcing the wearer's misdeeds, a ridiculous looking fool's cap with asses' ears, and a set of graded rods to inflict just the right degree of pain appropriate to an offense. Most of the book's illustrations depict transgressions (Little Charles throwing stones at someone) or humiliating punishments (Mr. Jennet tying Charles up). And in the end, Charles—who had worn all the medals and had been beaten with all the rods—proves incorrigible. As an adult he is a rotter, lonely and despised. Though Steward has a lively awareness of the variety and unpredictability of viewer response to pictures, he assumes too readily a clichéd and predictable response to books like *The Holyday Present.* Young readers—like their elders—find their delights where they may. In the very copy of the book whose frontispiece Steward reproduces from the Houghton Library at Harvard, that page and others describing the rewards of the good little children remain crisp and clean, whereas the pages graphically depicting the children's sins and their colorful punishments are grubby and worn, having no doubt been much-thumbed by young readers for all the wrong reasons. In a similar vein, Steward comments (echoing Gerald Gottlieb [35]) that Richard Ransome's *Good Boy's Soliloquy: Containing His Parents' Instructions Relative to his Disposition and Manners* is "touchingly naive" (157) in its expectations that readers will not imitate the colorfully described misdeeds it pictures. Yet it is hard to look at this delightful little book's illustrations and not perceive that the joke would have been obvious to anyone, young or old, who picked it up. Enjoying those misdeeds is the real point of the book, whatever the title might convey.

Steward seems ready also to go along with Mary Jackson's view that Blake intended his illustrations to Mary Wollstonecraft's *Original Stories* as an ironic counterpoint to the text. (See also Summerfield 229–33.) Steward suggests that Wollstonecraft had lost sight of the individual child, and that Blake was trying in his illustrations "to right this by showing himself on the side of the children: the tutor is inevitably depicted as self-conscious and studied, while the children look wistfully at the wider world denied them" (145). The 1791 edition has six Blake engravings. The one to which Steward refers shows the tutor, Mrs. Mason, with her charges. At the moment in the text that is illustrated, one of the girls (who tends to put off doing the good she might do) has become deeply upset while hearing the painful story behind the ruined estate she is visiting. Its owner was a man destroyed by such habits as hers. Mrs. Mason takes her hand and comforts and counsels her, suggesting it is time they leave this place. In the picture, the girl looks sadly over her shoulder—not at a wider world denied her, but at the decayed estate that symbolizes the bitter waste of timely opportunities to do good. Admittedly, in light of his highly personal and idiosyncratic use of visual signs, it is difficult to gauge possible ironies in Blake's work. And it has been suggested (Erdman 80) that one of the illustrations for *Songs of Innocence and Experience* is a parodic version of the cover of *Original Stories*. But the cover for Wollstonecraft's book can be read as a straight mythification of the story, with the tutor (stylized rather than studied and self-conscious) as a Christ-like cruciform figure and the girls posed like haloed angels in prayerful attitudes beside her. This angel motif is picked again up in the picture of Mrs. Mason's encounter with a Welsh harpist, and in a picture (mentioned without any reference to intended irony by Steward himself [169]) depicting a charitable visit. To a casual modern eye, the juxtaposition of caption and content in some of the pictures might well suggest ironies belied by the immediate context of the story. ("Indeed we are very happy!" is the perfectly apt caption to a scene in which everyone is in tears.) Nevertheless, the two remaining plates—a sentimental domestic moment and a tragic prison scene—don't seem to have any obvious ironic import. If Blake intended these pictures to undercut Wollstonecraft's text, I doubt many readers of it, young or old, have gotten the message—that is, if they really read the book carefully. Of course, in the spirit of Steward's critical approach at its best, resolving this question definitively would involve not only a close attention to the written text, but also a thorough survey of Blake's symbolic practice, specific historical information about the making of this text's illustrations, and a feeling for the reading practices of parents and children in the period, because the context of various eighteenth-century *individuals*—here the artist, the author, the publisher, and the reader—is crucial in any effort to understand the art of the past.

Steward makes much of the difference between the way eighteenth-century and modern viewers might see certain pictures. He concludes his book with a chapter on this matter, a consideration of the occasions in Georgian art when children were not treated as children. A good part of the chapter discusses "fancy pictures"—which are, for the most part, portraits of paid models posed in some emblematic fashion. Steward is especially interested in the way these pictures reflect "a complex relationship of complicity, projection, and domination between adult painter/viewer and child subject" (27). He believes that when confronted by such a picture "the generally sensitive viewer of today will almost certainly attach different meanings to it than would a visitor to the Royal Academy in 1770." Our heightened awareness of the pathology of power relations between children and adults may be one factor at work here. Discussing two fancy pictures by Reynolds, for example, Steward raises important questions about adult representation of children for their own, not always savory, purposes. These "misunderstood" pictures are, he suggests, "perhaps the most sexualized representations of small children to be painted by a society artist of the first rank" (209). The first picture, "Cupid as Link Boy" (1744), shows a winged child of five or six carrying a torch through the London streets. The association of link boys with prostitutes navigating the streets at night and their implication in illicit sexual activities would have been familiar to eighteenth-century admirers of Reynolds like the disreputable Duke of Dorset, who owned both "Cupid as Link Boy" and its companion piece "Mercury as Cut Purse." "Mercury" portrays a very similar little boy, perhaps the same model as in "Cupid," dressed as the God Mercury, with a winged cap. Mercury, Steward notes, was not only a messenger god but also a god of commerce who was often shown with a money bag. Steward thinks Georgian viewers familiar with Hogarth's before and after pieces would have understood that point because in Reynolds's picture "Mercury holds his purse limply . . . the picture becomes a kind of before and after pair, an infantine sexual progress from the erect to the pendulous" (210). But there are even darker implications in this pair of pictures than those Steward explicitly draws, because presenting Mercury as presiding over the aftermath of a sexual encounter would have been a clear hint in the eighteenth century that sexually transmitted disease was the result of this "sexual progress." The most painful aspect of the pair of pictures is the projection onto very young faces of such adult knowledge. Together, the images of children presented in Steward's gallery of pictures produce surprisingly diverse takes on childhood, and these last images add an important warning about how rash it is to indulge in clichés and generalizations about "childhood innocence" rather than to attend to individual art works in all their particularity.

The primary delights of *The New Child* are the gorgeous pictures and Steward's convincing demonstration that close reading and patient contextualization are an appropriate method for understanding them. Without the least mystification, he gently teases out the implications of each picture's details for the reader, casually sharing as much expertise in art history and traditional iconography as the task seems to demand. In Michael Baxandall's terms, this is a "democratic" and "sociable" way for an art critic to work (137). It is a brave way, too; for because he reproduces most of the pictures he discusses, Steward gives his readers the equipment they need to second-guess him—a process this text encourages. At every turn the reader is urged to question the materials presented—and sometimes to probe more deeply or range more widely than Steward's chapters allow. But ending up with more questions than answers simply means that Steward's intriguing studies of individual pictures and genres may serve as stimulating prolegomena to further study of the subjects they introduce with such verve and enthusiasm. Among the generous attributes of this lavishly produced volume are the most tempting, widest margins for personal annotation I have seen in some time, and I predict that anyone interested in the period, the problems, and the pictures treated here will find the book—and "talking back to it" in those margins—irresistible.

Notes

1. Some of the notions Steward has picked up are puzzling. Can he really think that Chesterfield's letters were so very appealing to Puritans (132)? How can he say (or think) that from the 1790s to "well into the nineteenth century" children's literature presented "wealthy children" as "always scrupulous and fair," "the highborn always generous and kindly" (177)? How can the story of Goody Two-Shoes possibly send "a message that charity can impede the discovery of one's truth, and that one might well be left, even as a child, to make one's own way" (170), when the young heroine gets so much help from kindly rich folk and when a whole chapter of her story is devoted to her ideas on creative ways that the rich can help the poor?

2. Students of children's literature using this book should be aware that Steward's citation of titles and dates is sometimes unreliable and that there are no references to standard journals in the field such as *Children's Literature, Children's Literature Association Quarterly,* or *The Lion & the Unicorn.*

Works Cited

Baxandall, Michael. *Patterns of Intention: On the Historical Explanation of Pictures.* New Haven: Yale University Press, 1985.

Erdman, David V. *The Illuminated Blake: William Blake's Complete Illuminated Works with a Plate-by-Plate Commentary.* New York: Dover, 1974.

Gottlieb, Gerald H., ed. *Early Children's Books and Their Illustration.* New York: Pierpont Morgan Library, 1975.

The History of Little Goody Two-Shoes. London: J. Newbery, 1765.

Jackson, Mary V. *Engines of Instruction, Mischief, and Magic: Children's Literature in England from Its Beginnings to 1839.* Lincoln: University of Nebraska Press, 1989.

Kilner, Dorothy. *The Holyday Present Containing Anecdotes of Mr. and Mrs. Jennet and their Little Family.* 3d ed. London: Printed for J. Marshall & Co. no. 4 Aldermary Church Yard in Bow Lane and no. 17, Queen St. Cheapside, [1788?].

Ransome, Richard. *The Good Boy's Soliloquy; Containing his Parents' Instructions Relative to His Disposition and Manners.* London: W. Darton, Jr., 1811.

Stanhope, Philip Dormer, 4th Earl of Chesterfield. *Letters Written by the Earl of Chesterfield to his Son, Philip Stanhope, Together with Several Other Pieces on Various Subjects, Published by Mrs. Eugenia Stanhope.* London: J. Dodsley, 1774.

Summerfield, Geoffrey. *Fantasy & Reason: Children's Literature in the Eighteenth Century.* Athens: University of Georgia Press, 1985.

Wollstonecraft, Mary. *Original Stories from Real Life; with Conversations, Calculated to Regulate the Affections, and Form the Mind to Truth and Goodness.* 1788. 2d ed. With six plates by William Blake. London: Printed for J. Johnson, no. 72, St. Paul's Churchyard, 1791.

Tellers and Tales

Patricia Pace

Tell Me a Fairy Tale: A Parent's Guide to Telling Magical and Mythical Stories, by Bill Adler, Jr. New York: Penguin, 1995.

Dreaming and Storytelling, by Bert O. States. Ithaca, N.Y.: Cornell University Press, 1993.

Creative Storytelling: Building Community, Changing Lives, by Jack Zipes. New York: Routledge, 1995.

Walter Benjamin observes that "storytelling is always the art of repeating stories, and [that] this art is lost when the stories are no longer [remembered]. It is lost because there is no more weaving or spinning going on while they are being listened to. The more self-forgetful the listener is, the more deeply is what he listens to impressed upon his memory. When the rhythm of work has seized him, he listens to the tales in such a way that the gift of retelling them comes to him all by itself" (91). Benjamin emphasizes the close relationship between working, making, and telling—the crafting of a community as well as a tale. For him, stories give us a glimpse of the earliest cultures, the person actively shaping experience through living, authentic speech. Although there is undoubtedly truth in his account of the oral tale and the storyteller, it also reveals a longing for a past beyond recovery. Later in his work, Benjamin takes a less nostalgic view of the teller and tale, writing that "The historical materialist leaves it to others to be drained by the whore called 'Once upon a time'" (262).

The conflicting views Benjamin demonstrates regarding the meaning of stories and their performance presage the complex and contested perspectives focused on "the art of the story" in contemporary culture. For many literary academics, storytelling in its many structural forms, from the sacred to the secular, is heralded as the quintessential human activity, one that defies death while imposing meaning and order on experience. Others, alert to the way stories may reify the ideological and commercial interests of those in power, are

Children's Literature 25, ed. Francelia Butler, R. H. W. Dillard, and Elizabeth Lennox Keyser, guest ed. Mitzi Myers and U. C. Knoepflmacher (Yale University Press, © 1997 Hollins College).

wary of the promise, of the wish come true. In popular literature as well, stories and storytelling are recommended as valuable self-help and spiritual aids—but only particular kinds of stories with particular virtuous or therapeutic aims are sanctioned. Three recent books about stories, each with varying definitions and perspectives on performance, offer different understandings of the work of story in the cultures that shape us: the realm of dream; the school setting; and that factory of stories and storytellers, the family.

With the publication of *Creative Storytelling: Building Community and Changing Lives,* Jack Zipes expands his interest in Marxist and feminist interpretation of tales into the field of critical pedagogy (an area of study often associated with the work of Henry Giroux). Not that Zipes is a newcomer; his twenty years of work with children, educators, and storytellers in the United States and England are documented in the storytelling exercises, suggestions for classroom approaches, and "theoretical reflections" that compose this book. Although Zipes characterizes the book as "an anti-manual, not to instruct but to share . . . methods and ideas . . . borrowed from many different critics, storytellers, teachers and children," the practical instructions for integrating stories with visual art activities and creative dramatics would be useful for teachers of children and youth as well as the teachers of would-be teachers in colleges and universities (2). His chapters provide familiar and unfamiliar stories for classroom use, as well as interesting variants on the tales that might prove time-consuming for the teacher to collect; the assignments themselves are detailed and supplemented with helpful material such as the structural functions and motifs in the fairy and folk tale and critical commentary on the various genres. The book progresses from performative approaches to familiar fairy tales to forms including "utopian tales" and science fiction. And most admirable of all, Zipes never patronizes his intended reader—the teacher with limited time and resources—who daily struggles to impart literacy and empower children.

As critical pedagogy, Zipes's classroom work is but a means to implement a more ideological project in which "story" is the vehicle by which "we become our own narrators, the storytellers of our lives, . . . to put the dreams of our lives into effect" (4). By a deft mix of classics and folk literature, a "real" storyteller can infuse students with enthusiasm and, through an emphasis on creative play, help children develop critical faculties and challenge authority. For Zipes, these goals mean specifically questioning the sexist stereotypes in fairy tales, the distorted materialism presented in TV versions of fantasy and fairy tales, and the commodification of animals, as well as the systematic abuse of children by adults and institutions, war, and burgeoning technology. Many of us would agree that these are worthy, even virtuous aims, but perhaps they are only auxiliary to the less programmatic project of art-making and storytelling itself.

Clearly Zipes believes in the power of art, in story or drama, to transform lives and communities: "Schools need to transform themselves constantly into cultural domains where work becomes play, play work" (10). Surely "play" does perform important "work" for culture, but perhaps it does so more effectively in an institutional setting where critical questioning is not the goal of storytelling or performance. In Zipes's estimation, storytellers are more important as members of the school community than as artists. Similarly, "a performance is just what it is, a performance, no matter how much the storyteller may care for children or love his or her art" (9). Although the author concludes his book with the injunction that "storytellers cannot and should not pretend to be therapists, gurus, or social workers . . . pretending that stories have a magic power of healing the woes of children and the community," he nevertheless insists, with Benjamin, that there is somehow a "genuine storyteller [sharing] his or her story with the listeners . . . for the benefit of the community" (Zipes 223, 225). Art-making, in story or performance, is profoundly ingenious; it is concerned with invention, artifice, craft. What *Creative Storytelling* lacks is any pedagogy grounded in an aesthetic theory of dramatic art, with aesthetic aims and criteria, in which self-discovery and empowerment may occur outside the ideological reaches of the left or the right.

If Zipes has a conflicted romance with story and storytelling, as many of us do, Bill Adler, Jr., has no qualms about appropriating the tale and the telling for commercial interests. Indeed, what is most interesting and most disturbing about *Tell Me a Fairy Tale: A Parent's Guide to Telling Magical and Mythical Stories* is what it reveals about the market for such books—and the way the publisher construes the contemporary family scene. It might go something like this: after a busy stressful day at the office/factory/salesroom, Mom and Dad (or a single parent) barely make it home in time to rescue their children from the TV/arcade/day care center, pausing only long enough to pack the family in the car for dinner at McDonald's/KFC/Pizza Hut. They return, exhausted with the demands of the day, but intent on some quality time with the children. The designated-nurturing parent watches the children in the bath while boning up on a fairy or folk tale presented in a much abbreviated form, which he or she can then "perform" before bedtime in the quik/lite/deluxe version—according to the available time or the guilt factor operable that night. Adler wrote the book to help parents like himself; "I didn't want to acquire a large collection of fairy tale anthologies. First, a complete collection would be expensive. Second, to actually read the tales aloud from a book would take half an hour each evening. . . . Finally, it's much more enjoyable to *tell* a story than to read one—especially if you already know the ending" (xiv).

The emphasis on time management throughout the book is its most distinctive and revelatory feature. In Adler's version of the popular imagination, fairy tales are like food or other items of consumption, part of our vast cornucopia of leisure and pleasure, although we have little time for sustained enjoyment. Fairy tales are, first of all, "fun." In this "anthology," they are "indispensable . . . for adults who want to remember their childhood." The tales contain gruesome elements that don't scare the kids, but "psychologists explain this behavior in a number of ways, none of which are terribly relevant to the telling of fairy tales." Anyway, if the plots make sense to the kids but not to the adults, "So what?" (xiii–xvii).

This book has little to offer the scholar of literature, although it may provide a wealth of material as a cultural artifact of our time. Each heading in the book is a story title, followed by a summary (the "quik" version), a list of the characters and their attributes, the plot (deluxe serving), and a section on "How to Tell This Story" (which may include the "lite" version, or some more exotic variation tailored to the parent's particular tastes in children's fantasy). The book is both intentionally and unintentionally funny. For example, Bluebeard "had the misfortune of growing blue whiskers before the Smurfs were popular"; the Prince is described succinctly as "Handsome, rides a horse"; and in "The Snow Queen" the parent can contemporize the tale "by making Kay a hotshot snowboarder and putting the Snow Queen into a superpowered snowmobile." Also humorous, or appalling, are Adler's attempts to appease parental anxiety by his suggested revisions of the tales. As with "The Snow Queen," many of the variations replace frightening or magical elements with the more familiar imagery of contemporary consumer life: a vain and fanciful girl with red shoes now wears a pair of Air

Jordans, the gingerbread house in "Hansel and Gretel" becomes "a place they were taken to because they were good or had eaten their dinners," Sleeping Beauty and the Prince may become Charles and Princess Di (22, 115, 127, 67).

Seen more positively, Adler's prescriptions are refreshingly devoid of the usual veneration for tales and telling; after all, the tales and tellers of old were practitioners of a vulgar art that was very much a part of the everyday lives of the workers (and shoppers?) of yesteryear. And his emphasis on the brevity of the tale and the economy of the telling may speak important truths about the workaday world of the contemporary family—realities we can easily criticize but much less effectively resolve. He includes a few stories from other cultures, he often has inventive spins on the tales and insights from his own experiences with his daughter, and, as he concludes his introduction: "*Tell Me a Fairy Tale* was completed just in the nick of time. Karen, who is now nearly three and a half and has never tired of stories, has a baby sister, Claire" (xviii).

Bert O. States's *Dreaming and Storytelling* is the most scholarly of the three books reviewed, for States extends and elaborates on narrative theory to examine the dream as text. He describes his approach, however, as phenomenological—as an attempt to "confront dream and poetic images . . . at their point of origin." His "comparative poetics" is combined credibly, if somewhat uncomfortably, with recent work on dreams from neurobiology and cognitive psychology (5).

Dreaming and Storytelling is organized into chapters that explicate and reflect upon the isolated features particular to dreams, and each offers insight into the role of story in human consciousness. In "The Problem of Bizarreness," we find that the improbable or fantastic element of dream, the interruption of the mundane that is a defining characteristic of the dream narrative, is also a condition of artistic form—the dynamic central to human expressiveness. In this way, dreams are like poetic images: they are unusual, bizarre, or distorted as a condition of their being. But unlike stories or poems, dream texts are not intrinsically interesting to anyone but the dreamer. A report of a dream is only a sequence of events, whereas the dream state is one in which we are the protagonists and experience the events with their attendant sensations and emotions as they happen to us—as lived experience. A good storyteller or writer is able to engage the emotions of the audience or reader to a rousing and satisfying end, but "a dream does not reach conclusions; rather, it worries relations among emotion-laden objects . . . [it] plays out emotion emotion-ally" (82). States challenges Freud's notion that distortion signifies censorship of repressed content, for there is no way of determining a censored dream from an uncensored dream; in waking life and in analysis we censor, whereas in dreams we singlemindedly "think" our emotional world.

Like stories, however, dreams impart structure and order to one's emotional world. States compares dream "types" to literary modes, specifically the epic, dramatic, and lyric forms. In lyric dreams, "the self always speaks to and of itself . . . in comparative isolation from the contingencies of interpersonal life . . . [like] the dream of flight" (89). An epic dream would manifest the episodic structure of daily life with all its minutiae: urgencies, residual worries, and all their attendant emotions. Structurally, such dreams resemble the "pica-resque—travel, picnicing, wandering through a strange or familiar city" (90). Dreaming in the dramatic mode produces those startling or frightening dreams in which "the dream situation [is carried] to its furthest possible extreme" and contains the Aristotelian devices of reversal of fortune and crisis (86). These dream narratives are acti-vated by events and emotions as well as by desire, and, according to States, they *find their form* (not only their content) in the organizing structures of lived experience.

States does not shy away from difficult, even unanswerable ques-tions. In "Scripts and Archetypes," he begins by asking "why would the self—waking or sleeping—want to tell a story in the first place? What have such falsehoods to do with understanding and general-ized knowledge?" (112). The answer might seem a tautology: the per-son creates narratives because personhood demands a way to index and structure experience, ergo narrative. States painstakingly dem-onstrates that dreams partake of the same "scriptural coherence" as do the narratives we organize in waking life. That is, dreams, like fiction, are rule-governed; "As dreamers we are like colonists who in-habit a new world but bring along all the forms and response systems we learned in the old world" (179). Operating according to the same structures as do fictions, dreams, as products of a different state of consciousness, allow access to a different kind of "sensory experi-ence" or "felt meaning" (203).

Although States is not a critic of Freudian psychoanalysis in the caustic manner of much academic writing, he clearly wants to counter Freud's emphasis on the dream text as an object of interpretation with manifest or latent content. Instead of understanding the images in the dream as evidence of sexual repression (the primitive or neurotic subject in civilization), States utilizes the dream state itself as his object of hermeneutical investigation and description. He finds in dreaming *expressiveness* (as opposed to concealment)—the artist or storyteller is at the foundation of human consciousness.

If we understand our history by estimating only those material objects available from archaeological excavation and analysis, we might designate our humanity as one determined by our propensity for tool-making or war. But our history as symbol-makers is more evasive and obscure; we cannot claim accurate historical knowledge about the origin of story in human civilization. We can, however, look for the origin of story in individual human consciousness—in dreams, "the *ur*-form of fiction . . . [preceding] the creation of written and oral fictions in both the historical life of the species and the personal life of the individual" (States 3).

Dreaming and Storytelling tells us, with great erudition, how dreams work and how (not what) they mean. It provides a philosophical validation, of sorts, for our preoccupation with story—as children, parents, and academics. A philosophical explication, unfortunately, doesn't make for a very good story in itself. It doesn't, as Jack Zipes's book does, compel us to consider "the story in the world," the social world, where children go to school, hear stories, and decide to be princesses or warriors, naughty Squirrel Nutkins or sweet fluffy bunnies. And philosophy is beyond the purview of the bedtime story, a ceremony seemingly observed in even the most harried contemporary family. Philosophy, like dreaming, is light-years away from that other impulse so essential to the artist, to the child and to the person — *homo ludens*—man playing, performing, underscoring the potential subversiveness of story even while honoring its power.

Work Cited

Benjamin, Walter. "The Storyteller." "Theses on the Philosophy of History." *Illuminations: Essays and Reflections.* Ed. Hannah Arendt. Trans. Harry Zohn. New York: Schocken, 1968.

Dissertations of Note

Compiled and Annotated by Rachel Fordyce

Arango, Geralyn Anderson. "A Content Analysis of the Portrayal of Homeless Persons in Children's Books: 1980–1993." Ed.D. diss. Temple University, 1995. 141 pp. DAI 56:1274A.

Arango concludes that "as homelessness has come to the forefront as a compelling social issue of the 1980's and 1990's, children's literature has, to an extent, reflected this concern and shared it with its audience in the form of picture books and chapter books which feature homeless characters in main or supporting roles." After an exhaustive search, however, Arango could only identify thirty-eight works that dealt significantly with the issue.

Chase, Laura Doster-Holbrook. "Social and Educational Values Regarding Women in Selected Literature for Young Readers in Nineteenth-Century Georgia." Ed.D. diss. University of Georgia, 1994. 466 pp. DAI 55:892A.

Chase searches twenty books written by women for children or given by women to children looking for "muted" stories within them. Her work suggests that the authors and givers "had far greater expectations concerning social and educational values than may have been imagined" and that they realized their gender differences within a "patriarchal society as . . . an asset for problem solving [through] care and responsibility"; a bond between women and girls; "a means within marriage and family of developing a companionable partnership, and . . . an asset to building community." She believes that nineteenth-century women in Georgia "were active agents in their lives both at home and in the world," except in politics, and that they viewed girls' education "as a valuable, progressive means to encourage females' active agency in life."

Chen, Hai-Hon. "Values in Children's Books: From Chinese, Chinese American and American Authors' and Children's Points of View." Ph.D. diss. University of Wisconsin, Milwaukee, 1994. 310 pp. DAI 56:1640A.

Using a large sample of 369 stories written by 137 Chinese authors, 112 Chinese American authors, and 120 American authors, Chen identifies traditional values and characteristics in stories by and about Chinese people; she also notes that each story embodied at least one of the characteristics she identifies. The positive values are "kindness, helpfulness, wisdom, bravery, loving, caring, filial piety, and perseverance." "Greed, meanness, selfishness, lack of wisdom, unkindness, evil, cruelty and stubbornness [are] associated with bad characteristics." She found that Chinese and Chinese-American authors stressed positive values more frequently than did American authors, and that Chinese authors stressed benevolence, love, filial piety, righteousness, gratitude, and retribution, whereas Chinese-American and American authors stressed wisdom and happiness.

Duan, Shu-Jy. "A Tale of Animals: The Changing Images of Animals in Animal Fantasy for Children from Aesop's Fables Through 1986." Ph.D. diss. Ohio State University, 1994. 233 pp. DAI 56:123A.

This study deals with "the didacticism in children's literature and the anthropomorphism in animal fantasy" and asks "Why have animal fantasies endured since Aesop on, and how have they been employed in the service of society in gen-

Children's Literature 25, ed. Francelia Butler, R. H. W. Dillard, and Elizabeth Lennox Keyser, guest ed. Mitzi Myers and U. C. Knoepflmacher (Yale University Press, © 1997 Hollins College).

eral and children in particular?" Duan observes that all animal fantasy is didactic and for animal characters to be successful, something of their intrinsic animal nature must be preserved in the writing about them. The work is essentially an historical overview of animal fantasy.

Immel, Andrea L. "'Little Rhymes, Little Jingle, Little Chimes': A History of Nursery Rhymes in English Literature Before *Tommy Thumb's Pretty Song Book*." Ph.D. diss. University of California, Los Angeles, 1994. 231 pp. DAI 55:2841A.

Immel shows that prior to the 1700s nursery rhymes were often used in polemics and seventeenth-century drama and "were not regarded affectionately as the innocent nonsense of childhood, but as the unsophisticated humor of the illiterate, with whom the young were classified. Nursery rhymes occur in elaborate insults embedded in early eighteenth-century stories on contemporary antiquarianism as well as in criticism championing native vernacular literature." Until the appearance of *Tom Thumb's Pretty Song Book,* they were considered "too raucous or crude" to be acceptable to children. Immel's solid documentary evidence queries the usual modern romanticizing of nursery rhymes.

Johnson, Kathleen R. "En-Gendering Anthropocentrism: Lessons from Children's Realistic Animal Stories." Ph.D. diss. University of Massachusetts, 1994. 197 pp. DAI 55:2576A.

Johnson is concerned with the degree to which humans are viewed as superior to animals and as the only rightful recipients of "direct moral consideration." She analyzes forty-eight children's realistic animal stories and concludes "that the texts send ambivalent and contradictory messages: while children's stories may serve to inform the reader about our actual and potential connections to other animals, they also contain elements that continue to privilege the dominant views. As a result, the stories represent a limited arena for considering or realizing an alternative to anthropocentrism."

Kerper, Richard Michael. "Three Children Viewing and Reading: Transactions with Illustrations and Print in Informational Books." Ph.D. diss. Ohio State University, 1994. 326 pp. DAI 56:123A.

Kerper analyzes informational books and "the paired sign systems of illustrations and words" in them. The results of his studies show that "children's viewing was a recursive process embedded in a linear process and was dependent upon purpose"; that children have needed more "familiarity with pictorial convention as more and more informational books are used in classroom instruction."

Makita-Discekici, Yasuko. "Criteria for Selecting Appropriate Children's Literature for Limited-English-Proficient Japanese Students and Their [sic] Use in ESL/Bilingual Programs at the Primary Level." Ph.D. diss. Southern Illinois University at Carbondale, 1994. 137 pp. DAI 56:878A.

In a study of children in kindergarten through third grade, Makita-Discekici stresses "high literary quality, artistic and supportive illustrations, the appropriateness of content, and the consideration of the needs and interests of Japanese students" as he discusses children's second language acquisition and its relationship to literature. He also notes that the selection of literature should not be based on oral proficiency; children comprehend much better than they can speak, so they should be challenged. Included is an annotated bibliography and each notation contains learning activities based on selected children's trade books.

Mathis, Janelle Brown. "Preservice Teachers' Perceptions of Themselves as Learners, Readers, and Teachers in a Children's Literature Classroom." Ph.D. diss. University of Arizona, 1994. 449 pp. DAI 56:1740A.

Mathis describes an experiential learning course entitled "Children's Literature in the Classroom" and analyzes preservice teachers' perceptions of the role literature plays in their own reading, learning, and teaching. Three case studies of students in the class "showed how class members who had very different perceptions of how they best learned were all supported in their construction of knowledge within the class."

Middlebrooks, Sally. "Signs Saying 'Under Construction': Children's Worldmaking in an Urban Environment." Ed.D. diss. Harvard University, 1995. 330 pp. DAI 56:3478A.

Working with New York city children ages eight to eleven who live in high-rises or tenements, Middlebrooks examines their imaginary play: how they transform or build spaces to play in, particularly in economically poor urban environments. She draws on the work of anthropologists, folklorists, and psychologists, and her "research suggests that a child's perspective on city life may differ from those of the adult, that poor children—despite living in a 'disadvantaged' and 'deficient' environment—may be resilient, and that all children are actively attempting to organize their worlds and constructing theories about them."

Murphy, James G. "'I Am Not Like Other Historians': Historical Revision in Nathaniel Hawthorne's Literature for Children." Ph.D. diss. Fordham University, 1995. 205 pp. DAI 56:1780A.

Murphy shows that *True Stories from History and Biography* illustrate Hawthorne's "countervailing view of American history and Jacksonian society and [that his stories] attack the prevalent commemorative history" that essentially treated children's literature as propaganda and a method of socializing children to think optimistically about the era in which they lived. In "The Whole History of Grandfather's Chair," the first section of his work, Hawthorne attacks "the militarism of romantic history and reverses the national typology that celebrated the Puritans as originators of democracy and religious liberty." He shows how the Puritan spirit of independence was motivated by bigotry and xenophobia. Hawthorne also sees the American Revolution as an example of "mob violence" and attacks Jacksonian society for its "militant, chauvinistic nationalism." Murphy shows that Hawthorne's views in the literature he wrote for children are consistent with those in his adult literature: Hawthorne unfailingly "illustrated the falsity of [the Jacksonian] vision of America and her past" and consistently attacked "the rhetoric [it employed] to support that false vision."

Niiler, Lucas Paul. "Green Reading: The Land Ethics of Lewis and Tolkien." Ph.D. diss. State University of New York at Buffalo, 1995. 156 pp. DAI 56:1370A.

Niiler demonstrates that "in their self-contained mythic universes" Tolkien and Lewis emphasize "stewardship of nature as heroic behavior. Tolkien's and Lewis's heroes transmit a paradigm of living ethically, or symbiotically, within nature: the Rings trilogy and the Chronicles of Narnia, in turn, give us glimpses into what Tolkien and Lewis believed was the key to the survival of our own world: a radical re-fashioning of our prevailing and defining myths concerning the relationship of the cultural with the natural." He believes that Lewis's work shows that by destroying nature we destroy our own nature, and that Tolkien's emphasis is on "healing—bridging the gaps between self and other . . . although such a move will require a radical refashioning of still-prevailing assumptions—myths—about the ontological status of the natural." Niiler further suggests that reading Tolkien is an "escape" from culture to nature.

O'Donnel, Barbara Kay. "The Influence of Nontraditional Books on Children's Gender Stereotypes About Adult Occupations and on Their Occupational Role Playing with Peers." Ph.D. diss. Purdue University, 1994. 230 pp. DAI 56:720A.

O'Donnel worked with five-year-olds and found that literature did not significantly change or modify their stereotyped views of traditional adult work roles. "In general, children's role play was stereotypical regardless of their gender stereotyped attitudes. That is, some children whose beliefs were high on gender stereotyping played nontraditional roles and vice versa. Finally, boys were less willing to take on gender nontraditional roles during play than were girls."

Phillips, Kathryn Bednarzik. "A Comparative Content Analysis of Illustrated African-American Children's Literature Published Between 1900–1962 and 1963–1992." Ph.D. diss. University of Oklahoma, 1995. 164 pp. DAI 56:1933A.

Phillips's study confirms the fact that only "a limited amount of illustrated literature with African-American content [was published] prior to the Civil Rights Movement," and it was generally negative, biased, or stereotyped. She examines the picture stories of W. E. B. Du Bois in his periodical *The Brownies' Book* as well as books following the Civil Rights Movement and finds these later works consistent with standards Du Bois had established.

Pynes, Penelope June. "Development of Language Varieties' Awareness and Attitudes in School Children: Analysis of a Study Conducted in Sandhausen, Germany." Ph.D. diss. University of North Carolina at Chapel Hill, 1995. 359 pp. DAI 56:2593A.

Pynes's object is to further knowledge "concerning the acquisition of stereotypical judgments toward language varieties and to ascertain at what age children are capable of recognizing language varieties not related to ethnic varieties. She worked with first-, third-, and sixth-grade students and concludes that "somewhere between the beginning of the third and end of the fourth grade German children become increasingly aware of attitudes toward and the prestige afforded the standard language, but the process is still not complete by the sixth grade."

Rodman, Nancy Mock. "Family Diversity and Family Housing Between 1943 and 1993: Content Analysis of Children's Picture Storybooks." Ph.D. diss. Texas Woman's University, 1994. 181 pp. DAI 56:2433A.

Because children are susceptible to the images in picture books, Rodman believes that illustrations of families and their homes have "life-long implications for consumer issues, relationships, and housing." In part she treats picture books as "social artifacts," although her sample of books mostly portrayed "traditional nuclear Caucasian families residing in non-urban single-family detached housing with family life portrayed in typical residential spaces." This image varies little over the fifty years studied in the dissertation.

Romalov, Nancy Tillman. "Modern, Mobile, and Marginal: American Girls' Series Fiction, 1905–1925." Ph.D. diss. University of Iowa, 1994. 441 pp. DAI 55:2604A.

Romalov notes that "between 1900 and 1920 over 150 different mass-marketed series novels for girls were launched by over 30 publishers" and that they appeared "at the crossroads of the early twentieth-century woman's movement, the rise of a mass-marketed children's book industry, and the institutionalization of various branches of the children's literature establishment." The effect on girls' reading was profound, and the phenomenon is a "striking example of the relationship of popular fiction to historical context." She examines the way these narrative forms developed, their appeal to girls, their ideology, and how they affected "gender formation at a time in history when such formation was in a great state of flux and accommodation." She draws from theoretical and historical studies about children's and popular culture, audience studies, feminist criticism, and women's history as well as the history of education, publishing, and children's literature criticism. "The study concludes that these new texts offered possibilities for girls to conceptualize gender in ways different from that found in the mainstream, librarian-sanctioned literature," but they also included stereotypes, "encouraged adherence to hegemonic images of femininity. . . , [and resulted] in textual ambiguities, contradictions and tensions."

Schneider, Barbara Kane. "Why and Under What Conditions Do Some Children Become Voluntary Readers? A Qualitative Study." Ph.D. diss. Kent State University, 1994. 186 pp. DAI 55:3148A.

This study attempts "to provide an in depth description of children who are voluntary readers, how they interact with literature, and what impact this might have on pedagogy." Schneider concludes that "children are socialized into reading as a result of a complex interaction that occurs between home and school contexts" and that the physical setting, the classroom environment, teachers who read and encourage reading, and role-model parents are significant.

Sheehan, Kevin James. "Two Childhoods." Ph.D. diss. University of Pennsylvania, 1995. 166 pp. DAI 56:1797A.

In 1862, Sheehan observes, "two Anglican gentlemen of religion turned to the children's story to debate the origin and end of evil. Because these writers shared the premise that ontogeny recapitulated phylogeny, their debate was in effect a debate about the relation of childhood to adulthood." He juxtaposes Charles Kingsley's *The Water Babies: A Fairy Tale for a Land Baby* against Charles Ludwig Dodgson's *Alice's Adventures in Wonderland* and finds that Kingsley defined childhood as a "stage to manhood"; and Dodgson "defended a view in which manhood was a fall from Childhood." But redemption, for Kingsley, demanded that childhood be sacrificed; for Dodgson, it required that childlikeness be preserved. Sheehan notes that both authors believed that Darwin's *Origin of the Species* supported his "cosmological-soteriological scheme." But *The Water Babies* is based on the premise that life evolved from simple forms, that sinners were only temporarily punished, and that "all fallen souls will ultimately be united with God in heaven." Dodgson's work, on the other hand, "is a Fall-story which argues that the Malthusian abyss over which life dances is the result of Original Sin." He concludes that the two works may appear to be a justification of the ways of God to man, but "they also attempt to justify the British class system: the inaugural works of the 'golden age' of children's literature were exercises in elitist theodicy-making."

Smandra-Williams, Michele Olga. "Censorship and Children's Literature." Ed.D. diss. Indiana University of Pennsylvania, 1994. 229 pp. DAI 55:3744A.

This dissertation discusses censorship of children's literature in Pennsylvania and analyzes "book selection and challenge policies . . . , challenge trends, and the use of trade books in reading/language arts curricula." She finds that the use of trade books is increasing in the classroom; and although one-third of the 390 respondents to her survey reported censorship cases, few teachers were aware of challenge trends, and few schools had challenge policies or written rationales for using trade books. The most frequently challenged books were Robert Cormier's *The Chocolate War*, *Go Ask Alice* by Anonymous, *One Day in the Life of Ivan Denisovich* by Alexander Solzhenitsyn, and *The Witch of Blackbird Pond* by Elizabeth Speare. The reasons for censorship were "language, religion, witchcraft, sexism, and sexuality."

Wadham, Timothy Rex. "Light from the Lost Land: A Contextual Response to Susan Cooper's 'The Dark Is Rising' Sequence." Ph.D. diss. University of Texas at Arlington, 1994. 312 pp. DAI 56:919A.

Wadham's thesis is that "Cooper's work draws on basic mythic archetypes and story patterns [and that she] recreates them as a statement of the nature of the universe for children which shows them the polar opposites of good and evil and how they are connected to the past and to their own humanity through myth and story." He analyses the influence on Cooper's writing of her childhood and the books she read, as well as the effect of historical events and Cooper's strong sense of place. He finds that her work can be characterized as a form of "magical realism" that uses archetypal rites of passage while leaning heavily on Arthurian myths. He also stresses the importance of music and visual art to Cooper's works and "how her themes connect to unconscious form."

Also of Note

Blyn, Roslyn. "The Folkgames of Celtic-Speaking Children: A History and Classification System." Ph.D. diss. University of Pennsylvania, 1995. 350 pp. DAI 56:1924A.

Blyn finds that the number of folk games commonly associated with "Celtic-speaking children's play" may be exaggerated or overrepresented in "collections of cultural and linguistic revivals."

Bonifer, M. Susan Elizabeth. "Like a Motherless Child: The Orphan Figure in the Novels of Nineteenth Century American Women Writers, 1850–1899." Ph.D. diss. Indiana University of Pennsylvania, 1995. 184 pp. DAI 56:1773A.

Bonifer explores the evolution of the orphan's tale, employing "feminist psychology, biography, cultural history, and feminist readings of this genre."

Boufis, Christina M. "Where Womanhood and Childhood Meet: Female Adolescence in Victorian Fiction and Culture." Ph.D. diss. City University of New York, 1994. 255 pp. DAI 55:3518A.

By examining the works of Elizabeth Gaskell, Charles Dickens, George Eliot, Anthony Trollope, and Rhoda Broughton written between 1830 and 1870, Boufis tries to determine the period's cultural and literary changes in attitude toward "girlhood." She concludes that "the figure of the girl is often used to project larger nineteenth-century social, political, and cultural issues."

Bush, Patricia Eileen. "Values in Children's Literature: Recognition by Adults and Fifth-Grade Children." Ed.D. diss. University of Central Florida, 1994. 223 pp. DAI 55:2305A.

Bush selected ten Newbery Award and honor books to find out whether children and adults could identify "decision points, points at which characters made a decision based on personal values." She concludes that they can.

Castillo, Lisa Carmen. "The Effect of Analogy Instruction on Young Children's Metaphor Comprehension." Ph.D. diss. City University of New York, 1994. 100 pp. DAI 55:3450A.

Castillo asked five- and six-year-old children "to explain sentences (metaphors) whose meanings had been 'disguised' in an attempt to enhance their ability to deal with analogies."

De Board, Roberta Jean. "An Investigation of the Control of Genre in Children's and Teachers' Writing." Ph.D. diss. University of Washington, 1994. 234 pp. DAI 55:2769A.

De Board is concerned primarily with how teachers and students identify genre, particularly narration, persuasion, exposition, and instructional writing.

Detemple, Jeanne McLean. "Book Reading Styles of Low-Income Mothers with Preschoolers and Children's Later Literacy Skills." Ed.D. diss. Harvard University, 1994. 154 pp. DAI 55:1817A.

Detemple examined the activities of fifty-five mothers while they read to their children at ages three-and-a-half, four-and-a-half, and five-and-a-half. She observes that the mothers' interaction with their children decreased as the children grew older, and that age three-and-a-half was the most susceptible to a beneficial influence on the children's later literacy skills.

Dorn, Linda Jean. "A Vygotskian Perspective on Literacy Acquisition: Talk and Action in the Child's Construction of Literate Awareness." Ph.D. diss. Texas Woman's University, 1994. 280 pp. DAI 55:3147A.

Dorn concludes that "talk and action worked together within the social and cultural fabric of the literacy event to shape the child's construction of literate awareness."

Fetzer, Lorelei. "Facilitating Print Awareness and Literacy Development with Familiar Children's Songs." Ed.D. diss. East Texas State University, 1994. 192 pp. DAI 56:500A.

Fetzer finds that the lyrics and rhythms of familiar children's songs play a significant role in a child's ability to remember text. Their use to improve reading indicates "a growing involvement, confidence, competence, and enthusiasm in reading behaviors."

Finkelstein, Marc D. "Mental Imagery and Musical Composition: An Inquiry into the Imagery Use of Prominent Composers of Children's Songs." Ed.D. diss. Rutgers University, 1994. 387 pp. DAI 55:1412A.

This dissertation examines "the potential of mental imagery as a component in the process of musical composition in an elite group of composers of children's songs." Both auditory and visual imagery were important to the composers.

Krumrey, Diane Martha. "The Eloquent Savage in Early American Narrative." Ph.D. diss. University of Connecticut, 1995. 227 pp. DAI 56:2237A.

Krumrey treats the works of James Fenimore Cooper, among others.

Meier, Daniel Reed. "'OK, I'll Show You How to Do It': The Nature of Children's Literacy Involvement During a Kindergarten Choice Time Event." Ph.D. diss. University of California, Berkeley, 1994. 158 pp. DAI 56:1647A.

"Through a careful and thoughtful crafting of the choice time event, and the use of certain behavioral routines, the teacher framed and guided children's choice time participation and involvement in literacy activities."

Miller, Margaret Bonnie. "We Don't Wear Aprons Anymore: A Content Analysis of the Description of Working Mothers in Contemporary Realistic Fiction for Children, 1976–1992." Ed.D. diss. University of South Dakota, 1994. 211 pp. DAI 55:3121A.

In her review of 117 books, Miller found that the depiction of working mothers had increased somewhat from 1976 to 1992, that for the most part mothers were depicted favorably, and that protagonists' relationships to their mothers were positive.

Oppenheimer, Sharon Rosalie. "Performing Arts in Education in Hawai'i: A History of Drama, Puppetry, and Creative Movement for Children and Youth from 1875 to 1994." Ph.D. diss. University of Hawaii, 1995. 326 pp. DAI 56:1586A.

Oppenheimer's work is primarily a history of the Honolulu Theatre for Youth, the Artists-in-the-Schools movement in Hawaii, the Alliance for Arts Education, the Hawai'i Alliance for Arts Education, the Performing Arts Learning Centers, and "the infusion of arts in the schools [corresponding] with the restructuring of Hawai'i's school system" in the 1990s.

Pachoud, Julia Virginia. "A Radical Romance: An Existential Phenomenological Investigation of Feminist Playwrights Whose Works Appeal to Children." Ph.D. diss. Southern Illinois University at Carbondale, 1994. 147 pp. DAI 56:33A.

Pachoud demonstrates that "playwrights who successfully dialogue with children via their texts accomplish the important task of privileging childhood experience and of speaking to childhood realities. As child audiences witness the privileging of their own discourse, they are both authenticated and empowered to claim voice and body. The playwrights themselves are authenticated as the creative experience connects them to an artistic community and to an audience." The dissertation concludes with a "praise of effective children's theatre in light of the thematic."

Pershey, Monica Gordon. "Children's Awareness of Pragmatic Language Functions in Narrative Text." Ed.D. diss. University of Massachusetts at Lowell, 1994. 380 pp. DAI 55:2334A.

Studying first-graders, Pershey concludes that "cultivating pragmatic awareness to promote comprehension of and response to narrative has shown pedagogical utility," although further research is suggested.

Rose, Sarah Elizabeth. "The Effects of Dalcroze Eurythmics on Beat Competency Performance Skills of Kindergarten, First-, and Second-Grade Children." Ph.D. diss.
University of North Carolina at Greensboro, 1995. 125 pp. DAI 56:2040A.

Thirty-two weeks of instruction had a significant effect on children's performance skills and neutralized the gender differences in rhythmic ability that were
apparent in Rose's pretest.

Sagehorn, Alice Catherine Hoffman. "Beyond Heroes and Holidays: The Integration
of Multicultural Children's Literature in the Elementary Classroom." Ph.D. diss. University of Arkansas, 1995. 129 pp. DAI 56:2594A.

Sagehorn studies what types of multicultural literature elementary school
teachers read in the classroom and finds that they primarily used multicultural
literature as "a read aloud book" distinct from a regular unit of study.

Salisbury, Daniele Tema. "Georges Darien du l'Enfance Volée. Etude du Recrit d'Enfance dans les Romans de Darien." Ph.D. diss. New York University, 1995. 235 pp.
DAI 56:1812A.

Salisbury analyzes Darien's narratives about childhood and also focuses on
children's criticism of childhood. She finds that Darien's narrative voice is more
critical of childhood when he uses a child's voice than when he uses the adult
voice of his later autobiographical work. The dissertation is an extended study of
the use of the child's voice in narration.

Sanger, Linda. "The Function of Questions and Answers in Mother Goose Nursery
Rhymes." Ph.D. diss. New York University, 1994. 95 pp. DAI 56:124A.

"The study involved a review of the rationale for children knowing . . . nursery rhymes, establishing the rhymes' cultural and educational implications." Instructions for teachers who use nursery rhymes in the classroom are included.

Seidel, Steven, " 'To Be the Complete Thing': A Case Study of Teachers Reading Children's Writing." Ed.D. diss. Harvard University, 1995. 292 pp. DAI 56:853A.

Seidel attempts to set guidelines for teachers who assess students' work
through portfolios.

Trotter, M. Louise. "Young Children's Conversations with Picture Books: A Case Study
of Two First Graders in a Reading Intervention Program." Ph.D. diss. Ohio State
University, 1995. 222 pp. DAI 56:2155A.

In a year-long reading intervention class, Trotter found that informational
books and wordless picture books produced more student discussion than other
types of picture books.

Truitt, Judi Crabtree. "The Communication of Help-Seeking Skills to Children." Ph.D.
diss. University of Kentucky, 1994. 105 pp. DAI 55:1743A.

In this dissertation in educational psychology, Truitt concludes that students
who viewed a videotape and a play about seeking help probably learned more
skills from the videotape.

Contributors and Editors

GILLIAN ADAMS is the editor of *Children's Literature Abstracts* and an associate editor of the *Children's Literature Association Quarterly*.

JULIA BRIGGS, professor of English at De Montfort University, Leicester, is the author of a history of the ghost story, *Night Visitors* (1977), a study of Renaissance literature in relation to history, *This Stage-Play World* (1983, 1997), and a biography, *E. Nesbit: A Woman of Passion* (1987). She is coeditor, with Gillian Avery, of *Children and Their Books: A Celebration of the Work of Iona and Peter Opie* (1989), and has contributed to Peter Hunt's *Children's Literature: An Illustrated History* (1995). She is currently at work on a study of Virginia Woolf, whose writings she edited for Penguin Books.

FRANCELIA BUTLER, professor emerita at the University of Connecticut, has published many books on children's literature, including *Skipping Around the World: The Ritual Nature of Folk Rhymes*.

JOHN CECH teaches in the English department at the University of Florida in Gainesville. His most recent book is *Angels and Wild Things*, a study of Maurice Sendak.

PATRICIA CRADDOCK, the former chair of the English departments of Boston University and the University of Florida, has published four books and numerous articles on the work of Edward Gibbon. She teaches not only children's fiction but also British and American adult fiction from Bunyan to Morrison, and has been an avid reader of children's novels old and new, British and American, for over fifty years.

RICHARD H. W. DILLARD is professor of English and chair of the creative writing program at Hollins College in Virginia. The author of several scholarly works, he is also a novelist and poet.

RACHEL FORDYCE, former executive secretary of the Children's Literature Association, has written five books, including *Semiotics and Linguistics in Alice's Worlds* with Carla Marello. She is a professor of English and the dean of humanities and social sciences at Montclair State University.

SUSAN R. GANNON is professor of literature and communications in the Dyson College of Pace University. She is coauthor of *Mary Mapes Dodge* (Twayne, 1992), and her research interests include nineteenth-century periodicals for children, illustration, Stevenson, and Alcott. She is currently coediting a collection of critical essays on *St. Nicholas Magazine*.

ANGELA E. HUBLER is assistant professor of English and women's studies at Kansas State University. Her research in literature for girls is motivated by a desire to identify sources of resistance to traditional female gender-role socialization. Her entry "Sexism" appears in *The Oxford Companion to Women's Writing in the United States*.

ANDREA IMMEL is curator of the Cotsen Children's Collection at Princeton University Library. Among her interests are the history of nursery rhymes and eighteenth-century and early nineteenth-century juvenile publishers. Her descriptive catalog of the Cotsen Collection's children's books of John Newbery and his successors is forthcoming.

SHERRIE A. INNESS is assistant professor of English at Miami University. Her research interests include nineteenth- and twentieth-century American literature, children's literature, popular culture, and gender studies. She has published articles on these topics in a number of journals, as well as in four anthologies. She is also the author of *Intimate Communities: Representation and Social Transformation in Women's College Fiction, 1895–1910*.

287

ELIZABETH LENNOX KEYSER is associate professor of English at Hollins College in Virginia, where she teaches children's literature, American literature, and American studies. Her book *Whispers in the Dark: The Fiction of Louisa May Alcott* won the Children's Literature Association Book Award.

U. C. KNOEPFLMACHER, Paton Foundation Professor of Ancient and Modern Literature at Princeton University, is the author of four books and numerous articles on Victorian literature. He has coedited three books, including a 1992 collection of fairy tales and fantasies by Victorian women writers. His *Ventures into Childland: Victorians, Fairy Tales, and Femininity* is scheduled to appear in 1998, as is an essay called "Repudiating 'Sleeping Beauty'" in a collection coedited by Margaret Higonnet and Beverly Clark.

LORRAINE JANZEN KOOISTRA is assistant professor of English at Nipissing University in North Bay, Ontario, Canada. A specialist in visual and verbal relations, she has published *The Artist as Critic: Bitextuality in Fin-de-Siècle Illustrated Books* (Scolar, 1995) as well as a number of articles on art and literature, some of which focus on illustrations for Rossetti's *Goblin Market*. She is presently working on a book-length study, "Christina Rossetti and Illustration."

MITZI MYERS teaches writing and children's and adolescent literature at the University of California, Los Angeles. She has published extensively on historical children's literature and on eighteenth- and nineteenth-century women writers, including Mary Wollstonecraft, Hannah More, Harriet Martineau, and Maria Edgeworth. She is currently completing *Romancing the Family: Maria Edgeworth and the Scene of Instruction,* which examines, among other topics, the intertextuality of the author's work for children and adults. She is also writing a literary life of Edgeworth and annotating several volumes of Edgeworth for the forthcoming Pickering and Chatto reprint.

PETER F. NEUMEYER is professor emeritus at San Diego State University. Author of five children's books and a volume of poetry, and editor of critical volumes on Kafka and on illustrations of children's books, he has recently published *The Annotated "Charlotte's Web,"* as well as articles on Maurice Sendak and Raymond Briggs.

PATRICIA PACE is associate professor of communication arts and director of theater at Georgia Southern University. Her essays on gender and childhood have appeared in *Text and Performance Quarterly* and *The Lion and the Unicorn.*

ALAN RAUCH, associate professor of literature, communication, and culture at Georgia Institute of Technology, specializes in the cultural study of nineteenth-century science. He recently edited and introduced Jane Webb Loudon's novel, *The Mummy! A Tale of the Twenty-Second Century* (1827) for University of Michigan Press (1994), and is the author of *Moral Responsibility and the Growth of Knowledge: Science in the British Novel, 1818–1860,* which is forthcoming from Duke University Press. His current research focuses on the encyclopedic movement and the dissemination of knowledge in the nineteenth century.

MAVIS REIMER is assistant professor of English at the University of Winnipeg, Canada. She has edited a collection of essays on L. M. Montgomery's *Anne of Green Gables,* entitled *Such a Simple Little Tale,* and has recently published articles on the school stories of L. T. Meade.

ERIKA ROTHWELL is an instructor at the University of Alberta, where she has just completed her doctorate. Her Ph.D. thesis dealt with eighteenth- and nineteenth-century women writers of children's literature and their place in the history of both children's literature and women's writing.

DONELLE R. RUWE is assistant professor of English at Fitchburg State College in Massachusetts, where she teaches British literature and poetry. She is on the governing board of the Eighteenth- and Nineteenth-Century British Women Writers Association, edits the association's newsletter, and is coediting the forthcoming essay collection, *Re-Presenting Power: British Women Writers, 1780–1900.* She has published poetry and fiction, articles on American Indian writers, and has forthcoming articles on women writers of the British Romantic era.

MINNIE SINGH is assistant professor of Children's Literature and Culture at the University of Pittsburgh. The author of critical assessments of four Indian poets and, most recently, of a piece on John Berger, she has worked on the relation between colonial literature and children's books and is currently converting her doctoral dissertation on Kipling's movement from adult narratives to children's fiction into a book tentatively entitled *The Making of Rudyard Kipling: From Gossip Tale to Imperial Pastoral.*

MAUREEN THUM teaches Honors and English at the University of Michigan, Flint, where she also is the coordinator of graduate resources in the College of Arts and Sciences. She has published articles on Chaucer, Milton, the Brothers Grimm, Wilhelm Hauff, and Kenneth Grahame.

Award Applications

The article award committee of the Children's Literature Association publishes a bibliography of the year's work in children's literature in the *Children's Literature Association Quarterly* and selects the year's best critical articles. For pertinent articles that have appeared in a collection of essays or journal other than one devoted to children's literature, please send a photocopy or offprint with the correct citation and your address written on the first page to Gillian Adams, 5906 Fairlane Drive, Austin, Tex. 78731. Papers will be acknowledged and returned if return postage is enclosed. The annual deadline is May 1.

The Phoenix Award is given for a book first published twenty years earlier that did not win a major award but has passed the test of time and is deemed to be of high literary quality. Send nominations to Alethea Helbig, 3640 Eli Road, Ann Arbor, Mich. 48104.

The Children's Literature Association offers two annual research grants. The Margaret P. Esmonde Memorial Scholarship offers $500 for criticism and original works in the areas of fantasy or science fiction for children or adolescents by beginning scholars, including graduate students, instructors, and assistant professors. Research Fellowships are awards ranging but from $250 to $1,000 (the number and amount of awards are based on the number and needs of winning applicants) for criticism or original scholarship leading to a significant publication. Recipients must have postdoctoral or equivalent professional standing. Awards may be used for transportation, living expenses, materials, and supplies but not for obtaining advanced degrees, for creative writing, textbook writing, or pedagogical purposes. For full application guidelines on both grants, write the Children's Literature Association, c/o Marianne Gessner, 22 Harvest Lane, Battle Creek, Mich. 49015. The annual deadline for these awards is February 1.

Order Form Yale University Press
P.O. Box 209040, New Haven, CT 06520-9040
Phone orders 1-800-YUP-READ (U.S. and Canada)

Customers in the United States and Canada may photocopy this form and use it for ordering all volumes of **Children's Literature** available from Yale University Press. Individuals are asked to pay in advance. We honor both MasterCard and VISA. Checks should be made payable to Yale University Press.

The prices given are 1997 list prices for the United States and are subject to change. A shipping charge of $3.50 for the U.S. and $5.00 for Canada is to be added to each order, and Connecticut residents must pay a sales tax of 6 percent.

Qty.	Volume	Price	Total amount	Qty.	Volume	Price	Total amount
___	10 (cloth)	$45.00	_____	___	19 (cloth)	$45.00	_____
___	11 (cloth)	$45.00	_____	___	19 (paper)	$17.00	_____
___	12 (cloth)	$45.00	_____	___	20 (cloth)	$45.00	_____
___	13 (cloth)	$45.00	_____	___	20 (paper)	$17.00	_____
___	14 (cloth)	$45.00	_____	___	21 (cloth)	$45.00	_____
___	15 (cloth)	$45.00	_____	___	21 (paper)	$17.00	_____
___	15 (paper)	$17.00	_____	___	22 (cloth)	$45.00	_____
___	16 (paper)	$17.00	_____	___	22 (paper)	$17.00	_____
___	17 (cloth)	$45.00	_____	___	23 (cloth)	$45.00	_____
___	17 (paper)	$17.00	_____	___	23 (paper)	$17.00	_____
___	18 (cloth)	$45.00	_____	___	24 (cloth)	$45.00	_____
___	18 (paper)	$17.00	_____	___	24 (paper)	$17.00	_____
				___	25 (cloth)	$45.00	_____
				___	25 (paper)	$17.00	_____

Payment of $_____ is enclosed (including sales tax if applicable).

MasterCard no. _____

4-digit bank no. _____ Expiration date _____

VISA no. _____ Expiration date _____

Signature _____

SHIP TO: _____

_____

See the next page for ordering issues from Yale University Press, London.

Volumes 1–7 of **Children's Literature** can be obtained directly from John C. Wandell, The Children's Literature Foundation, P.O. Box 370, Windham Center, Conn. 06280.

Order Form Yale University Press, 23 Pond Street, Hampstead, London NW3 2PN, England

Customers in the United Kingdom, Europe, and the British Commonwealth may photocopy this form and use it for ordering all volumes of **Children's Literature** available from Yale University Press. Individuals are asked to pay in advance. We honour Access, VISA, and American Express accounts. Cheques should be made payable to Yale University Press.

The prices given are 1997 list prices for the United Kingdom and are subject to change. A post and packing charge of £1.95 is to be added to each order.

Qty.	Volume	Price	Total amount	Qty.	Volume	Price	Total amount
——	8 (cloth)	£40.00	——————	——	16 (paper)	£14.95	——————
——	8 (paper)	£14.95	——————	——	17 (cloth)	£40.00	——————
——	9 (cloth)	£40.00	——————	——	17 (paper)	£14.95	——————
——	9 (paper)	£14.95	——————	——	18 (cloth)	£40.00	——————
——	10 (cloth)	£40.00	——————	——	18 (paper)	£14.95	——————
——	11 (cloth)	£40.00	——————	——	19 (cloth)	£40.00	——————
——	11 (paper)	£14.95	——————	——	19 (paper)	£14.95	——————
——	12 (cloth)	£40.00	——————	——	20 (paper)	£14.95	——————
——	12 (paper)	£14.95	——————	——	21 (paper)	£14.95	——————
——	13 (cloth)	£40.00	——————	——	22 (cloth)	£40.00	——————
——	13 (paper)	£14.95	——————	——	22 (paper)	£14.95	——————
——	14 (cloth)	£40.00	——————	——	23 (cloth)	£40.00	——————
——	14 (paper)	£14.95	——————	——	23 (paper)	£14.95	——————
——	15 (cloth)	£40.00	——————	——	24 (cloth)	£40.00	——————
——	15 (paper)	£14.95	——————	——	24 (paper)	£14.95	——————
				——	25 (cloth)	£40.00	——————
				——	25 (paper)	£14.95	——————

Payment of £ —————————————————————————————————————— is enclosed.

Please debit my Access/VISA/American Express account no. ————————————————

Expiry date ——

Signature ————————————————— Name ————————————————————

Address ——

See the previous page for ordering issues from Yale University Press, New Haven.

Volumes 1–7 of **Children's Literature** can be obtained directly from John C. Wandell, The Children's Literature Foundation, Box 370, Windham Center, Conn. 06280.